W9-BEU-671

The Kovels' Collector's Guide to American Art Pottery

Ralph & Terry Kovel

Crown Publishers, Inc. / New York

BOOKS BY RALPH AND TERRY KOVEL

The Kovels' Collector's Guide
to Limited Editions

The Complete Antiques Price List

Know Your Antiques

American Country Furniture 1780–1875

Dictionary of Marks—Pottery and Porcelain

The Official Bottle Price List

A Directory of American Silver,
Pewter and Silver Plate

© 1974 by Crown Publishers, Inc.

All rights reserved. No part of this book may be reproduced or
utilized in any form or by any means, electronic or mechanical,
including photocopying, recording, or by any information storage and retrieval system, without permission in writing from
the Publisher.

Inquiries should be addressed to Crown Publishers, Inc.,
One Park Avenue, New York, N.Y. 10016.

Library of Congress Catalog Card Number: 74–80295
ISBN: 0-517-516764

Printed in the United States of America
Published simultaneously in Canada by General Publishing
Company Limited

10 9 8 7 6 5 4

"The best book of all is the book dedicated to me."

To Kim, our best researcher
and
In lieu of all the "letters to Lee"

ACKNOWLEDGMENTS

Hundreds of people helped us with the research for this book and spent time and effort answering questions and giving us suggestions. We thank Mrs. W. J. Allan; Mrs. Walter S. Auman; Wilmot T. Bartle (The Newark Museum); Miss Carol E. Beattie (The State Historical Society of Colorado); Mrs. Charles G. Benham; Edwin Bennett; Elsie Binns; Robert Blasberg, Dennis R. Bodem (Michigan Department of State); Mrs. Joy R. Bogue; Richard Borges (New York State Historical Association); William A. Bostick (The Detroit Institute of Arts); Gervis Brady (Stark County, Ohio, Historical Society); Michael Brook (Minnesota Historical Society); Walter L. Brown (Arkansas Historical Association); Eugenie Candau (San Francisco Museum of Art); John B. Carmicheal (Kansas State Historical Society); J. W. Carpenter; Robert G. Carroon (Milwaukee County Historical Society); Veronica F. Cary (Free Public Library, Trenton, New Jersey); Mrs. Barbara Child; Mrs. Hugh D. Combs; Ruth Corry (Georgia Department of Archives and History); Paul E. Cox; A. M. Cranston; Bill Cullison (Tulane University Library); Charles F. Cummings (The Public Library of Newark, New Jersey); John D. Cushing (Massachusetts Historical Society); Sharon Darling (Chicago Historical Society); Mrs. Maxton R. Davies, Jr.; Chester Davis; Michael P. Davis (Stangl Pottery); W. K. Day (United States Ceramic Tile Company); Kenneth N. Dearolf (Kenosha Public Museum); Dedham Historical Society, especially Marion K. Conant; Susanne De Ferranti (The Cleveland Museum of Art); Eric de Jonge (William Penn Memorial Museum); Mrs. Frank A. Digaetano, Jr. (The Newark Museum); Robert L. Dimit (Stan Hywet Hall Foundation, Inc.); Ellen B. Donahue; Caroline Dunn (William Henry Smith Memorial Library, Indiana Historical Society); Mrs. Lawrence Duvall; The East Liverpool Historical Society, especially William H. Vodrey and H. B. Barth; Charles H. Elam (The Detroit Institute of Arts); Mrs. Raymond Ellis; Mrs. Bennet K. Eskesen; LeRoy Eslinger; William A. Fagaly (Isaac Delgado Museum of Art); John L. Ferguson (Arkansas History Commission); Zane Field; Mrs. Catherine Lynn Frangiamore (Cooper-Hewitt Museum of Decorative Arts and Design); Howard B. Frankenfield, Jr.; Franklin M. Garrett (Atlanta Historical Society); Dave and Kay Glover; Marion Gosling (Marblehead Historical Society); Jim and Maggie Gould; Susan W. Grady; Charles Grantier; Arlene and Paul H. Greaser; Richard A. Greene (Delaware County Historical Society, Indiana); Betty Grissom; Foster E. and Gladys C. Hall; Patricia Hall (Philadelphia Museum of Art); Haviland & Co. Incorporated; Mrs. Jane E. Heath (The Lakewood Public Library, Lakewood, Ohio); James J. Heslin (The New York Historical Society); Eugenia Calvert Holland (Maryland Historical Society); Mrs. Sam Horvitz; Mary D. Hudgins; Sadie Irvine; Ernest Jacoby (North Bennet Street Industrial School); Arno Jakobson (The Brooklyn Museum); Mary Gregory Jewett (Georgia Historical Commission); Miss Frances Follin Jones (The Art Museum, Princeton University); John W. Keefe (The Art Institute of Chicago); Michael F. Kidzus (Ravine Mineralogical Museum); Ralph H. Kistler; Mr. and Mrs. Charles Klamkin; Robert Koch; Ann Koepke; Lynn Koogle; Mrs. George M. Kurzon, Jr.; Robert Lafond (The Art Museum, Princeton University, Princeton, New Jersey); William Fisk Landers; Ted Langstroth; Mrs. Charles B. Lansing; Grady G. Ledbetter and J. T. Case (Pisgah Pottery); Ruth Lee (The Haeger Potteries, Inc.); Dr. Sherman E. Lee (Cleveland Museum of Art); Ruth Little (Neville Public Museum); Miss Wilhelmina V. Lunt (Historical Society of Old Newbury); Robert M. McBride (Tennessee Historical Society); Dr. Carol Macht (Cincinnati Art Museum); Cecil T. Malone; Phyllis Mattheis; Kenneth Mauney; Mrs. George R. Mercer, Metropolitan Museum of Art; Mrs.

Charles G. Meyers; Donald Miller (University of North Dakota); James R. Mitchell (The Carborundum Museum of Ceramics); Esther Mock (Salem Academy and College); Dr. Joel C. Moss (Fort Hays Kansas State College); Ruth Murphy; The Museum of Modern Art; Lester Myers; Mrs. E. B. Olson; Helen G. Olsson (The Newark Museum); Mrs. Suzanne Ormond; Glidden Parker; Mrs. John R. Pear (Michigan State University); Charles H. Peck, Jr.; Herbert and Margaret Peck; Craig Perrin (California Historical Society); Arlene Peterson (Ohio Historical Society); Jessie J. Poesch (Newcomb College, Tulane University); Kathleen R. Postle (Earlham College); Sharon Pugsley (The New Jersey Historical Society); T. A. Randall (State University of New York, College of Ceramics at Alfred University); Marvin Raney; Paul F. Redding (Buffalo and Erie County Historical Society); Irving G. Reimann (The Exhibit Museum of the University of Michigan); A. Christian Revi (*Spinning Wheel*); Kenneth W. Richards (State of New Jersey State Library); Peggy Richards (Louisiana State Museum); Bob, Chuck, and Rich Roan, Inc.; Roland Antiques; Mrs. Judy H. Rowe; Mr. and Mrs. Richard Russack; Ruth K. Salisbury (The Historical Society of Western Pennsylvania); Joan Seidl (Rock County Historical Society); Thomas Sellers (*Ceramics Monthly*); Les Senders (Senders Gallery, Cleveland); Clinton A. Sheffield (Dickinson State College); Mrs. C. B. Shipman; Erika H. Singsen (Allen Memorial Art Museum, Oberlin College); Lewis D. Snyder (Tennessee Arts Commission); Mrs. Bernice C. Sprenger (Detroit Public Library); Harry and Marian Stevens; K. W. Stevenson (Van Briggle Art Pottery); Robert Stone (R. S. Antiques, New York City); J. Herman Stotz (County of Bucks, Pa.); Studio International; Dr. Edmund B. Sullivan (University of Hartford); Betty Swanson; Alison M. Swift (Chicago Historical Society); Mr. and Mrs. Terry Turan; John Tyler (William Penn Memorial Museum); J. L. Vantine (State Historical Society of North Dakota); John E. Varlie (Robertson-American Corporation); Mrs. Robert W. Vose (Storrowton Village Museum); Nicholas B. Wainwright (The Historical Society of Pennsylvania); Peter C. Welsh (New York State Historical Association); Celeste E. Wenzel (Madison Township Historical Society); Robert G. Wheeler (Greenfield Village and Henry Ford Museum); Margaret Whittlesey; Benjamin F. Williams (The North Carolina Museum of Art); Howard W. Wiseman (The New Jersey Historical Society); John C. Wolfe, Jr.; Beverly Wolter (The North Carolina Museum of Art); John H. Wright (Essex Institute); Martha E. Wright (Indiana State Library); Mr. and Mrs. Elliot A. Wysor; J. Walter Yore Company.

Extra effort and time were offered by these people who deserve special thanks. Donald Alexander; Art Museum, Princeton University, especially Dr. Martin P. Eidelberg and David W. Steadman; Paul Brunner; The Cleveland Public Library, Fine Arts Department, especially Stephen G. Matyi, M. Elizabeth Gehring, Janet Graham, Russell A. Hehr, Jane E. Moss; Mrs. William Fisher; David A. Hanks (The Art Institute of Chicago); Pat H. Johnston and the *Pottery Collector's Newsletter;* Kim Kovel; The Ohio Historical Society Library; Norris F. Schneider; Helen R. Seeley; The Smithsonian Institution, especially Sheila Machlis Alexander, Renee Altman, J. Jefferson Miller II; The Society for the Preservation of New England Antiquities, especially Mrs. Barbara G. Teller; Margot T. Sullivan (Boston Public Library); The Western Reserve Historical Society, especially Jarius B. Barnes.

For help in checking accuracy and details in the chapter devoted to their special interest we thank Vi and Si Altman; Lawrence H. Clewell; Jean d'Albis; Mrs. Richard Wynn Irvine (Louisiana Crafts Council); Dale and Neil McCullough; Barbara White Morse; Arlene Rainey; B. A. Sarby (Hunterdon County Historical Society, Flemington, N.J.); Mrs. Joan Severa (The State Historical Society of Wisconsin); Professor David Seyler; Kenneth E. Smith; Kenneth Trapp; Thelma Frazier Winter; Jane Wyckoff (Hunterdon County Historical Society).

And for a job well done in manuscript preparation and double checking details thanks to Debby Herman and Terry Sirko.

Necrology: To these researchers who did the original work in many of the areas covered in this book we give special tribute. Their work has lived after them. Edwin Atlee Barber; Evan Purviance; and E. Stanley Wires.

INTRODUCTION

After spending eight years researching the material for this book, we wonder if there can be any one definition for "art pottery." The first American art pottery was made in Cincinnati, Ohio, during the 1870s. It was hand-thrown and hand-decorated, and deliberately produced to be artistic rather than commercial. Later products that are part of the art pottery movement were made with underglaze slip decoration, matte glaze, carved or molded decorations, and a variety of other techniques. The art pottery movement seems to have ended in the late 1920s, when studio potters made the more artistic wares. Many of the art potteries started as a one-man or one-woman operation. Some grew from such small beginnings to become large successful financial ventures with hundreds of employees. The studio potter of the 1920s and after usually had a small pottery with one or two potters. Many remained small by choice, so that their wares could continue to be made almost entirely by the artist.

This book has emphasized those aspects of each pottery that we felt would be of value to the collector. Makers, artists, dates, marks, and lines of pottery are described in detail, and we have given a general history of each pottery. For any further information about the historical aspects of a pottery, a bibliography has been included under each entry.

The material in this work is as accurate as possible and is based on all the information that we found available. New research will probably solve some of the mysteries that may still exist. In those instances when two reliable sources give conflicting information, we have included both in the text with our opinion about the accuracy of each. Facts have been checked and rechecked from many sources, including magazines and newspapers of the period, factory records, interviews with employees and relatives, study collections at museums, and any other possible sources. The main entries have been read by experts who have specialized in research into one factory; their corrections or comments on accuracy were most appreciated.

The book is arranged in alphabetical order by factory. Following this are sections, with individual entries, on Pottery Tiles and Miscellaneous Factories. The miscellaneous section is really the starting point for further research. It includes potteries that have appeared in various records, even if only with fragmentary comments.

We have tried to make no value judgments in this book. Pottery is described, but we do not attempt to evaluate its artistic worth. This is a job for each collector or for a trained artist or potter.

Any comments or additional facts about the pottery discussed would be welcome. Research is never completed.

Ralph and Terry Kovel
November, 1974

ARC-EN-CEIL

Arc-en-ciel is the French word for rainbow. (The founders evidently did not check the spelling.) The firm made cooking wares in stippled blue, brown, green, or mottled brown and yellow glaze. The finest product of the firm was their iridescent gold luster vases.

The Arc-en-ceil pottery was founded on Coopermill Road in Zanesville, Ohio, in 1903. The factory had originally been built by Albert Radford who made pottery there for about six months before Arc-en-ceil purchased the pottery. It is said that Radford built the pottery for them, but due to a delay, Radford operated the pottery before the final sale. The records show a trustee for the A. Radford Company, so perhaps the plant had some money difficulties and was forced to sell. J. C. Gerwick was president and C. G. Dillon was secretary. John Lessell (see Weller) was another of the incorporators and he managed the plant. Arc-en-ceil became the Brighton pottery in 1905 and made cooking ware and other dishes. The plant was closed in 1907.

Bibliography

Purviance, Evan, "American Art Pottery," *Mid-America Reporter* (November 1972).

Radford, Fred W., *A. Radford Pottery His Life and Works [sic]*. Privately Printed: Fred W. Radford, 1973.

Schneider, Norris F., "Many Small Art Potteries Once Operated in Zanesville," *Zanesville Times Recorder* (February 4, 1962).

———, "Veteran Mosaic Tile Employee Compiles Outstanding Display," *Zanesville Times Recorder* (October 30, 1960).

AREQUIPA

In 1911 about twenty-five patients at a tuberculosis sanitorium near San Francisco, California, began making pottery. Sales from their finished work would furnish some extra money for the patients. They were helped by Frederick Hurten Rhead, who had worked at Roseville from 1902 to 1908, and the director of the sanitorium, Dr. Philip King Brown. Arequipa was the name of the sanitorium and it was decided that the pottery should be marked with the same name.

A man was hired to throw the clay and do the jobs that

An Arc-en-ceil urn with a handle, glazed with iridescent copper-colored glaze. The vase is 1½ inches high and is marked with the incised name. (The Smithsonian Institution)

This mark is stamped in ink.

required strength or exposure to clay dust, while the patients, tubercular girls, were able to decorate the pottery sitting in a well-ventilated, sunny room. Arequipa Pottery was at least partially made from local clays. The pieces had a thick, sturdy look. Some were glazed and some had incised or raised designs.

Frederick Rhead continued supervising the technical aspects of the pottery work until 1914. Between Roseville and Arequipa Rhead had been at University City, St. Louis, Missouri (1908–1911). He also was at Santa Barbara, California. At University City he worked on porcelains with other well-known potters, such as Adelaide Alsop Robineau, editor of *Keramic Studio* magazine.

(Below left) A grayish plum glaze covers this 8-inch vase. (The Smithsonian Institution)   (Below right) This vase has an iridescent orange and a gray matte glaze. It is 6 inches in diameter and 8 inches high. (The Smithsonian Institution)   (Bottom) "Persian blue" glaze. The vase is 2½ inches high and is marked "AP." (The Smithsonian Institution)

(Above) Marks: Two-letter signature, the tree and jug symbol, and a paper label.   (Bottom) This Arequipa vase was purchased in 1916. It has a bright yellow iridescent glaze over a modeled, then case form. It is 4⅜ inches in diameter and 4 inches high. (The Smithsonian Institution)

Albert L. Solon, son of Louis Solon, author of books about English pottery, replaced Rhead until 1916, when a successful potter, F. H. Wilde, took the job. The pottery was just beginning to succeed with a line of tiles when the war of 1918 led to the closing of the operation.

Bibliography

Blasberg, Robert, "Arequipa Pottery," *Western Collector*, VI (October 1968), 7–10.

Henzke, Lucile, *American Art Pottery*, Camden, New Jersey, and New York: Thomas Nelson, 1970.

This Avon Pottery mug in rose is 4¾ inches high by 3⅛ inches in diameter. (The Smithsonian Institution)

AVON POTTERY

The Avon Pottery was founded in Cincinnati, Ohio, in January, 1886, by Karl Langenbeck, who was previously with the Rookwood Pottery. Artus Van Briggle, who later worked at Rookwood, was one of the artists. The firm made a ware from yellow Ohio clay with modeled and incised decorations and colored slip. It had a dull glaze finish. They made another type of ware from white clay with painted designs on the biscuit and covered with transparent glaze. Gradual shading of pink, olive, violet, blue, and brown were blended on the white body. Some of these pieces were made with modeled handles such as the horn and elephant hands found on a few pieces. One line of pottery resembled the Rookwood standard glaze line. The pottery closed in 1887 or 1888. Their glazed pieces were marked "Avon."

AVON

Avon Pottery mark.

Bibliography

Barber, Edwin A., *The Pottery and Porcelain of the United States*, New York: G. P. Putnam's Sons, 1893 (3d and rev. ed. 1909).

————, *Marks of American Potters*, Philadelphia: Patterson and White, 1904.

Peck, Herbert, *The Book of Rookwood Pottery*, New York: Crown Publishers, Inc., 1968.

AVON WORKS

Although Edwin Barber in his *Marks of American Potters* is very clear about the difference between the Avon Pottery of Cincinnati and the Avon Works of Wheeling, West Virginia, later writers have confused the records.

In November, 1900, a new company was organized as the Vance Faience Company in Tiltonville, Ohio. This

This Avon Pottery vase is marked "Avon, 1902." It is 5 inches tall and 6 inches wide. The vase is glazed in shades of green and blue with a raised white decoration. (Authors' collection)

Avon Works marks.

company planned to make faience, jardinieres, pedestals, and umbrella stands. Several other types of wares were made and sold. In 1902, the name of the pottery was changed to the Avon Faience Company, and William P. Jervis of England became manager (see Craven). Frederick Hurten Rhead also worked at the company (see Arequipa). According to Barber, in January, 1903, the Wheeling potteries company was organized by combining the Wheeling, La Belle, Riverside, and Avon potteries. Each of these four potteries became a department of the Wheeling Potteries Company. Artware was made at the Avon department.

One of the wares made by Avon was a glazed line decorated with white slip. It is thought to be the forerunner of the Jap-Birdimal line of Weller that was later introduced by Mr. Rhead.

The Avon department of Wheeling stopped making art pottery about 1905. Several marks were used by the Vance and Avon potteries. Early pieces were marked Vance; later the firm used at least three marks with the word Avon.

BIBLIOGRAPHY: See Avon Pottery.

BENNETT

The early history of the potteries founded by Edwin Bennett are not part of the history of American Art Pottery except as background information. James Bennett lived in Derbyshire, England, and worked in many potteries there before coming to the United States. In 1834 he obtained a job at the Jersey City Pottery.

He later went to Troy, Indiana, where he worked at the Indiana Pottery Company. He left because he had malaria and hoped that an East Liverpool, Ohio, location would be more healthy. With some money advanced by Anthony Kearns and Benjamin Harker he built a pottery in 1839. His pottery company made yellowware pieces

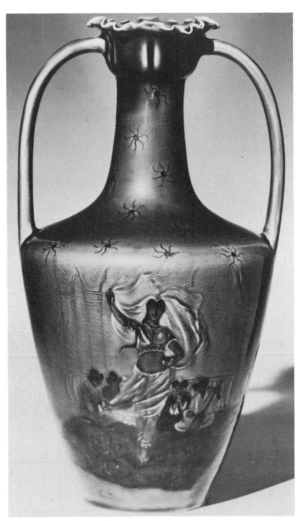

(Above) The bottom of the green glazed Bennett vase. The number 237937 is the museum accession number and is above the glaze. The other letters and numbers are below the glaze. (The Smithsonian Institution) (Right) The two-handled green glazed vase numbered 237937 was made by the Edwin Bennett Pottery Company, Inc., of Baltimore, Maryland. (The Smithsonian Institution)

which included mugs, pans, and other kitchen wares. The work was financially successful from the first batch, and James Bennett sent for his three brothers, Daniel, Edwin, and William. They came in 1841, and as Bennett and Brothers, they made yellowware and Rockingham ware. The success of this firm led to the founding of many other firms in the East Liverpool area such as the Harker Pottery, Salt and Mears, Knowles, Taylor and Knowles, John Goodwin's pottery, Woodward, Blakely & Co., Vodrey, and others.

In 1844, brother Edwin left the firm and went to Pittsburgh, Pennsylvania. In 1846, he started his own pottery, the E. Bennett Chinaware Factory, in Baltimore, Maryland. Two years later, his brother William joined him and the firm became E. & W. Bennett, until 1856 when William left the firm. Edwin Bennett continued to make pottery under the name Edwin Bennett Pottery from 1856 to 1890, and from 1890 to 1936 as the Edwin Bennett Pottery Co. Inc.

The firm, which continued operating under the

changes in name and personnel, made all types of pottery, including the famous "Rebekah at the Well" teapot, parian ware, Rockingham ware, porcelain, majolica, a type of Belleek, and others.

Art Pottery

The art pottery made at the factory was produced for only a short time, from 1895 to 1897. It was discontinued because of its poor sales. The line was called Albion. It was a slipware decorated with colored liquid clay on the green clay body of the piece. The body of the piece was green clay. After the design was built up from the colored glazes, the entire piece was covered with a clear glaze. Miss Kate DeWitt Berg was the chief decorator of these pieces. She made figures of hunting scenes in the desert and in the jungle, and they often pictured horses, camels, elephants, oriental figures, and related subjects. Another decorator of Albion ware was Miss Annie Haslam Brinton. Pieces were marked E Bennett, the date, often the initials of the artist, and the word Albion.

Bibliography

"Baltimore, Maryland's Bennett Pottery," *Spinning Wheel* (November 1958), 22.

Barber, Edwin A., *The Pottery and Porcelain of the United States,* New York: G. P. Putnam's Sons, 1893 (3d and rev. ed. 1909).

"Recent Advances in the Pottery Industry," *The Popular Science Monthly* XV (January 1892).

BROUWER AND MIDDLE LANE

The Middle Lane Pottery was operating in East Hampton, Long Island, by 1894. Theophilus A. Brouwer, Jr., was experimenting with luster glaze and he made pottery with unusual colors and metallic effects. One type was made with a glaze over gold leaf. This ware was called "Gold Leaf Underglaze." Another type was called "Fire Painting." The biscuit pottery was covered with a glaze that appeared to be a solid color until it was fired in a special manner. After firing, an iridescence plus a variety of colors were produced. Mottled pieces with a high gloss surface of reds and yellow, pale green and gold, or cream with mother-of-pearl were just a few of the possible colors created by "Fire Painting." No decoration was needed beyond the natural variation in glaze colors. A third type

A black and purple iridescent glaze is used over a lighter green glaze on this 7¼-inch vase. It is marked with the M under a whalebone arch. (The Smithsonian Institution)

(Above) This vase decorated with a snake has an iridescent glaze. It is 5 inches in diameter, 3½ inches high. The piece was made by the Middle Lane Pottery, East Hampton, Long Island. (The Smithsonian Institution)

A fiery orange yellow and brown glaze with iridescent effects covers this 7¼-inch vase. It is marked with the incised mark M under a whalebone arch, and the name Brouwer. It was made about 1903–1910. (The Art Museum, Princeton University, Princeton, New Jersey)

of pottery made was "Iridescent Fire Work." This pottery was glazed with a heavy coating with both the glaze and the metallic color in the same family. Extreme heat created a finished piece that resembled ancient rough glass. Pieces were made in various colors. "Sea-Grass Fire Work" was another glazed ware that was decorated through the action of the heat of the kiln. Lines that look like sea grass appear in green, brown, or gray on the plain glaze. "Kid Surface" ware was a pottery having a colored glaze in solid colors. Blue, white, brown, green, and gray were used. "Flame" was a special type of pottery combining several techniques. Each piece has a unique design and the mold was destroyed after a fine piece was made.

The factory moved to a new plant in Westhampton, Long Island, about 1903. It had a gate to the grounds made of a jawbone of a whale caught near Long Island. This bone plus the letter M was used as a trademark, and it was impressed on each piece. Also the name Brouwer was incised on the pieces that were made at Westhampton. Some pieces were also marked with the word "Flame" or a picture of a flame.

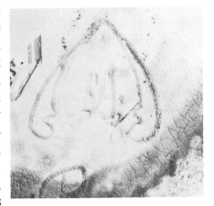

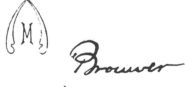

Brouwer marks.

Although Brouwer continued to make pottery, he had other business interests. He made a special type of "stone" figure from concrete, and in 1918, made concrete boats. In 1925, he incorporated The Ceramic Flame Company to make and sell pottery. In 1932 Brouwer died and the corporation was dissolved in 1946.

Bibliography

Barber, Edwin, *Marks of American Potters,* Philadelphia: Patterson and White, 1904.

————, *The Pottery and Porcelain of the United States,* New York: G. P. Putnam's Sons, 1909.

Benjamin, Marcus, "American Art Pottery—Part III," *Glass and Pottery World:* April, 1907, p. 35.

Clark, Robert Judson, *The Arts and Crafts Movement in America 1876–1916,* Princeton, N.J., Princeton University Press, 1972.

Evans, Paul, "Brouwer's Middle Lane Pottery," *Spinning Wheel,* December, 1973, 48–49, 54.

Jervis, W. P., *A Pottery Primer,* New York: O'Gorman Publishing Company, 1911.

BRUSH-McCOY POTTERY See J. W. McCoy Company

BRUSH POTTERY

(Above) Used from 1915 through 1925.   (Below left) Used from 1927 to 1929.   (Below right) Stamped mark used from 1930 through 1933.

In 1901, George Brush went to work as the editor of the *Owens Monthly,* a company paper of the J. B. Owens Pottery of Zanesville, Ohio. After a short time, he became the sales manager of the pottery, and in 1907, left the company to found his own firm, the Brush Pottery Company.

Brush started his firm in a plant that had been used by the Union Pottery Company. He used their molds to make bowls and kitchen wares. His firm continued in business until 1908 when it was destroyed by fire. Brush then became the manager of the J. W. McCoy Pottery of Roseville. By 1911, the firm became the Brush McCoy Pottery (see McCoy).

The Brush McCoy Pottery was reorganized, and in December 1925, changed its name to the Brush Pottery Company. George Brush became its president in 1931. He died in 1934 but the company is still working in Roseville, Ohio.

Just as there were two separate companies named Brush Pottery Company (one from 1907 to 1908; the other from 1925 through the present), there were two McCoy potteries: one, the J. W. McCoy Pottery, operating from 1899 to 1925 (when it changed its name to Brush); the other, the Nelson McCoy Pottery, which operated from 1910 to 1967 when it became part of the Mount Clemens Pottery.

Bibliography

Brush Pottery Company, Catalog, 1927, 1930, 1962.

Evans, Paul, "The Confusing McCoy Potteries," *Spinning Wheel* XXIX (January, February 1973), 8–9.

Schneider, Norris F., "Brush Pottery," *Zanesville Times Recorder* (September 9, 1962, September 16, 1962).

Zanesville Chamber of Commerce, Pamphlet, 1918.

(Above) Revised 1927 mark used from 1958 to 1968. (Below) Current mark in use since 1969.

BUFFALO POTTERY—DELDARE

The Buffalo Pottery Company made many types of pottery. The famous Deldare Pottery now is being classified with many of the art potteries although it was not hand potted or a uniquely decorated product, but rather a limited production line from a firm that made many types of chinaware.

The Buffalo Pottery was founded by the Larkin Soap Company. John Larkin and his brother-in-law Elbert Hubbard manufactured soap and sold it through a premium-purchase plan.

The Buffalo Pottery was built in Buffalo, New York, in 1901. The main purpose was to make dishes that could be given in exchange for certificates of Larkin soap. The Buffalo Pottery Company, now Buffalo China, Inc., is still in business.

The pottery of most interest to today's collector is Deldare Ware. The manager of the pottery was Louis Bown and the superintendent was George H. Wood; William Rea, a ceramic engineer, perfected the body. An olive-green base clay was developed by adding oxide of chrome to body clay made of English and Tennessee ball clay. The first pieces were made in 1908 and 1909. (Pitchers of the Deldare-colored body with black outline decorations are known, dated 1906 and 1907 and a later series dated 1923, 1924, and 1925.) The pieces were decorated with English scenes from two old books, *The Vicar of Wakefield* and *Cranford.* The etchings were copied and hand-

Stamped mark used on pitchers. The same mark was used for several years, so a different year may appear.

(Above) This stamped mark was also used on pitchers and may have a different year.   (Below) Mark used on Deldare Ware. Different years were used.

This Deldare humidor was made in 1909. On one side it says, "There was an old sailor and he had a wooden leg/He had no tobacco, nor tobacco could he beg." The other side says, "So save up your money and save up your rocks, And you'll always have tobacco in your own tobacco box." The humidor is 7½ inches high. (Authors' collection)

painted on the artware in mineral colors. A second series with its own backstamp was made in 1909 with the "Fallowfield Hunt" scenes. The only known piece of Deldare in 1910 was a calendar plate. A third series was made in 1911 with copies of etchings from "Tours of Dr. Syntax." This was a different Deldare ware that was called Emerald Deldare. Some Deldare, as above, was made in 1923, 1924, and 1925, but the cost of manufacturing made it unprofitable and the line was discontinued. The later Deldare was made in the same manner and often by the same artists, and the only difference was the date on the bottom.

Deldare ware was made in complete dinner sets, dresser sets, vases, pitchers, candleholders, punch bowls and mugs, and other shapes.

List of Known Design Titles

Ye Olden Days 1908, 1909, 1923, 1924, 1925: "All You Have to Do to Teach the Dutch English," "An Evening at Ye Lion Inn," "At Ye Lion Inn," "Breaking Cover," "Dancing ye Minuet," "The Great Controversy," "Heirlooms," "His Manner of Telling Stories," "Scenes of Life in Olden Days," "Scenes of Village Life in ye Olden Days," "Street Scenes," "Their Manner of Telling Stories," "This Amazed Me," "To Advise Me in a Whisper," "To Demand My Annual Rent," "To Spare an Old Broken Soldier," "Travelling in ye Olden Days," "Village Life in ye Olden Days," "Welcome Me with Most Cordial Hospitality," "Which He Returned with a Courtesy," "With a Cane Superior Air," "Ye English Village," "Ye Lion Inn," "Ye Olden Days," "Ye Olden Times," "Ye Town Crier," "Ye Village Gossips," "Ye Village Parson," "Ye Village Schoolmaster," "Ye Village Street," "Ye Village Tavern." *Fallowfield Hunt 1908, 1909:* "At the Three Pigeons," "Breakfast at the Three Pigeons," "Breaking Cover," "The Dash," "The Death," "The Hunt Supper," "The Return," "The Start."

Other pictures in this series are just entitled "The Fallowfield Hunt" or are uncaptioned. All of these pictures were done originally by Cecil Aldin as prints about 1900.

Designs

Emerald Deldare 1910, 1911: The Dr. Syntax scenes by Thomas Rowlandson were copied on the Emerald Del-

(Left) This sample plate was used to advertise the Buffalo Pottery Deldare Ware. (Right) "An evening at Ye Lion Inn" is a Deldare plate of 6¼ inches diameter.

At right. (Top) The Deldare designs were used later on a pink background plate called Rouge Ware. This 11-inch-diameter plate is decorated with the scene "Morgan's Red Coach Tavern." This ware was made after 1928. (Authors' collection) (Center) The Dutch jug was made in 1906 and 1907. This 6⅛-inch jug is marked 1906. The decorations are in shades of red, green, and blue. (Authors' collection) (Bottom) The Fox Hunt is a 7-inch-high pitcher marked 1907. It was offered for sale in the 1905 catalogue but was available in later years. (Authors' collection)

dare with minor alterations. The borders of the Emerald Deldare are art nouveau style or geometric. Some pieces have an art nouveau central design instead of the Dr. Syntax picture.

Abino Ware

Abino ware was made in 1911, 1912, and 1913. It was the art pottery that was made after Deldare. The shapes were the same as Deldare, but it had a transfer-printed, hand-decorated design showing boats, sea scenes and windmills. The designs were misty and soft with pale green and rust the main colors. Abino was marked with hand-printed black letters plus the date and a series number.

Pitchers

It seems necessary to include the pitchers made by Buffalo Pottery from 1905 to 1909, although these were not art pottery. These pitchers were made of semivitreous china and twenty-nine are known today. The decorations are transfer printed and often hand decorated. Many pieces had gold at the top edge and on the handles. The twenty-nine pieces include:

Art Nouveau	1908	The Buffalo Hunt
Blue Geranium . .	1905	. . . . undated

(Left) The Pilgrim pitcher is marked 1907. It is 8¾ inches high. One side shows Miles Standish, the other John Alden and Priscilla. (Center) The Roosevelt Bears pitcher was made in 1906, 1907, and 1908. This piece is marked 1907. The pitcher has pictures of the bears made popular through some children's books illustrated by Floyd Campbell. (Authors' collection)   (Right) The Blue Willow pitcher is not one of the special pitchers but is part of the Blue Willow dinnerware sets. This 6⅝-inch-high pitcher has an indistinct date mark. The fence in the front of this pitcher is dark blue although the catalogue shows this piece with a lattice fence. It was made about 1907. (Authors' collection)

Canton Blue Flowers
. . . . 1905
Chrysanthemum
. . . . undated
Cinderella. 1907
    (offered for sale—
        1905–1909—
        Larkin catalogues
Dutch Jug
. . . . 1906 and 1907
The Fox Hunt and the
Whirl of the Town
. . . . 1908
George Washington
. . . . 1907
Gloriana
. . . . 1907 and 1908
The Gunner. . undated
Holland. 1908
Hounds and Stag 1906
John Paul Jones. . 1907
The Landing of Roger

Williams 1907
Mason Jug. 1907
Melon-shaped China
Pitcher 1909
The Old Mill 1907
Orchids . . . . . . undated
Pilgrim 1908
Rip Van Winkle . 1907
Robin Hood 1906
Roosevelt Bears. . 1907
Sailing Ships and
Lightship 1906
Sailors and
Lighthouse 1906
Triumph (annual
poppy). . . . . . . undated
Vertical Stripe. . . 1906
The Whaling City—
New Bedford,
Massachusetts . . . 1907
Wild Ducks 1907

Bibliography

Altman, Seymour and Violet, *The Book of Buffalo Pottery*, New York: Crown Publishers, Inc., 1969.

Barber, Edwin A., *The Pottery and Porcelain of the United States,* New York: G. P. Putnam's Sons, 1893 (3d and rev. ed. 1909).

"Buffalo Pottery's Art Ware," *Spinning Wheel* XIX (May 1963) 20.

Garrett, Brice, "Buffalo Pottery and the Larkin Company," *Spinning Wheel* XIX (January, February 1963), 18–19.

Gernert, Dee Albert, "Buffalo Pottery's Deldare Ware," *Spinning Wheel* XIX (March 1963), 14–15.

"A Visit to the Buffalo Pottery." *The Pottery, Glass & Brass Salesman,* II (August 11, 1910), 27–28.

"Oakwood" is impressed on the bottom of both of these Cambridge Pottery vases. The larger vase at the left is 7½ inches high, glazed in shades of dark brown to tan. The smaller vase at the right is 6¾ inches high, glazed in mottled yellow to green to brown shades. (Authors' collection)

CAMBRIDGE ART POTTERY

One of the minor art potteries that developed in the southern Ohio area was the Cambridge Art Pottery of Cambridge, Ohio. The firm was started about 1895 and worked until World War I. The pieces made were very similar to the other brown-glazed decorated wares of the area, such as Weller, Louwelsa or Owens Utopia, or Rookwood. All types of floral decorations and some portraits were used to decorate the pieces. The artists who worked at this factory seemed to be well traveled and many of them also decorated at other Ohio factories.

CAMBRIDGE Guernsey.

Acorn   OAKWOOD

TERRHEA

Cambridge marks can appear either by themselves or with the acorn and/or cipher. When the name appears alone, it is impressed. When the acorn and/or cipher appears with the name the entire mark is printed.

This Cambridge pottery vase is mottled brown, green, and yellow. It is 10 inches high. (Authors' collection)

Bibliography

Barber, Edwin A., *Marks of American Potters,* Philadelphia: Patterson and White, 1904.

"Cambridge Glass Museum Opens," *The Antique Reporter* (August 1973).

Trade Marks of the Jewelry and Kindred Trades, New

1879–1886.

Printed in red or impressed, 1886–

C.A.P. Co.

Impressed, 1890–1891

York and Philadelphia: Jewelers' Circular-Keystone Publishing Co., 1904.

Wolfe, John C. Jr., Letter to the Authors (February 7, 1972).

CHELSEA KERAMIC ART WORKS
See Dedham Pottery

CHELSEA POTTERY U.S.
See Dedham Pottery

CINCINNATI ART POTTERY COMPANY

The Cincinnati Art Pottery Company was founded in Cincinnati, Ohio, in 1879 as a joint stock company, of which Frank Huntington was president. Thomas J. Wheatley (see Wheatley Pottery) worked for the firm until 1882. They made several types of pottery, at first underglazed decorated pottery, but later Barbotine ware, which was an applied pottery. That was discontinued and replaced by a ware called Hungarian Faience, which had an overglaze decoration on white clay. Their Portland Blue Faience was a dark blue glazed ware with gold decorations. The most important work of the company was Kezonta ware, an ivory-colored faience with natural floral colors and gold scrollwork decorations. The factory closed in 1891. Several marks were used by the firm. (See Pottery Club of Cincinnati.)

Bibliography

Barber, Edwin A., *The Pottery and Porcelain of the United States,* New York: G. P. Putnam's Sons, 1893 (3d and rev. ed. 1909).

(Left) White crackle glaze with cloisonné decorations of natural color flowers on a sky-blue background decorate this vase. It has gold trim. The vase is Kezonta ware made by the Cincinnati Art Pottery Company about 1895. It is marked with the word "Cincinnati" stenciled in a circle. (The Smithsonian Institution)   (Below) Cincinnati Art Pottery Company "Hungarian Faience" as pictured in *Popular Science Monthly,* Vol. 40, January 1892.

_____, *Marks of American Potters*, Philadelphia: Patterson and White, 1904.

Peck, Herbert, *The Book of Rookwood Pottery*, New York: Crown Publishers, Inc., 1968.

Perry, Mrs. Aaron, "Decorative Pottery of Cincinnati," *Harper's New Monthly Magazine*, LXII (May 1881), 834–845.

CLEWELL

Charles Walter Clewell of Canton, Ohio, made a unique type of pottery called Clewell Ware. A leaflet written by Clewell to be given out with pieces of the pottery said: "A number of years ago, while visiting the Wadsworth Atheneum in Hartford, I saw a small bronze wine jug in the J. Pierpont Morgan Memorial Collection. The bronze had been found at Boscoreale during the excavations which led to the finding of the famous silver treasure of the Louvre, was accredited to the Romans and dated 200 B.C. It was blue; a wonderful blue varying from the very light tones through turquoise to almost black with flecks of green and rustlike brown and spots of bare darkened metal.

"Seeing this little jug cost me more than two years of experimenting and a number of trips to Hartford to compare results, but finally the perfect blue appeared. It was a long hunt and particularly difficult; textbooks gave me no help."

The blue patina bronze that Clewell developed was used on Clewell ware after 1923. Mr. Clewell also developed a method of bronze coating on pottery. He could then treat the bronze in various ways to make it turn different colors. At a specific moment during the process when he felt the effect was ideal, he chemically treated the piece to stop the coloring and permanently fix the design and color. This meant that the Clewell ware could be washed later and the colors would remain.

Clewell started his experiments in 1899 and Clewell ware was made in very limited quantities from 1902 to 1955. He bought pottery blanks from such Ohio potteries as Roseville, Weller, Owens, Rookwood, Cambridge, Knowles, Taylor and Knowles, and others. They were covered with a thin coating of bronze and specially treated. Sometimes, the bronze was made to look as if it had been hammered. At other times, pieces looked as if they had been made with metal rivets. A few pieces had incised

The Cincinnati Art Pottery Company made this pitcher marked "KEZONTA." It has a yellow crackle glaze with gold overglaze decorations. The interior is covered with a clear glaze. It is 12 inches high, 6 inches in diameter. The gold decoration is credited to Jesse Dean of New York who worked from about 1870 to 1910. (The Smithsonian Institution)

The Clewell mark.

line designs. They were well suited for use as pitchers and vases because the pieces actually had metal on the outside and pottery on the inside. An ad for his work that appeared in the Burr McIntosh Christmas catalogue, 1908, suggested the purchase of a Holland Stein and Tankard set. The ad read: "These sets are faithful reproductions of the original old Holland Steins of four hundred years ago, made of hammered copper (brass or silver) with porcelain lining and hand made by a special process which we control. Sets furnished plain or quaintly marked with monogram or inscription."

After Clewell died, his daughter sold most of the stock that was left to nearby collectors and art institutes. It is said that less than three thousand pieces remained.

Pieces of Clewell were marked with an incised "Clewell" or an impressed "Clewell Metal Art Canton, O." or "Clewell Coppers" or "Clewell Canton, Ohio" or a "W" within a "C."

Clewell also cast bronzes that can be found signed with his name.

Clewell died in 1965. His formula for producing the blue patina on bronze was burned at his death and his method still remains a secret.

Bibliography

"The Bronze Productions of C. W. Clewell of Canton, O.," advertising leaflet.

Clewell, Lawrence H., correspondence with authors.

A vase with metal covering showing the characteristic aged coloring of the "patination" series by Clewell.

(Right) This Clewell mug was offered for sale by the Clewell Studio of 1956 E. 9th St., Canton, Ohio, in 1908 through a Christmas catalogue. It was part of a set called the Holland Stein and Tankard Set, made of hammered copper with porcelain lining, and handmade by a special process. The pieces could be furnished plain or marked with monogram or inscription. The mug is 4½ inches high, 3 inches in diameter. It is unmarked. (Authors' collection)

(Below) This Clewell vase has incised decorations and a dark metallic glaze.

The copper-covered mug has the words "Canton, Ohio" raised on the side. The bookend is also copper-covered and has the center initial "M" as part of the design. (Neil McCullough)

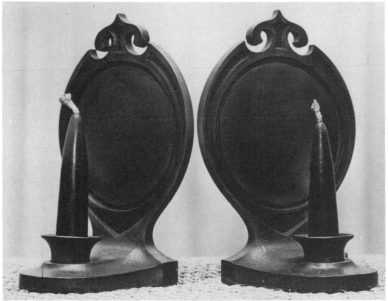

Clewell candleholders are unusual. This pair has a dark metallic glaze. (Neil McCullough)

Clewell, Ralph and Beulah, correspondence with authors.

Cranston, A. M., correspondence with authors.

McCullough, Dale and Neil, correspondence with authors.

Meyers, Mrs. Charles G., correspondence with authors.

CLIFTON POTTERY
See Lonhuda Pottery

The Cowan monogram as stamped in black and impressed on the bottom of a piece.

Pale green glaze was used on this plate by Thelma Winter with carved decorations of deer and dog. It is 11½ inches in diameter. The Cowan Pottery made these dishes for a short time, but so many were damaged in the kiln that the line was dropped. (Authors' collection)

COWAN POTTERY

R. Guy Cowan* was born in East Liverpool, Ohio, on August 1, 1884. His father and grandfather had been potters and he started to help in his father's pottery at a young age. He studied art in high school, graduated, and moved to Cleveland, Ohio, where he taught ceramics classes at East Technical High School. He took a few years off from teaching and completed a course in ceramic engineering at Alfred University in New York in 1911. He returned to teaching in Cleveland until 1913 when he opened his own pottery studio. During the years that he was teaching and studying, he often visited the studio of Horace Potter, a popular gathering place for many of the Cleveland artists.

In 1913, Guy Cowan built a kiln in his backyard at the corner of East 97th Street and Euclid Avenue. His work was exhibited and, with the help of the City of Cleveland and the Cleveland Chamber of Commerce, Cowan incorporated his business and built a larger studio. The new studio was opened at Nicholson Avenue in Lakewood, Ohio. Most of the early Cowan pieces were made from terra cotta and buff clays with lead glaze, probably obtained near East Liverpool, Ohio.

At the start of World War I, Guy Cowan closed his pottery studio and served in the Chemical Warfare Service as a captain. After the war, he was offered several jobs. He decided to reopen the Cowan Pottery Studio, and Wendell G. Wilson, an army major with whom he had served, came to manage it. The pottery received official recognition and first prize at the International Show at the Chicago Art Institute in 1917.

Soon after the pottery reopened the gas well at the plant ran out, so a new pottery was built at Lake Avenue and Linda in Rocky River, Ohio, in 1920. An old barn was used as the office and working plant. Nine gas kilns were built at this site.

Cowan briefly returned to school about 1921 and took courses at the John Huntington Polytechnic Institute in Cleveland, Ohio. In 1921, he began a large-scale commercial production, and over twelve hundred dealers in the United States, which included stores such as Marshall

*Reginald Guy Cowan was his given name, but Guy would not use it and was always known as R. Guy Cowan. (From a letter March 20, 1965, R. M. Hanna to Western Reserve Historical Society.)

Field of Chicago, Wanamaker of Philadelphia and Halle Brothers of Cleveland, sold his pottery. He also made tiles (the floor of the Solarium of the Cleveland Museum of Art was paved with Cowan floor tile and remained until 1958 when the floor was replaced. The tiles were made from buff clay from eastern Ohio). The pottery also made doorknobs, fountains, wall panels, and, of course, vases and figurines, flower holders, and the other commercial wares. The firm had forty employees by 1925.

The Cleveland City Directory of 1927 notes that the Cowan Pottery Studio, Inc., was incorporated in 1927 with a capital of $100,000. It was formerly the Cleveland Pottery and Tile Company. Officers were R. Guy Cowan, president; Harry J. Thompson, vice president and treasurer; and Jerome Fiske, secretary.

The designs at the pottery were usually done by Guy Cowan, but he often bought designs from other Cleveland artists and students at the old "Cleveland School of Art," now the Cleveland Institute of Art where he headed the Ceramic Department from 1928 through 1933. Two artists, Paul Bogatay and Thelma Frazier, were hired on a permanent basis.

The Cowan Pottery Studio started having money problems in 1929, and Guy wanted to reorganize it into an art center for a colony of artists. The firm was reorganized as Cowan Potters Incorporated. Howard P. Eells, Jr., was chairman of the board, Guy Cowan was president, and Charles C. Berry was their vice president and general manager. A group of civic-minded wealthy Clevelanders helped with the financing, including Mr. and Mrs. F. F. Prentice, William G. Mather, John L. Severance, H. G. Dalton, Mr. and Mrs. E. B. Greens, Mrs. Ben P. Bole, Lyman Treadway, and Mary Newberry. The new company planned to move the factory to a modern building in a nearby suburb where "spirit and physical beauty will be fitting and compatible with the artistic nature of its work" (*The Bystander* of Cleveland, September, 1929).

Most of the money problems continued into the depression and in December of 1931, Cowan Potteries, Inc., was closed. The remaining stock was sold to the Bailey Company, a department store in Cleveland. Guy Cowan continued working in Cleveland as a research engineer for Ferro Enamel until 1933 when he moved to Syracuse, New York, to become a consultant to the Onondaga Pottery Company. He continued to work and teach there until he died in March of 1957.

The dancer by Elizabeth Seaver Ness is glazed in a dark tan body color with royal blue hair and base and maroon and yellow pants. The figure is 9½ inches high. It is marked with the impressed Cowan insignia and the impressed word COWAN. This figure was also made in plain cream color. (Authors' collection)

This art deco bird head is a bookend made by Cowan. Gold and dark iridescent glaze covers the 5½-inch-high bookend. (Authors' collection)

Ducks and foliage are carved on the sides of this large maroon glazed vase. The 12-inch-high piece was made by the Cowan pottery in the 1920s. It is marked with the incised name Cowan and the circular Cowan mark. (Authors' collection)

A brilliant yellow crackle glaze covers this Cowan vase. The irregularities at the lower half of the form are caused by thicker glaze and are not part of the planned decoration. It is 7 inches high, 5 inches wide and marked with the Cowan circular impressed mark. (Authors' collection)

Product

The first pottery made by Guy Cowan was of red clay covered with lead glaze and hand signed. When the new kiln was built in 1920, a real porcelain body was used. It was made from English china clay, English ball clay, Maine feldspar, and Illinois flint. The English ball clay was shipped by boat to Philadelphia and brought to Cleveland by one or two train carloads at a time.

The equipment at the plant was the most modern of its day and the clay was ground, searched by magnets for iron, and filter-pressed into slabs. Jiggered clay was used on the potter's wheel and for hand modeling. Slip clay was used to pour into the molds. The artist made the original design using plaster or clay. A plaster cast was made and filled with plaster to form a new model and then the new model was reworked. Then the perfected model was used to make a block and case that formed many molds. Some of the molds were made in as many as twenty pieces.

Most of the pieces were made of porcelain and covered with a colored glaze. Tiles were made of tan clay from eastern Ohio.

The firm was making commerical wares and tiles in 1921. By 1925, Cowan had a full line of table settings, bowls, candlesticks, compotes, lamp bases, patterned dishes, teapots, cup and saucers, a line for the sickroom which included toast covers, and the usual figurines and vases.

The flower figurines were introduced in 1925. The table setting of bowl, flower holder, compotes, and candlestick became popular. An inexpensive line for the flower shops called Lakeware was introduced in 1928. It had the Cowan shapes, but different glazes. In later years, the Lakeware and Cowan glazes seem to have been interchanged. Cowan also made humidors, wine sets, sunbonnet girl bookends, plus a variety of statuettes for the tops of radio cabinets. A contest in 1930 where ten dollars was offered for the best planting promoted the strawberry jars. The R. Guy Cowan line was introduced for decorators. It included limited edition figures, thrown bowls, tiles, liqueur sets, service plates, and the king and queen decanters. Office items such as clips, inkwells, penholders, Wahl penbases, bookends, paperweights, and lamps were made. In 1931, the seahorse base line and informal decorated pottery were introduced.

The range of products by Cowan Potteries is certainly

far-reaching. They were not only art pottery, but also commercial pottery. Limited edition pieces were made to sell at high prices while some ashtrays were for sale for as little as fifty cents. Pieces were glazed in jade, la Garda, daffodil, oriental red, basalt, peach, apple blossom, larkspur, jet, blue delft, russet brown, plum, silver, feu rouge, May green, ivory, a light blue called clair de lune, the famous Egyptian blue, and crystal. In the fall of 1928, verd antique, October, and fawn glazes were introduced. In 1930, new matrix glazes were azure, plum, peach, and fir green; each gave a two-colored mottled effect. Lusterware was colored fire blue, marigold, sea-green and larkspur blue. Crackleware was glazed guava, spruce, terra-cotta, parchment, or Egyptian blue. Some pieces were coated with black slip and had designs cut through to the white body. Glazes were made in low gloss or flat glaze. Sometimes two glazes were used on the same piece and a new name was used in the catalogue; for example, ivory and nasturtium green made April, ivory and pink was apple blossom, and ivory and orchid was hyacinth.

"Madonna," made by R. Guy Cowan in 1928. It is 18⅝ inches high and 13½ by 5½ inches at the base. (The Cleveland Museum of Art, Dudley P. Allen Fund)

Artists and Designers

(Includes their known pieces; dates indicate reference in catalogues.)

Russell Barnett Aiken.

Elizabeth Anderson. (Married Hugh Seaver; later married Eliott Ness) Spanish dancers 1928, Pierrot and Pierrette, 1928.

Whitney Atcheley.

Arthur E. Baggs. Potter and ceramist, glaze expert (crystalline glazes), later headed Ceramic Department of Ohio State University, 1928–1935.

Alexander Blazys. 1927–1929. Sculptor—most important piece monumental sculpture in bronze, "City Fettering Nature," Cleveland Museum of Art, ceramic sculpture "Moses," "Russian Dancers," head of Sculpture Department, Cleveland School of Art.

Paul Bogatay. 1929–1930. Designer unique pottery in limited edition.

R. Guy Cowan. 1912–1931. Adam and Eve, Margarita, 1929, Madonna, 1929.

Dalzee.

Edris Eckert. Designer, well-known glass artist today.

This 10-inch-high cream-colored flower holder by Walter Sinz was shown in the 1931 Cowan catalogue. It sold for $5.00. The piece is marked with two different impressed Cowan marks. (Authors' collection)

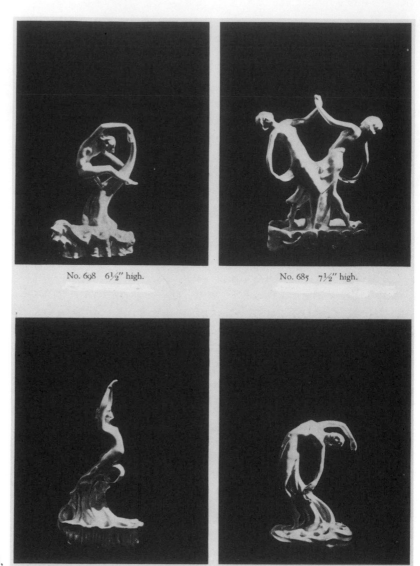

No. 698 6½" high.

No. 685 7½" high.

No. 683 8¼" high.

No. 700 6" high.

Flower holder, figurine No. 698, was created by artist Walter Sinz.

Waylande De Santis Gregory. 1932, Burlesque Dancer, Diana and the Two Fawns, Tors, 1929, beaten dog, relief decoration vase, 1930, U-19, Pan sitting on a toadstool, swan, Salome, Alice in Wonderland.

Richard Hummel. Ceramic technician, chemist, mixed glazes, made clay bodies.

A. Drexel Jacobson. 1928, Julia, 1932, Introspection, 1928, Antinea.

Raoul Josset. 1930, B-16 large bowl, relief decoration, sports figurines included football, polo, etc. French monumental terra-cottas with Chicago Terra Cotta Company. Was invited by Guy to work in pottery.

Mr. McDonald.

Jose Martin. 1930, French wood carver did intricate carvings on plaster molds for lidded jars, etc. Art Deco style. Invited by Guy to pottery.

22

F. Luis Mora. Sculptor and painter of the Southwest. Ceramic mold figures series of three: Indian Brave, 16" high; Seated Girl, 9" high; and Woman with Flower Basket, 16" high.

Elmer Novotny.

Margaret Postgate. 1929, 1932.

Victor Schreckengost. "Jazz" bowl, 1931.

UNIQUE PORCELAIN FIGURES FROM AN IMMORTAL BOOK

To meet a widespread demand for Cowan decanters and bottles we decided to create something that would have originality and artistic appeal as well as utility. That we succeeded far beyond our hopes is indicated by the instant popularity of the above pair.

You will recognize, of course, the famous King and Queen characters from Carroll's "Alice Through the Looking Glass". That they are decanters is cleverly concealed until the crown is removed.

These figures (X12, X13) retail at $5.00 each in Ivory, Black, or Oriental; or at $7.50 when hand decorated in several contrasting colors. They are glazed inside and leakproof.

Quite the most unique offering by Cowan in many years.

A page from the 1929 catalogue of the Cowan Potters, Inc., showing the King and Queen decanters by Waylander de Santis Gregory.

ADAM AND EVE   *By R. Guy Cowan*

Limited edition of 25—6 pair unsold.   Present Price $100.00
Terra cotta crackle glaze.   13½" high

Exhibited Cleveland Museum of Art, 1928. Pennsylvania Academy of
Art, 1929. Invited, jury free, to fall exhibition, National Painting and
Sculpture at Chicago Art Institute, 1929.

A page from the 1930 catalogue of the Cowan Potters, Inc., showing Adam and Eve, the limited edition figures.

Elsa Shaw. Instructor Design, Cleveland School of Art. Tile Mural—Grecian Figures, Art Deco style.

Walter Sinz. 1925–1930. Sculptor, Sculpture Department, Cleveland School of Art. Me and My Shadow, relief plates. Central figurines for table settings with bowls and candlesticks.

Jack Waugh. Mold maker.

Frank N. Wilcox. 1925. Designed Boy and Girl Bookends.

Edward Winter. 1930, designer limited edition pottery.

Thelma Frazier Winter. 1928–1930, designer limited editions of vases and plaques. Colorist in underglaze painting for F. Luis Mora's Indian Series (three figures, 16 to 18 inches high) and Elsa Shaw's large-scale tile murals. Service plates, limited edition, in pale blue green (opalescent glaze with raised white design) undersea design. Crackle plates, 1929–1930.

Limited Editions

(partial list): Antinea, 100, bust of a woman, 13⅞" high, Drexel Jacobson, 1928; Burlesque Dancer, 50, Waylande Gregory; Giulia, 500, A. Drexel Jacobson, 1928, bust of

Italian girl, 10⅝" high; Mary, 50, Margaret Postgate, 1929; Madonna, 50, Margaret Postgate, 1929; Adam and Eve, 25, R. Guy Cowan 1929, 13½" high terra-cotta glaze; Margarita, 50, R. Guy Cowan, 1929, shell-green glaze; Diana and the Two Fawns, 100, Waylande Gregory, 1929; Torso, 1929, Waylande Gregory; Moses, 1930, Alexander Blazys, blue glaze; service plates undersea designs pale blue green with raised white decorations; Thelma Frazier, Winter, 1930.

The circular impressed Cowan mark is found on this footed dish. It has a pink interior and cream exterior. (Authors' collection)

Among Cowan marks are "Cowan Pottery" incised on early redware pieces, often in conjunction with the artist's initials or Cowan's monogram; "Cowan" stamped in black; "Cowan Pottery" stamped in black; and "Lakeware" impressed on that line from 1927 to 1931.

Bibliography

Boros, Ethel, "Playing the Antique Market," *The Plain Dealer* (November 12, 1967).

Borsick, Helen, "Pottery Lights Up a Brilliant Ohio Epoch," *The Plain Dealer* (August 24, 1969).

Brodbeck, John, "Cowan Pottery," *Spinning Wheel* XXIX (March 1973), 24–27.

Clark, Edna Maria, *Ohio Art and Artists*, Richmond, Va.: Garrett and Massie, 1932.

Cowan Potters, Inc., The, Catalogues 1928, 1930, 1931, undated.

Milliken, William M., "Ohio Ceramics," *Design* (November 1937).

Robbins, Carle, "Cowan of Cleveland, Follower of an Ancient Craft," *The Bystander of Cleveland* (September 7, 1929).

Stiles, Helen, *Pottery in the United States*, New York: E. P. Dutton, 1941.

Western Reserve Historical Society File: artists list from Edward Winter, Jan. 4, 1965. "The Cowan Pottery Collection at the W.R.H.S."; "Cowan Potters, Inc."; letters from Rhoda M. Hanna, March 20, 1965, June 22, 1965, August 13, 1969; letter from Richard O. Hummel, January 27, 1966; information from Dr. William Milliken, Dec. 17, 1964.

Winter, Thelma Frazier, correspondence with authors.

(Above) An Egyptian-inspired design is carved on this blue glazed bowl made at the Craven Art Pottery. (Right) Jervis's mark on the Egyptian-inspired bowl.

Olive and vermilion glaze covers this vase made about 1905 by the Craven Art Pottery, East Liverpool, Ohio. It is 5¼ inches high and 5 inches in diameter. The bottom is marked with an impressed "J." (The Smithsonian Institution)

CRAVEN ART POTTERY

William Percival Jervis is a name known to pottery researchers because of his books: *A Book of Pottery Marks, Rough Notes on Pottery,* 1896; *The Encyclopedia of Ceramics,* 1902; and *A Pottery Primer,* 1911. He also had his own art pottery factory that created some unusual pottery during the early 1900s.

Jervis came to the United States from England before 1896. In 1902, he became manager of the Avon Faience (See p. 4). When the firm discontinued making art pottery in 1905 he left. That year the Craven Art Pottery Company of East Liverpool, Ohio, was organized by W. P. Jervis, and Albert Cusick. It is believed others were included. Jervis made faience with a matte glaze. His glazes were deliberately developed to produce a shaded effect because he felt that the shading was more true to nature. The glazes were in greens, blues, yellows, oranges, pinks, crimsons, and blacks. The body of the art pottery was Ohio yellowware clay and New Jersey marl. The pieces were made to be utilitarian and their shapes were determined by their use. Jervis would think of a flower for a vase and then design the vase to suit it.

There are pieces with raised designs. Many had incised writing as part of the decoration. Cutout sections and hand-painted flowers were used. Some of the pieces show the potters' absolute lack of skill, with bases that sagged and uneven walls. The pottery seemed highly experimental.

The exact date of closing of the factory is not known. The Record of the Pottery Industry of the East Liverpool District, p. 286. Vol. 24, No. 8, 1945, *Bulletin of the American Ceramic Society,* by William H. Vodrey, Jr., lists the Corns Knob Works at Laura Avenue in East Liverpool in 1890. About 1900, they sold out to Benty Brothers, who made artware until 1906 when they became known as Craven. Craven discontinued business and suspended operations about 1910.

Bibliography

American Commercial Pottery Marks, Installment No. 6 (author and publisher unknown).

Barber, Edwin A., *The Pottery and Porcelain of the United States,* New York: G. P. Putnam's Sons, 1893 (3d and rev. ed. 1909).

Benjamin, Marcus, "American Art Pottery—Part II," *Glass and Pottery World* (April 1907), 35.

Jervis, W. P., "American Pottery—Jervis Mat Glazes," *Sketch Book,* VI (November 1907), 307–310.

————, "Pottery Flower Vases."

Koepke, Ann, correspondence with authors.

Seeley, Helen R., correspondence with authors.

DEDHAM POTTERY

The Robertson family was actively making pottery for many years before the establishment of the Chelsea Keramic Art works in Chelsea, Massachusetts. James Robertson was born in Edinburgh, Scotland, the son of a potter at the Fife Pottery. James had worked in the same pottery, but when he was about sixteen years old, he went to Watsons Factory in Prestonpans, Scotland, where he married and then traveled with his wife to northern England. There he worked in several of the potteries. He managed a redware pottery, worked in a blackware factory, and in firms that made luster and transfer wares. In 1853 he emigrated to the United States, arriving in New Jersey with his family. They had planned to settle on a piece of land in Illinois that Robertson had purchased when he was in England, but it turned out to be a swamp and he was forced to remain in New Jersey. James first worked in South River, then in the shop of James Carr in South Amboy. He next worked in New York City and then returned to New Jersey, to the firm of Speeler, Taylor and Bloor in Trenton. By 1859, the family had moved to Boston, Massachusetts.

Robertson had a daughter and three sons. According to a city directory, his son George was in business with him

Marks:

A.W. & H.C.
Robertson

1868–1872

in Boston in 1859. Records of the day show that Robertson managed the "East Boston Pottery," a name that may have meant the New England Pottery Company. In 1860 he joined with Nathaniel Plympton to form the Plympton and Robertson Pottery and they won a prize for their work at an 1860 exhibition in Boston. But by 1862, the firm changed owners and the pottery was owned by a Mr. Homer. Robertson worked for him as company manager until his retirement in 1872. (In *Early New England Potters and Their Marks* it is said that James Robertson worked for the East Boston Crockery Manufactory from 1865 to 1871. No mention is made of the Plympton & Robertson Pottery.)

CHELSEA KERAMIC ART WORKS (1872–1889).—Following a family tradition, the three Robertson sons went into the pottery business. In 1866, in an old varnish shop at Willow and Marginal streets, Chelsea, Massachusetts, Alexander W. Robertson started a pottery making redware. The pottery was located on the Chelsea marshes near a fine deposit of red clay on the Snake River near Powder Horn Hill. In 1867, Hugh Cornwall Robertson went to work with his brother and they made red clay flowerpots and vases marked A. W. and H. C. Robertson. The pots were unglazed or coated with dark green paint. James Robertson joined his sons at the Chelsea Pottery on June 1, 1872. He made what is believed to be the first pressed clay tiles produced in the United States. The firm name became James Robertson and Sons.

From about 1875 until 1889 the company was known as the Chelsea Keramic Art Works. They made red bisque ware which was a new, more sophisticated type of pottery. It was similar to the Grecian terra-cotta pieces that were first made in 1875. The urn-shaped pieces had red

Marks:

(Above) 1872–1889 (The Smithsonian Institution)
(Left) 1880–1889 (The Smithsonian Institution)
(Right) 1880–1908. Robertson mark.

1881–1895. CPUS mark. The following is a letter by Milton Robertson dated November 17, 1947: "The plate you refer to has the letters in the Clover Leaf —CPUS, which stands for Chelsea Pottery, U.S. to identify it as against Chelsea Potteries in England. It is the old mark used at the Chelsea, Massachusetts, plant before it was removed to Dedham. However, as the impression was made in the clay, and considerable of the bisque ware was brought to Dedham undecorated and unglazed, some of the early Dedham ware carried the Chelsea imprint. As a matter of fact, toward the closing days of Dedham Pottery, I came across some of the old Chelsea plates with the Chelsea mark on them, but they also had the mark like the one in the corner of this letter." (The letterhead had the square mark with a rabbit and the word "Registered," seen on the following page. (The Smithsonian Institution)

figures on a black ground in the ancient style. The red clay color showed through undecorated and the black encaustic decoration filled in around the design. Each piece was polished and had a smooth texture that was sometimes ornamented with engraved lines. Other redware pieces were made with high-relief modeled designs of children and birds. Franz Xavier Dengler, the sculptor, made these pieces before his death at the age of twenty-five. Other artists who worked with the firm were John G. Low (who later founded the Low Tile Works [see]), Isaac Elwood Scott, and G. W. Fenety.

The public did not seem to want the art pottery produced by the Chelsea Keramic Art Works, so in 1877, the company introduced a new ware called the Chelsea Faience Floral designs. The decoration was either carved in relief or applied to the vase while it was damp. A soft glaze covered the entire piece. Some of the pieces were made of a buff-colored clay with a hammered effect or with cut designs filled in with a white clay which formed a sort of mosaic effect under the glaze. This pottery was popular but it was too expensive for the general public. Some of the pieces were modeled by Josephine Day, the sister-in-law of Hugh Robertson, but Hugh did many of the pieces himself.

In 1878, a creamware was made that took colored glazes. Another type of pottery made at this time was called Bourg-la-Reine of Chelsea. It was a faience that was made by covering the piece with colored clays, often blue and white slip. Robertson used a painting technique and covered it with a transparent glaze in the same manner as Limoges faience.

1893–CPUS, inside the border, handwritten under the glaze. (The Smithsonian Institution)

Inside the rim, artist's cipher "JLS" for J. Lindon Smith, 1893. (The Smithsonian Institution)

1896–1932.

1896–1943.

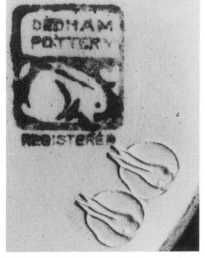

1929–1943. (The Smithsonian Institution)

1931

Stamped in blue on Fairbanks Memorial Plate.

In border, the mark of Maud Davenport.

CT no. 37

Probably Hugh Robertson test piece for developing glaze.

John Low left the firm in 1878 to start his own tile works. George W. Robertson went to work for him.

James Robertson died in 1880, but the company continued under the same name. Alexander W. Robertson retired in 1884 and the firm was then controlled by Hugh C. Robertson who years before had seen the Chinese sang de boeuf glaze at the Philadelphia Centennial Exhibition. He decided to try to find the secret of this red glaze. During the years that he experimented with this glaze, several other types of wares were made at the pottery, many of them the indirect result of his experiments. A dry glaze was developed about 1880. It was obtained by putting pieces into a kiln with those that required a high glaze. The heat was reduced and a full, satinlike glaze developed in a dull metallic color and shades of brown. A brown and blue mottled glaze was used on many pieces.

Hugh Robertson made many engraved or carved high relief stoneware plaques featuring designs from La Fontaine's fables, Dickens, or pictures of celebrities such as Dickens, Holmes, Byron, and Longfellow.

The company made a stoneware that was somewhat similar to parian in appearance. Experiments attempting to create a red glaze produced sea-green, peachblow shaded glaze, apple green, mustard yellow, blue green, purple, and maroon, all glazed with a hard brilliant finish. Also made were some pieces that had the Japanese style crackle with a gray and blue underglaze. It was a technique that often appeared in later products at the Dedham Pottery.

The discovery of the sang de boeuf glaze reads like a storybook drama. Robertson worked almost day and night in his pottery grinding the pigment and watching the kiln. He kept peering into the kiln at fifteen-minute intervals for sixty hours at a time. He had to be sure that the temperature was perfect. He supposedly used every dry bit of wood in his pottery to keep the kiln going. His method was primitive by today's standards; chemical formulas and temperature gauges were not available. He had a piece of old oriental sang de boeuf which he broke into small pieces and used for experiments. With this, he found that the ware could not be refired as he wished, so he kept making his own porcelain thimbles until he finally discovered the method. He named his red glaze "Robertson's blood."

Several other types of pottery were developed by Hugh Robertson during this period. He made large wall plaques that looked as though they were produced from carved wood. Figures were incised into the surface on some, while other types of plaques were made by carving bas-relief wet clay on a clay background. The figures were in high relief and some examples looked almost like sculpture work. A ware was also made by using raised clay decorations on a flat surface. Some pieces were glazed to look like the blue and white jasparware of Wedgwood.

All the inventive and artistic achievements of the Chelsea Keramic Art Works were acclaimed, but financial success never did come. The pieces required too much time and handwork by the artists, and money problems closed the firm in 1889. Fortunately, the art patrons of the area did not want to see Robertson stop making pottery so in 1891 they helped him form a new company. It was called the Chelsea Pottery U.S.

CHELSEA POTTERY U.S. (1891–1896).—Hugh Robertson was the manager of the newly formed company, the Chelsea Pottery U.S. Learning from the financial failure of his earlier pottery, Robertson and his directors decided that the firm should try making salable tablewares and avoid the expensive time-consuming art wares. Robertson remembered the crackleware glaze that he had achieved earlier on a few large vases. He worked on the process and within a few months after the formation of the new firm, he developed what is now the famous crackleware. The pieces were made in gray with freehand blue decoration. One known piece has the date 1891 and the initials JTC for J. Templeton Coolidge, one of the directors of the new firm. Several of these pieces were marked with the clover mark C.P.U.S. Joseph Lindon Smith, Charles E. Mills, Miss K. E. DeGoler, and others worked on the designs.

The work at the pottery seemed successful, but the kiln had always been on damp ground, and smoke from a nearby factory caused damage to some of the wares. In 1895, Arthur A. Carey, a director of the pottery, bought some land in East Dedham, Massachusetts, near a canal that ran from the Charles River to the Neponset River. The waterpower was useful for the crushing machinery and a railroad was nearby for the delivery of goods. A four-story brick building was built on the new parcel of land and the name of the firm was changed to the Dedham Pottery Company. The change in the name was partly to avoid confusion with the Chelsea Porcelain Company of England.

(Top) An unglazed red and terra-cotta bowl impressed CAW. It is 4½ inches high, 3¼ inches wide. (The Smithsonian Institution) (Bottom) Crimson, orange, red, gray, and green glaze covers this Dedham Pottery vase made by Hugh C. Robertson about 1899–1908. The 8-inch-high piece is incised Dedham Pottery with the cipher HCR. (The Art Museum, Princeton University, Princeton, New Jersey)

H. Robertson did this vase for the Dedham Pottery about 1900. It is 6½ inches high. (Collections of Greenfield Village and The Henry Ford Museum, Dearborn, Michigan)

DEDHAM POTTERY (1896–1943).—When Hugh Robertson arrived in Dedham, Massachusetts, to start work on his new pottery buildings, he brought most of the workers from the Chelsea Pottery U.S. The town of Dedham had no raw materials for the pottery, but the new firm's knowledge and designs of the earlier works made it possible for them to succeed. The clay came from Maryland and New Jersey; the feldspar from Maine; Iowa clay, English clay, Kentucky clay, and green cobalt were used.

The Dedham Pottery had two kilns. One was used to make the crackle glaze dishes that have become the best known of its works. The ware was fired at a high temperature so that a true procelain was made. It was hard with "a soft gray glaze and curiously crackled with a blue in-glaze decoration and fired at a heat of from 2000 to 2500 degrees." (Brochure of Dedham Pottery, 1896.)

In the second kiln, the firm made what were called "accidental glazes" or "volcanic ware." The pieces were fired ten to twelve times to produce the desired changes in the thick paste glaze that was applied to the top of the vases. The glaze ran and created mottled and striped effects. This process required skill because too much firing left unattractive bare spots on the red clay and the vase had to be refired. The vases were made in crimson, green, yellow, blue, slate, gray, mahogany, and other colors.

Hugh Robertson suffered for many years from lead poisoning which was the result of his glaze experiments. He died in 1908. There must have been some problems about the continuation of the Dedham Pottery because in Mr. Barber's 1909 edition of *The Pottery and Porcelain of the United States,* he stated: "At the present time, the Dedham Pottery is in course of reorganization, and all lovers of the beautiful in art will welcome its speedy reopening." The firm's problems must have been brief or Mr. Barber misunderstood the situation because a son, William A. Robertson, succeeded Hugh Robertson as head of the pottery. Unfortunately, William had suffered burns in a kiln explosion in 1905 and he had only limited use of his hands. He was able to run the pottery, but he could not design or model pieces. Consequently, most of the work after 1908 was produced from the old designs of Hugh Robertson. Some of the designers remained at the factory and two of them did some important work. Maud Davenport, of Dedham, started working in 1904. She occasionally signed her initials on the plate back or put a small "o" into the border design. She worked until 1929. Her brother

Three Dedham vases. *Left:* A 2¼-inch-high bowl of reddish brown slip made about 1880–1888. *Center:* A 4¼-inch blue green vase marked with the incised words "Dedham Pottery." *Right:* A 1½-inch-high blue green vase with incised decoration, marked CKAW. (The Smithsonian Institution)

joined the Dedham Pottery in 1914 and headed the decorating division. He made borders but he was also a sculptor and made some of the small animal pieces.

The factory continued to prosper until 1929 when William Robertson died. His son J. Milton Robertson continued the work at the factory until April 17, 1943. All of the remaining pottery was sold at Gimbels department store in New York City in September of the same year. The buildings remained until 1946. In a letter to Mrs. William W. Fisher on October 21, 1943, J. Milton Robertson, then a Navy Lieutenant Commander, added these facts: "The manufacture of the ware in the clay state ceased in Janu-

This olive green teapot is 7 inches high. It was made by the Chelsea Keramic Art Works about 1880–1888 and is marked CKAW. It was a copy of a known English teapot. (The Smithsonian Institution)

(Above left) Thick green glaze over light gray covers this "Volcanic Ware" vase made by the Dedham Pottery. The 7¾-inch piece is incised "Dedham Pottery" and "H R." (The Smithsonian Institution)   (Above right) An unusual piece of pottery. This plate has no crackle glaze. The blue decoration is similar to the designs made on the tableware of the Dedham Pottery. This 10-inch-diameter piece has a border design called "dolphin," but it is not the Dedham factory "dolphin" or "fish" pattern. Rather it must be an early attempt at the famous line of tableware. It is marked CPUS. (The Smithsonian Institution)

Dedham Pottery platter with wolves and owls, 12½ inches long, 7¾ inches wide. It has the typical white crackled glaze decorated with blue over the glaze, marked Dedham Pottery Co., Dedham, Mass. The pattern is not included in the list of tableware patterns of the factory. (The Smithsonian Institution)

ary, 1942, and at that time notified all our old customers, at the last known address. . . . We continued firing ghost kilns until last March and finally released the help on April 17, 1943. The pieces of crackleware were sent to the Society of Arts and Crafts, 32 Newbury St., Boston.

"It is not my intention to ever reopen the plant. It would be difficult getting artists and craftsmen and many repairs are necessary to the kilns. . . .

"Many people were disappointed but the threat of closing had been going on for so long, they rather thought that it was a sales talk. Actually I carried the load on that place over a period of years, when good business practice would definitely say close."

During the last five years the firm was in business, it did about three thousand dollars a year. Over 250,000 pieces of crackleware were believed made by the factory.

Another Robertson, Hugh's son Alexander, went to California in 1884 and founded his own firm (see Roblin Pottery).

George W. Robertson, after twelve years at the Low Tile Works, founded his own factory in 1890, the Chelsea Keramic Art Tile Works, in Mornsville, Pennsylvania. (See Robertson Art Company.)

Product

The most important ware made at the Dedham Pottery was the famous crackleware. Its manufacture gives a few clues to its age. Plates and other such pieces were made in hinged molds. Hugh Robertson decided that to keep the design uniform, the decorators should have some sort of guidelines. The molds for the rabbit plate, which was the first standard design, were made with a slightly engraved border that the decorators could follow. The decorators became so familiar with the pattern that the plates were finally made smooth. The pottery was fired, glazed, decorated freehand, and fired again. While the plates were still hot from the kiln, lampblack was rubbed on the piece so that it would darken the crackle of the glaze on the face of the piece.

Crackleware has several characteristic. The tablewares were made with repetitive borders with no pattern but the crackle lines in the center. The back of a dish has no crackle. It has an eggshell texture with black specks in the glaze. The foot rim of a plate is unglazed and there were almost always three fingerprints that can be seen where a hand held the plate while glazing. All the pieces are marked.

Dedham Pottery plates, in an owl pattern, 6 inches in diameter, and an elephant pattern, 7½ inches. (The Smithsonian Institution)

(Above left) Dedham Pottery plate, 8 inches, birds in potted orange tree pattern. (Authors' collection) (Above right) Dedham Pottery plate, 8 inches, magnolia pattern. (Authors' collection)

There were over sixty border designs, but only the rabbit design was kept in stock while the others had to be ordered. Thirteen designs were listed as standard in 1938.

The first of the border designs was the rabbit. A prize was offered to students at The Boston Museum of Fine Arts School in 1892 for the best design. Joseph L. Smith, a teacher, drew the winning design; the rabbits rest between what look like Brussels sprouts. There are ten rabbits to a plate, with the rabbit border originally going counterclockwise (Hugh Robertson soon reversed the direction). Smith also made the fish and poppy borders.

The pond lily border was designed by Maud Davenport after 1904. Her brother made several borders after 1914, which included the cat, dog, and chick, and designed a plate for the Republicans during the Teddy Roosevelt years. He was supposed to have designed the plate border with elephants, but when he got to the end, there was not enough space. To solve the problem, he drew a baby elephant and the design remained that way.

Denmann Ross made the tapestry lion and Charles Mills, the dolphin, magnolia, iris, and water-lily designs.

Border Designs of Dedham Plates

Apple, Azalea, Birds in Potted Orange Tree, Butterfly, Butterfly with Flower, Cat, Cherry, Chick, Clover, Clover (raised), Cosmos, Crab, Dolphin, Dolphin (upside down), Dolphin with Mask, Duck, Duck (tufted), Elephant, Fish, Flower (5 petals), Flower (7 petals), Grape, Grouse, Horsechestnut (3), Horsechestnut (raised), Iris (2), Lion (tapestry), Magnolia (2), Moth (3), Mushroom (3), Nasturtium, Owl (2), Peacock, Pineapple, Pineapple (raised), Polar Bear, Pond Lily, Poppy, Quail (raised), Rabbit (raised counterclockwise), Rabbit (one ear), Rabbit (two ears),

Rabbit (with monogram), Snowtree (3), Strawberry (2), Swan, Turkey (2), Turtles, Turtles Cavorting, Wild Rose.

Bibliography

"American Art Pottery," Bulletin of the Department of Commerce and Labor, *American Pottery Gazette,* V No. VI (August 10, 1907).

"Antiques for Investment," *Spinning Wheel* (September 1969).

Barber, Edwin A., *The Pottery and Porcelain of the United States,* New York: G. P. Putnam's Sons, 1893 (3d and rev. ed. 1909).

————, *Marks of American Potters,* Philadelphia: Patterson and White, 1904.

"Best American Pottery, The," *House Beautiful* II (1897) 87.

Bowdoin, W. G., "Some American Pottery Forms," *The Art Interchange* (April 1903) 87.

Clark, Robert Judson, *The Arts and Crafts Movement in America 1876–1916,* Princeton, N.J.: Princeton University Press, 1972.

Crowley, Lilian H., "It's Now the Potter's Turn," *International Studio* 75 (September 1922) 539.

Dedham Pottery Co., "A Short History of the Dedham Pottery," 3-fold pamphlet c. 1930, no author listed.

(Top) Dedham pottery bowl, grape pattern.   (Bottom) Dedham pottery bowl, swan pattern.

Dedham Pottery platter, rabbit pattern. (Dedham Historical Society, Dedham, Mass.)

Dedham pottery plates. The lobster plate is 6½ inches in diameter, the crab, 7½ inches. (The Smithsonian Institution)

(Left) Dedham Pottery covered bowl, rabbit pattern. (Dedham Historical Society, Dedham, Mass.) (Right) Dedham Pottery bowl, rabbit pattern. (Dedham Historical Society, Dedham, Mass.)

Evans, Paul F., "The Art Pottery Era in the United States 1870 to 1920, Part One," *Spinning Wheel* (October 1970).

_____, "The Robertson Saga, I. The Creative Years: 1866–1889," *Western Collector* (April 1967).

_____, "The Robertson Saga, II, The Commercial Years: 1891–1943," *Western Collector* (May 1967).

"Field of Art—American Pottery, First Paper," *Scribner's Magazine* (November 1902) 637, Second Paper (March 1903), 381.

Fisher, Mrs. William, correspondence with the authors.

Foster, Edith Dunham, "Dedham Pottery, II," *House Beautiful* 36 (September 1914), 117.

Hawes, Lloyd E., *The Dedham Pottery and the Earlier Robertson's Chelsea Potteries*, Dedham, Mass.: Dedham Historical Society, 1968.

_____, "Hugh Cornwall Robertson and the Chelsea Period," *Antiques Magazine* (March 1966), 409.

(Left) Dedham Pottery pitcher, rabbit pattern.   (Right) Dedham Pottery plates. *Back row:* Rabbits (counterclockwise) at ends and rabbits (two ears) at center. *Center row:* Clover (raised), clover, pineapple (raised). *Front row:* Clover (raised), rabbit (two ears), pineapple (raised). (*House Beautiful*, September, 1914)

Dedham Pottery, *left to right:* pitcher, Night and Morning pattern, 5 inches high. Facing side, Morning, shows rooster, hens, and sun. Night side has an owl and moon. Covered sugar bowl, rabbit pattern, 4-inch diameter. Plate, iris pattern, 8½-inch diameter. Rabbit knife holder, 2½ inches high. The knife blade rested between the ears. (The Smithsonian Institution)

Left to right: Duck plate, azalea plate. (*Victorian Antiques.* Thelma Shull)

Ray, Marcia, "A B C's of Ceramics," *Spinning Wheel* (June 1967) 18.

"Rise of the Pottery Industry, The," *The Popular Science Monthly* 40 (December 1891), 158.

Watkins, Lura Woodside, *Early New England Potters and Their Wares,* Cambridge: Harvard University Press, 1950.

DENVER CHINA AND POTTERY
See Lonhuda Pottery

DORCHESTER POTTERY

Stoneware was made by George Henderson in New Haven, Connecticut, in 1884. He had taken over the management of S. L. Pewtress Pottery and changed the name to Henderson and O'Halloran. Henderson left New Haven in 1895 and founded the Dorchester Pottery on Victory Road in Dorchester, Massachusetts. There, he made many types of stoneware pieces, which were in great demand and are still being made.

In 1940 the Dorchester Pottery began making a line of decorated pottery ware in blue and white from New Jersey clay. Full dinner sets were made. The pieces were decorated in cobalt blue with either a painted decoration, sgraffito, or by covering the entire piece with a cobalt glaze and scraping a portion away, which showed the light-colored body beneath. The pieces were molded or thrown. They often had traditional designs that included pussy willows, scroll, pinecone, stripes and codfish, colonial lace, and blueberry plus a few other designs, usually flowers. At one time, some of the pieces were decorated with bayberry green or a gold glaze, but they were made only to special order.

The decorators and potters signed the pieces and, of course, the Dorchester name is on each example.

Henderson died in 1928; his son Charles Henderson died in 1967. The pottery was run by Mrs. Charles Hill Henderson, designer and superintendent; her brother Charles Hill, decorator and glazer; Lilli Yeaton, her sister; and Nando Ricci, a potter, whose family has worked for the Dorchester Pottery for generations. It closed in 1979.

Bibliography

"Dorchester Pottery, The," *National Antiques Review* (October 1969), 44.

Evans, Paul F., "Stoneware and the Dorchester Pottery," *Western Collector* VI (May 1968), 7–11.

FRACKELTON

Susan Stuart Goodrich Frackelton was a decorator of china and pottery, a writer, and the founder of a pottery. She was born in Milwaukee, Wisconsin, in 1848, the daughter of a banker who later ran a brickyard. She went to a New York finishing school but she also studied art with Heinrich Vianden of Milwaukee. From 1867 to 1891 Mrs. Frackelton operated a china, glassware, and stoneware shop where she also taught china decorating. Her invention of a gas-fired kiln that could be used at home made it possible for many women to make pottery as a hobby. Her best-known work was a bowl made of cream-colored brick clay. The piece she molded was fifteen inches long, with modelings of grape vines for angles and clusters of grapes at the edge. It won a medal at the Philadelphia Centennial Exposition of 1876.

In 1882 Mrs. Frackelton helped design a big brick

An olive jar made from stoneware by Susan Stuart Goodrich Frackelton. (*The Pottery and Porcelain of the United States* by Edwin Barber, 1909)

house at Case Street and Ogden Avenue, in Milwaukee. It was in this house that she continued to hold classes in china decoration, made pottery, and carried on other artistic pursuits. (She once did illuminations for a book.) She married her husband Richard in 1896. He became a dealer in chinaware.

SF cipher for Susan Frackelton.

Mrs. Frackelton's pottery was made from Milwaukee brick clay or of gray and blue stoneware with relief and underglaze blue decorations. She did the molding, firing, and decorating herself. She died in 1932.

Bibliography

Barber, Edwin A., *The Pottery and Porcelain of the United States,* New York: G. P. Putnam's Sons, 1893 (3d and rev. ed. 1909).

_____, *Marks of American Potters,* Philadelphia: Patterson and White, 1904.

Carroon, Robert G., "The Pottery Industry in 19th Century Milwaukee," *Historical Messenger of the Milwaukee County Historical Society* 27 (March 1970).

Crowley, Lilian H., "It's Now the Potter's Turn." *International Studio* 75 (September 1922) 539.

Stover, Frances, "Susan Goodrich Frackelton and the China Painters," *Historical Messenger of the Milwaukee County Historical Society* 10 (March 1954).

FULPER POTTERY

Drain tiles were being made in 1805, in Flemington, New Jersey. Samuel Hill (1793–1858) came to Flemington from New Brunswick in 1814 to work as a potter. He made earthenware and drain tiles. One of his workmen, Abraham Fulper, bought the firm in 1858 when Mr. Hill died. At first, Fulper made only drain tile, but soon he made both earthenware and stoneware. Vinegar jugs, pickling jars, bottles, beer mugs, butter churns, bowls, and "drinking foundations for poultry" were produced.

Martin Stangl became the ceramics engineer in 1910 and, with the firm now under the direction of William H. Fulper II (son of Abraham), they began making artware. Stangl left in 1914 to work for Haeger, of Dundee, Illinois. (There is considerable disagreement about these dates. All written records were destroyed and the information is based on recollections by Stangl and Fulper employees). The Fulper Pottery won several awards at the 1915 San Francisco Panama Pacific International Exposition. Their

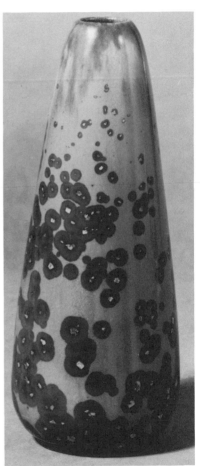

Brown to olive glazes cover this Fulper vase. Black and gray crystals with light centers appear on the glaze. It is 5½ inches high. The piece is marked with an original paper label: "Vasekraft, Slender Ovoid, Leopard skin $1.00, Vasekraft, emblem of a potter, Fulper 1905" (1905 is probably not a date; the museum acquired the piece in 1914). (Newark Museum, Newark, New Jersey)

art line was called "Vasekraft." The line included "famille rose," a copy of the famous Chinese pattern, "Mirror Glaze," a high-gloss, crystalline glaze, and "Mission Matte," a brown black glaze with shaded greens. According to the catalogues, other colors were "cat's eye," mustard matte, "elephant's breath" (gray), "cucumber green," "blue wisteria," plum, yellow, café au lait, mulberry, verte antique, mission matte, and "violet wisteria." The firm made lamps, lampshades (often set with glass), ashtrays, cigarette boxes, vases, bowls, and other giftwares. The shapes were made of "clay wrought into odd —sometimes too odd forms" (*Pottery in America, The American Magazine of Art,* February, 1916, Vol. VII, No. 4, p. 3).

John Kunsman and Edward Wyckoff were two of the Fulper potters who worked on the art line. At the same time, the firm was making the "Fulper Germ-Proof Filter," a set of jars that held cold drinking water. They even made dolls' heads for a short time. In 1920, the firm introduced the first solid color glazed dinnerware produced in the United States; green was the only solid color made until 1930 when other colors were added.

The Fulper Pottery continued to expand, and in 1926 they acquired the Anchor Pottery Company of Trenton, New Jersey. A fire in 1929 destroyed the Fulper Pottery buildings in Flemington and the firm decided to move most of their operations to their Trenton plant. Artware was still made on a small scale in Flemington until 1935.

The firm name was changed to the Stangl pottery in 1929. In June of 1972, the company was purchased by Frank H. Wheaton, Jr., of Wheaton Industries.

A vertical Fulper mark, printed in black, and a 1916–1918 label.

Bibliography

Blasberg, Robert, "Twenty Years of Fulper," *Spinning Wheel* (October 1973), 14–18.

Fulper Pottery Company, *Vasekraft—Fulper Catalogue,* after 1915.

"Hill-Fulper-Stangl Pottery Gallery Proposed for Doric House Museum," *Hunterdon Historical Newsletter,* Winter, 1973.

Rawson, Jonathan A., Jr., "Recent American Pottery," *House Beautiful* 31 (April 1912), 148.

Stangl Pottery, *Stangl: A Portrait of Progress in Pottery,* New Jersey, privately printed, 1965.

Stuart, Evelyn Marie, "Vasekraft—An American Art Pottery" (Reprint from *Fine Arts Journal,* 1914).

Wyckoff, Jane, and Sarby, B. A., correspondence with authors.

(Above) This unusual vase has a center holder for flowers. The green glaze with some crystalline formations was dripped over a dark tan. The piece is marked with the Fulper printed mark, a paper label for Fulper, and the paper label for the Panama Pacific International Exposition, 1915. (Authors' collection)

(Below, left) A Fulper lamp made of pottery with leaded glass. The pottery is glazed blue and gunmetal in glossy glazes. The glass is green, yellow, and blue. Made about 1911–1915. The height is 19 inches. Fulper in a vertical rectangle is printed on the lamp. (The Art Museum, Princeton University, Princeton, New Jersey) (Below, right) This 6⅞-inch-high vase has a green crystalline glaze. It is marked with the Fulper stamp in a vertical rectangle, and an original paper label: "Vasekraft, med. Globular Bottle, Leopard Skin, crystal $4.40, Vasekraft, emblem of a potter, Fulper 1904" (1904 is probably not a date). (Newark Museum, Newark, New Jersey)

Dark green and black glazes with silver crystalline formations were used on this 8½-inch vase. It has the printed Fulper mark in the vertical rectangle and an original paper label: "Vasekraft, Med. double Ori., form Cucumber Green, $4.40 Vasekraft, emblem of a potter, Fulper 1905." (1905 is probably not a date.) (Newark Museum, Newark, New Jersey)

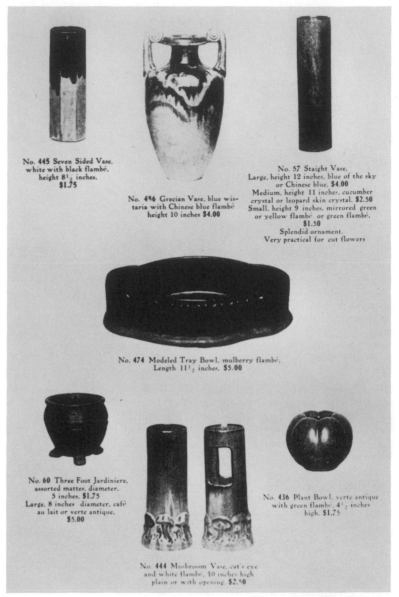

No. 445 Seven Sided Vase,
white with black flambé,
height 8½ inches,
$1.75

No. 486 Grecian Vase, blue wistaria with Chinese blue flambé
height 10 inches $4.00

No. 57 Staight Vase,
Large, height 12 inches, blue of the sky
or Chinese blue, $4.00
Medium, height 11 inches, cucumber
crystal or leopard skin crystal, $2.50
Small, height 9 inches, mirrored green
or yellow flambé or green flambé,
$1.50
Splendid ornament.
Very practical for cut flowers

No. 474 Modeled Tray Bowl, mulberry flambé,
Length 11½ inches, $5.00

No. 60 Three Foot Jardiniere,
assorted mattes, diameter,
5 inches, $1.75
Large, 8 inches diameter, café
au lait or verte antique,
$5.00

No. 436 Plant Bowl, verte antique
with green flambé, 4½ inches
high, $1.75

No. 444 Mushroom Vase, cat's eye
and white flambé, 10 inches high
plain or with opening, $2.50

Page 16 from Vasekraft catalogue, date unknown. (Hunterdon County Historical Society, Flemington, New Jersey)

The name Fulper is stamped in a vertical rectangle on this vase. The glaze of the 8½-inch-high vase is light to dark green iridescent. (Authors' collection)

(Right) A blue flambé glaze was dripped over the mustard matte of this vase. It is 4 inches in diameter, 3½ inches high, marked with the Fulper imprint in a vertical rectangle. (Authors' collection)

(Right) This small Fulper ewer is 4½ inches high. On the bottom is a paper label that is printed with the name Fulper in a vertical rectangle. In pen is written "38C Dipstick, Ashes of Roses, $1.00." (Authors' collection)

Page 4 from Vasekraft catalogue, date unknown. (Hunterdon County Historical Society, Flemington, New Jersey)

No. 498 Heraldic Bowl, café au lait with green and mahogany flambé, dia. 8¾ inches, $4.50

No. 501 Handled Bowl, Venetian blue, dia. 7 inches, $2.00

No. 500 Iris Bowl, mustard matte with green flambé or blue wistaria with green flambé, diameter 10 inches, $6.00

No. 503 Modeled Bowl, verte antique with mahogany and white flambé, diameter 9 inches, $4.00

No. 504 Bowl with flower holder, verte antique with Chinese blue and white flambé, diameter 8 inches, $3.50

No. 484S Bowl with flower holder, verte antique with white flambé, dia. 8 in. $3.00
No. 484L Blue wistaria with white flambé, diameter 10½ inches, $4.50

No. 456 Penguin Self-contained Flower Holder, naturalistic, height 7 inches, $1.75

No. 424 Lily Pad, naturalistic glaze, $ .50

No. 451 English Castle Flower Holder, naturalistic glazes, height 5 inches, $1.50

No. 438 Flower Bowl with effigy feet, blue matte, with blue of the sky lining, or mustard and mission matte with yellow flambé 10½ in. diameter. $6.00

No. 58 Ovoid Bowl, mustard matte with brown and black flambé. $4.50

No. 443 Cat-tail Vase, café au lait or verte antique, height 12½ inches. $4.00

No. 468 Peacock Bowl, Chinese blue and white flambé, diameter 10 inches. $5.00

No. 50 Modeled Square Vase, height 8 inches, blue matte or verte antique. $1.50

No. 76 Fernery and insert, café au lait, height 4 inches. $1.70

No. 26 Fool's Cap Vase, tall, height 10½ inches, green flambé or cucumber green. $2.50
Fool's Cap Vase, medium, height 7½ ins., green mirrored. $1.50
Fool's Cap Vase, Small, height 5½ inches, mulberry flambé $1.00

No. 489 Urn Vase, mahogany and Chinese blue flambé, height 8 inches. $3.00

No. 20 Tall Ovoid with neck, Chinese blue or green flambé, height 13 inches. $6.00

(Right) A page from the Vasekraft catalogue, date unknown. (Hunterdon County Historical Society, Flemington, New Jersey)

GAY HEAD POTTERY

Gay Head Pottery was made in Martha's Vineyard at Cottage City, Massachusetts, about 1879. W. F. Willard made vases using the multicolored clays found on the island. Red, blue, slate, and buff-colored clays were mixed, and they gave a marbleized effect to the finished vase. The pieces were dried in the sun and not baked because firing would destroy the color. The pottery was impressed "Gay Head" on the side of each piece.

Bibliography

Barber, Edwin A., *The Pottery and Porcelain of the United States,* New York: G. P. Putnam's Sons, 1893 (3d and rev. ed. 1909).

Evans, Paul F., "The Niloak Pottery," *Spinning Wheel* (October 1970).

Watkins, Lura Woodside, *Early New England Potters and Their Wares,* Cambridge: Harvard University Press, 1950.

GONDER POTTERY

Gonder Pottery was the former Zane Pottery that had been purchased from the McClelland family by Lawton Gonder in 1941. Gonder's parents worked at the Weller plant. He had worked at the Ohio Pottery Company, the American Encaustic Tiling Company of Zanesville, Ohio, Cherry Art Tile Company of Orlando, Florida (1926), the Florence Pottery Company of Mt. Gilead, Ohio, and as a consultant for Fraunfelter China and the Standard Tile Company of Zanesville, Ohio. After he bought the Zane Pottery, he renamed it Gonder Ceramic Arts, Inc.

The firm made high-priced and good quality art pottery. Gonder hired talented artists to do the designing. Several innovations in ceramics were developed. They made a flambé glaze and a gold crackle glaze, a Chinese crackle glaze, and a line of old Chinese pottery reproductions.

The company expanded and in 1946, opened another factory where they made lamp bases under the name Elgee Pottery. The plant burned in 1954 and Gonder added on to his other plant. They stopped making ceramics in 1957. (See also *Peters and Reed.*)

GRUEBY FAIENCE COMPANY

William H. Grueby was born in 1867, and as a boy of fifteen began to work at the Low Art Tile Works of Chelsea, Massachusetts, where he remained for about fifteen years. However, the record is confused on this point. Grueby was supposed to have had charge of an exhibit of tile at the Chicago World's Fair in 1893 (*Arts and Decoration,* Vol. 1, Nov., 1910). It was at this fair that he saw some of the foreign work and decided to experiment with his own glazes. Another source (*Pottery and Glass,* Jan., 1909, Vol. 11, No. 1) has Grueby associated with John Low for fifteen years in the clay works. But if Grueby joined Low at age fifteen, or in 1882, then he remained associated with him until 1897, which is after the date of the founding of the Grueby firm. It seems more likely that, at the time of the 1893 Fair, Grueby was working with the Boston Terra Cotta Company of Boston, Massachusetts (Barber, *Pottery and Porcelain,* 1893 ed.). Grueby and a Mr. Atwood were working in the production of architectural faience at the firm, which may be the Boston Art Pottery Company mentioned in the article "Grueby Art Pottery by Robert Blasberg, *Antiques Magazine,* August, 1971. It may also be the Boston Firebrick Works.

It is clear that Grueby was working in the ceramic tile industry in the Boston area when in 1894 he decided to develop his own glaze. He experimented and soon had a glaze that was similar to the French *Grès flammé* (earthenware dipped in opaque enamel and fired until vitrification). It had a matte finish rather than the gloss popular with other potteries of the time. The glaze was given a dull finish, not by sandblasting or acid treatment as had been done before, but by the method of firing in the kiln.

He decided to form his own company and in 1897 the Grueby Faience Company was incorporated ("Grueby Faience Co., glazed brick" is listed in the Boston City Directory of 1895). Lura Watkins, in *Early New England Potters and Their Marks,* calls it the Grueby Faience and Tile Company. The company included George Prentiss Kendrick, the designer of the pottery shapes and ornaments; and William H. Graves. Circulars for the company for 1899–1900 mention the designs as being done entirely by Kendrick. A comment in a 1902 article, "American Pottery" (*Scribner's Magazine,* Nov., 1902, 32:637), says "there is no change in the arrangement yet known." Another important decorator at the factory was Addison B. Le Boutillier, a French architect.

The pottery was made by hand, although a few examples such as the scarab paperweight may have been molded. The pieces were thrown on a foot-powered wheel and then the modeling was done by one of the young girls or boys hired by the firm. Most of these artists were graduates of the Museum of Fine Arts School in Boston, the Normal Art School, or the Cowles Art Schools. The initials of some of these artists can be found on pieces of Grueby ware.

In 1900, at the Paris Exposition, Grueby won two gold and one silver medal, winning over some pieces of Rookwood pottery. It achieved renown in America a year later at the Pan American Exposition in Buffalo.

In 1908, the firm divided. The Grueby Pottery Company made the garden furniture, pottery, and tiles for construction, while the Grueby Faience and Tile Company continued to make art pottery.

Too much success seemed to doom the firm. The Grueby style of pottery with simple lines and a dull finish became the style, and dozens of cheaper copies were made at other factories. The firm finally had to close the art pottery in 1910. (The Grueby Faience and Tile Company was declared bankrupt in 1908, but a new firm by the same name continued to make tile.) The tile and ar-

Marks (impressed):

Backs of tiles. (Smithsonian Institution)

Craftsman Magazine, December, 1914, pictured this Grueby tile bathroom wall. (Left) The magazine caption read: "The interesting tile design . . . is from the Grueby Faience and Tile Company and is a panel in the bathroom of Mrs. Searls in San Francisco: In color, arrangement and decoration this is probably the most elaborate and beautiful bathroom in America. It is entirely fitted up with Grueby Tiles. The floor is in dull green tile with a border in a pond lily decoration. The design about the walls is growing fleurs-de-lis in rich natural colors. The background of this varied and beautiful decoration is in harmonious soft tones. So well is this fleur-de-lis pattern designed that the very sense of the plant growing up from pools of water is manifest. A more appropriate design for an elaborate bathroom could hardly be imagined and if extravagance is to be shown in house fittings what more delightful than to bathe in a room surrounded by rich-hued flowers in the midst of verdure." (Below) A set of four tiles was made with the emblems of the four Gospels. One 7½-inch tile of blue with green relief shows a winged ox holding a book, the emblem of St. Luke. The other tile, of orange with green relief, shows an eagle holding a book, the emblem of St. John. (The Smithsonian Institution)

chitectural pottery part of the firm burned in 1912,* but must have continued to work until 1920, the last year it is listed in the Boston City Directory. It was purchased by the C. Pardee Works of Perth Amboy, New Jersey.

Pottery Shapes, Colors, Etc.

The most important type of art pottery made by the Grueby Faience Company was the matte glaze ware developed by William Grueby. These pieces were modeled by hand. The veining of the leaf was added to the vase as a thin piece of clay. The additions were tooled onto the wall of the vase. Some incised lines were also used.

The designs featured natural shapes such as the mullen

*E. Stanley Wires, who purchased the William Smith Tile Shop in the building housing the Grueby Boston office in 1908, wrote about the effects of the fire in a letter: "After the fire between 1910–1912, the company couldn't make a profit due to their inability to duplicate the glazes in the old brick kilns they were using. Mr. Graves had a nervous breakdown and left the company. At that time, they attempted to start a Hartford Faience Co. in Conn. which ended about 1913. Soon after this Grueby went with the C. Pardee Works in Perth Amboy, New Jersey. I think he was with them when he died in 1931."

leaf, the lotus, the tulip or marsh grasses, the plantain, and the acanthus leaf. The hand tooling on the clay gives a surface that appears rough, but is really smooth to the touch.

The glaze was applied about 1/32 of an inch thick. Most pieces were of a single color or a blended monotone. Green was favored, but the firm also made pieces of pink, yellow, brown, blue, gray, grayish purple, and creamy white. Some pieces were made with a flower motif glazed in a different color, such as yellow on a green or blue ground. One writer describes the ware as follows: "The surface of Grueby enamels has much the character of a watermelon or cucumber, or the warm brown of a russet apple, and is full of delicate veining and mottling which give it an individuality of its own. The forms, of which there are several hundred, run from small cabinet bits to great jars three feet high and new ones are constantly added." (*Pottery and Glass,* Jan., 1909, Vol. II, No. 1, page 14.)

Grueby also made lamp bases for Tiffany, Duffner, Kimberly, Bigelow Kinnard & Company, and he made many types of tiles. Grueby tiles were decorated with floral and geometric patterns, annuals, medieval knights, illustrations from Carroll or Kipling, and specially ordered designs. Some tiles were made with cloisonné walls of clay to hold colored glazes in a stylized design. This technique is occasionally found on the art pottery. One ware that created great comment in the early 1900s was a white crackleware of a quality claimed to be equal to that of old Korean pottery.

Of course, the method of manufacture with the handwork of the potters and artists meant no two pieces of Grueby ware were exactly alike.

According to the *American Pottery Gazette* (Aug. 10, 1907, p. 47), the clays for all Grueby products were from America, coming from deposits in New Jersey and at Martha's Vineyard. And *Keramic Studio,* (Vol. 6, Feb., 1905) said that "the business of the Grueby pottery, everyone knows, was originally the making of drain and sanitary piping, etc. The art ware necessarily must have been of the same materials to avoid too great complexity of production."

Bibliography

"American Art Pottery," Bulletin of the Department of Commerce and Labor, *American Pottery Gazette,* August 10, 1907, Vol. V, No. VI.

(Top) Geometric patterns of yellow, ocher, and white matte glazes appear on this 7½-inch-high vase. It was made about 1892–1902. The vase has the impressed circular mark: Grueby Faience Co., Boston, U.S.A. It also has an original paper label with a lotus flower (as on Grueby tiles) and the notation "price $18, No. B." (Newark Museum, Newark, New Jersey) (Bottom) Modeled tulip leaves and flowers of green and yellow matte glaze decorate this 8⅝-inch vase. The piece is marked with the Grueby Pottery, Boston, USA, impressed circular mark. It is also marked with the cipher MJC (?) 36; and the painted notation X. (The Art Museum, Princeton University, Princeton, New Jersey)

Grueby Faience Company

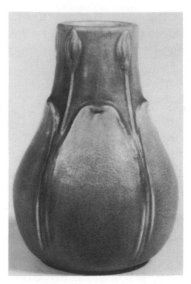

(Left) Modeled leaves and flower buds of dark green and yellow matte glaze decorate this Grueby pottery vase. It is 12 inches high, marked with the impressed circle, lotus mark, and the symbols 20, AL. It was probably made by Annie V. Lingley about 1899–1910. (From the collection of David Hanks)   (Right) Stylized stems with buds and leaves are modeled on this Grueby vase. It is 7³⁄₁₆ inches high, glazed with a pale blue matte glaze. The vase, made about 1898–1902, is marked with the Grueby Faience Co. Boston USA impressed circular mark. (Newark Museum, Newark, New Jersey)

This tall, 21⅞-inch vase was exhibited at the Paris World's Fair in 1900. It has a green matte glaze. The decoration is stylized flower buds and leaves. The paper label says "Grueby Museum, $50.00, 9542." (The Art Museum, Princeton University, Princeton, New Jersey)

(Left) Wilhelmina Post was the artist for this dark green pottery vase with modeled decorations of leaves and buds made about 1898–1902. The vase, 7⅞ inches high, is marked with the impressed circular mark "Grueby Faience Co., Boston, U.S.A." and the symbols W.P. and L. (The Art Museum, Princeton University, Princeton, New Jersey)   (Right) Five modeled leaves form the decoration on this light green matte glazed vase. The 10⅝-inch piece was exhibited at the Paris World's Fair in 1900. It is marked with the impressed circular mark with the lotus flower, Grueby Pottery, Boston, U.S.A., and the number 172 and cipher RE. It was made by Ruth Erickson. (Newark Museum, Newark, New Jersey)

(Right) This green Grueby vase was acquired by the Smithsonian Institution in 1906. It is 6¾ inches high. (The Smithsonian Institution)

(Top left) Buff stippled glaze is the only decoration for this 2¾-inch-high unmarked Grueby vase made about 1905. (Smithsonian Institution)   (Bottom left) This scarab pottery paperweight was made by Grueby for the St. Louis World's Fair in 1904. It has a green semimatte glaze. The scarab is 4 inches long by 2¾ inches wide by 1¼ inches high. It is marked with the impressed circle and lotus mark, Grueby Faience Co. Boston, USA. (Smithsonian Institution)

(Top left) Green, blue, and brown trees decorate this Grueby tile made about 1900. It is marked Grueby Faience and Tile Co. Boston, Mass. The tile is a 6-inch square, 1 inch thick. (Smithsonian Institution)   (Top right) Green, brown, blue, lavender, and ocher glazes form the painted design of this tile. It was made about 1906. The tile is 13 inches square. (The Smithsonian Institution)

(Left) Yellow daffodils are modeled against a green background on this 12¼-inch-high Grueby vase. It is marked with the impressed mark "Grueby Pottery, Boston, USA" and the number 170. The vase was made about 1891–1901.

Barber, Edwin, *The Pottery and Porcelain of the United States,* New York: G. P. Putnam's Sons, 1893 (3rd and rev. ed. 1909), 502–503.

Belknap, Henry W., "Another American Pottery," *Pottery and Glass,* Vol. II, No. I (January, 1909).

Blasberg, Robert, correspondence with authors.

_____, "Grueby Art Pottery, *Antiques,* August, 1971, 246.

Bowdoin, W. G., "Some American Pottery Forms," *The Art Interchange,* April, 1903, 87.

Clark, Robert Judson, *The Arts and Crafts Movement in America 1876–1916,* Princeton, N.J.; Princeton University Press, 1972, pp. 36, 137, 138, 139, 140, 141, 142–143.

"The Crafts: In the Potter's House," *Current Literature* (Vol. 30) June, 1901.

Dudley, Pendleton, "The Work of American Potters," *Arts and Decoration,* Vol. 1, November, 1910, p. 20.

"The Field of Art—American Pottery," *Scribner's Magazine,* November, 1902, Vol. XXXII, 65, 637.

Gray, Walter Ellsworth, "Latter-Day Developments in American Pottery," *Brush and Pencil,* Vol. 9, 1902, 236.

"Louisiana Purchase Exposition Ceramics, Grueby Faience," *Keramic Studio,* V. 6, February, 1905.

Luther, Louise R., "Tribute to a Remarkable Woman, Another Dimension of Grueby Pottery," *Spinning Wheel,* March, 1972, 40–41.

McDowell, C., "Grueby: American Art Pottery," *A Collectors Annual,* No. 5, 102–103.

"Notes on the Crafts," *International Studio,* V. 24, February, 1905, p. xci.

"The Potters of America: Examples of the Best Craftsmen's Work for Interior Decorations: Number One," *Craftsman,* December, 1914, V. 27, p. 295.

Ruge, Clara, "American Ceramics—A Brief Review of Progress," *International Studio,* March, 1906, V. 28, 21–28.

_____, "Development of American Ceramics," *Pottery & Glass,* August, 1908, V. I, No. 2, p. 3.

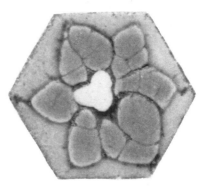

(Top) A stylized flower of dull yellow is on this blue tile. Each edge is 4 inches long. (Smithsonian Institution)

(Center) This tile with a tan border shows a deer on a blue green background. It is 4 inches square. (Smithsonian Institution)

(Bottom) This hexagonal tile is yellow with green and white floral decoration. Each edge is 3 inches long. (The Smithsonian Institution)

A green stylized rabbit and plant decorate this off-white Grueby tile. It is 4 inches square. (The Smithsonian Institution)

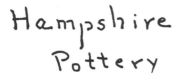

Mark used on pieces designed by Cadmon Robertson in tribute to his wife, Emoretta Robertson.

Marks:

Sullivan, Margot T., Boston Public Library, Social Sciences Department, correspondence with authors.

Watkins, Lura Woodside, "The Art Potteries," *Early New England Potters and Their Wares*, p. 222, Cambridge: Harvard University Press, 1950.

HAEGER POTTERIES, INC.

The Haeger Brick & Tile Company of Dundee, Illinois, was founded in 1871 by David Haeger. His son Edmund H. Haeger decided to produce an art pottery in 1914. The name of the firm was changed to The Haeger Potteries, Inc. A florists' line of pottery was made in addition to a line of art pottery. The firm is still operating.

Bibliography

Haeger Potteries, Inc. *1871–1971: Haeger—the Craftsmen for a Century*, Dundee, Illinois, 1971.

Rogers, Jo Ann, "Haeger Potteries 100 Years Old," *Collector's Weekly* (November 30, 1971).

HAMPSHIRE POTTERY

James Scollay Taft was born in Nelson, New Hampshire, in 1844. He began working in 1863. His first job was in a mill, then a grocery, and finally, in 1871, he purchased an old clothespin factory in Keene, New Hampshire, where he started making pottery. It was the first year of operation of the Hampshire Pottery Company. Taft's uncle, James Burnap, joined him in the business. Keene was an ideal location for a pottery because of the large deposits of feldspar and clay. At first the firm made redware, mainly flowerpots, later it added stoneware. A majolica type glazed ware was soon added. The majolica ware was evidently the result of the knowledge of Thomas Stanley, an English potter who began working at Keene in 1879. The pieces were made with green, yellow, brown, and blue glazes on a white body.

The new line of pottery was a success and other types were added. The firm was enlarged and a new kiln was added in 1883. Wallace L. King was the artist in charge of all the decorative work made in the new kiln. The most famous new product was the Royal Worcester type glaze. It had a creamy pink tone and it was used on all types of baskets, jugs, jars, cuspidors, rose bowls, tea sets, etc. The glaze took five firings and the ware was decorated with transfer designs in black. They were often pictures of local views. Two of the most popular pieces made with this glaze were the famous Longfellow jug and the witch jug made to be sold in Salem, Massachusetts. The souvenirs were such a success that a new line of colored glazed wares of blue, mahogany, and olive green was added. These pieces had a grained effect on the finish that was caused during the firing. The name of the resort or locality was put on the souvenir pieces with gilt. Most of the shapes were copied from early Greek and Egyptian styles.

Impressed mark.

The green matte finish was particularly popular. It is interesting that while Grueby (*see*) was credited with making the first popular matte finished art pottery in America, the Hampshire Pottery used this glaze in 1883, four years before Grueby.

At this time, about forty employees worked at the plant, of whom roughly half were decorators. Many of the pieces were made to be left undecorated and sold to amateur home decorators.

The firm grew and made many types of specialties and souvenir pieces, plus a new decorative line designed by a Japanese artist (name unknown) employed by the pottery.

Cadmon Robertson, Taft's brother-in-law, joined the firm in 1904 and soon afterward was in charge of all the manufacturing. Robertson (no relation to the other famous art pottery Robertsons of Chelsea Keramic Co.) was born in Chesterfield, New Hampshire, where he was educated as a chemist. He developed over nine-hundred glaze formulas while at the Hampshire Pottery. He was responsible for the famous colored matte glazes and also for many designs. His death in 1914 created problems for the firm; Wallace King, the artist in charge of decoration had retired in 1908, so the firm's only important remaining executive was James Taft. In 1916, Taft sold the Hampshire Pottery to George Morton, a Bostonian who had worked at the Grueby Pottery. Taft died in December, 1923. Morton made over a thousand items and stayed with the firm for only one year, returning to Grueby; it was the time of World War I and a limited demand for the pottery so the factory closed.

Morton reopened the firm after the war and added some machinery for the manufacture of white hotel china. Soon after, he added presses for making mosaic floor tiles, and from 1919 to 1921 the tiles became the main items of the Hampshire Pottery.

The plant closed in 1923 after the competition from the

This vase was made by the Hampshire Pottery Company, Keene, New Hampshire, about 1900. (The Art Institute of Chicago)

(Left) This green glazed bowl has a white glaze on the bottom. It is 9½ inches in diameter, 3 inches high. The plant is in high relief. (The Smithsonian Institution) (Right) Dark orange brown glaze decorated with brown flowers covers this Hampshire ewer. It is 6¼ inches high, marked J.S.T. & Co. Keene, N.H. (Authors' collection)

Ohio and New Jersey potteries made it impossible to continue at a profit. The New England plant had to import coal while many of its competitors were using natural gas, which was much cheaper.

Product

Redware followed by stoneware were the earliest products of the firm. Majolica ware was started in 1879 and was decorated in colors, then glazed in a variety of colors on a white body. Some pieces were cast in molds, giving the appearance of relief designs. Mugs with a dark green glaze shading to red and with a relief border near the rim were common. Brown glaze pitchers and tea sets shaped like ears of corn were made. Some marmalade dishes were shaped and colored like oranges. Many vases were made in brown, orange, or green with white.

The 1883 Royal Worcester glaze was made on a semi-porcelain body. The finish was a dull pale cream with pink overtones. The other souvenir pieces made at this time in blue, mahogany and olive green had a graining caused by firing.

The factory made baskets, jugs, cracker jars, chocolate sets, cuspidors, comb and brush trays, bonbon dishes, powder boxes, rose bowls, pitchers, tea sets, and umbrella stands. Souvenir items were a very important part of their production. White ware was made, either decorated or left plain.

All of the many glazes developed by Cadmon Robertson were used after 1904. He had matte glazes in green, blue, gray, bronze, yellow, and peacock blue which shaded from green to blue. The body was semiporcelain and it was fired at a high temperature. Foreign clay (often English) was used although New Jersey and Florida clays were the most popular. The firing caused minute white crystals in the glaze that gave a soft appearance. The interiors of many of the pieces were brightly glazed, which made them practical for daily use. The pottery made an extensive line of artwares that included candlesticks, vases, lamps, bowls, and dishes.

After the war the firm continued with many of the old shapes and colors but added some new colors. All types of lamps, candlesticks, jars, vases, and tea sets were made. During the later years, much of their ware was not art pottery but hotel china and mosaic floor tile.

Artists

Eliza Adams, Blanche Andrews, Mrs. John Dennison, F. L. Gillride, Marion Grinnel, Ida Jefts, Wallace King, and Emma Mercure.

Marks

Among the Hampshire marks are HAMPSHIRE KEENE N. H. printed in red; J. S. T. & CO., KEENE N. H. impressed; JAMES S. TAFT & CO. KEENE, N. H.; HAMPSHIRE; HAMPSHIRE POTTERY, KEENE N. H.; KEENE, N. H.; J. S. TAFT, KEENE N. H.; and HAMPSHIRE POTTERY. See the preceding pages for some other original markings. Also, a paper label was used, and Wallace King, the head artist, sometimes signed his work.

(Left) Green matte glaze was used on this 3½-inch-high vase with raised leaves. It has two marks placed over each other, the incised word "Hampshire" and the gold over glaze mark "Mt. Washington." (Authors' collection)   (Right) This 3¾-inch-high vase was made with dull brown glaze and a mottled effect on the raised leaves. (The Smithsonian Institution)

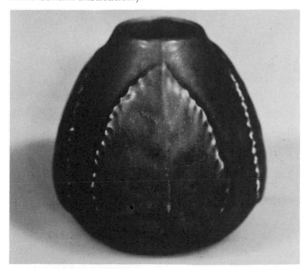

This pitcher shows the Landing of the Pilgrims. The design is a transfer. The pitcher is cream colored with black and gold decorations. It is 7½ inches high and is marked with the circular red Hampshire mark. (Authors' collection)

Bibliography

"American Art Pottery," Bulletin of the Department of Commerce and Labor, *American Pottery Gazette*, V (August 10, 1907) 3.

Barber, Edwin A., *The Pottery and Porcelain of the United States*, New York: G. P. Putnam's Sons, 1893 (3d and rev. ed. 1909).

———, *Marks of American Potters*, Philadelphia: Patterson and White, 1904.

Evans, Paul F., "Hampshire Pottery," *Spinning Wheel* (September 1970).

"First Hampshire Pottery Was Made 100 Years Ago," *Antique Trader* (December 21, 1971).

Pappas, Joan, and Kendall, Harold A., *Hampshire Pottery Manufactured by J. S. Taft & Company, Keene, New Hampshire*, New York: Crown Publishers, Inc., 1971.

Rawson, Jonathan A., Jr., "Recent American Pottery," *House Beautiful* 31 (April 1912) 148.

"Recent Advances in the Pottery Industry," *The Popular Science Monthly* 40 (January 1892).

Watkins, Lura Woodside, *Early New England Potters and Their Wares*, Cambridge: Harvard University Press, 1950.

HAVILAND POTTERY *(The art pottery movement in America began at the Haviland factory in France. The factory is included in the listing because its influence is mentioned in many other parts of this book.)*

The inspiration for the design of the beginning of American art pottery in the United States can be traced to the Centennial Exhibition in Philadelphia, Pennsylvania, in 1876. The slip-decorated artware from Haviland and Company, of Limoges, France, was seen and almost immediately imitated by three American potters: Charles Volkmar, of New York, Hugh Robertson, of Massachusetts, and Mary Louise McLaughlin, of Ohio. These potteries then became the inspiration for other factories. The potters often moved and changed jobs so the original influence of the Haviland Pottery traveled to many of the art potteries throughout the United States. But even before that, the Haviland Porcelain Co. had been known in

(Left) A young girl holding a garland of flowers is modeled in high relief at the top of the vase. The foliage is olive green, the flowers rose red, the draperies blue. The vase is by Aube, 15¾ inches by 19¾ inches. It is marked "Haviland & Co Limoges $\frac{45}{2}$." (Collection of Mr. Jean d'Albis, Limoges, France)   (Right) Blue, green, and brown leaves and brown grapes are modeled in high relief on this pottery vase marked "Haviland & Co. Limoges." It is signed E. Lindeneher. The vase is 19 inches by 19¾ inches. (Musée Adrien Dubouche, Limoges, France)

America. It had been making tableware in France for the American market since 1842.

Haviland art pottery had its beginning in 1872 when Charles Haviland decided to make a pottery that was very different from all styles currently in vogue in France. He went to Paris where in 1873, he hired M. Félix Bracquemond, an engraver, to supervise the building of a pottery studio at 116 Rue Michel-Ange in Auteuil (Paris), France. It was at this pottery from 1873 to 1876 that the art pottery models were designed. Some of the finished pieces were then made in a rented factory in Limoges, France.

Charles Haviland became acquainted with the artists who were the founders of the then emerging new schools of design. He was impressed by the Japanese movement in art, and the impressionism of the day.

Some examples of Auteuil pottery were sent to the Centennial Exposition in Philadelphia in 1876. So few pieces had been made that the firm sent all of their finished pieces as well as mock-ups in plaster and watercolor. The artists first made faience, but it was not too long before a common pottery with a lead glaze was preferred.

Bracquemond contacted a friend, Ernest Chaplet, who had developed a technique of decorating with slip mixed with colors. The slip was painted on the piece in the same

(Above) A gold phoenix flies over some branches on this black vase. It is 11½ inches by 13 inches and is marked $^{H\ \&\ Co.}_{\ \ \ L}$ and signed M.C. (Collection of J. d'Albis, Limoges, France)   (Right) The "harvesters" is a stoneware vase, 23¾ inches by 13½ inches decorated with pastel colors on a brown slip glazed background. It is marked H & Co. in a circle, signed Hexamer et. ED. (Collection of Maria and Hans Jorgen Heuser, Hamburg, Germany)   (Below) A dog's face is part of the decoration on this green, gold, white, and brown 13-inch-high vase. The artist's initials LF for Félix Lafond is on the side. The bottom of the vase is impressed Haviland & Co. Limoges No. 8. (Authors' collection)

manner as oil on a canvas. This slip or painted-on paste made it possible to raise certain parts of the design.

When Haviland terminated his contract with Bracquemond in 1881, he moved the kiln and Chaplet took over the management of the plant. He made tin-glazed whiteware. During the period of Chaplet's management, a search for an oxblood glaze similar to one on the early Chinese porcelains was a prime project. The glaze was finally perfected in 1884 and it was used on vases with Chinese shapes. Haviland stopped production at the pottery in 1885 because it was not a financial success.

Most of the vases made between 1878 and 1882 were marked with the impressed letters "H & Co." and then signed by the artist. The Museum of Limoges at Limoges, France, has a collection of this pottery. See Massier for another French artist who influenced the American pottery movement.

Bibliography

D'Albis, Jean, "La Céramique Impressionniste, à l'atelier de Paris-Auteuil (1873–1885)," *Cahiers de la Céramique du Verre et des Arts du Feu,* Numero 41 (1968).

_____, "Haviland et L'Impressionnisme en Céramique," *Paragone* (November 1972).

_____, "Histoire de la fabrique Haviland de 1842 à 1925," *Bulletin de la Société Archéologique et Historique du Limousin,* Tome XCVI.

_____, "Some Unpublished Ceramics of Dalou," *The Connoisseur* (July 1971), 175–181.

_____, correspondence with authors.

HULL POTTERY

The Acme Pottery Company was formed in Crooksville, Ohio, in 1903. It was in existence for only a short time when, in 1905, it was purchased and became the A. E. Hull Pottery Company. In 1917 the factory began making art pottery. Their wares were sold to florists and appropriate gift shops in all parts of the country. Hull Pottery was selling so well by 1921 that Addis E. Hull traveled to Europe to buy pottery in France, England, and Germany to be sold through the Hull pottery outlets. One Hull plant was converted to making tile in 1927 but by 1929 it was closed and the importation of pottery ended. In 1923 the Hull pottery built a continuous kiln 310 feet long. It cost $75,000 and by 1925, the firm was credited with making more than three million pieces a year.

In 1937 Hull contracted to make eleven million pieces for the Shulton Company of New York, and the A. E. Hull Pottery expanded to 450 employees.

The pottery burned to the ground in 1950. By 1952, the firm was restored and headed by J. Brandon Hull but the name was changed to the Hull Pottery Company. The firm is still working, but they are no longer making artware.

The A. E. Hull Pottery made many types of wares including artware, lamp bases, novelties, blue band kitchenware, and Zane Grey kitchenware and stoneware.

Pieces of the pottery are marked Hull Art U.S. or Hull U.S.A. and some were marked with a paper label. Pieces made after 1952 have been marked "hull." The artware includes numbers stamped on the pieces: 100 is the dou-

This Haviland jug has a pewter hinge for the pottery top. It is 12 inches high. The background glaze is tan with light blue highlights added as decoration. The leaves are dark brown or green with terracotta berries on the trim. The vase is marked CM on the side. The incised mark H & Co. is on the bottom. (Collection of Mrs. Sam Horvitz)

ble rose pattern; 300, orchid; 400, iris; 500, dogwood; 600, poppy. Butterflies, figurines, birds, and animals also appear.

Bibliography

Crooks, Guy E., "Brief History of the Pottery Industry of Crooksville, 1868–1932," *Crooksville-Roseville Pottery Festival Souvenir Program* (1967), 37–38.

Foraker, David, "Hull Pottery, Crooksville, Ohio," *Western Collector* IX (January–February 1971) 4–8.

Weiss, Grace M., "Hull Art Pottery," *The Antique Trader* (September 25, 1973) 46.

JUGTOWN POTTERY

The tradition of pottery in North Carolina goes back to the 1750s. Household wares and whiskey jugs were made by many potteries through the eighteenth and nineteenth centuries. The pottery was made in the ancient potters' tradition that has been known in all countries and the results were honest and simple with classic shapes and glazes.

In 1915 Juliana and Jacques Busbee became interested in what by then had become a dying art in North Carolina. They searched the state and either bought or photographed many good examples of pottery. They also encouraged any potter they could locate and soon set up a training and sales organization for what they named "Jugtown Pottery." (The term jugtown originally had unflattering connotations as it meant any town where jugs for whiskey were made, especially during Prohibition. But a "jugtown" potter was the unschooled but skilled potter the Busbees required for making their wares.)

The Busbees opened a tearoom at 60 Washington Square in Greenwich Village, New York City, to sell their pottery. By 1919 the tearoom was popular both for its pottery and for the caliber of its guests from the art and literary worlds. During these years, Mrs. Busbee remained in New York at the tearoom while Mr. Busbee worked with the potters in North Carolina.

By 1921, Jacques Busbee decided that it was time to build a shop at Jugtown, North Carolina. And because the older potters proved to be unable or unwilling to learn about the new shapes or to produce pottery on schedule, he hired Ben Owen as a potter in 1923. Owen turned the pieces and Busbee determined the shapes and did the glazing. Several other local men were hired to help mix clay, cut wood, and tend the kilns.

The pottery sold well and soon the tearoom or Village Store was moved to 37 East Sixtieth Street in New York City. Sales increased as the pottery received publicity from many magazines, including *Country Life, House Beautiful, The New Yorker,* and others.

As a market grew, other potters near the Jugtown Pottery began developing their wares and keeping up with the new shapes and glazes, and an industry was established in North Carolina. Juliana Busbee sold the New York store in 1926 and moved into a log cabin near the Jugtown Pottery.

The Busbees were eccentric but interesting people, and they attracted visitors from all over the world. Mrs. Busbee wore clothes made only of handwoven fabrics from North Carolina. She always asked her guests to help her with the dishes and ignored the comments of others. Mr. Busbee wore the first Bermuda shorts seen in the area.

During the depression, the potters kept working and the Jugtown Pottery continued to prosper. Jacques Busbee died in 1947. After his death, Juliana Busbee and Ben Owen continued to run the pottery. Juliana became ill in 1958, when the pottery was having financial problems, and the state considered taking over the property. She said she had willed the Jugtown Pottery to Ben Owen, but no will was found and she was too mentally ill to make a new one. The pottery ended production in 1958 and Owen left to start his own. Friends of the pottery organized to save it as a nonprofit organization for the state.

Stamp JUGTOWN WARE for original Jugtown Pottery. Ben Owen thought he had taken the only stamp with him, but it has been used by the present company in Jugtown.

Two green blue vases made by the Jugtown Pottery. (North Carolina Museum of Art)

A selection of Jugtown Pottery from the Jacques Busbee Memorial Collection. The pieces show Korean, Chinese, and Persian influences. Notice the thick white and clear black glazes. (North Carolina Museum of Art)

In December of 1958, the deeds were signed for Jugtown Incorporated. Through the confusion of Juliana Busbee's illness, another corporation was also formed, but with a John Mare. Legal problems arose, with each corporation wanting to be the one to save the pottery, and in 1959 it closed. In April of 1960, the legal problem was resolved and the pottery reopened. Mrs. Busbee died in March of 1962.

The Jugtown Pottery is still operating and is under the direction of Nancy Sweezy. It is owned by Country Roads, Inc., a nonprofit organization. The old marks, described in the preceding pages, are still in use.

Wares

The Jugtown wares were all of simple shapes. The early pieces were utilitarian adaptations of early pottery. Jugs, crocks, pie plates, sugar and cream dishes, plates, candlesticks, bean pots, tea sets, stew pans, pickle jars, and preserve jars were made. Later pieces were for the New York market and included oriental inspired pottery and decorative types. All of the Jugtown wares were glazed.

Rockingham ware and the stoneware of early days were early inspirations. A red clay was used to make an orange-colored ware. Gray stoneware with blue or white decorations was made. Black, white, dark brown, Chinese blue and green or "frogskin" glazes were used on the "Chinese" style pieces. The clay was local. A few pieces were decorated with flowers, incised designs, of impressed patterns such as thumb prints.

The pottery was handmade, thrown on a kick wheel, and then glazed and fired. Pieces were marked "Jugtown Ware" impressed in a circle from the early days of the factory, probably about 1922 or 1923. The name was not registered until 1959.

Bibliography

Breese, Jessie Martin, "Jugtown, N.C.," *Country Life* XLII (October 1922) 64–65.

Crawford, Jean, *Jugtown Pottery: History and Design,* Winston-Salem: John F. Blair, 1964.

———, "Jugtown Pottery," *Western Collector* VI (July 1968).

Goldsmith, Margaret O., "Jugtown Pottery," *House Beautiful* 52 (October 1922) 311, 358, 360.

Hoagland, Jane, "Jugtown Pottery," *Art Center New York Bulletin* I (April 1923) 167–168.

"Interested in Jugtown Ware?" *Pottery Collectors' Newsletter* I No. 1 (October 1971).

Mock, Esther, "An American Craft with a Pedigree," *Early American Life* (June 1973) 42–43, 86.

———, "The High Craft of Jugtown," *Hobbies* (November 1972).

———, correspondence with authors.

Salem College Collection, Winston-Salem, N. Carolina.

Stiles, Helen E., *Pottery in the United States,* New York: E. P. Dutton & Co., 1941.

KENTON HILLS

The failing Rookwood Pottery of Cincinnati, Ohio, laid off many skilled potters and decorators. In 1937, a group from the company headed by Harold Bopp, a chemist, founded the Harold Bopp Pottery in Erlanger, Kentucky. In 1939, the company was refinanced by George Seyler, father of David Seyler, an artist. Added to Seyler, art director, and Bopp, chemist, were William Hentschel and Arthur Conant, designers; Rosemary Dickman and Alza

Artists:

Julian Bechtold. Made very few pieces.

Harold Bopp. Made very few pieces.

Paul Chidaw. Part time.

Arthur Conant. Made very few pieces.

Rose Brunner Dickman. **RBD**

Rosemary Dickman.

Charlotte Haupt. Made very few pieces.

William Hentschel.

Leo Murphy. Part time.

Harold Nash. Part time.

David Seyler.

Alza Stratton.

Unknown

Stratton, decorators; John Reichart, moldman, and Mayo Taylor, kilnman. The company was renamed Kenton Hills Porcelains, Inc., or, unofficially, Kenton Hills Pottery.

The lines resembled those from the closed Rookwood Pottery. A high-fired soft paste porcelain was made, plain glazed with either underglaze brown slip or colorful hand decorations. The glazes included the most popular Spanish red, catseye green or blue, Danish blue, and oxblood; also celodon, mossy green, poplar green, morning blue, dusty pink, Persian blue, mandarin yellow, jungle black, hard white, decorator white, shell white, and savage coral. Native clays were used.

In 1941, the workmen left for war work and the stock was sold, and property rented. It was sold in 1945. All molds were destroyed.

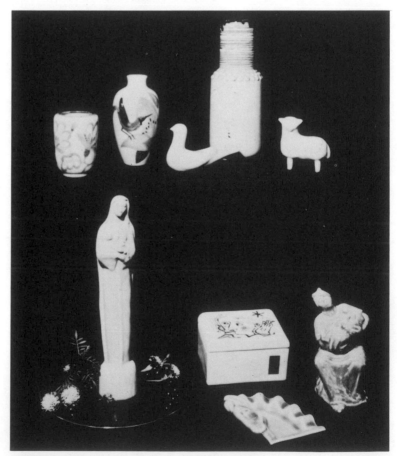

A selection of pieces in the Kenton Hills catalogue of 1941: (Top row) *Left to right:* vase decorated by David Seyler; vase decorated by Alza Stratton; bird sculpture by David Seyler; vase decorated by William Hentschel; animal sculpture by David Seyler. (Bottom row) *Left to right:* Three pieces designed by David Seyler; sculpture of sitting woman by Charlotte Haupt.

TRADE MARK

The experimental Harold Bopp pottery mark.

Marks (*left to right*): showroom label, not used on pottery; trademark impressed and often used with a label; and another Kenton mark.

David Seyler, now head of the Department of Sculpture at the University of Nebraska, states that the pieces were marked as follows:

1. Every Kenton Hills piece was impressed on the base with either the experimental HB lotus blossom or the KH tulip blossom. Neither mark dates a piece.
2. An impressed number is the mold shape number.
3. Impressed initials or a signature designate the designer or sculptor who created the form or added slip decoration to the clay shape.
4. An impressed circle in the base center was always used on some molds as a lamp drill guide if required.
5. Underglaze painted initials are those of the decorator. The words "Unica" or "Serica" added on decorated pieces imply a unique piece or one of a limited edition (usually lamp bases).
6. The letter S (special) indicated an experimental shape, usually one of a kind for a test kiln.

Bibliography

Cox, Warren E., *The Book of Pottery and Porcelain. Volume I,* New York: Crown Publishers, 1944.

Seyler, David, correspondence with authors.

Tomc, Thomas M., correspondence with authors.

Marks.

KNOWLES, TAYLOR AND KNOWLES

The history of the Knowles, Taylor and Knowles Company of East Liverpool, Ohio, does not really belong in a book about art pottery because the firm made many types of porcelain. But they did make one rare form of pottery, Lotus ware, and it is for this reason that a short history is included.

Isaac W. Knowles founded a pottery in East Liverpool in 1853 to make Rockingham and yellowware. In 1870, John N. Taylor and Homer S. Knowles (son of Isaac Knowles) joined the firm and it became known as Knowles, Taylor and Knowles. In 1888, Joseph G. Lee and Willis A. Knowles were added as partners, but the name remained as before. The firm incorporated in January of 1891 and the name then included the word Company.

Ironstone ware was made in 1872, the first in Ohio. Most of their products were hotel china. It was usually thicker than home-use china, but it was made of porcelain. They made many types of china and the company

(Below) A lotus ware vase painted and gilded in East Liverpool about 1890. Notice that the body of this vase is very similar to another lotus vase seen here. The decorations were often "one of a kind." (Collections of Greenfield Village and The Henry Ford Museum, Dearborn, Michigan)

(Below) Lotus ware vases from Knowles, Taylor and Knowles: (*left*) decorated with red, blue, and gold lattice decoration, 9¾ inches high, 6⅛ inches in diameter; (*right*) with applied decorations of the type used on the art pottery made by the factory, 7½ inches high, 4½ inches in diameter. (The Smithsonian Institution)

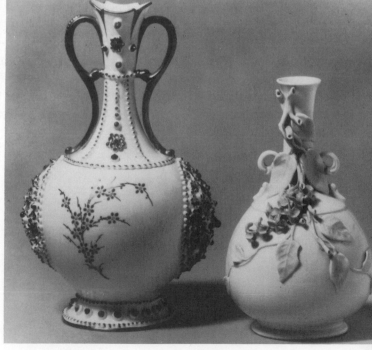

A page from a part of the Knowles, Taylor and Knowles Company catalogue, circa 1890, showing examples of "white flowers on olive body." Also pictured are "white flowers on a celadon body" and the more common white lotus ware. (East Liverpool Historical Society, East Liverpool, Ohio)

was the world's largest. Pieces were marked K. T. & K.

Lotus ware was made from about 1891 to 1896. It was named by Will Rhodes, one of their salesmen who thought one piece resembled a lotus leaf. Homer Knowles, one of the partners, and Joshua Poole, a plant superintendent from Ireland, developed the formula for Lotus ware. Poole had been a manager of the Belleek Pottery in Ireland and he helped develop a true Belleek ware for Knowles, Taylor and Knowles by 1889. But that November the pottery factory was destroyed by fire and the Belleek ware was discontinued. This was not Lotus ware, but a true Belleek which is even rarer today than Lotus. It was marked with the round Knowles, Taylor and Knowles mark and the word Belleek.

The first set of Lotus ware was made in 1889. It was a bone china that was actually made with animal bones. George and William Morley, from England, and Henry Schmidt, from Germany, were brought to the firm to assist in the production. Kenneth Beattie was the chief modeler at the pottery.

Schmidt worked in secrecy in a small workshop where he personally applied the leaves, flowers, "jewels," and filigree to the pieces of Lotus ware. He worked with the pieces in the hard green (unbaked) state. After the decorations were applied, the Lotus ware was baked in the same kilns as the commercial hotel wares. There was much breakage in the kilns both during the firing for the bisque state and after the decorating, and eventually the line was discontinued because of its high cost.

Lotus ware was displayed at the World's Columbian Exposition in 1893. A few pieces of undecorated Lotus ware were made from molds taken from commercial objects. One dish shaped like a fan behind a reclining lady was molded from an identical brass dish.

Pieces were made and decorated at the factory, but the ware was also sold plain and decorated by amateur china painters. The ladies of East Liverpool returned their decorated pieces to the kiln to be baked so the colored decorations have remained. Some pieces have been found with the color peeling. These were decorated out of town and not properly baked.

Although the name Lotus ware means a very white bone china to most collectors, only a limited amount of pottery was made and marked in the same manner. Lotus ware pottery had a dark green glaze on a chocolate pottery body with applied white china decorations of leaves, branches, and flower tendrils.

Most Lotus ware was marked with the round Knowles, Taylor and Knowles emblem and the words "LOTUS WARE."

Bibliography

Barber, Edwin A., *The Pottery and Porcelain of the United States*, New York: G. P. Putnam's Sons, 1893 (3d and rev. ed. 1909).

———, *Marks of American Potters*, Philadelphia: Patterson and White, 1904.

Crutcher, Jean, "Lotus Ware," *Antique News* 2 (October 1964).

East Liverpool, Ohio, Pottery Festival Catalogue, 1968–1972.

Garrett, Brice, "Ohio's Lotus Ware," *Spinning Wheel* (January–February 1966) 16–17.

"Lotus Ware," *Spinning Wheel* (November 1967).

Ramsay, John, "East Liverpool Ohio Pottery in the Museum of the East Liverpool Historical Society," *American Collector* (April 1948).

———, "Lotus Ware," *Glass and China* 47 (October 1942) 55–57.

LONHUDA POTTERY

Artists and Their Marks:

 Laura A. Fry.

 Helen M. Harper.

 Mr. W. A. Long.

 Sarah R. McLaughlin.

 Jessie R. Spaulding.

William Long of Steubenville, Ohio, founded the Lonhuda Pottery Company in 1892. Long was born in Ohio on July 18, 1844. After serving in the Civil War, he was discharged in 1865 and married a nurse whom he had met in a military hospital. The Longs eventually moved to Steubenville where he became a druggist. They had two sons, Charles and Albert. Life as a small-town druggist seemed to lack something, and Long found a new interest when he saw the pottery displayed at the Philadelphia Exposition of 1876. He set up a laboratory in the back of his drugstore and began experimenting with glazes. In 1892 he decided to form a pottery company with Mr. W. H. Hunter, editor of the Steubenville *Gazette,* and Alfred Day, Secretary of the U.S. Potters Association. The first letters of the names of the three men were used to form the company name, Lonhuda. The records are confused, but either William Long developed a brown underglaze of the type used by Rookwood or he was licensed to use a process developed by Laura Fry in 1889. Contemporary records show both Long and Rookwood bought licenses from Laura Fry (*China Glass and Pottery Review,* August 15, 1897).

The Lonhuda Pottery hired Laura Fry, Sarah R. McLaughlin, Helen M. Harper, and Jessie R. Spaulding as artists. Other artists who may have worked at the factory are Elizabeth Ayers, Charles John Dibowski, and Mary Taylor. The company made underglazed pieces with a slip decoration and the familiar brown background. The pottery was sold in all parts of the United States and also shipped to Europe. Lonhuda was exhibited at the Chicago World's Fair in 1893.

Samuel A. Weller (*see*) was attracted by the pottery and immediately decided that it would fit into his future pottery plans. He had a plant in Zanesville and was able to convince Long to make Lonhuda at the plant. A new firm was formed in January of 1895 by Long and Weller and it was called the Lonhuda Faience Company. The factory made Lonhuda for about a year, by which time Weller no longer needed Long and his secrets. (The pottery made by Weller after Long left was the Louwelsa line.) After the two separated, Long went to work for the J. B. Owens Company of Zanesville, Ohio. IIe stayed there four years. After he left, Owens continued to make the pottery under the name "Utopian."

Long moved to Denver, Colorado, in 1900 where he

1893.

 LONHUDA
1892.

 LONHUDA
268
1896.

 DENVER

Clifton mark.

Yellow violets decorate this chocolate-brown glazed Lonhuda vase. It is marked "Lonhuda, 1893, 115," including Sarah McLaughlin's cipher and identifying numbers. (The Benjamin Collection, The Smithsonian Institution)

organized the Denver China and Pottery Company. This pottery worked until 1905 when Long moved to Clifton Street, Newark, New Jersey, and founded the Clifton Pottery. He worked there from 1905 to 1908 making a line called "Crystal Patina." In need of work in 1909, Long moved back to Zanesville and again worked for Weller, until 1912. A short time later, he went to work for the Roseville Pottery and by 1914, he was working with the American Encaustic Tiling Company. He was hospitalized soon after and died in 1918.

Product

The Lonhuda Pottery was inspired by the forms of American Indian pottery. Not only did William Long admire the shapes of the pottery, but he used an Indian head as part of his mark. His pieces were made of colored clay with a slip decoration added to the unfired pieces. Reds, browns, yellows, and grays were used. The clay was usually an imported yellow. The high-gloss brown glaze was his most famous. A clear glaze and a matte glaze were also used. Pieces were made with decorations picturing Indians, famous people, dogs, seascapes, landscapes, fish, birds, and flowers.

The art pottery at the Denver China and Pottery Company had a matte glaze and it was often green. It was slightly iridescent with molded relief designs of Colorado flowers or art nouveau geometric patterns. The line was called "Denaura." The firm also made a general line of pottery.

The Clifton Art Pottery made several types of white clay pieces covered with crystalline glaze that resembled old bronzes. This was the "Crystal Patina" line. They also made Clifton Indian ware, a line of pottery made from red New Jersey clay and resembling early Indian pieces. The interiors of these pieces were often glazed black.

Bibliography

Barber, Edwin A., *The Pottery and Porcelain of the United States,* New York: G. P. Putnam's Sons, 1893 (3d and rev. ed. 1909).

_____, *Marks of American Potters,* Philadelphi: Patterson and White, 1904.

Hall, Foster E. and Gladys C., "The Lonhuda Pricing Formula," *Newsletter,* 1972.

"Denaura Denver" is marked on this 1903 vase made by the Denver China and Pottery Company. It has a green glaze on a majolica body. The design is in relief. The vase is 8½ inches high by 4¾ inches wide. (The Smithsonian Institution)

(Left) The 7¾-inch-high by 5-inch-diameter vase, made about 1905, is glazed with a gray green. It is marked "Clifton Art Pottery." (The Smithsonian Institution)   (Right) A replica of a Pueblo pottery vase from Pueblo of Homolobi at Holbrook, Arizona. It was made by the Clifton Pottery about 1905–1907. The colors are brown, black, buff, and brick red. The vase is 6⅛ inches high by 8½ inches. (The Smithsonian Institution)

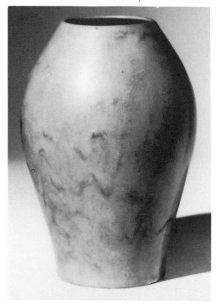

Gray green and yellow green and olive glazes are on this Clifton vase. It is impressed "Clifton Pottery Company 1906," and is 5 inches by 4⅛ inches. (The Smithsonian Institution)

"Lonhuda," *Spinning Wheel* (November 1967) 17.

"Lonhuda Pottery," *Mid America Reporter* (December 1971).

Purviance, Louise; Purviance, Evan; and Schneider, Norris F., *Weller Art Pottery in Color,* Des Moines: Wallace-Homestead Book Co., 1971.

_____, *Zanesville Art Pottery in Color,* Leon, Iowa: Mid-American Book Co., 1968.

Schneider, Norris F., "Lonhuda: Originated by William A. Long," *Pottery Collector's Newsletter,* I No. 4 (January 1972) (reprint from *Sunday Times Recorder,* Zanesville, Ohio, 1971).

_____, "Weller Pottery," *Zanesville Times-Signal* (March 16, 1958).

LOW ART TILE

John Gardner Low was a skilled artist of known talent long before he began producing tiles in Chelsea, Massachusetts. He was born January 10, 1835, in Chelsea, the son of John Low, a civil engineer. His artistic ability was

(Above left) This mark features the crossed keys. (The Smithsonian Institution)   (Above right) Used with or without dates 1881, 1882, 1883, 1884, 1885. (The Smithsonian Institution) (Left) About 1881. (The Smithsonian Institution)

apparent while he was still a boy. At the age of twenty-three, John went to France for three years and studied in Paris with Thomas Couture and Constantine Troyon. Many of his oil paintings of landscapes and peasants were auctioned in Boston in April, 1861.

Low hoped to make his living as an artist and for several years he did paintings and murals, one of which included a drop curtain for the Chelsea Academy of Music. He did not make enough money as a painter, so in 1870 he began working in ceramics. (The Low Tile Catalogue at the Boston Public Library has a chronology giving 1873 as the date.) Low first joined the Chelsea Pottery, operated by James Robertson. He worked there a year or more, learning the techniques and experimenting with his own ceramic projects. It was a visit to the Centennial Exhibition in 1876 that led him to use new colors and oriental designs. In 1877, his father financed a tile works and the building began for the J. and J. G. Low Art Tile Works. The building was located at 948 Broadway which was on the corner of Stockton Street. It was a well-equipped factory and not just a small craft shop. J. G. Low hired George W. Robertson to work at the tile works in 1878. He was paid $75 per week, a high salary at that time. The first firing of tile took place on May 1, 1879. The quality was excellent, and five months after the first tiles were made Low Art Tile was awarded a silver medal at the Cincinnati Industrial Exposition.

In 1880, Low was awarded a gold medal in Crewe, England, for the best English or American tiles shown at the exhibit of the Royal Manchester and Liverpool Agricultural Society Exhibition. This award caused much comment in the industry (as reported by *Popular Science Monthly*, Jan., 1892, p. 308): "This record, probably unsurpassed in ceramic history, serves to illustrate the remarkably rapid development of an industry new in America, but old in the East; it shows the resources at command of the American Potter." Recent researchers have found no record of the award in England, as noted by Barbara White Morse in *Spinning Wheel* (July–August, 1971, p. 27) in an article entitled "John Gardner Low and his Original Art Tile Soda Fountain."

Low tiles and "plastic sketches" were exhibited again at the Fine Arts Society of London, England, in 1882. The work was praised for its artistic and ceramic skills.

In 1883 John Low retired from the business and his grandson John Farnsworth Low, joined the company. The

Marks:

Used beginning 1883 when Low retired and J.F. succeeded him. (The Smithsonian Institution)

Mark used by Arthur Osborne.

Other marks included the registered trademark with a small circle enclosing the crossed keys; J & G Low with the city and state in a rectangle and "Pat'd/Feb 18/ 1879" in a circle. Sometimes the tile is marked with the name of the firm that sold it, for example, J. S. Conover & Co.

firm name was changed to J. G. and J. F. Low Art Tile Works. In addition to tiles, other forms of pottery were introduced, including a new major product, art tile soda fountains. The firm worked until 1902, but was not liquidated until 1907. They may have been forced out of business by the new tariff laws that permitted foreign kaolin into the country at a low price. The tile works survived a disastrous fire that burned much of Chelsea in 1908. John G. Low died in 1907.

Product

J. G. Low tiles were made by several methods. When John Low first began operations in 1877, he probably had never seen tile made mechanically in a factory. He experimented with various methods, glazes, and clays and he finally developed a relief tile via a method that had been used for years in England. The "dust" process had been a popular way to make ceramic buttons, and the technique was patented in England about 1840. Dry powdered clay was slightly moistened and subjected to great pressure in a machine press with a die. The design of the die was impressed on the tile. Then the tile was fired and glazed. Low also made "wet" or "plastic" tiles. The method was similar to making any sort of pottery. The damp or "plastic" clay was pressed into molds where it was allowed to dry and shrink. The tile was then easily removed from the mold, and it had a raised design on one side. The tiles were placed on cloth-covered plaster blocks where they were allowed to dry for a day. Artists often touched up the relief design by undercutting it with hand tools. The tiles were placed in drying rooms for several weeks and then they were fired and glazed. These tiles were unmarked and indented in the back to follow the curves of the tile design.

(Below) This Low Art Tile modeled by A. Osborne is 7¾ inches by 24 inches. It is glazed a yellow green. The design for this tile appears in the book *Plastic Sketches of J. G. and J. F. Low, 1887*. It has the words "Copyright 1881, JG and JF Low" and the title "Eureka" printed on the face of the photograph. (The Smithsonian Institution)

(Above) Stove tiles were used as decorations, as at the top of this "Sterling Stove" made at the Rice Stove Works in Rochester, New York, about 1886. The round tile had a small notch so that it could be held in place. The center tile is turquoise, the sides are yellow. (Collection of Greenfield Village and The Henry Ford Museum, Dearborn, Michigan)

John Low also developed an original method of tile manufacture. He called it the "natural" process. First, a flat tile was shaped. Then, a leaf, grass, lace, or some other similar delicate object was placed on the tile and forced into the clay surface with pressure from a screw press. A piece of tissue paper was then placed over the impressed tile. Clay dust was put on the tissue paper and pressed against the paper by the same screw press. The result was a sort of sandwich of two tiles, with the paper in between. The bottom tile had an impressed design, the top tile had a raised design. The two tiles were separated and both the relief and intaglio versions were completed with glaze. He later improved the method by making an impressed tile of paraffin wax which he coated to make into a mold to be used for hundreds of relief tiles.

The J. G. and J. F. Low Art Tile Works also made hand-modeled tiles. They were made by workmen who pressed them by hand into a mold and then undercut the design by hand, making a very high relief product. These tiles often have rough backs and show the fingerprints of the workmen. They are also marked on the back with the name of the factory impressed on ridges (from "Tiles to Treasure, Low Art Tiles," Barbara White Morse, *Spinning Wheel*, March, 1969, p. 18).

This framed tile is signed A in a circle. The 6-inch-square green tile has the same design as one of the plastic sketches shown on the next page. It is marked on the back "J. & J. G. Low Patent Art Tile Works, Chelsea, Mass. U.S.A. copyright 1881 J. & J. G. Low." (Authors' collection)

Although positive proof is not available, it seems logical that Arthur Osborne of the Low Art Tile Co. is the same Arthur Osborne who made this sterine wax plaque. The 8-by-6-inch plaque has a raised design colored in a lifelike manner. The front of the plaque is marked with the AO cipher found on Low tiles. The back of the plaque is stamped "Osborne (copyright) Made in England." (Authors' collection)

(At right and on opposite page) Two pages from the book *Plastic Sketches of J. G. and J. F. Low, 1887.* Notice that the tiles are shown unglazed, unlike the finished product. The cipher AO for Arthur Osborne appears on almost every piece. (Boston Public Library photograph)

All of the tiles were made from Connecticut feldspar, Carolina kaolin, and clays from Missouri and New Jersey. Tiles were made in many sizes, but the most common were six by six inches or four by four inches. Narrow border tiles were used on stoves or as trim. The round tiles were also used on stoves and were made in quantity. The round tiles are often unmarked.

A special product of the tile company was what Low called "plastic sketches." These were low-relief pictures made by an artist using clay instead of oil paints. Nearly all the sketches were made by Arthur Osborne, an English

artist who had worked for the Chelsea Keramic Art
Works. He was hired by Low soon after the Low tile plant
was built and he continued working with them until 1893
or later. Osborne was an imaginative artist who designed
tiles and did the sketches inspired by the cultures of Ori-
entals, Moors, African natives, Egyptians, and from nature, mythology and many other sources. Plastic sketches
up to eighteen inches in length were of farm scenes, animals, birds, monks, cupids, and beautiful women. Each
was signed "AO" on the face of the sketch. The identical
signature seems to identify him as the same Arthur Os-

(Above) An ornate cast-iron frame, apparently original, was used for this Low tile made about 1885. The tile is 6 inches square, glazed yellow brown.   (Top right) This 6-inch-square brown tile is marked "J. and J. G. Low Patent Art Tile Works Chelsea Mass, U.S.A. copyright 1881 by J. & J. G. Low." (Authors' collection)

(Bottom right) This 6-inch tan Low tile is marked J. & J. G. Low/ Patent/Art Tile Works.

borne who signed his pieces AO and copyrighted a process of making "Sterine" wax plaques in England in 1909, 1910, and 1911. (Books called "Plastic Sketches" by J. and J. G. Low, 1882, and J. G. and J. F. Low, 1887, showing many of these designs can still be found in the Boston Public Library.)

John G. Low began working on his tile soda fountain in 1883. He applied for a patent for his designs in 1888. Earlier soda fountains had been made of marble, but Low felt glazed tiles would be an improvement and would reduce the cost. His patent was not accepted at first, but with a few changes and the services of several lawyers, it was finally granted in 1889. The Low tile soda fountains were sold in all parts of the country. The most elaborate one ever made was shown at the Columbian Exposition in Chicago in 1893. It was sixteen feet high, twenty feet long and was covered with panels picturing cupids, human figures, and dolphins.

The factory also made pottery for several years starting about 1882. Their pottery included clock cases, ewers, flower holders, fireplace tiles, planters, and inkwells. Candlesticks, boxes, paperweights, lamps, and trivets were made of brass with tile decoration. Stoves were of cast iron with tile inserts. Vases and cups were styled in the Japanese manner with designs of flowers, animals, leaves, or scrolls ("American Pottery," *Scribner's Magazine,* Nov., 1902, 32:637). The pieces were small to medium in size ranging up to about ten inches in height. The body of the piece was made of clay similar to the white

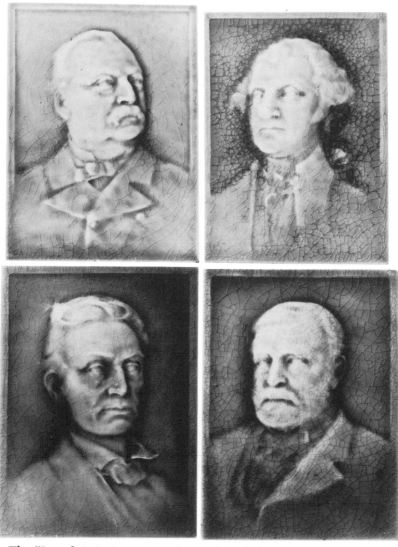

The "J. and J. G. Low Art Tile Works, Chelsea, Copyright 1885" is marked on the back of these four political tiles. Each tile is 4½ by 6¼ inches. *Clockwise:* The Grover Cleveland tile is glazed pale green, George Washington pale blue, and U. S. Grant and Lincoln medium blue. (The Smithsonian Institution)

tile. The body surface was decorated with glazes in many colors ranging from dark cream to chocolate and with shades of red, green, blue, gray, and yellow. Several colors were often used on one piece. Low ware was often mistaken for oriental pottery.

The tiles were made in many colors which included yellow, gray, brown, orange, blue, rose, and white, but most of their colors favored the earth tones of greens and browns.

"The Lows never imitated other work, either domestic or foreign. They have never made hand-painted, mosaic, printed, encaustic, or floor tiles, and they have never employed men who were trained in other tile works. Consequently, their products are characterized by a marked

Quick Meal was the name of a stove. The trademark chicken emerging from an egg is shown on this oval blue green tile 3¼ by 3 inches. The back of the tile shows it was made by impressing the clay into a mold in the manner of Low tiles. Other clues from the Quick Meal Company suggest that this was a Low tile. It is unmarked. (Authors' collection)

originality, both in style and design, which has caused them to be extensively imitated, both at home and abroad." (*Pottery and Porcelain*, Edwin Barber, p. 353, 1909 edition.)

Bibliography

Barber, Edwin, Marks of American Potters, Philadelphia: Patterson and White, 1904.

Bernard, Julian, *Victorian Ceramic Tiles*, Greenwich, Conn.: New York Graphic Society Ltd., 1972.

"Charles Dickens 1812–1870," *Antique Dealer & Collectors Guide* (December 1972).

Clark, Robert Judson, *The Arts and Crafts Movement in America 1876–1916*, Princeton, N.J.: Princeton University Press, 1972.

Dillingham, Charles T. 1887. *Plastic Sketches of J. G. & J. F. Low*, New York: Boston, Lee & Shepherd Publishers.

Evans, Paul F., "Victorian Art Tiles," *Western Collector* (V. 11), (November 1967).

"The Field of Art—American Pottery," *Scribner's Magazine* (V. 32–65, 637), (November, 1902).

King, Emma D., "Low Tiles," *Spinning Wheel* (January, 1957) (14).

Low, J. G., and J. F. Art Tile Works, *An Illustrated Catalogue of Art Tiles*, Chelsea, Mass., 1884.

———, "Low Art Tile," *Spinning Wheel* (December 1970).

———, "Low Art Tile," *Western Collector* (November 1967).

———, "Low Tiles," *Spinning Wheel* (November, 1967).

McClinton, K. M., *Collecting American Victorian Antiques*, New York: Charles Scribner's Sons, 1966.

Millet, F. D., "Story of Low Tile," *Century Magazine*, 1882.

Morse, Barbara White, "Buying a Low Art Tile Stove, Part One," *Spinning Wheel* (November, 1970), 28.

———, "Chelsea Ceramic Charm and Comfort," *The Antiques Journal* (October, 1972), 13.

———, "I Collect Low Art Tiles," *Yankee* (November 1970), 132.

———, "John Gardner Low and His Original Art Tile Soda Fountain, Part One," *Spinning Wheel* (July–August, 1971), 26.

———, "John Gardner Low and His Original Art Tile Soda Fountain, Part Two," *Spinning Wheel* (September, 1971), 16.

———, "Low 'Art Tiles' Today, A Primer for the Novice Collector," *National Antiques Review* (September, 1973), 26.

———, "Tiles to Treasure, Low Art Tiles," *Spinning Wheel* (March, 1969), 18.

Newark Museum Association, "New Jersey Clay Products" (date unknown).

"Recent Advances in the Pottery Industry," *The Popular Science Monthly* (January, 1892).

Sargent, Irene, "Potters and Their Products," *The Craftsman* (4, 3), (June, 1903), 149.

Watkins, Lura Woodside, "Low's Art Tiles," *Antiques Magazine* (14, 5), (May, 1944), 250.

———, "The Art Potteries," *Early New England Potters and Their Wares,* Cambridge: Harvard University Press, 1950, 222.

LYCETT

Edward Lycett (1833–1910) was one of the most famous china decorators in the United States. He also made art tiles for a short time.

Lycett was born in Newcastle, England. He worked at the Copeland Garrett pottery where he studied art and decorated vases. He painted, and his work was exhibited several times. After moving to New York in 1861, he opened a shop that decorated porcelains and porcelain panels for furniture manufacturers. The panels were decorated with figures and with heavy gold. In 1865, he was commissioned to decorate the second set of Lincoln china for the White House.

The painting of china became a popular pastime for wealthy women. Edward Lycett had a studio plus a staff and it was there that he took prominent, wealthy women as students and taught them the art of decorating porcelains. Maria Longworth Nichols of the Rookwood Fac-

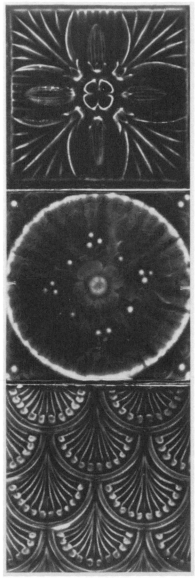

Three tiles made with iridescent glaze by Edward Lycett. The top tile is brown, the middle green, the bottom blue. (The Smithsonian Institution)

The Marblehead ship mark. (The Smithsonian Institution)

tory was believed to have sent some of her early works to be fired at the Lycett kilns.

In 1877 Lycett was invited to teach a class in china painting at the St. Louis, Missouri, School of Design. He took the job and left his company, Warrin and Lycett, which at the time, was under the direction of his son William. After one year in St. Louis, Edward Lycett moved to Cincinnati for a few months where he taught china painting. After his short stay in Cincinnati, he moved to East Liverpool, Ohio, where he opened a decorating business, with plans to establish his own manufacturing company in Philadelphia. While in East Liverpool, in 1879, he decorated some underglaze stoneware cups and saucers that were made by Homer Laughlin. The Philadelphia factory had just started when Shakespeare Laughlin, the main force behind the project, died. Lycett decided to return to New York City and resume the china painting business.

He joined the Faience Manufacturing Company of New York City in 1884. It was there that he experimented with glazes, bodies, and new shapes. A fine grade of porcelain was made including large vases with elaborate decorations. While experimenting with glazes, Lycett developed an iridescent glaze which he called "reflet metallique." This was said to resemble the ancient Persian glazes. Some tiles were also made using this special glaze. In 1890 he retired and moved to Atlanta, Georgia.

His three sons, Joe, Frank, and William, were also china decorators. William had a china decorating firm in Atlanta, and Edward did some of the work there. Records show that Edward Lycett also decorated for the Jersey City Pottery in New Jersey and the Union Porcelain Works in the Greenpoint section of Brooklyn, New York. His work ranged from six-foot panels for the front of a New York building to roses on chamberpots and reproductions of royal services. He made a special type of plate called "anamorphosis" for children. A distorted group of fine lines was drawn that if held at the proper angle, appeared as an animal. He developed a special gold, a mazarine blue, and the iridescent glaze.

A fine 1908 vase by the Marblehead Pottery was this one with ships and waves in tones of gray and blue. It was designed by A. E. Baggs and A. I. Hennessy. (*Keramic Studio*, June, 1908, p. 30)

Bibliography

Barber, Edwin A., *The Pottery and Porcelain of the United States*, New York: G. P. Putnam's Sons, 1893 (3d and rev. ed. 1909).

(Left) Stylized flowers of green, brown, and orange matte glaze decorate this vase. The flowers are incised and painted. The piece, 3¼ inches high, is marked with the Marblehead Pottery ship mark and the incised and conjoined letters AB,T. (The Art Museum, Princeton University, Princeton, New Jersey)

————, *Marks of American Potters.* Philadelphia: Patterson and White, 1904.

Lycett, Lydia, "China Painting by the Lycetts," *Atlanta Historical Bulletin,* VI, No. 25 (July 1941).

St. John, Wylly Folk, "Hand Painted China," *Atlanta Journal and Constitution Magazine* (February 12, 1967).

MARBLEHEAD POTTERY

Marblehead Pottery was started in 1905 by Dr. Herbert J. Hall in connection with a sanitarium he ran in Marblehead, Massachusetts. Dr. Hall thought that the work would be of help to his patients and so he developed a series of crafts for them that included wood carving, weaving, metalwork, and pottery. Clay was located very close to the sanitarium. The pottery was installed in the sanitarium, called the Devereux Mansion. The pottery had a kick wheel, turning lathe, and a six-burner kerosene kiln. By 1908 there were three designers, a decorator, a thrower, and a kiln man. Their output was two-hundred pieces per week. During the first two years the patients were instructed by Jessie Luther of Providence, Rhode Island. She taught all of the crafts. After that, the pottery was separated from the sanitarium and Arthur E. Baggs was made the director. Previously, he had worked under Professor Binns of Alfred, New York. Baggs was a fine artist and designer and he used the experimental glazes

(Top) Incised and painted geometric patterns of black decorate this speckled blue green vase. The piece is 3¾ inches high. It is marked with the Marblehead Pottery ship emblem and the incised letters HT for Hanna Tutt. (The Art Museum, Princeton University, Princeton, New Jersey) (Bottom) A vase with dark mustard-colored background is decorated with brown, green, orange, and blue geometric designs. The interior is glazed with glossy blue green. The vase is marked with the Marblehead ship mark. (The Smithsonian Institution)

and methods of decoration to make an artistic product. Arthur Baggs became the owner of the pottery in 1915 and he continued its work. When more space was required, the pottery moved to 111 Front Street, in Marblehead. The pottery was always a small operation; only six people were at the factory in 1916. The factory continued working until 1936. After it closed, Baggs became a teacher at Ohio State University.

Many artists were associated with the pottery. Arthur Irwin Hennessey and Maude Milner were designers there, working before 1912. Annie Aldrich and Rachel Grinwell, though not on the staff, did designs. Mrs. E. D. (Hanna) Tutt was a decorator and E. J. Lewis was a kiln man. John Swallow was an English thrower working in 1916, and before, and his wife sometimes helped. John Selmer-Larsen was a designer and Benjamin Tutt was a workman at the factory.

Product

At first, the pottery made a Marblehead that was designed to avoid the naturalistic in favor of a conventionalized design. There were no realistic flowers or scenes on the pottery. Conventionalized marine forms such as seaweed, ships, sea horses, and fish were used. Later pieces did include flowers, but in a more realistic style, particularly on plates and tiles. Conventionalized birds, fruit, and animals were also used.

The body was a mixture of New Jersey and Massachusetts clay. Colors were chiefly metallic oxides with matte glaze and stippling. Many of the bowls were enameled on the inside with a different color from the exterior. The most famous glaze used was Marblehead blue, a deep turquoise shade. Pieces were also made of gray, yellow, green, brown, or lavender (wisteria). A few pieces with red glaze and experimental pieces of tin enameled majolica and luster were also made. Special colors could be ordered. Designs were worked in three or four colors.

(Top) In 1908, *Keramic Studio* published an article about Marblehead Pottery. This vase, with conventionalized peacock feather design in blue and green, was designed by A. E. Baggs. (*Keramic Studio*, June, 1908, p. 30)

(Left) Hanna Tutt also decorated this vase with incised geometric patterns and green and dark green glazes. The Marblehead Pottery vase is 8⁹⁄₁₆ inches high. It is marked with the impressed Marblehead ship mark and an incised H. (The Art Museum, Princeton University, Princeton, New Jersey)

Sometimes, the design was incised and at other times it was left flat.

The pottery offered a special new ware about 1912. This consisted of a tin enameled faience with a cream-colored background. The new ware evidently was not a success as it does not appear in any later records. Arthur Baggs mentions a body type he developed that looked like porcelain although fired at a low heat. He made bowls of this material, which was perforated and glazed like the rice pattern china of the Chinese.

The pottery made a variety of items, which included tiles, pitchers, lamps, jars, garden sculpture, ornaments, tableware, bookends, and candlesticks. Their vases remained relatively undecorated. Marblehead pottery is marked with the stylized picture of a ship flanked with the letters "M" and "P".

Hanna Tutt executed this Marblehead vase about 1908–1910. It is modeled and painted with decorations of conventionalized flowers of green, brown, black, and yellow matte glazes. It is 7 inches high, and marked with the Marblehead ship mark and an incised HT, and includes an original paper label, "Marblehead, A-5, Pottery." (Newark Museum, Newark, New Jersey)

Bibliography

Baggs, Arthur E., "The Story of a Potter," *The Handicrafter,* I & II (April 1929), 8–10.

Binns, Charles F., "Pottery in America," *The American Magazine of Art,* VII No. 4 (February 1916), 131.

Crowley, Lilian H., "It's Now the Potter's Turn," *International Studio,* 75 (September 1922), 539.

Hall, Herbert J., "Marblehead Pottery," *Keramic Studio,* 10 (June 1908), 30–31.

Little, Flora Townsend, "A Short Sketch of American Pottery," *Art & Archaeology,* 15 (May 1923), 219.

MacSwiggan, Amelia E., "The Marblehead Pottery," *Spinning Wheel* (March 1972).

Marblehead Historical Society, "Marblehead Pottery—An American Industrial Art of Distinction" (reprint from Marblehead Pottery Catalogue, 1919).

Marblehead Potteries, The, *Marblehead Pottery Supplementary Catalogue 1924,* Marblehead, Mass., 1924.

"Modern Majolica," *Handicraft,* 5 (June 1912), 42–43.

"Pottery at Marblehead, The, " *Arts and Decoration,* I (September 1911).

Rawson, Jonathan A., Jr., "Recent American Pottery," *House Beautiful,* 31 (April 1912), 148.

Russell, Elizabeth H., "The Pottery of Marblehead," *House Beautiful,* 59 (March 1926).

MASSIER   *(Massier pottery of France was part of the important influences of the French Art pottery movement on the American factories. It is included to clarify other references in the book.)*

Clément Massier was another French artist who influenced the American art pottery movement. In 1881, he built a factory down the coast from Cannes in Golfe-Juan, France. His pottery had an iridescent glaze which was inspired by Hispano-Moresque pots he had seen in Italy. One of his pupils was Jacques Sicard, who later worked at the Weller Factory in Ohio. The iridescent glaze and art nouveau designs of Sicard were learned from Massier.

Massier's art pottery was marked Clement Massier on the side of the piece, impressed Clément Massier, Golfe-Juan or M. C. M. G. J., Clément Massier died in 1917. See Haviland Pottery.

(Left) Underglaze slip decorations of butterflies and branches are on this 4-inch vase. The butterflies are black and white, the leaves green, the background tan on brown. There is gold decoration at the top. The vase is marked on the bottom "Clément Massier" in gold on the rim and "C. M." in black in the center. (Collection of Betty Grissom; *Spinning Wheel* photograph)   (Right) This Massier pottery vase is decorated with stylized flowers and foliage. It is colored deep amber to pale yellow. The 12-inch piece is signed C.M. (Collection of Betty Grissom)

(Left) Honeysuckles cover this bronze, green, and gold luster vase. It is signed on the bottom "Clément Massier" in gold and impressed "Clément Massier, Golfe-Juan" in a V shape. (Collection of Betty Grissom; *Spinning Wheel* photograph) (Right) Purple, pink, and green luster glaze on this vase has an allover design of circles. It is marked M.C.M. G. J. a.m. (Collection of Betty Grissom; *Spinning Wheel* photograph)

Bibliography

Grissom, Betty, "Clément Massier—Master Potter," *Spinning Wheel* (September 1971).

J. W. McCOY COMPANY

The J. W. McCoy Pottery was founded in 1899 by James McCoy in Roseville, Ohio. The firm made commercial wares and a line of art pottery that included such items as mugs, jardinieres, pedestals, and tankards. The factory was destroyed by fire in 1903, but was soon rebuilt, and in January of 1905, the firm was incorporated and had new working capital.

George S. Brush became manager of the firm in 1909 after the destruction of his own pottery that year. Brush had worked for the Owens Pottery from 1901 to 1905 but

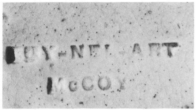

The impressed mark "Loy-Nel-Art" appears on the bottom of this large 10½-inch-diameter by 8½-inch-high jardiniere. The glaze is the typical dark brown with yellow pansies and green leaves. The interior is shaded brown to yellow. (Authors' collection)

left to organize the Brush Pottery Company in 1907 where he made stoneware and art pottery until the 1908 fire. In 1911, the McCoy pottery became the Brush-McCoy Pottery Company. However, there is confusion about this date. A Zanesville Chamber of Commerce booklet printed in 1918 says the firm started in 1913.

In 1912 Brush-McCoy bought the A. Radford Pottery of Clarksburg, West Virginia. Several of the lines made by Radford were continued and the firm also expanded to make pottery in the former J. B. Owens Pottery in Zanesville, Ohio. Several of the old Owens molds were kept and Brush-McCoy made these pieces too. The Zanesville pottery burned to the ground in 1918.

The pottery changed its name to the Brush Pottery Company in.1925 (not the same firm as a Brush Pottery that worked in Roseville from 1907 to 1912). George Brush died in 1934. The firm is still working in Roseville and makes florist pottery, cookie jars, and novelties.

Brush-McCoy Lines 1902–1930

Art Vellum: mottled ware, 1920.

Basket Weave: blue bird, 1912.

Bristol: white and blue kitchen ware.

Columbian: blue-banded yellow bowls, 1915–1918.

Corn: realistic corn design, later made by Shawnee Pottery, before 1912.

Dandy-line: standard yellow cooking ware, 1915–1918.

Egyptian: 1923.

Grecian: 1916.

Green Woodland: Higloss: 1923.

Jetwood: black tree designs on shaded background, 1923.

Jewel: high-gloss jewel design, matte body, 1923.

Loy-Nel-Art Line: designed by J. W. McCoy. Named for McCoy's sons, Lloyd, Nelson, and Arthur. Standard brown glaze similar to Weller Louwelsa or matte green, hand decorated with embossed and incised decoration, ca. 1906.

Lucila: toilet wares, white body, pink roses on ribbon bow design, 1916.

Marble Ware: before 1912.

Matte-green line: dull green glazed ware similar to Grueby glaze. Vases, jardinieres, dishes, umbrella stands, cuspidors, introduced in 1908.

Mount Pelee Ware: dull black lava-type pottery with

This 4½-inch vase is glazed dark brown with yellow flowers. It is marked Loy-Nel-Art McCoy. (Authors' collection)

some iridescence. It was inspired by the pottery found in some ancient ruins. First made in 1902, much destroyed in 1903 fire.

New Navarre: made from Owens molds for Henri Deux line, matte green and white, 1912.

Nuglaz: 1923.

Nurock: Similar to English Rockingham, 1915–1918, brown kitchen ware.

Old Egypt: Egyptian beetle decoration, 1915.

Old Ivory: before 1912.

Onyx: 1923, high glaze.

Radford's Radura: matte glazed, green, 1912.

Radford's Ruko: similar to jasper ware, 1912.

Radford's Thera: Matte glaze with slip decoration, 1912.

Radio Bug: ceramic bug with a crystal radio enclosed, 1927.

Roman: green or brown low-priced ware decorated with fluted effect and flower festoons, 1930.

Stonecraft: gray body, fluted sides, decorated top, 1920.

Sylvan: relief trees, similar to Weller Forest ware, 1915.

Venetian: no information available.

White Stone: cooking and toilet wares, 1915–1918.

Woodland: 1916.

Yellow Dandy: kitchen ware.

Zuniart: high-gloss Zuni Indian type decoration, 1923.

See also Nelson McCoy Pottery.

Bibliography

Coates, Pamela, *The Real McCoy,* Cherry Hill, N.J.: Reynolds Publishers, 1971.

Evans, Paul, "The Confusing McCoy Potteries," *Spinning Wheel* XXIX (January, February 1973) 8–9.

Lynn, Evelyn, "What About McCoy?" *The Antique Trader* (January 23, 1973) 50–51.

Nilson, Marianne, "The Nelson McCoy Sanitary Stoneware Company," *Joel Sater's Antiques News* (February 11, 1972).

Schneider, Norris F., "Brush Pottery," *Zanesville Times Recorder* (September 9, 1962, September 16, 1962).

Zanesville Chamber of Commerce, Pamphlet, 1918.

Mark used from 1934 to late 1930s. In the early 1940s the initials USA or Made in USA were added to this mark.

The impressed mark used during the early 1940s. The same mark, embossed, was used from the 1940s to the 1960s.

Impressed mark used during the 1940s.

(Right) Mark used from the late 1940s to 1966. (Far right) Current mark since Nelson McCoy Pottery became affiliated with D.T. Chase Enterprises.

NELSON McCOY POTTERY

James McCoy of the J. W. McCoy Pottery backed his son Nelson in a pottery in Roseville, Ohio, in 1910, founding the Nelson McCoy Sanitary and Stoneware Company. At first the firm made stoneware kitchen utensils, but by 1926 they began making artware. The name was changed to the Nelson McCoy Pottery in 1933. In 1945, the company founder, Nelson McCoy, died and his nephew Nelson McCoy Melich became president. Melich had been working for the company since 1924. He died in 1954 and the new president was Nelson McCoy, Jr. He is also the president of the Mount Clemens Pottery of Mount Clemens, Michigan, which purchased the firm in 1966. The Roseville plant, which is still working, in 1972 became the Nelson McCoy Division of D. T. Chase Enterprises of Hartford, Connecticut. *For bibliography, see J. W. McCoy Company.*

MERRIMAC POTTERY

In 1897 the Merrimac Ceramic Company was founded in Newburyport, Mass., where they made inexpensive drain pipes, florists' containers, and enameled tiles. The firm was reorganized in 1902 as the Merrimac Pottery Company and after this date made some art pottery that is of interest to collectors.

T. S. Nickerson was the founder of the firm. He had studied in England with William Crookes. He later worked alone in Massachusetts developing the glazes that characterize the best of the Merrimac work. At first the firm made small vases and ornamental pieces to be used in the home, but realizing the demand, Nickerson began to make quantities of decorative garden pottery.

Product

The art pottery vases for home use made by Merrimac Pottery were glazed in tones of green, violet, or dull grape

Pictures of Merrimac pottery from *The Craftsman*, a magazine published in 1903. (*Craftsman*, Vol. IV, 1903)

Paper label.

Impressed.

color, dull rose, brownish red, dull black, yellow, orange, and metallic glazes of blue or purple that slightly resembled polished iron. The colors were sometimes applied as a crackled glaze. The crackleware ranked as the best pieces made.

The garden pottery was made of white clay or a natural terra-cotta color. One of the most famous lines was their Etruscan pottery which was a reproduction of pieces found in the Boston Museum of Art. The vases copied were Arretine ware made by the Romans. It was of terra-cotta with decorations in low relief.

Marks

A paper label appeared on all pieces of Merrimac Ceramic Co. work made from September, 1900, to August, 1901. After that, an impressed mark of a sturgeon was used.

The name Merrimac, which is the Indian word for sturgeon, derives from the river that flows through Newburyport.

Bibliography

Barber, Edwin, *Marks of American Potters*, Philadelphia: Patterson and White, 1904.

Bowdoin, W. G., "Some American Pottery Forms," *The Art Interchange* (April, 1903), 87.

Lunt, Miss Wilhelmina V., Curator, Historical Society of Old Newbury, Newburyport, Mass. (correspondence with authors, May, 1972).

"Merrimac Pottery," *Keramic Studio* (6), (April, 1905).

Sargent, Irene, "Some Potters and Their Products," *Craftsman* (V. IV), (1903), pp. 248–56.

MORAVIAN POTTERY AND TILE

Impressed.

MORAVIAN

Stamped in the clay.

The family of Henry Chapman Mercer arrived in Bucks County, Pennsylvania, in 1684. Henry was born in Doylestown in 1856. His family had wealth and position; they were members of Congress, judges, and businessmen. Henry was sent to a local boys' boarding school, then to Mohegan Lake School near Peekskill, New York. He went to Harvard University and was graduated in 1879. Although he started at the University of Pennsylvania Law School, he soon left. In spite of this, he was able to practice law for several years. In the 1880s, Henry Mercer

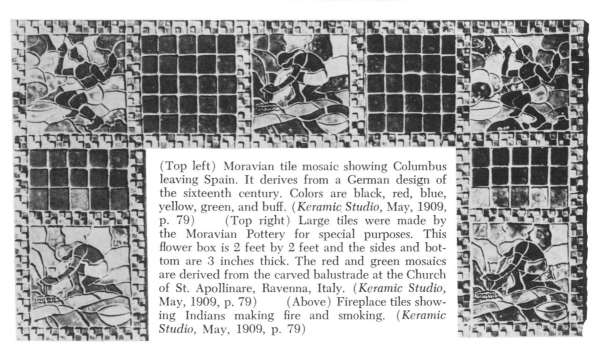

(Top left) Moravian tile mosaic showing Columbus leaving Spain. It derives from a German design of the sixteenth century. Colors are black, red, blue, yellow, green, and buff. (*Keramic Studio*, May, 1909, p. 79) (Top right) Large tiles were made by the Moravian Pottery for special purposes. This flower box is 2 feet by 2 feet and the sides and bottom are 3 inches thick. The red and green mosaics are derived from the carved balustrade at the Church of St. Apollinare, Ravenna, Italy. (*Keramic Studio*, May, 1909, p. 79) (Above) Fireplace tiles showing Indians making fire and smoking. (*Keramic Studio*, May, 1909, p. 79)

became interested in antiquities and he helped found the Bucks County Historical Society. He published a book in 1885 about the Lenape Stone. For the next ten years, he worked in the fields of archaeology and anthropology and he became Curator of American and Prehistoric Archaeology at the Museum of the University of Pennsylvania. In 1893, he was the Associate Editor of the *American Naturalist* and a member of the United States Archaeological Commission for the Columbian Exposition. Money was given to him for an expedition to the Yucatan in 1895 and,

(Top left) This Moravian mural panel was made about 1922. (*International Studio*, March, 1922, p. 77)   (Top right) Moravian perforated tile mosaic, 2 feet by 2½ feet. The design is copied from the Balcony of Desdemona in Venice. Colors are black, buff, red, and green. (*Keramic Studio*, May, 1909, p. 79)   (Above) This "Bible Fireplace" was featured in an article about tiles in *International Studio* in 1922. (*International Studio*, March, 1922, p. 74)

although he worked for several months, he could find no evidence of prehistoric man. In 1897, he began to write about Colonial America and published an article about tools.

That same year he started experimenting with the manufacture of tiles in Doylestown, another of his many interests during a lifetime of varied activity. Anyone who has visited the famous Mercer Museum in Doylestown can appreciate the unusual scope of this famous collector.

Tools were a hobby of Mercer and he bought quantities of all types with the hope of comparing American tools with those made in other countries. While searching for the tools, he visited many factories, including many pottery companies. He studied the potters' tools, and during the process became interested in the manufacture of pottery. There was no one to tell him about the difficulties in manufacturing pottery or of the problems in building a working kiln. Henry Mercer experimented and tried several potters and potteries before he decided to go to Germany where he could learn the proper way to make pottery from the experts.

A kiln was built soon after he returned home and Mercer made a few goblets, pots, and many tiles. He realized that tiles were the items that would sell. He called his pottery the Moravian Pottery and Tile Works because the earliest tiles were Moravian inspired. Tiles were made for floor pavements (like those at the Capitol building at Harrisburg, Pennsylvania), fireplaces, walls, and ceilings, and the firm also made large decorative tile panels.

He built a huge concrete "castle" which was completed in 1910, when the Moravian Pottery and Tile Works burned down. Then he began work on a new fireproof building for his pottery. The concrete building was finished in 1912. It incorporated tile decorations and included a high, vaulted ceiling that some contemporary architects said would collapse. He built a third as a museum in 1916. Mercer's strange concrete buildings still stand, as museums, and include his tool collection. The buildings continue to prove to the public the advanced architectural construction of Mercer's design.

The Moravian Pottery and Tile Works was a small plant with about sixteen artists and workmen. When Mercer

A Moravian Pottery tile in green, brown, red, yellow, and black, 15 by 22 inches. This is the same design of Adam and Eve as in the upper right-hand corner of the "Bible Fireplace." The tiles were assembled into sets to tell a story, with the selection the decision of the buyer. (The Smithsonian Institution)

(Top) About 1910, the Moravian Pottery and Tile Works made this tile called "Dragon Pattern." It is glazed blue and yellow tan, 3³⁄₁₆ inches high by 3½ inches wide. (Newark Museum, Newark, New Jersey)   (Bottom) A relief pattern of a lion in blue green, tan, and buff glazes decorates this tile called "Etin," c. 1910. It is 5⁵⁄₁₆ inches .square. (Newark Museum, Newark, New Jersey)

died in 1930, he willed the company to Frank King Swain. Swain died in 1954 and his nephew Frank H. Swain became manager. Swain sold the pottery in 1956 to Raymond F. Buck who made ordinary tiles. The county bought it in 1968 and there is now an attempt to return the production to its earlier quality.

Product

The first wares made at the Moravian Pottery and Tile Works came from the common red clay that was found nearby. This clay was too soft and was unsuited for pots, but it was very satisfactory for tiles. The tiles were covered with a heavy glaze. Other tiles were made from white clay from New Jersey. The white clay tiles were usually colored blue or green. The red tile was glazed with other colors. The body color sometimes showed through the glaze and changed the apparent shade so Mercer tried to use a body color that would not interfere with the glaze color.

The designs for the tiles were created by Mercer. His first designs were inspired by the Moravian stove plates that he had collected from the Pennsylvania region. Later, he made medieval, Indian, and other tile designs, such as of flora and fauna. Inspiration came from English floor tiles and German and Spanish tile designs of the earlier centuries, as well as from tapestries and archaeological fields.

The tiles were made by new methods. The colored clay was cut into small units, making designs in silhouette. The designs were often set in concrete. The overall effect was that of a mosaic decoration, but the pieces were large slabs, not the tiny mosaic pieces of early days. Some of the tiles were glazed and some were made from colored clay without glaze. Consequently, some tiles had a shiny finish, while others had a matte appearance. Some floor tiles were half glazed, the raised unglazed portion protecting the glazed surface from wear. Mercer used all techniques, including smear glaze, modeling, sgraffito, and slip-decoration. No attempt was made at uniformity or realism. Colors were placed arbitrarily, sometimes resulting in an orange sky or a yellow tree. The pieces of tile were often not square but cut to the shape of the figure in the design. Square tiles were dried on racks or metal trays and were often irregular in shape. The installation of the tiles required wide joints and many critics objected to this look.

Plain tiles in geometric shapes glazed brown, black,

An armored knight on a charging horse is the relief pattern on this Moravian Pottery tile. It is glazed with glossy ocher and blue. The tile is 4½₁₆ inches high by 7⅝₁₆ inches wide. The pattern, made about 1910, was called "Knight of Margam." (Newark Museum, Newark, New Jersey)

green, blue, buff, or red were also available. And special designs featuring the customer's business or family were made. The tiles usually included the company mark or the word "Moravian" stamped into the clay. The Moravian Pottery and Tile Works also made a few other wares such as inkwells, cups, penholders, sconces, vases, and bowls.

Bibliography

Barnes, Benjamin H., "The Moravian Pottery Memories of Forty-Six Years," Doylestown, Pennsylvania: The Bucks County Historical Society, 1970.

Blasberg, Robert W., "Moravian Tiles Fairy Tales in Colored Clay," *Spinning Wheel* (June, 1971) 16.

The Bucks County Historical Society. "The Mercer Mile," Doylestown, Pennsylvania: The Bucks County Historical Society, 1972.

Crowley, Lilian H., "It's Now the Potter's Turn," *International Studio* (75), (September, 1922) 539.

Fox, Claire Gilbride, "Henry Chapman Mercer: Tilemaker, Collector, and Builder Extraordinary," *Antiques* (October, 1973) 678.

Ruge, Clara, "American Ceramics—A Brief Review of Progress," *International Studio* (V. 28) (March, 1906), 21–28.

Tachau, Hanna, "America Re-Discovers Tiles," *International Studio* (March, 1922) 74. (V. 75).

MATT MORGAN POTTERY

Matt Morgan opened an art pottery company in Cincinnati, Ohio, in 1883 (other information makes this date

Dark blue glaze and gold overglaze cover this Matt Morgan vase. It is 4⅜ inches high, 2⅝ inches wide. The vase is one of a pair, each marked with the Matt Morgan impressed mark, and the numbers 323. One of the pair has a paper label for the factory. (Authors' collection)

appear too late but it is the date given in *Pottery and Porcelain in the United States* by Edwin Barber, 1903 revision). Morgan was an English artist who had arrived in the United States only a few years earlier. He met and became friendly with George Ligowsky, who was the inventor of the clay pigeon. How or why the two decided to open a pottery is still unknown, but the artist and the maker of sportsman's targets joined forces. Ligowsky made the clay and Morgan decorated the pieces to resemble Moorish wares. Their pieces were covered with incised designs, and colors were applied to the raised portions. Shiny and matte glaze finishes were used.

Several fine decorators worked for the firm and they put their initials on the bottom of the pieces they made. Herman C. Mueller (See Mueller Tile Co.) and Matt Morgan were the principal designers and decorators. Matthew Andrew Daly worked for the firm but he soon left to join the Rookwood Pottery. N. J. Hirschfield, another decorator, left the Matt Morgan Pottery at the same time to go to the Rookwood Pottery. Daly left Rookwood in 1903 and became the head of the art department at the U.S. Playing Card Co., holding that job until 1931. He died in 1937.

Matt Morgan Pottery lasted in business for only a year; it closed because of money problems. The firm used several impressed marks.

Bibliography

Barber, Edwin A., *The Pottery and Porcelain of the United States*, New York: G. P. Putnam's Sons, 1893 (3d and rev. ed. 1909).

Initials of the decorators were scratched in the clay. For example, N.J.H. were the initials of Mr. N. J. Hirschfeld.

(Top) Mark for the vase shown here. (Bottom) The paper label used by Matt Morgan.

Impressed.

Impressed.

———, *Marks of American Potters,* Philadelphia: Patterson and White, 1904.

Peck, Herbert, *The Book of Rookwood Pottery,* New York: Crown Publishers, Inc., 1968.

MOSAIC TILE COMPANY

The Mosaic Tile Company of Zanesville, Ohio, was started by Karl Langenbeck and Herman Mueller in 1894. The two men had been working for the American Encaustic Tile Company, Langenbeck as a chemist and Mueller as a modeler, but they wanted a larger share of the profits. A group of investors joined them in forming the Mosaic Tile Company, and a building and kiln were built and a staff was hired.

The firm grew and they added buildings. At first, only floor tiles from local buff clay was made. The firm used a new method of manufacture that employed perforated patterns to apply clay. This made production less expensive. Soon other types of tiles were added, including "Florentine mosaic, a dull finish floor tile inlaid with colored clays under pressure." The floor tiling was popular with the building trades and the firm opened an office in New York City in 1901. Langenbeck and Mueller left the firm by 1903.

William M. Shinnick who worked at the plant continued to become more active in the management until he became general manager in 1907. He was interested in new methods and new products but it was not until 1918 that faience tiles were made for walls in a variety of pastel colors. Other plain and ornamental vitreous and semivitreous tiles were produced including ceramic mosaic, art mosaic, white wall tiles, and fireplace tiles. The firm continued to grow and prosper, and by 1918 they had branch offices in New York, San Francisco, Boston, Baltimore, and Philadelphia. About 1920, Harry Rhead of the Roseville Pottery Company was hired to supervise the manufacture of the faience tiles. He left in 1923 to found the Standard Tile Company of South Zanesville, Ohio.

The Mosaic Tile Company continued to grow and many important structures featured their tiles: The hotels Stevens, Drake, Morrison, and Sherman in Chicago; Roosevelt Mansion in Hyde Park, New York; the Will Rogers Memorial at Fort Worth, Texas; and the New York subways, among others.

The depression slowed the construction business so the

Lincoln's profile appears in raised white clay on a blue background on a tile that has six edges, each 1¾ inches long. The reverse of the tile has the Mosaic Tile mark. (Authors' collection)

General Pershing is pictured on this blue and white oval tile, 5 by 3½ inches. Note the reverse of this tile. (Authors' collection)

firm began to make hot plates, badges, boxes, bookends, souvenirs, and wall panels. In 1959, the firm stopped making faience tile, and in 1967 the Mosaic Tile Company closed.

Artists

Ruth Axline (also worked at Weller), Harry Ayres, Ira Chandler, Sydney Cope, from England, 1929–1934 (Nelson McCoy Pottery 1934–1961), David Fink, George D. Ford, Kenneth Gale (?), Kenneth Garrison, Roy Greene, Robert Hartshorne (also worked at AET Co.), Cecil Jones, Karl Langenbeck, chemist (see American Encaustic), Horace M. Langley, Charles Lenhart, Herman Mueller, modeler (see American Encaustic), Gordon Mull (also worked at Weller), Alfred Nicklin (also worked at AET), Harry M. Northrup (see American Encaustic), Peter Patterson, Charles Penson, Harry Rhead, Supervisor (see Roseville), James Riley, David Schaum, William Shinnick, General Manager, Byron Shrider, Mary Vore, Bernard West.

Special Tiles

Aesop Fable Tiles; Simon Bolivar, 3¼-inch hexagonal, blue basalt with white bust; Abraham Lincoln, 3¼-inch hexagonal, blue basalt with white bust; Charles M. Lindbergh, rectangular, printed picture; General Douglas MacArthur, printed tile, 4-inch, brown; William McKinley, 3¼-inch hexagonal, blue basalt with white bust; General Pershing, 3¼ x 5 inch oval, blue basalt with white bust; Pilgrim, 3¼-inch hexagonal, blue basalt with white bust; Franklin D. Roosevelt, plaque, 12 inches, brown; William Shinnick, round printed tile; Woodrow Wilson, 3¼-inch hexagonal, blue basalt with white bust; Zanesville Sesquicentennial, 1947.

Bibliography

Bernard, Julian, *Victorian Ceramic Tiles,* Greenwich, Conn.: New York Graphic Society Ltd., 1972.

Dawson, B. A., "Zanesville Is a Tile Town: Mosaic Tile Co. Is Large Industry," *The Zanesville (O.) News* (November 5, 1939) 9.

Mosaic Tile Company Catalogue (1959).

Newark Museum Association, "New Jersey Clay Products," date unknown.

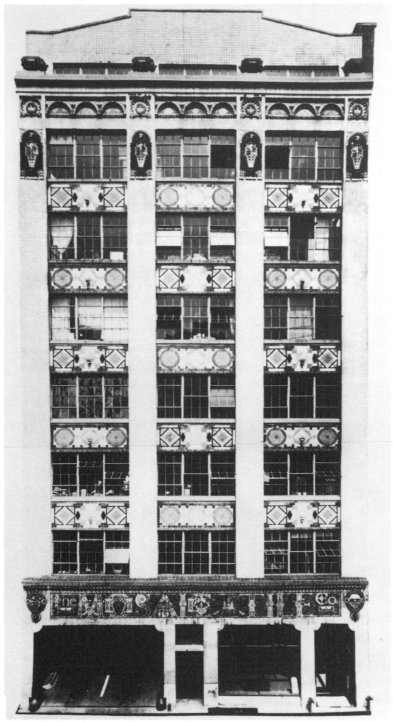

The Mosaic Tile Company building at 445 West 41st Street, New York, New York. It was built in 1928 and torn down in 1954. (Ohio Historical Society Library)

Ohio Historical Society Library, *The Mosaic Tile Company Historical File* (August, 1967).

Purviance, Louise, and Schneider, Evan and Norris F., *Zanesville Art Pottery in Color,* Des Moines, Iowa: Wallace-Homestead Press.

Savino, Guy, "Colorful Skyline Marker Falls in 3d Tube Clearing," *Newark* (N.J.) *News* (April 27, 1954).

Mosaic Tile Company

This beige, brown, black, and green tile was made by the Mosaic Tile Company about 1905–1915. It was both matte and semimatte glazed. The 5-inch-square tile has a molded design of an elephant standing on a ball with the company monogram. (Collection of Carol Ferranti Antiques; photo The Art Museum, Princeton University, Princeton, New Jersey)

These three racks contain sample border tiles made by the Mosaic Tile Company about 1920. The racks are 17½ inches by 6 inches. The tiles are removable. (Authors' collection)

Schneider, Norris F., "Mosaic, Largest U.S. Tile Plant," *Zanesville Times Signal* (September 10, 1944).

_____, "Mueller Co-Founder of Mosaic Tile Company," *Zanesville Times Recorder* (March 7, 1971).

_____, "Veteran Mosaic Tile Employee Compiles Outstanding Display," *Zanesville Times Recorder* (October 30, 1960).

_____, "Souvenir Tile," *Zanesville Times Recorder* (October 30, 1966).

Wires, E. Stanley, "Aesop Great Fables, How Tiles Have Interpreted," *Antiques Journal* (May, 1970), 10.

Zanesville Chamber of Commerce Booklet (1918).

The Zanesville Signal, "Zanesville History Recorded in Tile," Zanesville, Ohio, March 19, 1940.

MUELLER MOSAIC TILE COMPANY

The Mueller Mosaic Tile Company of Trenton, New Jersey, was organized by Herman Mueller in 1909. The firm made mosaic tiles for bathrooms, swimming pools, mantles, walls, and floors, as well as art faience panels and decorative signs. The firm closed in 1938 and Mr. Mueller died in 1941. See Mosaic Tile Company.

Mueller mark.

This gaping turtle is really a fountain spout tile. It was made by the Mueller Mosaic Tile Company of Trenton, New Jersey, about 1910. It is glazed brownish green, and measures 6 by 6 by 3½ inches. (The Smithsonian Institution)

EXTERIOR DOOR FRAME IN POLYCHROME FAIENCE.

POLYCHROME FAIENCE EMBLEM.

9

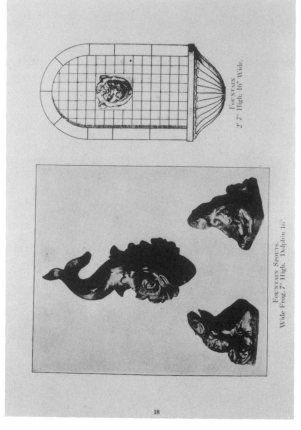

FOUNTAIN 2'7" High, 16" Wide.

FOUNTAIN SPOUTS.
Wide Frog, 7" High. Dolphin 10".

18

Pages from a Mueller catalogue, date unknown. (Courtesy the New
Jersey State Museum)

BULKHEAD, JEWELERY STORE.

POLYCHROME SHIELDS FOR EXTERIOR DECORATION.
Top Row: Designs 900, 901, 902, 903.
Bottom Row: Designs 904, 905, 906, 907.
Size 12"x9".

35

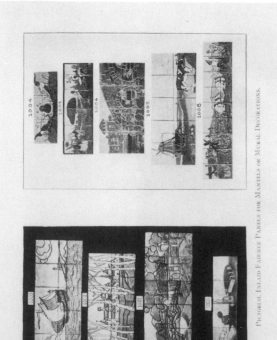

PICTORIAL INLAID FAIENCE PANELS FOR MANTELS OR MURAL DECORATIONS.

43

Bibliography

"Adding Color to Our Architecture," *Trenton* (March, 1926), 1–3.

Clark, Robert Judson, *The Arts and Crafts Movement in America 1876–1916*, Princeton, N.J.: Princeton University Press, 1972, p. 157.

"Mueller Tile," Mueller Mosaic Company, Manufacturers, Trenton, New Jersey.

MUNCIE POTTERY

The Muncie Pottery was founded by Charles Benham in Muncie, Indiana, in 1922 to produce a standard line of pottery for florists and department stores. The 1926 catalogue of the firm lists it as The Muncie Clay Products Company. The vases they produced were made with a variety of glazes in shiny and matte finishes. The name Muncie was incised on the bottom of each piece. Sometimes the letter A was used. Like many others, Muncie was a victim of the depression and it closed in 1939. The building and most of the records were destroyed by fire in 1951.

MUNCIE

The incised Muncie mark.

Bibliography

Benham, Mrs. Charles G., Muncie, Indiana (correspondence with authors, November, 1972).

Henzke, Lucile. "Muncie Pottery," *Pottery Collectors' Newsletter* (II, 4), (February, 1973), pp. 53–54.

Muncie Clay Products Company, *Artistic Pottery*, Muncie, Indiana: Muncie Clay Products Company, 1926.

NEWCOMB POTTERY

New Orleans was a center of culture and industry when Ellsworth Woodward arrived there in 1885 from Massachusetts. Woodward, who believed in vocational education for women, felt that with training, some young ladies would continue working as a career. Others of course, would marry, but because of their training, they would appreciate the fine arts and help create a market for many of the items made at arts and crafts schools.

The first school organized by Woodward had classes in brasswork, stenciling, woodcarving, and clay modeling. The thirty students who joined the clay modeling group

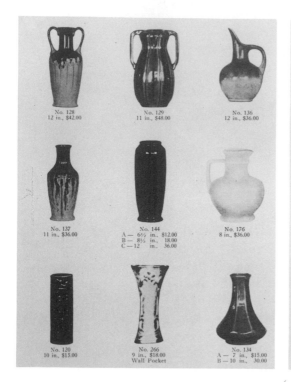

Four pages from the catalogue, *Artistic Pottery*, 1926, Muncie Clay Products Company, Muncie, Indiana.

Newcomb Artists:

To date pieces of Newcomb Pottery, it helps to know not only the dating systems but also the dates that some of the artists worked. The following is an alphabetical list of artists and potters who worked at the Newcomb Pottery (the listing is incomplete as no record of the artist was kept). The date given in parenthesis is the year the person is known to have been at the pottery or the date of an article which mentioned his or her name. When known, the mark is given next to the artist's name.

Esther Augustin (Godat). c. 1920.

Aurelia Arbo.

Vincent Axford. 1920–1926. Ceramic engineer.

Mrs. Avery

Henrietta Bailey. 1902–1903, (1905)–1915. Listed in 1917 exhibit.

Mary F. Baker. (1904).

Gladys Bartlett. 1910–1911.

Eunice Lea Bate (Coleman). 1917.

Maria Benson. c. 1905.

Selina E. Bres. 1895–1897. Potter. See Selina E. B. Gregory.

Mary W. Butler. 1900–1901, (1904).

Corinne Chalaron (Cotinae M. Chalmron?). 1928.

Frances H. Cocke. (1904)

Paul Cox. (1910–1918). Director.

Marie Delavigne. Listed in 1917 exhibit for embroidery.

Olive W. Dodd. (1904).

May Dunn. 1909–1910.

Esther Huyer Elliott. (1904). Before 1899.

Bessie A. Ficklen. (1904).

Gabry. (1895). Potter.

Jane Gibbs. 1905.

Esther Augustin Godat. c. 1920.

Juanita Gonzalez. Teacher.

Angela Gregory. Teacher.

Selina E. Bres Gregory. (1904)

Cecile Heller.

Sarah Henderson. (1904).

Hoerner. See Julia Michel.

Sally Holt. Before 1899.

Emily Huger. (1904).

Jonathan Hunt. 1928–1940. Potter.

Sadie Irvine. (1903–1906) student; 1906–1952 decorator and teacher. Listed in 1915 exhibit.

Frances Jones. (1904).

Hattie C. Joor. (1904).

Harriet Joor. Harriet and Hattie may be same person.

Irene Keep. (1904).

Roberta B. Kennon. 1897–1898.

Katherine Kopman. 1894–1895, (1904).

Maria Le Banc. May be Maria Hoe Le Blanc.

Maria Hoa (Hoe?) Le Blanc. 1897–1898, (1904–1905). Misspelled in 1904 list.

Jeanette Le Buef. 1940.

Leonard.

Sarah B. Levy. 1898–1899.

Francis E. Lines. (1904).

Cynthia Littlejohn. 1905–1906. Listed in 1917 exhibit.

Roberta Lonegon.

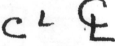

Ada Lonnegan. About 1900–1905.

Corinne Luria.

Alma Bourke Mason. Listed in 1917 exhibit.

Joseph Meyer. 1896–1931. Potter.

Julia Michel (Hoerner). 1916.

Mr. Miller. Potter after 1920.

Robert Miller. Potter before 1900.

C. Sliger Millspaugh.

Hilda Modinger. 1917–1918. Potter, decorator.

May Morel. c. 1910–1917.

Leona Nicholson (Mrs. Bentley Nicholson). 1900–1901 (1904–1905). Misspelled in 1904 listing.

George Ohr. Potter before 1900.

Charlotte Payne. 1900–1910.

Beverly Randolph. (1904).

Mary W. Richardson. 1900–1901, (1904).

Martha (Maude?) Robinson. Before 1905.

Elizabeth G. Rogers. 1899–1900, (1904).

Mr. Rogers. Potter after 1920.

Amelie Roman. 1895–1896, (1904, 1905).

Desiree Roman. 1889–1890, (1904).

Medora Ross.

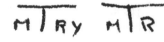

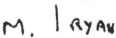

Mazie T. Ryan. 1898–1899, (1904)–1905.

Raymond A. Scudder. (1904).

Sewells. 1900–1910.

Mary Sheerer. 1898–1931. Teacher.

Efie Shepard.

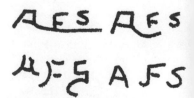

Anna Frances Simpson. 1910–1931.

Carrie Sliger. 1894–1895.

Gertrude R. Smith (1904). Listed in 1917 exhibit for embroidery.

Kenneth Smith. Manager about 1945; ceramic engineer, professor of ceramics, potter.

Mary S. Smith. Listed in 1917 exhibit for embroidery.

Mary Sommy.

M. W. Summey. Same as Mary Sommy?

Rosalie Urquhart. 1900–1901.

Mr. Walrath. Potter after 1920.

George Wasmith. Potter before 1896.

Sabina (Sabrina) E. Wells. (1905).

Hermione Weil.

Louise Wood. 1894–1895.

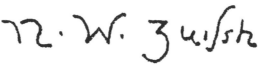

N. W. Zulish. c. 1905.

Additional marks, probably artists' but unidentified:

c. 1905

c. 1905

E HE

Before 1910

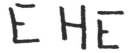

May be Esther Huyer Elliott

c. 1912

Unknown

RK

c. 1906. May be Roberta Kennon

c. 1905

Unknown

G N

Unknown

FQ

Unknown

E M

Unknown

S.E.W

c. 1905. May be Sabina Wells

:Newcomb College Factory mark.

GX33: Code number for glaze, size, inventory, etc.

JM: Joseph Meyer, potter's mark.

258: code number.

AFS: A.F. Simpson, artist's mark.

Rare factory marks:

Incised.

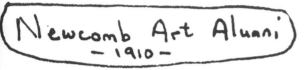

NEWCOMB COLLEGE

 Early mark.

Code marks:

$a1 - a2 - etc -$

Registration mark.

Q   Buff clay body before 1910.

W   White clay body before 1910.

R   Clay mixture.

U   Clay mixture.

soon formed the Ladies Decorative Art League (called the Art League for Women in some sources), meeting at 249 Baronne Street.

In 1886, with his brother William, he organized the New Orleans Art Pottery Company. The firm had one hundred subscribers at ten dollars per share of stock. The thirty young ladies from the league joined the firm and took shares in exchange for their labors. The pottery rented a building at 224 Baronne Street, built a kiln, outfitted the room with the thousand dollars that was subscribed, and hired two potters to produce the clay bodies the ladies decorated.

Joseph Fortune Meyer, the first of the potters, had extensive training before he came to work for the New Orleans Art Pottery Company. His father had been a potter and he and a partner had made and sold peasant types of pottery produced from local clays. They knew every process in making pottery: they located the clay, built the kilns, fired them with wood, made the glaze from private formulas, and then sold the pieces at the French Market.

Meyer came from his native France when his father moved to Biloxi, Mississippi, before the Civil War. The boy was nine when he made the three-month ocean trip. It left Joseph with a love of the sea and sailing, which influenced some of his later works. He had no formal

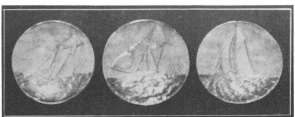

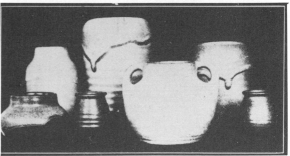

(Left, top and bottom) Vases and bowls made by the New Orleans Art Pottery Club. (*Ceramic Age*, April 1935)   (Below, top) Newcomb Pottery plaques made by Joseph Fortune Meyer about 1900. (*Ceramic Age*, April 1935) (Below, bottom) Vases and bowls in copper red glazes by Joseph Fortune Meyer, made before 1910. (*Ceramic Age*, April 1935)

education, but he read incessantly and is credited with almost total recall. As a youngster, he had no religious beliefs, but he married a Catholic. The marriage produced no children, but he and his wife raised a servant girl's child as their own. Joseph Meyer was a shrewd businessman and very careful about money. He was an active potter through much of the Newcomb period, dying in 1931.

The other potter hired by the New Orleans Art Pottery Company was George Ohr. He was an eccentric but gifted potter who remained only a short time and then founded his own pottery firm (Ohr Pottery).

The New Orleans Art Pottery Company, with the help of two potters and thirty young ladies, made jardinieres, lawn pots, and a few other items which were sold in Len-

(Top) Lamp pictured in *Craftsman Magazine*, October 1903, in an article about the Newcomb Pottery. (Bottom) Amelie Roman was the artist, Joseph Meyer the potter of this vase with painted abstract designs in green and blue. The 3⅜-inch vase has a glossy glaze. It was made about 1900–1910. The piece is marked with the impressed cipher N within a C, the conjoined cipher JM, the painted artist's cipher AR within a rectangle and the number 1 within a shield. (The Art Museum, Princeton University, Princeton, New Jersey)

nox, Boston, and Chicago. The firm was dissolved after five years because of money problems.

The records of the closing of the New Orleans Pottery Company and the start of the Newcomb College pottery classes are confused. The New Orleans Art Pottery Company is supposed to have closed in 1891, but the record also claims that William Woodward became a professor of art at Tulane University in 1890. He was on the faculty in 1883, and in charge of drawing and design at Tulane's School of Architecture and professor of painting in the Newcomb School of Art in 1890. His Brother Ellsworth supervised fine arts at Sophie Newcomb College from the beginning of that school, which is today part of Tulane. Perhaps the two men each held two jobs for a year or so. It has been verified that in 1895, the Woodward brothers, especially Ellsworth, convinced the college to start a pottery class and sell the product made by the students.

The board of trustees of Sophie Newcomb College agreed to the novel experiment of an art course in which the developed product could be sold. They approved funds and Ellsworth Woodward began the class in October of 1895. The money was used to furnish a room in an abandoned chemistry laboratory. Woodward installed a round kiln with four fireboxes, a kick wheel, drying shelves, tubs for clay, decorators' smocks, glaze pots, and a hand mill for grinding. Some of the saggers and perhaps other equipment came from earlier New Orleans potteries such as the Hernandez pottery and the Saloy porcelain factory.

Mary G. Sheerer, who had studied at the Cincinnati Art Academy and Art Students League, was hired to teach the classes in the decoration of pottery and its appreciation. Miss Sheerer had worked in Cincinnati and knew some of the decorators from the Rookwood factory. She favored the slip painted decoration, but when slip painting was found too difficult to control in the warm, drafty New Orleans building, she switched to biscuit painting. After 1900 the girls decorated by one of the approved methods after the slip and biscuit methods failed. It was a type of cut or carved design. Joseph Meyer was the potter who threw the shapes designed by Miss Sheerer.

In Miss Sheerer's accounts of the school, she mentioned that a potter from the Golfe-Juan Pottery at Cannes, France, was hired to make the forms on the wheel and to supervise the glazing and firing. Evidently this was M. Gabry, a Frenchman who had worked with the Hernandez porcelain factory in New Orleans. Unfortunately, Gabry committed suicide in December of 1895 and another potter, George Wasmith, was hired. He did not remain long because in 1896 Joseph Fortune Meyer, who had earlier worked for Woodward and the New Orleans Pottery Company, was hired. He remained at the school as chief potter until 1925, throwing almost every piece that was decorated at the factory. George Ohr, the eccentric potter, also worked at Newcomb for a short time, but he was fired because he was "not fit" to instruct young ladies. Robert Miller was another potter who worked there for a short time.

In 1910 a new technician, Paul E. Cox, was brought in to assure a more uniform product. He had been trained at Alfred University in New York State and in 1904 was the second graduate of the second college of ceramics in the United States. Cox was concerned with the technical problems of glaze, clay body, and the control of the product in a way his predecessors could not be. Early potters worked by trial and error and rarely had written records to guide them. Glaze and clay formulas were carefully guarded family secrets.

Cox improved the quality of the clay by adding feldspar and flint. He developed a raw lead glaze with a semimatte texture for underglaze. He found that three firings were needed to get the best effect from this new glaze. The first coat was dipped, with the next two sprayed. His blue and green matte glazes were so popular that the shiny glazes used earlier were rarely seen on pieces after 1910. During his years at the school, he built a modern kiln with enough mechanized production so that all of the decorators were able to make a better wage. Cox remained with the school until 1918.

In 1929, Kenneth E. Smith was the manager of the Newcomb Pottery and Professor Lota Lee Troy was in

This vase has glossy green and blue fleur-de-lis designs. It is 6⅞ inches high. The base is marked with NC, Q, JM, Lonnegan. It is the work of Ada Lonnegan about 1900. (Newcomb College, Tulane University, New Orleans, La.)

Three pictures of Newcomb pottery pictured in *Brush and Pencil*, 1900.

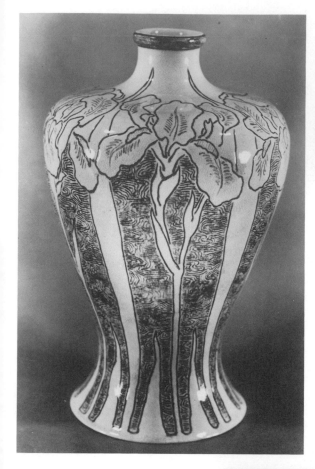

(Left) Mary Sheerer was the decorator of this vase made about 1898. It is decorated with incised and painted irises in blue and cream shades and glossy glaze. The 10¼-inch piece is marked Newcomb College. (Cincinnati Art Museum, Eden Park, Cincinnati, Ohio)   (Above) This 5½-inch glossy glazed vase was made by Marie Hoe Le Blanc. The trees and road are colored in blue and blue green tones. The vase is marked with the Newcomb NC cipher, JM (for Joseph Meyer, potter), MHL cipher, and Emhl cipher and the numbers 121x. (Newark Museum, Newark, New Jersey)

The crocus-decorated vase is glazed blue, green, and white. It is marked NC, BT 3 JM MRobinson. The 4½-inch-high vase was made about 1905. The blue gray mug has a semigloss glaze and carnation designs. It is marked with the Mazie T. Ryan mark. The mug was made about 1905. (Newcomb College, Tulane University, New Orleans, La.)

charge of all the activities at the Newcomb School of Art where the girls continued to decorate for the pottery. Under their direction, the pottery earned about twenty thousand dollars per year through the 1930s. In 1931, Ellsworth Woodward and Miss Sheerer returned to the pottery for a short time. Robin Feild and John Canady headed the art school after Miss Troy. In 1952 Sadie Irvine retired and Kathrine Choi became head of the pottery department. Pottery was made under her direction.

(Left) Blue and gray stylized blossoms decorate this vase of semi-matte glaze. It is 6⅞ inches high. The piece was made by Sadie Irvine about 1910. The vase is marked with the impressed cipher NC, the incised cipher SI, KS, UQ88, and an original paper label "Newcomb College Designs are not Duplicated, Subject_____, No. UQ88 Price $6.00, New Orleans." (Cincinnati Art Museum, Cincinnati, Ohio)   (Above) This three-handled mug was made about 1900–1910. It has a green and buff glossy glaze. The 6¼-inch mug is marked with the impressed cipher NC, the cipher JM, and the initials WL.

Wares

The long history of pottery made at Newcomb College shows the changes in each style with the change in potters or chief designers. It is possible to classify the pottery pieces in five main chronological divisions.

First Period (to 1899)

From the start of the factory until about 1910, the main influences on the design and quality of the work were those of Mary Sheerer and Joseph Meyer. The basic rules had been set by the Trustees of the University and the Sophie Newcomb Art Department. All the finished products had to be approved by Miss Sheerer to maintain quality. The designs used by the young ladies reflected the natural environment of the New Orleans area. Plants were popular as design motifs although the very early pieces sometimes had geometric patterns. Typical subjects were tall pines, palm trees, jasmine, wild rose, syringa, fleur-de-lis, orange, plum, magnolia, lotus leaves and flowers, water lily, moss-draped cypress, snowdrop, spider wart, iris, alisa, march maple, and the popular live oak and moon design. Floral designs were always kept simple. The whole plant was shown, not just a flower or a detail.

Newcomb Pottery mugs as shown in *Craftsman Magazine*, October 1903.

This lidded jar is 4¾ inches high. It is glazed green with a pinecone motif. The piece is marked with the NC mark, EHE, JM, Q, KK3. It may be the work of Esther Huger Elliott, and was made before 1910. (Newcomb College, Tulane University, New Orleans, La.)

The clay was taken from Bayou Tchulakabaufa in Mississippi and St. Tammany Parish (county), Louisiana. Both a white clay and a buff clay body were used before 1910. Miss Sheerer also mentions a red clay that was used for the undecorated terra-cotta pieces.

Every piece had to be original and never duplicated. It had to be marked with the initials of the college, the designer, and the potter. Each girl was given 50 percent of the sale price of her pieces. If a decorator showed promise, she was given two years of free study plus a free studio after graduation. Many of the decorators needed the money that they obtained through the sale of the pottery, which they continued to make after leaving school.

Color selection was the choice of the decorator, but the blue green tones seem to have become a Newcomb Pottery characteristic, and the girls preferred those shades.

The shapes of the pieces were determined by Miss Sheerer and later by Sadie Irvine. The ladies selected the pottery shapes from a book, the potter threw them on a wheel, and the clay vases were stored in a damp room until they were needed for decorating.

From about 1895 to 1900 the designs were slip painted on the bisque with a transparent glaze over the decorations. The designs were usually green, blue, or yellow with the cream color of the body showing. Some buff clay pieces were decorated with white slip.

Second Period (1900–1910)

Some early pieces were glazed with colors, the decoration the result of the accidental blendings in the kiln. The slip

painting proved unreliable, so during the second period
of the pottery, they used incised carving in the unfired
clay. The damp clay vase was smoothed and stored until
the young ladies scratched a design on the surface. The
scratches were then worked into deeper cuts. After the
incised decoration was finished, the piece was sponged to
remove any marks. The sponging also brought fine silica
to the surface of the clay and added to the misty effect
that is prized in this period of Newcomb pottery. The
piece was then colored with underglaze colors which

(Right) Mazie T. Ryan was the artist and Joseph Meyer the potter
for this Newcomb pottery vase in blue, green, yellow, and buff. It is
11¾ inches high, with a glossy glaze. The piece is marked with the
impressed cipher NC, the cipher MTR, the cipher JM, and the painted
numbers AT84. A paper label identifies the vase as "wild tomato."
(The Smithsonian Institution)

(Below left) This 9-inch jardiniere is decorated with blue and green
glossy glazed trees. It is marked with NC, the LN cipher for artist
Leona Nicholson, JM AY 29. It was made before 1906. The tall vase
is 12½ inches high. It has the syringa motif in blue gray glossy glaze.
The piece is marked with the Newcomb NC, the cipher for Maria Hoe
Le Blanc, CP72 JM. (Newcomb College, Tulane University, New
Orleans, La.)   (Below right) This inkstand is 3⅞ inches high. It
is glazed in blue, green, and brown glossy glaze. The piece is marked
with the NC mark, JM, IID Q I D1-81. It was made about 1905.
(Newcomb College, Tulane University, New Orleans, Louisiana.)

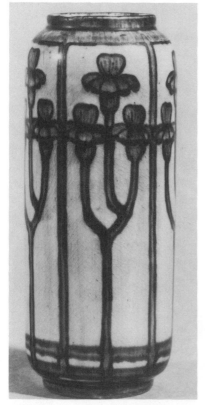

(Top left) Marie Hoe Le Blanc decorated this mug. Joseph Meyer was the potter. It was made with a landscape scene of trees and a road in blue and green glossy glaze. The 5½-inch-high mug was made about 1900–1910. It is marked with the impressed cipher NC, the cipher JM, the incised cipher MHL, and the painted cipher EM HL, and the numbers J21 X. (The Art Museum, Princeton University, Princeton, New Jersey) (Top right) Leona Nicholson made this vase for the Newcomb pottery about 1900–1910. It is decorated with designs of stylized flowers in blue, green, yellow, and white. The 5½-inch glossy glazed vase is marked with the impressed cipher NC, the cipher JM, LN, painted numbers BZ-72, and an original paper sticker "BZ-72 $3.50." (Newark Museum, Newark, New Jersey) (Left) Conventionalized flowers of blue and green glossy glaze decorated this 6½-inch Newcomb pottery vase. The artist is C. Payne, the potter, Joseph Meyer. The vase is marked with the impressed cipher NC, the cipher JM, the incised mark C. Payne and the painted cipher CP. (The Art Museum, Princeton University, Princeton, New Jersey)

were heavier in the deeper cuts. Black underglaze was occasionally used in the incised lines. The entire piece was then dipped into transparent glossy glaze. All these pieces have colored outsides and cream-color interiors.

Although the pottery was described as artistic and well made by many of the magazines of the day, at least one (*Scribner's*, March, 1903) seemed to disagree: "The characteristic look of the larger pieces is peculiar and not pleasing to all persons as the surface is streaked and spotted with pale gray in a way that suggests inadequate technical treatment, the patterns being very dark blue or in

(Left) The cup and saucer are decorated with blue gray rice designs in glossy glaze. They were made by Maria Bensen about 1905. The plate, with blue glaze and white flowers, was made by Ada Lonnegan about 1905. (Newcomb College, Tulane University, New Orleans, Louisiana) (Bottom left) The black incised carving of the stylized treelike motif is characteristic of the best of the 1900–1910 vases made at the Newcomb Pottery. (Newcomb College, Tulane University, New Orleans, Louisiana) (Bottom right) Green and blue glossy glazed water lilies decorate this 9¼-inch-high vase. It is marked with a Newcomb Pottery paper label, the impressed cipher NC, ZZ71, the artist's name, N. W. Zulish. (Newcomb College, Tulane University, New Orleans, Louisiana)

(Top) A blue and white vase decorated with irises is 5 inches high and has a glossy glaze and the marks NC, ground out, JM B QocG, A191. (Newcomb College, Tulane University, New Orleans, Louisiana)   (Bottom)   Newcomb pottery vase from *Craftsman Magazine*, October 1903.

the light gray relieved on the dark blue, the darker color itself being applied in the same streaky way."

Most of the wares from the second period had the characteristic blue green color with incised decoration, often emphasized with black.

Third Period

A new design technique, used from 1910 to about 1930, was developed under the guidance of Paul Cox. The low molded relief designs were made in the pottery while it was damp and a matte glaze intended to resemble Rookwood was added. The color was applied underglaze on the bisque ware and dipped in a semitransparent matte glaze so the finished glaze had underglaze decoration, and a soft misty effect remained. The inside was glazed without color.

Fourth and Fifth Periods (1930–1945)

Design elements and glaze techniques overlapped from period to period because making pottery was an ongoing business. When a particularly popular design was developed, it remained in the line for a while. The favorite Newcomb pottery design (1920–1930) was probably the pale blue and green tree dripping with Spanish moss reflected in the moonlight. The motif supposedly was first used by Sadie Irvine in one of the early periods, and the design remained popular.

The Newcomb Pottery made many types of vases, mugs, and other salable items, such as tea sets, candlesticks, and lamps. The leaded glass, bead, and metal shades were also made at the art school. See the Bibliography for a very comprehensive paper by Paul Cox on the technical aspects of making glaze, firing, etc.

Marks (See page 114)

The rules of Newcomb Pottery required that every piece be marked. This practice was continued at least through the 1920 period. The artist's initials, potter's initials, "NC" for the pottery, code numbers for the type of clay body and glaze formula number, and the inventory number were incised by hand in the bottom of each piece. The cut-in lines were sometimes filled with color to make them more legible.

Before 1910, the clay bodies were marked "Q" for buff clay and "W" for white clay body. A scratch through the pottery mark means the piece is a second. If the mark is obliterated, it means the piece is unendorsed by the pottery. The pottery symbol, an "N" within a "C," was used on almost all pieces. A few pieces are known by the incised words "NEWCOMB COLLEGE." Some pieces were also marked with a paper label that said: "Newcomb Pottery, New Orleans, Designs are not duplicated." The price was also on the paper label. A few unmarked pieces are known. If the glossy glaze popular before 1910 was used, the entire piece was glazed over the marks. The matte finished pieces made after 1910 had impressed marks made by dies, and were left unglazed.

Newcomb Pottery was considered an artistic success in its day. Proof of this is the numerous awards that were given to the pottery at exhibitions and fairs: 1900, Paris; 1901, Buffalo Pan American Exposition; 1902, Charleston West Indian Exposition; 1904, St. Louis Fair; 1905, Portland, Oregon, Lewis and Clark Centennial Exposition; 1907, Jamestown Tercentenary Exposition; 1913, Knoxville, Tennessee; 1915, San Francisco, California, Pan Pacific Centennial Exposition.

Bibliography

Baker, Mary F., "The Newcomb Art School and Its Achievements," *The Sketch Book* (V. 4), (June, 1905), 264.

Barber, Edwin, *Marks of American Potters*, Philadelphia: Patterson and White, 1904, pp. 156–157.

———, *The Pottery and Porcelain of the United States*, New York: G. P. Putnam's Sons, 1909, pp. 499–502;

Benjamin, Marcus, "American Art Pottery—Part III," *Glass and Pottery World* (April, 1907), 35.

Binns, Charles F., "Pottery in America," *The American Magazine of Art* (V. 7, No. 4), (February, 1916), 131.

Blasberg, Robert W., "Newcomb Pottery," *Antiques* (V. XCIV, No. 1), (July, 1968), pp. 73–77.

———, "The Sadie Irvine Letters: a Further Note on the Production of Newcomb Pottery," *Antiques* (August, 1971), 250–251.

Bowdoin, W. G., "Some American Pottery Forms," *The Art Interchange* (April, 1903), 87.

Bulletin of the Department of Commerce and Labor, "American Art Pottery," *American Pottery Gazette* (V. V, No. VI), (August 10, 1907).

Joseph Fortune Meyer at the potter's wheel. (*Ceramic Age*, April 1935)

This Newcomb bowl is of light blue matte glaze with a band of raised lilies of the valley. It is 6 inches in diameter, 4½ inches high. The vase is marked with the impressed cipher NC, the artist cipher AFS, and C M, 288. (Authors' collection)

Blue matte glaze and a green trickle glaze cover this thrown and turned Newcomb vase, 7⅜ inches high. It was glazed and fired by Paul Cox. The piece was purchased by the Smithsonian Institution in 1916. (The Smithsonian Institution)

Capers, Roberta M., *Two Decades of Newcomb Pottery*, New Orleans: Art Department, Newcomb College, Tulane University, 1963.

Clark, Robert Judson, *The Arts and Crafts Movement in America 1876–1916*, Princeton, N.J.: Princeton University Press, 1972.

Collier, Alberta, "She Unveiled Vistas for Others," *Dixie* (March 14, 1971), 8–10.

———, "Newcomb, The Pottery That Brought Fame to a College," *Dixie* (August 6, 1972).

Cox, Paul E., "Potteries of the Gulf Coast," *Ceramic Age* (V. 25, No. 4) (date unknown).

———, "Technical Practice at the Newcomb Pottery," *Journal of the American Ceramic Society* (V. I, No. 7), (July, 1918).

———, Baton Rouge, Louisiana (correspondence with authors, April, 1968).

Crowley, Lillian H., "It's Now the Potter's Turn" *International Studio* (V. 75), (September, 1922), 539.

Frackelton, Susan Stuart, "Our American Potteries— Newcomb College," *Sketch Book* (V. 5) (July, 1906), 430.

Grady, Susan W., Isaac Delgado Museum of Art, New Orleans, Louisiana (correspondence with authors, March, 1972).

Henzke, Lucile, "Newcomb Art Pottery," *Spinning Wheel* (September, 1968), 12.

———, "Newcomb College Pottery," *Pottery Collectors' Newsletter* (V. 1, No. 4) (January, 1972), 51.

Irvine, Mary Ellen, New Orleans, Louisiana (correspondence with authors, March, 1972, April, 1972).

Irvine, Sadie, New Orleans, Louisiana (correspondence with authors, April, 1968).

Jervis, W. P., "A Pottery Primer," New York: O'Gorman Publishing Co., 1911, p. 180.

Kendall, John Smith, "History of New Orleans," Chicago and N.Y.: Lewis Publishing Company (V. II), 1922.

Little, Flora Townsend, "A Short Sketch of American Pottery," *Art & Archaeology* (V. 15), (May, 1923), 219.

"Louisiana Purchase Exposition Ceramics—Newcomb College," *Keramic Studio* (V. 6), (April, 1905).

"Newcomb Pottery," *The House Beautiful* (V. 5), (March, 1899), 156–158.

Ormond, Mrs. Suzanne, New Orleans, Louisiana (correspondence with authors, March, 1972).

Poesch, Jessie J., Associate Professor, Department of Art, Newcomb College, Tulane University, New Orleans, Louisiana (correspondence with authors, February, 1972).

Rawson, Jonathan A., Jr., "Recent American Pottery" *House Beautiful* (V. 31), (April, 1912), 148.

Richards, Peggy, Director of Louisiana State Museum, New Orleans, Louisiana (correspondence with authors, March, 1972).

Ruge, C., "Development of American Ceramics," *Pottery & Glass* (V. 1, No. 2), (August, 1908), 3.

Scribner's Magazine. "The Field of Art—American Pottery, Second Paper" (V. 33–44), (March, 1903), 381.

Sheerer, Mary G., "Newcomb Pottery," *Journal of the American Ceramic Society* (V. 1, No. 7), (July, 1918), 518.

Smith, Kenneth E., Manager, Ceramic Division, American Art Clay Co., Inc., Indianapolis, Indiana (correspondence with authors, March, 1972).

———, "The Origin, Development and Present Status of Newcomb Pottery," *American Ceramic Society Bulletin* (V. 17), (June, 1938), 257.

Stiles, Helen, *Pottery in the United States*, New York: E. P. Dutton & Co., Inc., 1941.

(Top right) Anna Frances Simpson was the artist and Joseph Meyer, the potter of this iris-decorated vase in glossy blue and blue green. The 12³⁄₁₆-inch piece was made about 1904–1910. It is marked with the impressed cipher NC, the cipher JM, the painted letters AFS, DI, DO-15. (The Art Museum, Princeton University, Princeton, New Jersey)   (Bottom right) The most popular design ever made at the Newcomb Pottery was this oak tree and moss decoration first used by Sadie Irvine. This vase is 8 inches in diameter, 16 inches high. It has blue, green, and pink matte glaze. The piece is marked with the impressed cipher NC, the cipher JM, the cipher SI, and the number 147. It was made about 1917. (Newcomb College, Tulane University, New Orleans, Louisiana)

Swanson, Betsy, New Orleans, Louisiana (correspondence with authors, March, 1972).

Woodword, E., "The Work of American Potters," *Arts and Decoration* (V. 1), (January, 1911), 124.

NEW MILFORD POTTERY

The New Milford Pottery Company was established in New Milford, Connecticut, in 1886. The name was later changed to The Wannopee Pottery Company. The pottery made a mottled glaze ware and porcelain and semi-porcelain pitchers with a dull glaze. They made one type with relief medallion heads of Beethoven, Mozart, and Napoleon. The pitchers were white except for two bands of leaves which were brown and greenish yellow.

Pieces were marked with a square and the letters "NMPCo." or "LS" (Lang and Schafer, New York agents who ordered the ware) in a circle.

The same management ran the Park Lane Pottery, which made an art pottery called "Scarabronze." Scarabronze had a metallic type of glaze that resembled old copper. A. H. Noble, the manager of the pottery, developed the ware accidentally while trying to create something entirely different. Scarabronze ranges from dark bronze to sage green and reddish copper. The body is made from Connecticut red clay. The pieces were adaptations of old Egyptian forms. Some pieces also have slip-painted Egyptian characters and figures.

"Scarabronze Ware" from Edwin Barber's *The Pottery and Porcelain of the United States*, 1909 edition.

Bibliography

Barber, Edwin. *Marks of American Potters.* Philadelphia: Patterson and White, 1904.

———, *The Pottery and Porcelain of the United States.* New York: G. P. Putnam's Sons, 1909, p. 504.

Watkins, Lura Woodside, "The Art Potteries," *Early New England Potters and Their Wares,* Cambridge: Harvard University Press, 1950, p. 222.

NILOAK POTTERY

Niloak (pronounced Ni'lŏk) Pottery was made in Benton, Arkansas, from 1909 to 1946. Their special marbelized art

NILOAK

Trademark.

pottery line is of great interest, but the factory also made case and molded wares.

J. H. Hyten had a pottery in Boonsboro, Iowa, and moved to Arkansas for his health. He worked at a pottery, which he finally bought and renamed the Eagle Pottery. The hills in the area had good potting clay of many colors and a natural gas supply to heat the kiln. But Hyten died within a few months and his widow married a potter who ran the pottery until 1895 when they moved to Ohio.

After Hyten's death, his eighteen-year-old son, Charles D. "Bullet" Hyten, worked in the stoneware pottery, decided to stay in Arkansas and run the pottery. His two brothers joined him and the firm became known as Hyten Bros. Pottery. In 1909, Charles began making a new type of pottery of different colored clays. The mixture of clay was put on the potter's wheel and a multicolored spiral design of the natural color clays was formed. At first, the pieces were glazed inside and out, but Hyten decided to glaze only the inside of the pieces so that they could hold water. The exterior remained in the natural matte finish of the multicolored clays, and it was finished with a sandpapering process. The end result was ware with an almost satin finish.

To manufacture this marbelized pottery required several special processes. Different clays shrink at different rates. To avoid this, Hyten developed his own process. He

A tubular vase made of a marbelized mixture of blue, cream, and terra-cotta-colored clays. It is 9 inches high. (Authors' collection)

A 5½-inch- and a 4-inch-high vase made after 1913. Both of these marked pieces of Niloak are made of brown, blue, and white clays. (The Smithsonian Institution)

(Top) Niloak vase 3½ inches high by 3½ inches in diameter. It is of marbelized blue, cream, and terra-cotta-colored clays, marked with an incised "Niloak." (Authors' collection)   (Bottom) An 8-inch-high vase marked Niloak. It is made from blue, gray, cream, and terra-cotta-colored clays. (Authors' collection)

added whiting, ground flint, and, when needed, coloring pigments to the liquid clay. Then the clay was worked in the more usual ways, but the baking process also was different. The pottery was fired for 36 to 49 hours in a steadily increasing heat. The temperature finally reached about 2100 degrees Fahrenheit. This process was eventually patented by Charles Hyten. He applied for the patent in June of 1924 and received it January 31, 1928. Patent 1657997 read, "the invention, more specifically speaking has to do with the production of clay pottery of a decorative character by virtue of the use of clay of different colors." It explains the process and also the coloring agents added to the clay.

Several articles claim that all of the Niloak Pottery was made from natural-colored clays dug from the Saline County Hills near Benton, Arkansas. Blue, red, white, gray, brown, and beige clays were found. When unavailable colors were needed, oxides were added to white clay, cobalt oxide for blue, ferric oxide for red, and chromic oxide for gray, as stated in the patent.

In 1910, Hyten decided to market the art pottery under the name Niloak, which is "kaolin" spelled backwards. Koalin has been used for making porcelain since early times in the Orient.

Niloak pottery was offered for sale in a local jeweler's window. Business was so good that in 1911 the Niloak Pottery Company was formed. Stock was sold and the money was used to build a two-story plant with modern equipment. Hyten was superintendent. The stoneware line of the earlier Eagle Pottery and some glazed wares were made, but the colored clay marbelized pieces were about 90 percent of the output.

In 1912, the sales force had been increased and Niloak pottery sold well in all parts of the country. In 1918 Hyten bought total control of the company. The firm made 75,-000 pieces in its most productive years. Six potters were employed at various times but Hyten made most of the pieces. Stores in all parts of the United States and in Cuba, Europe, and the Far East sold Niloak. It was part of a display at the 1934 Chicago World Fair.

With the depression, sales fell because the pottery was expensive. So the firm began to make castwares in several types of high-gloss and semimatte finishes and some hand-turned pieces were also made. The castware line, called "Hywood," included both solid and multicolored pieces. At first, the new line was stamped with the name Hywood as well as Niloak, but soon it was marked simply Niloak.

During the depression years the building and properties were mortgaged and Hyten lost control of the business. He continued as a salesman until 1941 when he joined Camark Pottery as a salesman. Marbelized Niloak was made until 1942 and the pottery continued until 1946. Charles Hyten died in 1944.

Product

The swirled mixed clay pottery made by Niloak and first developed by Charles Hyten in 1909 is the most popular of the company's wares collected today. A few of these early pieces were glazed both inside and out; most of the marbelized wares were glazed only on the inside. The soft, sandpapered, satiny finish of the natural clay was preferred.

The colors of the pieces depended on the supply of clay on hand and the skill of the potter. Two or more colors were used, usually blue and brown. It is unusual to find a piece that is predominately white, although white was sometimes included in the mixture. It is thought that the earlier pieces were of dark brown, cream, and blue. Later pieces show green, blue, and pink mixtures. Early pieces are possibly a bit less colorful. The clays used were of natural color whenever possible, but some of the pieces were made with tinted clay.

All types of pottery shapes were made: vases, candlesticks, tobacco humidors with lids, wine and ale bottles with corks, fruit bowls, lamps, mugs, tiles, umbrella stands, ashtrays, pitchers, clock cases, fern dishes, smoking sets, steins, tankards, match holders, jardinieres, and lamps.

The Hywood line was entirely different from the other ware. This was a cast or molded pottery, not hand-thrown. The Hywood pieces were small animals such as squirrels or frogs, small vases, pitchers, and other inexpensive items. Hywood was not an art pottery.

Marks

Both impressed marks and paper labels were used. Although it is often claimed that all Niloak was marked, unmarked pieces are known. This may be because the piece had a paper label at the factory and the label has disappeared.

The impressed marks were the name of the factory, NILOAK, in either art style or printed form. The word Niloak sometimes appears in raised letters under glaze.

Paper labels.

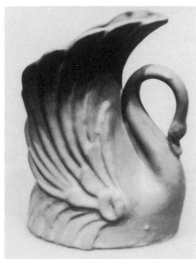

(Top) This 5½-inch-high Niloak vase is marked with a paper label: "The Gift Shop, Biggs Art Store, of Hot Springs, National Park, Ark." The label is pasted over the incised Niloak mark. Made from blue, cream, brown, and terra-cotta clays. (Authors' collection)   (Bottom) This swan is marked with the raised "Niloak." It is a molded vase, 7½ inches high, with a green and pink matte glaze. (Authors' collection)

This was part of the mold. The year and date also sometimes appear on pieces made in 1928 after the patent was granted. The name NILOAK was registered No. 195889, Nov. 3, 1924.

The paper labels were of several types, either "Niloak Pottery" in a circle or "From the Niloak potteries at Benton, Arkansas" on a jug. Often a model number was included in the center of the circle. The Hywood pieces were marked with the words "Hywood by Niloak." and later with the word "Niloak." These were stamped in black or in raised letters on the piece. Sometimes a patent number was included.

Bibliography

Crowley, Lilian H., "It's Now the Potter's Turn," *International Studio* (V. 75), (September, 1922), p. 539.

Dixson, Jeannette H., "Niloak Pottery," *Hobbies* (March, 1973), p. 109.

Dunnahoo, Pat, "Cheap Glass Killed Once-Thriving Pottery Industry," *Arkansas Gazette* (June 28, 1970), p. 4-E.

Evans, Paul F., "The Niloak Pottery," *Spinning Wheel* (October, 1970), p. 18.

Goolsby, Erwin, "Niloak Pottery," *Old Bottle Magazine* (April, 1970), p. 35.

Heissenbuttel, Orva, "Niloak Pottery Little Known Ware of Art Nouveau Period," *Tri-State Trader* (March 13, 1971), p. 1.

Johnson, Gini, ' "Mission" Control, Don't Call It "Mission"!' *Pottery Collectors' Newsletter* (V. 2, No. 2), (November, 1972), p. 21.

Johnson, Virginia Coleman, "Niloak Pottery," *The Antiques Journal*, (July, 1973), p. 28.

Kistler, Ralph H., Salt Lake City, Utah (correspondence with authors, January 24, 1970).

Malone, Cecil T., Little Rock, Arkansas (correspondence with authors, July, 1970, November, 1970, and January, 1972).

Mauney, Kenneth, "Arkansas Man Collects Ozark Pottery," *Collectors News,* Grundy Center, Iowa (date unknown).

_____, Dumas, Arkansas (correspondence with authors, February, 1970; September, 1970; December, 1971; January, 1972).

Rainey, Mrs. Arlene, Benton, Arkansas (Her letter appeared in *Spinning Wheel,* June, 1971.).

_____, (correspondence with authors, December, 1971; February, 1972; June, 1972).

Shipman, Mrs. C. B., Mount Lake Terrace, Washington, (correspondence with authors, January, 1972).

Weiss, Grace, "Niloak Pottery," *The Antique Trader* (April 17, 1973), p. 63.

NORSE POTTERY

The Norse Pottery Company founded in Edgerton, Wisconsin, in 1903 moved to Rockford, Illinois, in 1904. Pottery was made to resemble ancient Norse pottery and was glazed in dull metallic glaze. The company closed in 1913. The company produced replicas of ancient relics, and although (Below) This black Norse pottery vase was made about 1909. It is 7⅝ inches high and 12⅛ inches wide. The original advertisement labeled this bowl "from the bronze era." It is a copy of a piece from Bornholm, Denmark. (The Smithsonian Institution)   (Top right) This footed jardiniere is one of the Norse line that has the "semblance to the bronze originals preserved in a dull metallic glaze with the effect of verdigris preserved in the corners and crevices and the sunken lines of the etching." The jardiniere shows the Greek influences on the Norse. (*Pottery and Glass,* March, 1909, Vol. II, No. 3, p. 134) (Bottom right) Another Norse jardiniere, a copy of a piece from the Stone Age. (*Pottery and Glass,* March, 1909)

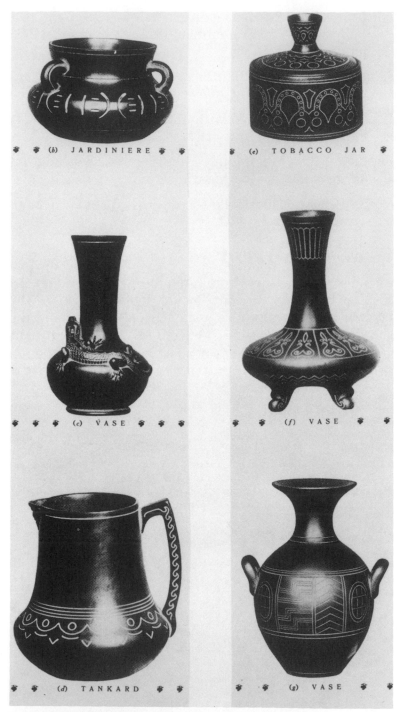

Norse pottery examples include: (b) a copy of a jardiniere from the Middle Bronze Age, the original found at Bornholm; (c) a vase from the Iron Age, the original found at Jutland; (d) a tankard copied from one of the Late Bronze Age; (e) a tobacco jar adaptation with early Egyptian motif; (f) a vase influenced by the Stone and Bronze Ages; (g) a vase with early Greek influence. (*Pottery and Glass,* March, 1909)

not art pottery in the true sense, they were outstanding examples of pottery of the period.

Bibliography

"Norse Pottery," *Pottery & Glass* (V. II, No. 3), (March, 1909).

NORTH DAKOTA SCHOOL OF MINES

The North Dakota School of Mines was established in 1892 at the University of North Dakota. (Prior to that Dean E. J. Babcock was making summer surveys by buckboard or bicycle in search of mineral resources.) Thereafter the university hired a trained potter, made pottery, and offered instruction in working with clay and ceramic materials and in the methods of forming clay wares, glazing, firing, etc. But first, in 1904, Marcia Bisbee had modeled a small leaf-shaped ashtray from some of the clay that Dean Babcock had discovered. And that year, a collection of pottery made from North Dakota clay had been exhibited at the St. Louis World's Fair. It had been made by a New Jersey potter, and most people would not believe it was North Dakota clay.

In 1910 Margaret Kelly Cable was hired to teach pottery making and the value of North Dakota clays. She had been trained at the Handicraft Guild in Minneapolis, Minnesota, in the potteries of East Liverpool, Ohio, and studied both with Charles Binns of the New York State College of Ceramics and Frederick Rhead, art director of the Homer Laughlin Pottery. Miss Cable remained at the

(Left) This pink vase with carved floral decorations has the circular mark of the University of North Dakota and is incised "Millard-Huck-2557, Prairie Rose." It is 6¼ inches high by 6¾ inches wide. Huck is the artist Flora Huckfield. (Author's collection) (Right) Stamped factory mark with the incised name "Millard-Huck."

Several pieces in a photograph from the University of North Dakota archives. The lidded vase is dated 1919.

University of North Dakota until her retirement in 1949. She died in 1960.

Julia Mattson of Kensington, Minnesota, taught ceramics from 1924 to 1963. She studied at the University of North Dakota, the Art Institute of Chicago, the Taos School of Art, and the University of New Mexico. She died in 1967.

Margaret Pachl of Lincoln, Nebraska, taught ceramics from 1949–1970. She trained at the Kansas Art Institute, North Texas Agricultural College, and Alfred University of the New York State College of Ceramics. She also taught at Alfred University and in 1948 at the Kalamazoo Institute of Arts.

All of the pieces produced at the University of North Dakota were made from local clays. The design of the work varied through the years from strongly colored art nouveau and art deco designs to the simpler modern utilitarian style. Some of the pieces were produced by a cutaway technique that made the finished work resemble the acid-cut cameo glass of Frederick Carder. Others had borders or overall designs of an intaglio type. Many were plain, solid-colored glazed pieces. Flowers and animals of North Dakota have been favored in the designs, as have green, brown, blue, orange, pink, lavender, and other matte glazes. Pieces stamped with the university name were made until 1963. Since then, only the students' names have appeared on the pottery.

Each piece has an incised mark in a circle in cobalt blue under the glaze: "University of North Dakota Grand Forks, N.D. Made at School of Mines N.D. Clay." A few are marked "U.N.D. Grand Forks, N.D." Records exist so that it may be possible to date pieces of the pottery from the glaze number and form. The chairman of the ceramics department at the university has had success with this method. The university has an almost complete set of records of the glazes. They also have some dated mold shapes.

Artists

Margaret Kelly Cable (see text), 1910–1949.

Agnes Dollahan, c. 1946.

Flora Huckfield, 1923–1949, signed Huck.

Julia E. Mattson (see text), 1924–1963, marked JM.

Margaret Pachl (see text), 1949–1970.

Bibliography

Cable, Margaret, "Post-War Ceramic Opportunities in North Dakota" (publication and date unknown).

————, "The Development of Ceramic Work at the University of North Dakota," *Journal of the American Ceramic Society* (reprint), (V. 5, No. 3), (March, 1922) 140–145.

Dommel, Darlene, "University of North Dakota Pottery," *Spinning Wheel* (June 1973), 30–31.

Grand Forks (N.D.) Herald, "Ceramics Veteran to Retire July 1" (May 29, 1949), 21.

————, "Ceramist Mrs. Pachl Retires to the Ozarks" (June 7, 1970).

A 1935 collection. (University of North Dakota archives)

An undated collection. (University
of North Dakota archives)

———, "Former Ceramics Head at U Honored" (April 25, 1951).

———, "Julia E. Mattson" (obituary), (January 7, 1968).

———, "Rites Conducted for Miss Cable" (November 4, 1960).

Grantier, Charles, correspondence with authors.

Miller, Donald (Chairman of Ceramics Department, University of North Dakota, Grand Forks, North Dakota), correspondence with authors.

Spinning Wheel, Letter to Editor from Mr. Charles Grantier (October 1972).

University of North Dakota and clippings from their files on Margaret Kelly Cable, Julia E. Mattson, and Margaret Davis Pachl.

OHR POTTERY

Eccentric artists are a part of the tradition, but none can claim a stranger career than the almost unknown American potter George E. Ohr. Ohr worked as a potter for many years in Biloxi, Mississippi. He was recognized as an artists in his own time, yet he sold almost none of his work; he donated about twelve pieces to the Smithsonian Institution. In 1906, Ohr closed his pottery and stored six thousand pieces in the pottery shed as his legacy to his children. He and his family believed this pottery would be purchased someday by the United States government. Even as early as 1902, W. P. Jervis in *Encyclopedia of Ceramics* expressed Ohr's feelings about his pottery: "Mr. Ohr with an unbounded confidence in his own genius is laying up at Biloxi a vast store of ware in the hopes that it may be purchased entire by the nation as an example of his prowess. Did we but accept him at his own estimate he is not only the foremost potter in America, but the whole world. He said so and he ought to know."

This collection remained in storage until 1972 when it was purchased for resale by an antique dealer, J. C. Carpenter. The collection included the pottery, molds, records, and family photographs.

George Ohr was far from a modest man. He wrote his biography for an art magazine in 1901. The language and choice of incidents reveals the eccentricity of the writer. It is almost an allegorical tale as he says of his birth: "I

(Top) Special mark used on inscribed cup. (Center) This mark was used in uppercase or lowercase letters, with or without "Miss." and sometimes alone. (Bottom) Hand script signature used from 1899 to 1906.

"A visitor asked me for my autograph and since then "1898" my creations are marked like a check. The previous 19 years mark is like any old newspaper type just like this G. E. OHR/Biloxi, Miss."

J. Harry Proctman (Portman?), a foster brother of George Ohr, worked at the pottery for a short period. A few pieces are known that are signed "J.H.P." and with a George Ohr mark.

came on the second schooner and knocked the nose out of joint of the first one, and kept it so, as the other three storks that came in town were nothing to brag about and that completed the programme (3 hens, 1 rooster and a duck, I'm that duck. . . .)."

Evidently, George Ohr, who was born in 1857 to a blacksmith and a German woman from Wurtemberg, felt he was always in trouble or, as he says, "in very hot aqua and evaporated liquified air." His family lived in Biloxi, but when he was old enough, probably eighteen, he ran away to New Orleans. He worked at a ship chandler's store where he was given free room and board plus soap for washing. By the third year, he was paid fifteen dollars per month, and still given free soap. He felt he was entitled to $1.50 per day for the fifteen hours of daily work he was doing, so he went back to Biloxi.

Over the years, he worked as an apprentice in a file cutter's shop, in a tinker's shop, and in the ship's store.

He was sent a letter, probably about 1885, by an old friend, J. F. Meyer, who later was a potter at Sophie Newcomb College. Meyer offered Ohr ten dollars a month plus the chance to learn a trade. Ohr hopped a ride on a freight train and went back to New Orleans to become a potter. Meyer was then making simple pottery on a wheel. (See postscript at the end of this entry.)

Ohr worked as a potter long enough to gain some skill and then spent two years traveling to sixteen states to see other potters and their potteries. He returned to Biloxi with $26.80 and equipped his own pottery. Ohr was able to make the most of the equipment because of his earlier training in ironwork. Most of his money was spent on the bricks for the kiln. The less than humble Ohr in his autobiography details how he made the mortar, built the kiln, sawed the pine trees, floated them to town, built the shop, and did all the other necessary jobs.

The first year he claims to have worked alone as a potter is 1883. He made over six hundred pieces of his unique pottery and then exhibited them at the New Orleans Cotton Centennial Exposition where, evidently, the pottery was stolen. But he kept making his "mud fixings" and kept displaying it at fairs.

He also seems to have worked for a while at the New Orleans Pottery Company and perhaps at the Crescent City Pottery. (A pot exists with the names George Ohr and Crescent City Pottery marked on it.)

Ohr's pottery shop burned in 1893 and he rebuilt it by

George Ohr made this vase for his wife. (J. W. Carpenter)

(Above) An 1895 display of George Ohr's pottery. (J. W. Carpenter)

(Left) Gunmetal and pewter finished wares in a display about 1895. (J. W. Carpenter)

Ohr was proud of his flowing mustache. This picture was taken about 1895. (J. W. Carpenter)

An eccentric, he enjoyed posing for strange pictures of himself and did as much for his friends. These two show him in a playful mood. (J. W. Carpenter)

1894. This building was well known in the area and was even pictured on souvenir plates made in Europe. George Ohr continued to make pottery in Biloxi and probably spent a brief time at the Newcomb Pottery working under Joseph Meyer. He was evidently fired because he was "not fit to teach young ladies" (from a thesis prepared at

Ohr made many early pieces with incised inscriptions as part of the decoration. This cup with mottled dark gray, green, and brown glaze is inscribed, "Here's your good health and your family's and may they all have long lives and prosper." There are three signatures at the bottom of the inscription, H. W., O. J. Herson, and Aug. The cup is marked with an impressed "G. E. Ohr Biloxi, Previous to No. 14 not numbered" and "3-8-1896 No. 37." (Authors' collection)

Another inscribed piece is this umbrella stand 14½ inches high by 10 inches in diameter. The pot's entire surface is decorated with words from a letter to the Smithsonian: "Biloxi Miss. Dec 18, 1900. To the Smithsonian Wash. As kind words and deeds never die, such words and deeds are fire, water and water acid. and time proves when recorded on mother earth or clay. This is an empty jar just like the world solid in itself yet full on the surface. Deed and thoughts are but the instigation and shadows fade and disappear when the sun goes down. Mary had a little lamb Pot Ohr E George has had a little pottery now where is the boy that stood on the burning deck. This pot is here and I am the potter who was." It is signed "G. E. Ohr." (Collection of J. W. Carpenter)

Sophie Newcomb College; date, title, and author un-known).

In 1906, Ohr decided to give up making pottery. His son had bought a Cadillac dealership and the family went into this new business. George Ohr died in 1918, still convinced he was the greatest potter who ever worked.

His eccentricities are well known. He was sometimes called the "Mad Potter of Biloxi," partly because of his appearance, which was unusual. He had long hair that he knotted on top with a brass pin. His beard, very long, was tucked into his shirt to keep it from interfering with the clay on the potter's wheel. And his amazing moustache was so long that he kept it out of the clay by placing the ends behind his ears. It is said that a cast of his muscular arm is still to be found at the Newcomb School of Art as part of the models for students to draw.

Ohr often played jokes. He once appeared in a Mardi Gras float in a nightshirt, leaning against a large cross, and he left his family a collection of pictures showing him as twins, making faces, and in other comical poses. Perhaps his most interesting eccentricity was to name his seven children Leo, Lio, Zio, Oto, Clo, Ojo, and Geo so their initials would also be their first names.

(Left) This 6½-inch-high vase has an orange glaze that is slightly iridescent. It is decorated on the side with the inscription "Mr. J. R. Alexander, Biloxi, 1898." It is impressed on the bottom "G. E. Ohr, Biloxi Miss." (Authors' collection) (Center) The Ohr Pottery made some early pieces in molds, like this 7½-inch-high pitcher with the word "Biloxi" scratched on the bottom. The molded panel decorations are of women in flowing drapery. The piece is glazed a dark brown. (Authors' collection) (Right) The same pitcher was sometimes glazed in pale blue and dark blue glazes with brown. This piece is unmarked but the original mold for the pitchers was found with the collection of pottery discovered in 1972. (Authors' collection)

(Left) Snake decorations were often used by the Ohr Pottery, as on this 7-inch vase. It has a green-speckled, slightly iridescent glaze. The handle is applied. The piece is marked with the script signature "G. E. Ohr" and "Biloxi, Miss." (Authors' collection)   (Center) Bright pink glaze with a very bubbled dripped glaze of dark gray and green covers this vase with the folded, crimped top. It is 7 inches high and signed "G. E. Ohr" in script. (Authors' collection)   (Top right) A yellowish beige glaze with green mottling covers this folded vase. It is 3½ inches high and 6 inches wide. The piece is incised with the typeset style mark "G. E. Ohr, Biloxi, Miss." (Authors' collection) (Bottom right) The varicolored glazes on this free-form pitcher shade from green to gold to blue. The interior is glazed in shades of green-yellow. The 3-inch-high piece is marked with an impressed typeset "G. E. Ohr, Biloxi, Miss." (Authors' collection)

(Left top) This free-form vase is 3 inches high and 4 inches across. It is glazed light and dark green with red mottling. The piece is marked with the typeset-style mark "G. E. Ohr, Biloxi, Miss." (Authors' collection)   (Left center) A speckled glaze was favored by Ohr for a time. This 5½-inch folded vase is covered with a yellow glaze speckled with green. The interior is yellow. The piece is marked with the typeset-style mark "G. E. Ohr, Biloxi, Miss." (Authors' collection)   (Left bottom) Mottled yellow and green glaze was used on this bowl with folded edges. It is 5 inches by 3 inches wide and 3 inches high. It is marked "G. E. Ohr, Biloxi, Miss." in typeset style. (Authors' collection)

Postscript

The records are confused about the exact dates that George Ohr and Joseph Meyer worked together in New Orleans. Mr. Ohr, in an article dated 1901, claims to have learned his trade from Meyer before 1883 when he exhibited at the New Orleans Cotton Centennial. The Centennial opened in 1884 and closed in 1886. (Could he have meant the Atlanta Cotton Exposition in 1875?) Mr. Meyer and his fellow workmen at Newcomb Pottery, in several articles written before 1905, claim that Mr. Ohr assisted at the New Orleans Pottery Company two years, between 1886 and 1890. It is also stated that Ohr worked at Newcomb Pottery after it was started in 1896. Perhaps Mr. Ohr wanted to ignore his short stay as a potter at Newcomb because he was fired; probably he confused the dates.

Mr. Barber, in his book written in 1904, mentions Ohr, but he did not mention him in the edition of 1893. It is our belief that the dates given by Mr. Ohr are wrong and that he began to pot after 1885, possibly showing his pieces in public about 1891 to 1895. He then probably worked by himself, except for the very short return to the Newcomb Pottery after 1895. His work was well known by 1901.

Product

Some of the pottery made by George Ohr was unlike any of the other American art pottery forms. Pieces varied in size from the height of a thimble to that of a man. He usually used a local clay, often red or yellow, fired at low temperature in the wood-burning kiln. Sometimes he would try clay from other cities such as New Orleans or Mobile, Alabama. Pieces made from these strange clays were usually marked to explain where the mud had been found.

He made molded wares probably early in his career. Pieces showed Art Nouveau-style girls, fishermen, a girl on a bicycle, and a steamboat. Some of the molds still exist. Only pitchers and a shaving mug made in these molds are known today. Some of the hand-thrown pieces had molded handles and spouts.

Hand-modeled pieces were probably made for sale at fairs. A large variety of hats, inkwells shaped like houses, artists' palettes, cannons, mule heads, busts of presidents, banks, and even chamber pots and puzzle mugs were made. These were souvenir type items of small size with varied glazes in yellow to brown tones.

The most unusual of the Ohr pieces were made of what appears to be twisted clay. This was very thin clay that was twisted, crushed, folded, or dented into odd shapes. Some examples were pleated before they were twisted. Some were made with edges that had been pinched to their thinnest or chipped before glazing. Each piece was different in both shape and glaze. Some were made from marbelized clay covered with a clear glaze.

(Top) A gray and mottled green bubbled glaze was used on this scalloped-top vase. It is 3¾ inches high, marked "G. E. Ohr, Biloxi, Miss." in typeset style. (Authors' collection) (Bottom) An orange glaze mottled with green and browns decorates this 6-inch vase. Notice the pleatlike effect at the center of the vase made by folding the clay while it is wet. The mark is "G. E. Ohr, Biloxi, Miss." (Authors' collection)

(Top left) A white glaze was used with green and brown mottling at the top. The body is made of a red clay. It is 3½ inches high, signed "G. E. Ohr" in script. (Authors' collection)   (Top center) This free-form bowl has remarkably thin edges. The glaze is orange and brown. The height at the highest point is 3¼ inches. It is marked "G. E. Ohr, Biloxi, Miss." (Authors' collection)   (Top right) A pale yellow green glaze covers this vase. The edge of the vase was chipped when the clay was dry and the vase sides were folded in one area. Then the entire piece was glazed. It is 3½ inches high, marked "GEO E OHR, Biloxi, Miss." in typeset style. (Authors' collection) (Left) The clay for this vase was pleated like material, then the entire vase was formed and bent into its irregular shape. The brown glaze has brown speckling. It is 2½ inches high, 5 inches in diameter, marked "G. E. Ohr, Biloxi," in typeset style. (Author's collection)

(Bottom left) George Ohr evidently took the edge of the wet clay of this bowl between his fingers and pinched it, drawing the clay as thin as possible as he pulled the edge. The glaze is an iridescent brown. The metallic-finish vase is about 5 inches in diameter. It is marked "G. E. Ohr, Biloxi, Miss." in typeset style. (Authors' collection)   (Bottom center) The Ohr pottery made many styles of hats. This green and brown hat is 4½ inches long. It is marked on the crown with the impressed mark "G. E. Ohr, Biloxi." (Authors' collection)   (Bottom right) Not every artist would make a statue of a potato, but George Ohr did. This green glazed figure is 10 inches high. It is marked "G. E. Ohr" in script. (Authors' collection)

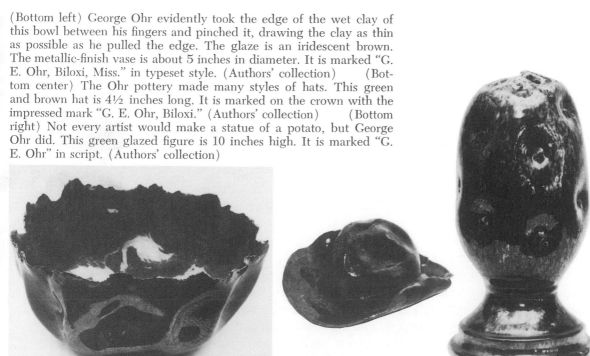

(Top left) Inkwells of many shapes were modeled, not molded, by Mr. Ohr. This donkey head has a hole at the top for the pen. It is glazed an orange brown. The 5½-inch piece is marked "Geo. E. Ohr, Biloxi, Miss." (Authors' collection)   (Top right) An inkwell shaped like an artist's palette, with pen, tubes of paint, and a pot used for ink. The palette is 6¼ inches long. It is marked "Geo. E. Ohr, Biloxi, Miss." in typeset style. (Authors' collection)   (Bottom left) Inkwell glazed a dark brown is shaped like a log cabin. It is 3 inches long, 2½ inches high, marked "G. E. Ohr, Biloxi" in typeset style. (Authors' collection)   (Bottom right) A realistic printer's type holder was made by Ohr of brown-glazed pottery for the wooden parts, and dark metallic glaze for the type. Notice the "screw." The "wood" is inscribed in script "Jackson News 5-10-95." The "type" says:

> The poet sings in dainty rhyme
>   Of summer days and sunny clim
> Of beauteous maideens passing fair
>   With witching eyes and waving hair
> Till near the end you're apt to C
> A welcome to the pot-Ohr-E.
>   Resp'y
>   GEO E OHR
> Biloxi, Miss. 5-12-95

The back of the piece is marked "G. E. OHR BILOXI" in capital letters and with the inscribed letter H. The piece is 5½ inches long. (Authors' collection)

(Top left) A joker like George Ohr would enjoy making puzzle pieces. This coffeepot is 7¼ inches high. It has two separate compartments and could hold coffee in one, tea in the other. (The Smithsonian Institution)   (Top right) This pink and green glazed double pot has four spouts. It is filled from the top or the bottom through a hole. The liquid can come out of only one spout on each side and the pot must be turned over to pour from the second spout. It is the form of a double cadogan pot. Single cadogan pots were also made. The piece is 8 inches high and 10 inches across from spout to spout. It is marked "Ohr" on one spout. (Authors' collection)   (Bottom left) Puzzle mugs were made in quantity by Mr. Ohr. This mottled green, red, and gold mug has raised decorations on the handle. The bottom is signed "G. E. Ohr" in script and has the screw top impression he often used on these mugs. (Authors' collection)   (Bottom right) Two more puzzle mugs by Ohr. To drink from these mugs, you held a finger over a hole in the handle, then sipped on the handle as if it were a straw. (Collection of J. W. Carpenter)

Modeled snakes and lizards were sometimes used as decorations on the vases. These were made with a body that looks like a looped ribbon. Sometimes a vase had added ruffles of clay or applied looped handles. Edwin Barber, in his *Pottery and Porcelain Development Since 1893,* mentions seeing modeled designs of crabs, seashells, wildcats, lizards, serpents, and dragons. Incised decorations of flowers or inscriptions are on some pieces. Some teapots had surface dents that resemble hammer marks on metal. We own a statue of a potato.

The glaze used by Ohr is as varied as his pottery shapes. Brown, red, purple, blue, yellow and green lusters and metallic glazes were used. A bright pink with drip designs of another color, and a mottled or speckled effect are found on some wares. Many of the glazes are flawed or even burned. Most of the pieces found in storage were of brown to yellow coloring.

Bibliography

Barber, Edwin, *The Pottery and Porcelain of the United States,* New York: G. P. Putnam's Sons, 1909, pp. 498–499.

Blasberg, Robert W., *George E. Ohr and His Biloxi Art Pottery,* privately printed, Port Jervis, New York: J. W. Carpenter, 1973.

Carpenter, J. W., correspondence with authors.

———, "Geo. Ohr's 'Pot-Ohr-E'," *The Antique Trader Weekly* (September 19, 1972), 42.

Kovel, Ralph and Terry, "The Mad Potter of Biloxi," *The Western Collector* (X, 5), (May, 1972) 18–20.

Ohr, George E., "Some Facts in the History of a Unique Personality. Autobiography of Geo. E. Ohr, the Biloxi Potter," *Crockery & Glass Journal* (V. 54. No. 23), (December 12, 1901).

OVERBECK POTTERY

Overbeck mark

Four sisters founded an art pottery of merit in Indiana. The Overbeck Pottery was established in their family home located in Cambridge City, Indiana, in 1911. All of the work was done by four sisters, daughters of John Overpeck. (The four girls changed their names to Overbeck in 1911 after their parents died.) One of them, Margaret, was on the art faculty at De Pauw University, Greencastle, Indiana. She had previously worked at a pottery in Zanesville, Ohio, and had studied under Arthur W. Dow at Columbia University. Her sister Mary studied at Columbia with her. Her sister Elizabeth studied pottery in 1909 and 1910 in Alfred, New York, with Charles F. Binns. Hannah, the fourth sister, was the principal designer. All of the sisters but Elizabeth studied at the Art Academy in Cincinnati, Ohio. Margaret, the guiding spirit in founding the pottery, died shortly after the pottery opened.

The work at their studio was more or less divided among the three surviving sisters. Hannah was a decorator and she did most of the designs. Elizabeth was the technician and she worked with the clay and the glazes and executed the designs. Mary designed and glazed.

Examples of Overbeck pottery as pictured in *International Studio,* September 1922. (*Connoisseur Magazine*)

All the sisters were capable of filling any of the jobs required in making pottery. After Hannah's death, the others kept working and when Elizabeth died Mary continued to make the pottery alone until her death in 1955.

The pottery was made from a mixture of feldspar from Pennsylvania, kaolin from Delaware, and ball clay from Tennessee. Some pieces were made with local clay. The wares were glazed in raspberry, turquoise, lavender, creamy yellow, dark gray, pink, blue, green, and a wide range of other colors. Commercial and art pottery were made at the same time. The pots were made on a wheel. With the exception of the molded cups and saucers and a few small figurines, all the pieces were one of a kind. The glaze was either matte or shiny. Designs were incised, carved, or glazed in patterns.

After 1911 the pottery was marked with the Overbeck monogram. The initials of the designer and potter were added. Earlier pieces were marked with the incised name of the artist.

Bibliography

Crowley, Lilian H., "It's Now the Potter's Turn." *International Studio* (V. 75), (September, 1922), 539.

International Studio (September, 1922), 546.

Little, Flora Townsend, "A Short Sketch of American Pottery," *Art & Archaeology* (V. 15), (May, 1923), 219.

Postle, Kathleen R., correspondence with authors.

———, "Overbeck Motifs Drawn from Nature: Were Made at Cambridge City, Ind." *Tri-State Trader* (July 24, 1971).

———, "Overbeck Pottery" *Spinning Wheel* (May, 1972), 10–12.

———, "Overbeck Pottery Collection Sold: New Value Scale Set," *Tri-State Trader* (date unknown).

"Overbeck Home Purchased by Hagerstown, Ind., Couple Recently" (publication and date unknown).

OWENS POTTERY COMPANY

J. B. Owens was born near Roseville, Ohio, in 1859. He discovered at an early age that he was a good salesman, and while in his twenties became a traveling salesman for a line of stoneware. By 1885, he was making pottery and stoneware at his own plant in Roseville. He moved to Zanesville, Ohio, in 1891 and built a plant where within a year he resumed making stoneware.

Artists and other Employees (* Artists listed in Barber):

Virginia Adams—also worked at Weller, Roseville

*Estelle Beardsley

*Edith Bell

*Fanny Bell

*A. F. Best—also worked at Weller (Roseville?)

*Cecilia Bloomer

*Lillian Bloomer

John Butterworth—also worked at Roseville (Weller?)

C. M. C.—unknown

Charles W. Chilcote?—also worked at Weller, Zane

Chilectsi

Daniel Cook—also worked at Rookwood

*Cora Davis

*Walter I. Denny

E—unknown

*Harrie (Harry?) Eberlein

*Hattie Eberlein—also worked at (Roseville?)

*Cecil Excel

J. F.—unknown

Frank Ferrell—also worked at Roseville, Weller, Peters & Reed; designer 1907

Charles Fouts—also worked at (Weller?)

*Charles Gray—also worked at (Weller?)

*Martha E. Gray

*Delores Harvey

*Albert Haubrich—also worked at Weller

Hugo Herb—modeler 1906, also worked at Weller

John Herold—also worked at (Weller ?), Roseville

*Roy Hook—also worked at (Weller?)

*H. Hoskins

H. I.—unknown

Guido Howarth

Karl Langenbeck—chemist

*Harry Larzelere—also worked at Roseville

John Lessell (also spelled Lassell), foreman 1905—also at Weller

*A. V. Lewis—also worked at (Weller?)

William A. Long—also worked at Lonhuda, Weller

Mc—unknown

R. M.—unknown

*Cora McCandless

*Carrie McDonald

B. Mallen—also worked at Roseville

Hattie Mitchell—also worked at Owens (Roseville?)

*Miss Oshe

Bert Owens—potter mark B. 01

*Mary L. Peirce—also worked at Weller

Albert Radford—also worked at Weller, Radford

Marie Rauchfuss—also worked at Rookwood, Weller

*Harry Robinson—also at Weller

*Hattie M. Ross—also worked at Weller

*R. Lillian Shoemaker—also worked at Roseville

Helen Smith—also worked at Roseville, Weller

*Ida Steele

Tot Steele—also worked at Weller, Roseville

*William H. Stemm—also worked at Weller

*Mary Fauntleroy Stevens

C. Minnie Terry?—also worked at (Roseville?) Weller

*Mae Timberlake—also worked at Weller, Roseville

*Sarah Timberlake—also worked at Weller, Roseville

*Arthur Williams—also worked at Roseville

Marks:

Owensart Utopian.

Owensart.

J. B. OWENS/UTOPIAN

Impressed

OWENS UTOPIAN   HENRI DEUX

OWENS FEROZA

According to Edwin Atlee Barber, "Sometimes other marks will be found on pieces from this establishment. These are experimental marks, of no significance to the purchaser, but relating to certain records at the factory. The more common of these are here figured. The last one represents a series of such marks in which any letter plus a figure or number may be used."

Art pottery was made at the J. B. Owens Pottery Company from 1896 to 1906. Mr. Owens hired many potters and artists. Karl Langenbeck was hired as the head chemist in 1891. Langenbeck had much experience in the field of art pottery as he had worked with Maria Longworth Nichols of Rookwood fame and he was also the founder of the Avon Pottery Company. John Lassell, the foreman in

This 10½-inch bottle-shaped Owens vase has a brown to green to gold glaze. The lifelike daffodils were painted by Delores Harvey whose initials D. H. appear at the base of the vase. The impressed mark J. B. Owens, Utopian, 1010B appears on the bottom. (Collection of LeRoy Eslinger)

The Owens Pottery made a variety of art ware. *Left:* Blue flowers in relief decorate this 10¼-inch-high vase marked Owens. *Center:* A matte lavender glaze was used on this 4-inch-high vase with the dragonfly decoration. It was made about 1905. *Right:* 6½-inch-high bottle with Owens Utopia glaze made about 1885. The flowers are orange and brown. It is marked "Owens Utopia 117." (The Smithsonian Institution)

1905, developed iridescent glazes. Hugo Herb (1907), Guido Howarth, and Frank L. (Di) Ferrel (1) also were employed. W. A. Long, who made Lonhuda, worked for the J. B. Owens Pottery Company from 1896 to about 1900. He was the artist who developed the Utopian line that was similar to Weller's Louwelsa Pottery, also developed by Long.

The Owens Pottery burned in March 1902, but Owens rebuilt his plant and continued in business. The pottery made many types of art pottery using Ohio and Tennessee clay. Eventually there were two plants, one in Zanesville and one in New York City. Their 1904 catalogue alone lists eight hundred items. The pottery was awarded four gold medals at the Lewis and Clark Exposition in Portland, Oregon, in 1905. The company perfected a continuous type kiln that helped keep the wares uniform. Similar kilns were eventually used by many other potter-

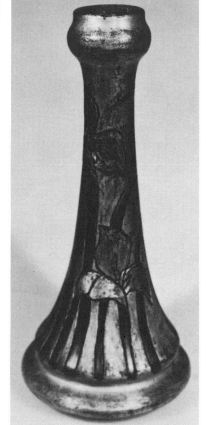

(Left) This Owens bottlelike swirl vase is 4½ inches high. It has a dark to light brown glaze with green and orange floral decoration. The incised Owens mark appears on the bottom. (Collection of LeRoy Eslinger)   (Center) An Owens vase meant to look like a pottery vessel by an American Indian. It is 6½ inches long, 5 inches high, and 4 inches wide. Terra-cotta with black and brown designs. (The Smithsonian Institution)   (Right) A rare Owens vase covered with copper and gold metallic glaze. The incised iris decoration was evidently part of the work done at Owens, but the glaze was by the Clewell Pottery of Canton, Ohio. The 12½-inch-high vase has the embossed Owens mark and a Clewell paper label. We have also seen an Owens vase with a thin sheet copper overlay made by Clewell. (Authors' collection)

ies in the United States. In 1907 Owens stopped making art pottery and began producing tiles. He had a successful tile operation, the J. B. Owen Floor and Wall Tile Company, until 1928 when the plant again burned. (The plant sometimes was referred to as the Empire Floor & Wall Tile Co. The Zanesville Chamber of Commerce booklet of 1918 has a picture of the J. B. Owens Floor & Wall Tile Co. and says it is six years old.) Ignoring the advice of others, Owens rebuilt the plant and during the depression lost everything. He moved to Homestead, Florida, where he died in 1934.

Product

The art pottery made by J. B. Owens was of high quality, with a special type of glaze for each line. No general characteristic identified all Owen Pottery, though some of the lines can be easily recognized even if unmarked.

(Top left) A pair of floral decorated brown glazed Owens vases. *Left:* Red, orange, and yellow cherries decorate this brown to orange high gloss piece. It is 13½ inches high and 6¼ inches wide, and marked Owens in block letters. *Right:* This 10½-inch-high example features orange and yellow nasturtiums on brown to green high-gloss ground. The name Owens is impressed in block letters. (Top right) This 13-inch-high Owens vase has a medium brown to orange glaze with a nasturtium flower in orange and green. It is incised "Owensart." (Collection of LeRoy Eslinger) (Left) An Owens scalloped-top vase decorated with an orange flower. This 9- by 11-inch piece is signed by artist Cora Davis.

Aborigine, 1907. Matte glaze finish; crude; American Indian inspired designs.

Alpine, c. 1897 (?) 1905 (?). Matte glaze, shaded gray or brown background. Artist freehand slip decoration in blue, green, others usually flowers, fruit (Example marked Steele).

Aqua Verdi, 1907. Slightly iridescent glaze, usually green, embossed stylized decoration.

Art Vellum. Orange, brown, other earth-tone colors, vellumy finish, underglaze decoration.

Corona. Bronze colored.

Corona Animals 1905. Animal figures in natural colors, from life-sized garden figures to small indoor decorative pieces under five inches. Unglazed.

Cyrano, 1898. Blue, red, black, or dark brown background with raised white lacey decorations. Glossy glaze.

Delft, 1904. Bucket-shaped blue and white ware with Dutch scences.

Feroza, 1901. Coating like hammered metal.

Gunmetal ware, 1905. Unglazed, resembles dull gunmetal, engraved decoration.

Henri Deux, 1900. Art nouveau designs cut into clay, filled with color.

Lotus, 1907. Underglaze decoration, natural subjects, light shaded background, high gloss glaze.

Matt Utopian, 1905. Light color matte finish.

Mission, 1903. Matte glaze, designs of old Paris missions, landscapes, etc. each came with a weathered oak stand.

Opalesce Inlaid, 1905. (Opalesce Utopian) Solid colored background of light color, overglaze irregularly spaced wavy lines of olive green or light color on copper, gold, or silver, floral decorations inlaid and outlined in black.

Poster. Brown tones of background like Utopian, Greek actors, musicians.

Red Flame, 1905. Red glazed background, embossed floral decorations.

Rustic, 1904. Imitation tree trunks, stumps, matte glaze.

Soudanese, 1907. Ebony black background glaze, inlaid decoration of flowers, animals, birds in shades of lavender, white, etc., high gloss glaze.

Sunburst, 1906. High gloss glaze similar to Utopian.

Utopian, 1897. High gloss dark brown background, under glaze slip painting of flowers, portraits, Indians, animals. Also made in light shades of blue, pink, and brown.

Utopian Opalesce, 1905. Descriptions vary: either a corolenelike decoration on gold or like opalesce, but with no gold wavy lines.

Venetian, 1904. Iridescent metallic glaze on indented surface.

Wedgwood Jasper, 1903. Resembles the English Wedgwood Pottery.

Bibliography

Benjamin, Marcus, "American Art Pottery—Part III," *Glass and Pottery World,* April, 1907, 35.

Cobb, Lura Milburn, "A Visit to Some Zanesville Potteries," *The Southwestern Book* (V. II, No. 12), (December, 1905).

Hall, Foster E. and Gladys C., Punta Gorda, Florida, *The Owens Pricing Formula,* (date unknown).

Purviance, Evan, "American Art Pottery," *Mid-America Reporter,* Leon, Iowa, October, 1972, 18.

Purviance, Louise and Evan, and Schneider, Norris F. "The J. B. Owens Pottery Company," *Zanesville Art Pottery in Color,* Des Moines, Iowa: Wallace-Homestead Press, 1968, plates 12 and 13.

Schneider, Norris F., "Veteran Mosaic Tile Employe Compiles Outstanding Display," *Zanesville Times Recorder,* October 30, 1960.

Spinning Wheel, "J. B. Owens Pottery Co.," January–February, 1968.

Zanesville Chamber of Commerce Booklet, "J. B. Owens Floor and Wall Tile Company," 1918.

C. PARDEE WORKS

The C. Pardee Works of Perth Amboy, New Jersey, was founded before 1893. They made paving bricks, sewer

These two tiles were made by the C. Pardee Works, probably as campaign items in 1884. Both tiles are glazed purple 6-inch squares. *Left:* James G. Blaine, vice-presidential candidate. *Right:* Grover Cleveland, presidential candidate. (The Smithsonian Institution)

pipe, and floor and glazed tile. Art tiles to be used as wall decorations were made by 1893. These tiles included intaglio modeled heads of Emperor Wilhelm, President Benjamin Harrison, President Grover Cleveland, and James G. Blaine. Printed tiles were made as souvenirs of Niagara Falls, Plymouth Rock, Salem, and many other places of interest. The firm made hand-painted underglaze tiles, printed underglaze and overglaze tiles, and inlaid and relief pattern tiles.

Bibliography

McClinton, K. M., *Collecting American Victorian Antiques,* New York: Charles Scribner's Sons, 1966.

Newark Museum Association, "New Jersey Clay Products" (date unknown).

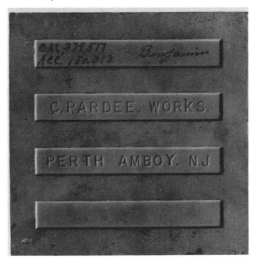

Pardee mark. (The Smithsonian Institution)

PARK LANE POTTERY: See New Milford Pottery
PAUL REVERE POTTERY: See Revere
PAULINE POTTERY

Pauline Pottery was made at two separate factories: one the Chicago-Edgerton establishment from 1883 to 1893, and the other in Edgerton, Wisconsin, from 1902 to 1909. Mrs. Oscar I. (Pauline) Jacobus was one of the many women who became interested in painting china during the last quarter of the century. She not only painted china, but also gave lessons in the art. While studying at the Chicago Art Institute early in the 1880s, Mrs. Jacobus saw an exhibit of Sarah Bernhardt's sculpture. China painting had been interesting, but here was a new tech-

Marks:

Incised.

Incised.

Incised.

nique Mrs. Jacobus could apply to pottery. A short time later, she opened her own studio to make and decorate art pottery.

Her kiln, which had been sufficient for hardening china paints, was not adequate to fire pottery and she set out to learn the proper techniques. She enrolled at Rookwood, the home and studio of Mrs. Maria Longworth Nichols of Cincinnati, Ohio. It was there that she began to learn all the techniques of the pottery business, including mixing clay, shaping, throwing, molding, glazing, and firing.

Mrs. Jacobus's husband was a member of the Chicago Board of Trade. While she was studying in Cincinnati, he wrote her that there was a group of women who planned to open an art pottery studio in Chicago. Mrs. Jacobus was determined to be the first to make art pottery in her hometown, so she rushed back with John Sargent, a qualified kiln maker. In 1883, she sent out invitations for her first exhibit of art pottery in Chicago. The entire pottery staff consisted of Mrs. Jacobus, one presser, and two student decorators. One of her original decorators was a woman named "Springer" (one of her pieces is in the Wisconsin State Historical Society Collection marked with her name and the date, 1883.)

Mrs. Jacobus's pottery was named "Pauline" by Mr. Jacobus, and a few pieces were marked with the script name "Pauline Pottery." At the first exhibit, some Pauline Pottery was purchased by Tiffany of New York, who continued to sell it for many years. Marshall Field of Chicago, and Kimball's of Boston, were two other early retailers of Pauline Pottery.

The early pieces of Pauline Pottery were made of a dense Ohio clay. The clay was shipped to the Chicago pottery and was the only clay used. The glazes were mostly matte and there was much incised and gilded work as buff or red color wares.

The Pauline Pottery Company operated from a small Chicago shop from 1883 to 1888. It was overcrowded and the student decorators were soon replaced by a staff of artists. It was apparent that the operation would soon have to move to larger quarters.

Mr. Jacobus had heard about a bed of superior pottery clay 125 miles from Chicago near Edgerton, Wisconsin. The clay had been used from the 1850s to make building bricks. But a layer of cream-colored clay that was discovered beneath the brick clay was what interested the Jacobuses. The advantage of building a pottery near the clay and not having to ship clay from Ohio was obvious to both of them. In November, 1887, Mr. Jacobus met with several men from Edgerton and convinced them of the economic soundness of pottery. A contract he held from the Bell Telephone Company to make porous battery cups would give employment to about thirty men. Also, the fame of Pauline Pottery and its sales were known, so many of Edgerton's businessmen were interested. Three men, W. W. Babcock, F. W. Coon, and Andrew Jenson went to Chicago and reported back that it seemed a worthwhile business venture. Eleven thousand dollars was raised in two weeks and a final eight thousand dollars was soon added, probably by Mr. Jacobus. The pottery corporation was formed with W. W. Babcock, president; C. F. Mabbett, vice president; and Thomas Hutson, treasurer; plus five directors: O. I. Jacobus, J. P. Towne, Andrew Jenson, Henry Marsden, and M. L. Pelton. The Pauline Pottery was incorporated on February 14, 1888 with capital stock of twenty thousand dollars (when the extra thousand dollars was raised is unknown.) The stock was divided into four hundred shares of fifty dollars each. The E. C. Hopkins Warehouse was purchased by the end of March, and John Sargent was hired from Cincinnati to built the kilns. He built four, three cone-shaped for the battery cups and one square kiln for firing the art pottery at a different temperature. Claywashers, pressers, lathes, a forty-horsepower engine, and all the other needed machinery were purchased. Mr. Jacobus was the superintendent of the battery cup works on the first and second floor, and Mrs. Jacobus continued to make her art pottery on the third floor.

Incised (used after 1891).

Thirteen ladies were hired to decorate the art pottery. All of the decoration was underglaze and the painting was done in mineral colors with a brush in what contemporary artists called the Japanese style.

Twenty-two other people were employed at the firm. In 1891, Thorwald P. A. Samson and Louis Ipson came from Denmark. Samson was an artist and modeler; Ipson a molder; most of the Pauline pottery at the time was made in molds. The two Danes worked only a year and then formed the American Art Clay Works in Edgerton, Wisconsin, making terra-cotta figures and busts of local red clay.

An interesting sidelight in the history of the Pauline Pottery is the part played by Wilder Pickard of Pickard China. Pickard saw some Pauline pottery in Marshall

Incised.

Incised.

Mark of the Edgerton Pottery Company. Not a Pauline Pottery mark.

Field's. He contacted the pottery and in March of 1889 was given a contract to sell the decorated ware in Indiana, Michigan, Illinois, Missouri, Iowa, Wisconsin, and Minnesota. Before he became their sales agent, the pottery had been sold only to order restricted to a few of the larger cities. There is a note reported in the *Wisconsin Tobacco Reporter,* Edgerton, Wisconsin, Nov. 20, 1891, that in November of 1891, "Mr. Pickard has sold more goods for the Pottery this season, than all other years put together."

In May of 1893, Mr. Jacobus died and the business ran into problems. The battery cup part of the business lost money because the dry cell battery had been invented and the demand for cups fell. There were also some problems regarding a patent infringement. Mrs. Jacobus lost control of the business and in May of 1894, five of the stockholders of the original Pauline Pottery of Edgerton incorporated as the Edgerton Pottery Company and continued to use the plant. They made an artware of lower quality than the Pauline Pottery and the business failed. By 1902, the original plant was sold for scrap value and the Edgerton businessmen who had financed the factory lost all of their investment.

Mrs. Jacobus bought the kiln and remaining clay at the sale. She could not find a kiln builder so she marked each brick of the kiln and with the help of a local brickmason rebuilt it in the backyard of "The Bogert," the family home. She put the clay and potter's wheel in the basement of the house. Decorating and glazing was done in a low building at the back of the yard. Some of the clay supposedly was dug from the flower beds behind the house.

Mrs. Jacobus was able to do every job connected with making art pottery. She hired student decorators and in the summer ran a type of boardinghouse. The following appeared in *Sketch Book,* Vol. 5, 1906: "PAULINE POTTERY, near Edgerton, Wisconsin, study and recreation combined, summer school during July for practical instruction in art of Pottery. Number of pupils limited, for rates and further particulars address Mrs. Pauline Jacobus." The course cost twenty dollars for four weeks plus seven dollars for room and board. The boardinghouse-pottery was well run and had many Chicago guests. Mrs. Jacobus made the pottery forms in the summer and did the decorating, firing, and glazing during the winter. This small studio version of the Pauline Pottery continued from 1902 to 1909 when Mrs. Jacobus closed the pottery operation. During the years she worked with clay she washed, molded, threw, cast, glazed, decorated, and filled and fired the kiln. The heavy manual labor required to fill and lift the saggars and to seal and brick the kiln was quite an accomplishment for a woman.

She was such a proper Chicago lady, with such formal manners, that the locals rather feared her. When her house caught fire on July 19, 1911, a young man pounded on her door to tell her. But evidently by the time he overcame his timidity and told his story the fire had got out of control. The house was totally destroyed, leaving only the kiln and the log cabin where she had sold some of the seconds. Mrs. Jacobus then went to live with her daughter and son-in-law, Jenny and John Coons. When they moved to Texas Mrs. Jacobus went with them but she returned to Edgerton in 1927 for a visit. The last few years of her life were spent in the Masonic Home at Dousman, Wisconsin. She died in 1930, and is buried in Oak Woods Cemetery, Chicago, in the Dow Bogert vault.

Product

The variety of wares produced at the Pauline Pottery in Chicago as well as at Edgerton makes it difficult to cite one or two types as characteristic. The early pieces made from Ohio clay were heavy and grayish in body color. Matte glazes were preferred. At the same time, a redware was made that was decorated with incised designs, then gilded over the glaze.

The clay from the beds at Edgerton was considered a yellow clay, but it fired to a near white color. Many of the pieces appeared light yellow because of a transparent lead glaze that was applied over the painted decoration. The decoration was always underglaze. The clay body was soft, as the pottery was fired at a low temperature. A chip shows a chalk-colored base with a pale honey-yellow glaze. The glaze very often "crazed." The fine network of lines on the glaze was caused by what a potter would call a poor "fit"; the glaze and the clay expanded at different rates causing the crazed surface. These lines have often allowed water to seep into the clay body. Some pieces are badly discolored because water has remained in a bowl that was used for flowers or other such purpose.

The pale yellow pieces decorated with colors reminded some early contemporary experts of old Italian faience. Designs of garlands, scrolls, and griffons, dragons, flowers and fruits add to this effect. Bertha Jaques in *Sketch Book,*

Decorators' Marks:

Unknown decorator.

Unknown decorator.

E A H

Eugenia A. Hutchinson.

Fannie

Scratched on bottom of piece.

Unknown.

Unknown.

Vol. 5, June, 1906 features a picture of such a pitcher, numbered 18.

A dark blue to green glaze was another popular style. The color seems to have been sprayed onto the pieces. The blue green wares are known from 1906 and earlier. Other pieces were of brown into yellow, yellow into dull green, olive green into rose pink, or dark blue into rose pink.

The underglaze decorations were of many types. Floral patterns of a characteristic style were done with freehand brush painting. The flowers were outlined with a thin black line. Often designs seemed to "bleed," which was the result of glaze flooding, and was not intentional. Nearly all Pauline decorations have a "pattern book" quality, although some are drawn with more freedom. Most pieces were made with the yellow-toned glaze and decorated with flowers in muted tones, with everything outlined in black. Some wares had raised leaves or heads that protruded from the sides of the vases in high relief. Another type of ware reminded purchasers in the early 1900s of the majolica ware of the 1880 period. Sponged or brushed gilding was often used on the edges or around the decorations. The gilding was put on over the glaze. A red-brown band that shades from the rim into the base was also popular.

Pauline pottery was made with two firings. First the body clay was fired to bisque, then decorated, glazed, and fired the second time. Because each piece was decorated by hand, no two are exactly alike, even though some designs were repeated over and over.

A few pieces that were made of red clay are known. This is a local Edgerton clay and is traditionally thought to have been dug from the garden at Bogert.

Marks

The most familiar mark on Pauline Pottery is the crown made from two "P"s, one of them reversed. The mark was not recorded with federal copyrights prior to 1891, but it was probably used before that date. The mark was originally inscribed by hand. It may have been used in Chicago, but so far no records have appeared to prove this. The frustrating aspect of dating by mark is that a piece occasionally appears to confuse the records. The State Historical Society of Wisconsin at Madison owns a bowl with a high relief band of oak leaves and a matte glaze. It is marked with the printed crown and a shape number 166, but it is not made from Edgerton clay. It may have been that some Ohio clay was sent to Edgerton, although there is no record that this was done. It may even be an Ohio clay piece from the Chicago period.

The crown mark appears either with "o" "p" or "c" in the center. The words "Trade mark" appear with the crown after 1891.

Early pieces had the name of the pottery stamped or incised by hand. Later ones were sometimes in blue or green underglaze. There were model numbers (the smaller the number, the older the piece) as well as decorators' symbols or initials on some pieces. A few pieces were made with the name Pauline Pottery and a date. One known piece is marked in this manner and dated 1883. A large covered vase at the State Historical Society of Wisconsin and a rose jar with lid at the Neville Public Museum are marked with the crown and the words "trade mark" and "made for M.F. & Co" meaning made for Marshall Field of Chicago.

Many books have erroneously listed a different crown with the letter "G" in the center. There is no evidence that this was a Pauline Pottery mark.

Artists' signature marks are still, in most cases, unidentified. Many of the artists and students were trained at the Chicago Art Institute.

> Other decorators: N. F. Mears (appears on a plaque); T. H. Samson 1899 (appears on a plaque), L. H. Towne (appears following the word "Copyright" on a plate); and Mary Thompson (no marked example known).

Bibliography

Allan, Alice, "Pauline Pottery" (undated article).

Barber, Edwin, *The Pottery and Porcelain of the United States*, New York: G. P. Putnam's Sons, 1909, pp. 332–337, 431.

Dearolf, Kenneth N., correspondence with authors.

Jaques, Bertha, "The American Potteries—The Pauline Pottery," *Sketch Book* (V. 5), (June, 1906) 377–381.

Platt, Dorothy Pickard, *The Story of Pickard China*, Hanover, Pennsylvania: Everybodys Press, Inc., 1970.

Severa, Mrs. Joan, correspondence with authors.

Shull, Thelma, "The Pauline Pottery," *Hobbies* (V. 48) (October, 1943), 56–58.

Sketch Book (V. 5) (1906).

Whyte, Bertha Kitchell, "Pauline Pottery of Edgerton, Wisconsin" *Spinning Wheel* (April, 1958), 24–26, 38.

The Pauline Pottery made this gray covered jar and plate. The jar is 7⅛ inches in diameter. Both bear the crown mark over 136. (The Smithsonian Institution, Washington, D.C.)

A hand-painted jardiniere by Peters and Reed Pottery Company as shown in *Pottery and Glass,* June, 1909.

PAUL REVERE POTTERY. See REVERE

PETERS AND REED

John D. Peters and Adam Reed founded the Peters and Reed Pottery Company in 1897. The two men had been working for Sam Weller and decided to open their own pottery company. They started in an old building that had been used by the Clark Stoneware Company. The building was rented from a bank with a "buy later" option. The Roseville Pottery bought the plant when the Peters and Reed Company could not raise the money.

Peters and Reed Pottery was incorporated in 1901, with Adam Reed president and J. D. Peters treasurer. The firm worked at a new location in South Zanesville. They made flowerpots at first because there was a ready market: the Weller factory had stopped making flowerpots about 1897 and began concentrating on the manufacturing of art pottery. After a short while, Peters and Reed added jardinieres with painted decorations. To improve the quality of their pottery, they asked Frank Ferrell, one

(At Bottom) *Top, left to right:* Light green appliqué man smoking pipe on dark brown ground, 4 inches high, 5½ inches wide; green wreath around lion's head appliqué on dark brown ground, 2½ inches high, 4 inches wide; red and green floral appliqué on brown ground, 6 inches high, 5 inches wide; red and green appliqué on dark green ground, 3 inches high, 5 inches wide; gold lion's head with grapevine appliqué on dark green ground, 4 inches high, 4 inches wide. *Bottom:* Light green wreath appliqué on dark green ground, 9 inches high, 4 inches wide; red and green cherry sprig on dark brown ground, 9 inches high, 4 inches wide; ram's head appliqué on brown to green ground, 4½ inches high, 4 inches wide; yellow lion's head and red and green appliqué on dark brown ground, 14 inches high, 8 inches wide. All of the pieces are Peters and Reed. (From the collection of J. Walter Yore Company, Toledo, Ohio)

(Above) This "sewer tile" vase is brick red with green glaze. It has raised roses as the decoration. The piece is 12 inches high. Although the bottom is unmarked, notice the name Ferrell as part of the design on the front of the vase. (Authors' collection)

Three pages from an undated Peters and Reed Pottery Company catalogue (ca. 1910) showing three types of wares. (Ohio Historical Society Library)

This 5-inch-diameter bowl is brick red with green. It has a glossy interior. The piece is marked "Zane Ware, Made in USA" in a rectangular arrangement (Authors' collection)

The impressed Zane Ware mark and cipher.

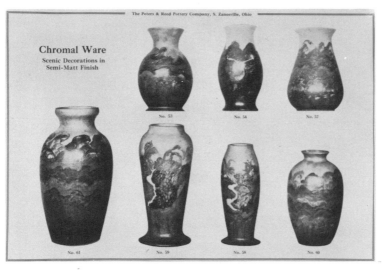

(Above) Zane Ware vase with Landsun glaze in shades of blue and yellow. The vase is 6¾ inches high. It is signed. (Authors' collection)

(Right) An undated Gonder Ceramic catalogue page. (Ohio Historical Society Library)

(Above) Zane Ware vase with Landsun glaze in shades of blue and yellow. The vase is 6¾ inches high. It is signed. (Authors' collection)

of the designers at Weller, to sell them some ideas. In 1905, when Ferrell left Weller, he did some designing for Peters and Reed, later becoming a full-time salesman and designer for them. In 1917, Ferrell went to work for the Roseville Pottery.

Moss Aztec was the most famous line that Ferrell designed for Peters and Reed. It had a red clay body that was glazed and then dipped in a mixture of paraffin and coal oil, which gave the piece a green cast. The 1921 catalogue describes it as "The quiet effect of the rich red brown tones of the Historic Aztec Indians coupled with the apparent mossy deposit of nature."

The firm made many other lines that also sold well. The description in the catalogue of some of the wares reads:

Chromal."The Chromal ware resembles the landsun line with the exception that beautiful scenic effects are portrayed in a very effective manner."

Landsun."The Landsun ware is finished in blended effects of different colors, which makes many very beautiful pieces, each piece being different."

Montene."The Montene ware is made in two decorations. The rich copper bronze iridescent and the green variegated semi-matte finish."

Pereco."The Pereco ware has a semi-matte finish, in plain green, orange, and blue colors, which harmonize with any scheme of decorations."

Persian."The Persian ware is made in blue and brown, plain semi-matte finish."

Adam Reed and Harry S. McClelland (then the company secretary) bought the plant in 1920. They changed the name to the Zane Pottery Company. See *Zane Pottery* and *Gonder Pottery.*

Bibliography

Barber, Edwin, *The Pottery and Porcelain of the United States,* New York: G. P. Putnam's Sons, 1909.

Clark, Edna Marie, *Ohio Art & Artists,* Richmond, Garrett, and Massie, 1932, p. 170.

Gonder catalogs, 1943, 1950, others undated.

Peters & Reed Pottery Company, The, undated catalog.

Pottery and Glass, "Peters & Reed Pottery Co." (V. 2, No. 6.), (June, 1909) p. 302.

Schneider, Norris F., "Lawton Gonder," *Zanesville Times Signal* (September 22, 1957) page unknown.

_____, "LePere Plant," *Zanesville Times Signal* (November 11, 1956) page unknown.

_____, "Peters & Reed Pottery," *Zanesville Times Signal* (September 15, 1957), page unknown.

Zanesville Chamber of Commerce, booklet, 1918.

PEWABIC POTTERY

Many of the famous American art potteries, such as the Pewabic Pottery of Detroit, Michigan, were started by talented women. Pewabic Pottery was founded by Mary Chase Perry (Stratton). She was born in Hancock, Michi-

Impressed in the ware.

MCP

Initials for Mary Chase Perry.

PEWABIC DETROIT

Impressed.

Also used was "PEWABIC POTTERY DETROIT." A few museum quality pieces were marked "M1M2," especially labeled for Mr. Freer.

(Below right) Mary Chase Perry at work in her studio. (*Keramic Studio*, February, 1905)   (Below left) Flowing matte glazes on vases by Miss Perry. Notice the lamp on the right in the doorway. (*Keramic Studio*, February, 1905)

gan, in 1868. After her father was killed (murdered by a man who mistook him for someone else), her mother moved the family to Ann Arbor, Michigan, and then to Detroit.

Miss Perry went to art school in Cincinnati and New York where she worked in clay sculpture and china painting. It was in 1903 that she decided to join her next door neighbor, Horace James Caulkins, and make pottery. Horace Caulkins was in the dental supply business and he had developed a kiln for making dental enamel. It was in this kiln that their tiles and vases were fired. The first shop was built in a coach house at the back of a mansion located at John R. and Alfred streets in Detroit. The name Pewabic was the Indian name for a nearby river and it was only after many years that Miss Perry learned Pewabic meant "copper color in clay."

Miss Perry wrote in an article (*American Ceramic Society Bulletin,* October 15, 1946, Vol. 25, No. 10) that at first she had no training and just experimented with the glazes. The first items made at the pottery were bowls and jars characterized by a dark green matte glaze. These were ordered by a Mr. Burleigh, a Chicago dealer, for one thousand dollars. She also sold an architect some three-by-six-inch tiles with rounded edges and uneven surfaces.

(Right bottom) A Pewabic "Crocus" vase made about 1900. It is 3⅝₁₆ inches high. (Collections of Greenfield Village and the Henry Ford Museum, Dearborn, Michigan)   (Top left) This vase with modeled decorations of tulips and leaves was covered with a green matte glaze. Made by Miss Perry about 1903–1905, it is marked with the impressed "Pewabic" in an arc surmounted by five flames. (The Art Museum, Princeton University, Princeton, New Jersey) (Top center) This iridescent glazed vase in tones of gold, purple, gray, and green was made about 1914. It is 10 inches high. (Newark Museum, Newark, New Jersey)   (Top right) Gold iridescent glaze over blue glaze decorates this 18¾-inch vase made about 1910–1912. (The Detroit Institute of Arts, Gift of Charles L. Freer)   (Right center) This 4¾-inch-high Pewabic vase has an iridescent heavy glaze of tan, white, and yellow shades that flowed to form irregularities on the surface. The vase was purchased by Potter and Mellen, Cleveland, about 1920. The artists at the store made a brass cover with a citrine quartz handle, and the finished piece was sold. (Authors' collection)

(Top left) Brown and yellow glazes were used on this Pewabic pottery vase made about 1905. It is 4½ inches high. (The Smithsonian Institution)   (Top right) *Left:* An 11½-inch-high vase with blue-black glaze and iridescent markings. *Center:* A pear-shaped vase, 13⁵⁄₁₆ inches high, with greenish-black matte glaze and a slightly pitted surface. *Right:* A matte brown glaze under a lavender drip glaze on a 9½-inch Pewabic Pottery vase. All three are marked "Pewabic Detroit." (The Detroit Institute of Arts, Detroit)   (Left) This 1925 Pewabic vase is 8⁵⁄₁₆ inches high. (Collections of Greenfield Village and the Henry Ford Museum, Dearborn, Michigan)   (Bottom left) This Pewabic vase was made about 1925. It is 9½ inches high. (Collections of Greenfield Village and the Henry Ford Museum, Dearborn, Michigan)   (Bottom center) A 1930 Pewabic vase, height 4⁹⁄₁₆ inches. (Collections of Greenfield Village and the Henry Ford Museum, Dearborn, Michigan)   (Bottom right) A Pewabic tile, 6¹⁄₁₆ inches square, dated 1930. (Collections of Greenfield Village and the Henry Ford Museum, Dearborn, Michigan)

And small square jars with covers were made in a tile machine using the clay dust method. The machine was operated by hand. Varying shrinkages made the fit of the covers an unsure thing and it was often hard to find the right lid for a jar. The jars were made with a shiny dark blue glaze and sent to South America, filled with cosmetics.

In 1907, Perry and Caulkins built an English-type studio and laboratory building. They bought a miniature Crossley clay outfit from the Chicago Fair and set it up in the basement. Three years later, they had a full-size blunger, filter press, and pug mill.

Their pottery gained fame throughout the world, especially for its tiles. Building friezes and panels of colored mosaic with matte glaze were made for Ford buildings in Detroit, New York, Brooklyn, Omaha, and San Francisco. Tiles were made for St. Paul's Cathedral in Detroit, and floors and decorations were made for churches in Pittsburgh, Evanston, St. Paul, Philadelphia, and Washington; an irregular tesserae ceiling was made for the Oberlin College Art Gallery, Oberlin, Ohio; fountains, alcoves and stair risers for the Detroit Institute of Art; and faience tiles and trim for the Union Guardian Building in Detroit. The pottery also made elaborate bathroom, fireplace, and floor tiles, and fountains, friezes, and entrance doorways for shops, church altars and even swimming pools.

Mary Perry married William Buck Stratton in 1918. She continued her work at the pottery and decorated her home with tiles. Horace Caulkins died in 1923 and Mrs. Stratton ran the Pewabic Pottery alone. Several of the most important orders for tile for building interiors came after this. The depression affected the pottery and in 1931 orders were scarce, but through Mrs. Stratton's efforts, the pottery continued. The Strattons moved from their large home to a small one in 1937 and a year later Mr. Stratton died in a streetcar accident.

Ira Peters and his wife, Ella, worked with Mary Stratton at the pottery until her death in 1961. The Pewabic Pottery became the property of the Michigan State University and has been continued as an adult ceramic center and museum.

Product

About 1903, Mary Perry developed an iridescent glaze that was one of the most famous glazes used by the Pewabic Pottery. It was still being used when she died.

The pottery had a hard white body covered with heavy opaque enamels of many colors. The clay was fired at a high temperature and was so hard, that it was, one article claimed, "neither earthenware nor Porcelain" (*American Pottery Gazette,* Vol. V, No. VI, August 10, 1907). It was made from clay from Florida, Michigan, North Carolina, and Virginia, and some from England. Ivory, brown, blue, and gray glazes were used, usuallly in matte finish. Other pieces were green, purple, yellow or white. On some pieces crystalline spots of a light color were found. Some examples had a heavy glaze that trickled down the side of the vase. Other early wares were decorated with relief forms of leaves and plants with a dull matte glaze.

In the early days of the Pewabic Pottery prior to 1910, when these glazes were first being used, Miss Perry and Mr. Caulkins employed a man to throw the forms on a wheel and an errand boy who did much of the other routine work. Miss Perry was the artist and did all of the high relief decorations and designs.

She continued experimenting with glazes through the years and kept some of the best pieces for collector Charles Lang Freer. Many of these examples eventually were given to museums. Her famed blue jar in the Peacock Room of the Freer Gallery in Washington was one of these special pieces.

Although vases were made through all the years of the pottery, the only dishes produced were a set for Teacher's

(Above) Bas-relief of a lunette in the Della Robbia manner made for the Church of the Most Holy Redeemer, Detroit, Michigan. (*The American Magazine of Art,* January, 1926)   (Right) A Pewabic tile in the wall decoration of the shrine of the Immaculate Conception, Washington, D.C. (*The American Magazine of Art,* January, 1926)

(Left) Storytelling tiles made by the Pewabic Pottery adorn this fireplace in the Children's Room of the Detroit Public Library. (*The American Magazine of Art*, January, 1926)

(Left) This fireplace is still to be seen at Stan Hywet Hall, Akron, Ohio. It was ordered from the Pewabic Pottery August 4, 1915: "Frank Seiberling, Akron Ohio porch floor and Fountain at about $1,350.00." It is thought to represent the legend of St. Keyne. The fountain was made by Mrs. Stratton, and records still exist to show her notes and thoughts. She also made the tile floor of the Della Robbia room, and the tiles for a bathroom at the house. (Stan Hywet Hall, Akron, Ohio)
(Right) Detail of the fountain. (Stan Hywet Hall, Akron, Ohio)

College at Columbia University. The Pewabic Pottery made sixty dozen plates, cups, and saucers, with a broad blue band, to signify the Palisades, and a green wavy line below to symbolize the Hudson River.

The architectural features and tiles made by Mrs. Stratton were always specially designed and the architects knew her designs would be suitable.

Two lamps made by Mary Chase Perry pictured in *Keramic Studio*, February, 1905. The lamp on the top has three peacocks with tails forming the base. The shade is decorated with eyes of the feathers in golden brown glass. The bottom lamp is decorated with the leaf stems and puff balls of the dandelion. The glass shade is made with a pale blue ground and deep blue flowers with fine leading.

Pewabic mosaics were made in a unique manner. "The Pewabic mosaic is made with a clay body, with or without sand or grog, and comes out of the kiln in long strips, in an unglazed, a bright glazed and an iridescent glazed state. The long strips, about three-eighths of an inch wide, are broken into little squares which are pasted face up (an improvement on the old method of pasting them face down) on the design, and are arranged and rearranged by the artist until the desired color effect is obtained. When the design is perfected, a paper is pasted on the face, the first paper sponged off and the sheet pressed into cement." (*American Magazine,* Art, Vol. 17, January, 1926.)

Bibliography

Antiques, "Ceramics" (March, 1965), 324.

———, "Pewabic Pottery Detroit" (June, 1966), 849.

Art Digest, "Pewabic" (V. 3), (June, 1929) 20.

Benjamin, Marcus, "American Art Pottery—Part III," *Glass and Pottery World* (April, 1907), 35.

Binns, Charles F., "Pottery in America," *The American Magazine of Art* (V. 7, No. 4), (February, 1916), 131.

Bulletin of the Department of Commerce and Labor, "American Art Pottery," *American Pottery Gazette* (V. V, No. VI), (August 10, 1907).

Clark, Robert Judson, *The Arts and Crafts Movement in America* 1876–1916, Princeton, N.J.: Princeton University Press, 1972, pp. 173–175.

Dimit, Robert L., correspondence with authors.

Flu, E. B., "The Pewabic Pottery at Detroit—A Unique Institution," *The Ceramic Age* (January, 1927), 13–16.

Hegarty, Marjorie, "Pewabic Pottery," *Detroit Institute of Arts Bulletin* (V. XXVI, No. 2), (1947), 69–70.

Holden, Marion L., "The Pewabic Pottery," *The American Magazine of Art* (V. 17), (January, 1926), 22.

Impresario, Magazine of the Arts, "Michigan State University Revives Pewabic Pottery" (February–March, 1968), 16.

Keramic Studio, "Mary Chase Perry, Potter," (V. 6), February, 1905), 219.

Lacey, Betty, "Pewabic Pottery in Detroit," *National Antiques Review* (March, 1971), 22.

National Antiques Review, "Letters to the Editor" (June, 1971), 6.

Pottery Collectors' Newsletter, "Pewabic Pottery, An Introduction to the MSU/Pewabic Pottery" (V. 1, No. 10), (July, 1972), 135.

Stratton, Mary Chase, "Pewabic" *American Ceramic Society Bulletin* (V. 25, No. 10), (October 15, 1946).

PISGAH FOREST POTTERY

Walter Benjamin Stephen was born in Clinton, Iowa, on October 3, 1876. His family moved to Chadron, Nebraska, when he was ten. Both of his parents were artistic; his father was a stonecutter and his mother an artist. After ten years in Nebraska the family moved to western Tennessee. There Walter and his father, Andrew, were stonemasons. In 1901, they dug a well and found a clay that was of an unusual color. Walter and his mother made boxes and figures from the clay. They built a kiln and a kick wheel and the two experimented with the making of pottery.

They called the firm the Nonconnah Pottery. Mrs. Stephen decorated the pieces with raised designs of light clay. Her decorations included covered wagons, Indians, buffalo hunts, and other early American scenes.

Walter Stephen's parents died in 1910, and by the summer of 1913, he moved near the foot of Mount Pisgah in North Carolina. C. P. Ryman became his partner and the two men built a shop and kiln. They dissolved the partnership in 1916.

Walter Stephen began to experiment with pottery again in 1920 and by 1926 had his own pottery, with equipment to make his fire-vitrified ware. Walter Stephen died in 1961 but the Pisgah Pottery continued in business under the direction of Tom Case and Grady Ledbetter. The firm is still working, though part time.

Product

The early pieces made by Walter Stephen were dark glazed pots with cameolike decorations. Dark green, blue, and other colors were used for the background, with white decorations. One type of Pisgah Forest Pottery was made with a crystalline glaze in ivory, silver, or other shades. The general line of pottery was glazed turquoise, or wine, the most popular colors ivory, pink, green, yellow, and brown.

All marks were raised and several variations used: with or without the potter figure and with or without the name Stephen. These are dated 1931, 1934, and 1937.

This mottled vase has green and maroon specks in the glaze. It is 6½ inches in diameter, 5½ inches high. It bears the impressed mark showing the man at the forge and "Pisgah, 1937." (Authors' collection)

The pottery made vases, teapots, jugs, candlesticks, tea sets, mugs, bowls, and even miniature cream and sugar sets.

Early pieces were marked "Stephen" or "W. B. Stephen." After 1926, the Pisgah pieces were marked "Pisgah Forest." Some were marked with the picture of a potter at his wheel. All of the marks were raised on the piece.

(A source of confusion for the pottery collector may be other potters who worked in the Pisgah Mountain area. O. L. Bachelder made pottery during the same years, but even though it was made at Mount Pisgah, it was called Omar Khayyam Pottery.)

Bibliography

Camp, Helen B., "A Craftsman of the Old School," *International Studio* (V. 78), (October, 1923) 54.

Duvall, Mrs. Lawrence, correspondence with authors.

Johnston, Pat H., "O. L. Bachelder Omar Khayyam Pottery," *Pottery Collectors' Newsletter* (V. 1, No. 11), (August, 1972) 145–148.

Ledbetter, Grady G., and J. T. Case, correspondence with authors.

Ray, Marcia, "Pisgah Forest Pottery," *Spinning Wheel* (January–February, 1971), 16.

Monogram of Clara L. Poillon. It was also used without the circle.

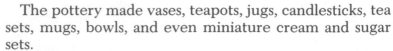

POILLON POTTERY

The Poillon Pottery was founded in Woodbridge, New Jersey, about 1904. Mrs. Clara L. Poillon and H. A. Poillon ran the pottery, which made a variety of ware like majolica, with blue, green, or yellow glazes. Gold luster, orange luster, and matte glazes were also used. The pottery garden tubs were made in red or cream terra-cotta with bold relief carvings. The firm also made breakfast and luncheon sets, lamps, and vases.

The Poillon Pottery exhibited at the Art Palace at the St. Louis Exposition in 1904. They showed a vase by Joseph Insco and a jardiniere by T. H. Pond (Keramic Studio No. 6, April, 1905).

Poillon Pottery red terra-cotta tub to be used on a terrace. (*Arts and Decoration*, August, 1911)

Bibliography

Keramic Studio, "Poillon Pottery" (V. 6), (April, 1905).

(Right) Raised figures of men seated at a table decorate this Poillon Pottery vase. The piece is 12½ inches high. It has a yellowish brown crackled glaze. See picture below of mark that appeared on the bottom of the vase. (The Smithsonian Institution)

Noel, Margaret, "Work of American Potters, Article V. Poillon Pottery Indoors and Out," *Arts and Decoration* (V. 7), (August, 1911), 412.

POTTERY CLUB OF CINCINNATI

The beginning of art pottery in America was probably in Cincinnati, Ohio, at a ladies' china-painting meeting. Benn Pitman of the Cincinnati School of Design started a class for a group of ladies in 1874. His school did not have china painting as part of the curriculum, so he hired Maria Eggers as a teacher and formed a class in his office after school hours. The original members of the class were Mrs. William Dodd, Mrs. George Dominick, Mrs. E. G. Leonard, Miss Charlotte Keenan, Miss Florence Leonard, Miss Clara Newton, Miss Georgie Woollard, and Miss M. Louise McLaughlin.

The painting done by the group was an overglaze decoration on porcelain. It was a popular pastime for the ladies of the day.

The instructor, Edwin Griffith, began his class in overglaze painting in 1877. He had a room with an oven to fire the work in a building on Fifth and Race streets. That same year, one of the students, Miss McLaughlin, published a book about china painting on porcelain. She also began experimenting in an attempt to make pottery similar to some she had seen at the Centennial Exhibition of 1876 in Philadelphia. The French pottery that she saw was produced at the Haviland Factory and was made by artists as one-of-a-kind pieces. Miss McLaughlin had some success and a few pieces were made in 1877. She worked on her pottery at the firm of P. L. Coultry and Company, whose staff helped her, as did Joseph Bailey and his son Joseph of the Dallas Pottery Co.

Miss McLaughlin obtained some colored glazes from Paris but also tried some of the glazes from Coultry and Company. Her clay came from Ohio. She finally was able to make some pottery that could be shown at the Paris Exposition of 1878. A deep blue colored faience vase with underglaze decoration was given an honorable mention, although it has been said that it had earned a medal until the judges learned the maker was a woman.

(Above) *Left:* The white background of this plate is decorated with painted blue underglaze decorations. It was made in 1877 and is 8 inches in diameter. A paper label on the plate says this is the first successful piece of underglaze blue decoration made by M. Louise McLaughlin. *Right:* The 10¼-inch-high vase is decorated with painted underglaze decorations of the "French style." The flowers are in shades of pink, black, and gray. It was made by M. Louise McLaughlin about 1877. (Cincinnati Art Museum)   (Left) M. Louise McLaughlin made this vase about 1880. It is called the Ali Baba vase and was one of three of this large size (37¼ inches high) made in 1880. The underglaze decoration represents hibiscus flowers in red and yellow against a shaded green background. (Cincinnati Art Museum)

Encouraged by her success, Miss McLaughlin founded the Pottery Club of Cincinnati which was composed of twelve women, later increased to twenty-five. Two kilns were built for firing at the Frederick Dallas Pottery in 1879. This and other expenses were paid by Miss McLaughlin and Mrs. Maria Longworth Nichols. Mrs. Nichols was not a member of the club, but she later became the founder of the Rookwood Factory (see the entry for Rookwood Pottery). It was the work of the club that led to many of the other art pottery factories in the Cincinnati area. The members of the Pottery Club often signed their names or initials to their work. The original members were Miss McLaughlin, Miss Clara Chipman Newton, Miss Alice B. Holabird, Mrs. E. G. Leonard, Mrs. Charles Kebler, Mrs. George Dominick, Mrs. Walter Field, Miss Florence Carlisle, Miss Agnes Pitman, Miss Fannie M. Banks, Mrs. Andrew B. Merriam and one vacancy believed to be for Mrs. Nichols. Honorary members were Mrs. M. V. Keenan, Miss Laura Fry, and Miss Elizabeth Nourse. Mrs. W. P. Hulbert, Mrs. C. A. Plimpton, Mrs. Adelaide Nourse, Mrs. D. Meredith, Miss Hennrietta Leonard, Mrs. William Dodd, Mrs. Frank R. Ellis, and Miss

(Above) Maria Longworth Storer made this vase in 1897. The modeled decoration depicts three seahorses. The seven-inch-high vase is covered with dark red glaze. It has a painted mark, "M.L.S. 1897." (Cincinnati Art Museum)   (Top right) Laura A. Fry made this pitcher in 1881 while with the Cincinnati Pottery Club. The pitcher has blue decorations and is incised on the bottom with the cipher "LAF, 1881, Cin. Pottery Club." (Cincinnati Art Museum)

(Bottom right) Mrs. C. A. Plimpton made this 16½-inch vase in 1881 as a member of the Cincinnati Pottery Club. Her husband designed the Arabian scene. The design was made by inlaying colored clays into the body of the piece. The clays in tones of cream, brown, and terra-cotta came from Ohio; the black clay came from Indiana. (Cincinnati Art Museum)

K. DeGolter were other women who exhibited Cincinnati Art Pottery of the same type. This last group either worked in the same building or may have been later members of the club, although each of the artists worked in a unique style. Pieces of work by the Pottery Club of Cincinnati members are usually without any mark to indicate their group's affiliation. All the pieces were of either red, yellow, or cream Ohio clay. Incised work, relief modeling, and glaze designs were used in all colors, including gold. The slip was applied with a brush to a damp clay pot. This was a very different method from that used in France, although the effect was similar. The use of red clay by these ladies was not of importance at first because the clay was completely covered with slip. (The Rookwood artists went back to the red clay and left it exposed so that the new brown red color of the Ohio Art Pottery was developed.) The club was disbanded in 1890 for lack of money.

Miss McLaughlin, an artist of many interests, decided to try to develop a true porcelain from Ohio clay. She built a kiln on her suburban Cincinnati property and began experimenting despite her neighbors' complaints about the smoke. The clay came from the Ohio River Valley, near the Kentucky state line. She made the first pieces of what she called "Losanti" ware in 1900. L'Osantiville was an early name for Cincinnati. Losanti is not an art pottery, but a true porcelain. It was marked with the name Losanti or the initials L M^c L. The porcelain was decorated with relief carving and slip painting under the glaze. Some pieces were made with the colored clay inlay that was known as "grain of rice." The ware had a cutout space which was filled with a translucent glaze. Losantiware was discontinued in 1904.

Miss McLaughlin continued her varied interests. She did wood carving, portrait painting, landscape painting, lace making, embroidery, weaving, and she made art jewelry of metal and stones.

Bibliography

"American Art Pottery," Bulletin of the Department of Commerce and Labor, *American Pottery Gazette,* V (August 10, 1907).

Barber, Edwin A., *The Pottery and Porcelain of the United States,* New York: G. P. Putnam's Sons, 1893 (3d and rev. ed. 1909).

———, *Marks of American Potters.* Philadelphia: Patterson and White, 1904.

Bowdoin, W. G., "Some American Pottery Forms," *The Art Interchange* (April 1903), 87.

Clark, Edna Maria, *Ohio Art and Artists,* Richmond, Virginia: Garrett and Massie, 1932.

Crowley, Lilian H., "It's Now the Potter's Turn," *International Studio,* LXXV (September 1922), 539.

Evans, Paul F., "Cincinnati Faience: An Overall Perspective," *Spinning Wheel,* XXVIII (September 1972), 16–18.

"Field of Art, The—American Pottery," *Scribner's Magazine* (March 1903), 381.

Langstroth, T. A., letter to the authors, April 14, 1968.

Little, Flora Townsend, "A Short Sketch of American Pottery," *Art & Archaeology,* XV (May 1923), 219.

"Louise McLaughlin," *Keramic Studio,* XI (March 1906).

Nelson, Marion John, "Indigenous Characteristics in American Art Pottery," *Antiques,* LXXXIX (June 1966), 846.

"Overtures of Cincinnati Ceramics," *Cincinnati Historical Society Bulletin,* XXV (January 1967), 72–84.

Peck, Herbert, *The Book of Rookwood Pottery,* New York: Crown Publishers, Inc., 1968.

Perry, Mrs. Aaron, "Decorative Pottery of Cincinnati," *Harper's New Monthly Magazine,* LXII (May 1881), 834–845.

"Personalities," *Hampton-Columbian Magazine,* XXVII (January 1912), 835–36.

"Rise of the Pottery Industry, The," *The Popular Science Monthly,* XL (December 1891), 158.

Ruge, C., "Development of American Ceramics," *Pottery & Glass,* I (August 1908), 3.

"Some Potters and Their Products," *Craftsman,* IV (1903), 330–33.

A. RADFORD POTTERY

Albert Radford was born in Staffordshire, England, in 1862. He was one of a family of potters dating back many

Albert Radford's letterhead.

generations. Some of the Radford family worked at the Wedgwood factory in England, but it is still uncertain whether Albert Radford had ever worked there or at another pottery in England.

Albert moved to the United States in 1885 and took a job at the Haynes Pottery Company in Baltimore, Maryland. There he met and married Ellen Hackney, another employee of the pottery. A year later, they moved to Trenton, New Jersey, where he worked for the Eagle Pottery Company. While there, Radford received an award for his work from the Pennsylvania Museum and School of Industrial Art.

About 1890 Radford and his family moved to Broadway, Virginia, where he started his own firm, A. Radford Pottery Company. His first pieces came from the kiln in 1891 but the records do not tell what type of pottery was made at this plant.

About 1893 the Radfords moved to Tiffin, Ohio, and Albert began working at the Sanitary Pottery of Tiffin. At the same time, he build a kiln on his own property where he made Radford Tiffin jasperware, which resembled Wedgwood jasperware. The Sanitary Pottery of Tiffin closed about 1898 and Radford moved to Zanesville, Ohio. The city directory of Zanesville first lists Albert Radford in 1901.

Radford worked in Zanesville as a modeler at the S. A. Weller Pottery. He left Weller and went to work as the general manager of the Zanesville Art Pottery. When the Zanesville plant was destroyed by fire in 1901 Radford went to the J. B. Owens Pottery as superintendent and modeler.

He started his own firm again in 1903, the A. Radford Pottery Company of Zanesville, Ohio. (According to Fred W. Radford, Albert Radford's grandson, Albert Radford never worked at this pottery; the work was done by Albert's father, Edward Thomas Radford.) The firm started early in 1903 and by August was sold to the Arc-en-Ceil

Pottery. It is unclear whether the sale had been planned or the Radford Pottery was forced to sell. A trustee handled the sale.

The A. Radford Pottery made Zanesville jasperware. A piece of glazed pottery marked A. Radford Pottery has been located, but it may have been a test piece and not part of the commercial production.

In 1904 Albert Radford left Zanesville for Clarksburg, West Virginia, where he helped establish another pottery. This firm made the Ruko, Radura, and Thera pottery. Radford died in August of 1904. The pottery was also called the A. Radford Pottery Company and it remained in business after his death, until 1912. Albert Haubrich, who had worked for the Weller and Owens potteries, was manager of the decorating department.

Product

The first Radford pottery was the Radford Tiffin jasperware made about 1893. The body of the ware was made from English China clay, English ball clay, silica, barium, and other chemicals. Color was added to the clay. Tiffin jasperware was made in royal blue, light blue, olive green, and two shades of gray. The body of the ware was fine-grained and was either cast or turned. Radford modeled the cameo by hand. A mold was made of clay and plaster and the cameos were cast and put on the jasperware body. Some of the cameos were apparently molded from Wedgwood cameos, but most were designed by Radford.

Tiffin jasperware was sometimes impressed "Radford Jasper," with die-cut letters. Radford made bonbon dishes, jewel boxes, nut bowls, flowerpots, cracker jars, card receivers, plaques, comb trays, pitchers, pin trays, fern dishes, butter dishes, cheese covers, cookie jars, sugar bowls and creamers, and ring stands of Jasperware. All of these items were listed in the Tiffin pottery price list.

Zanesville jasperware was made in 1903 at the plant that became the Arc-en-Ceil Pottery. It was made from ball clay, feldspar, and silica and required less heat in the firing. Most of the cameos were molded with the vase. The cameo was painted with solid colored slip. A few pieces were made with separately cast cameos. These were probably made by Albert's father, Edward Thomas Radford.

Some of these pieces were painted inside with a slip to give the finished piece a different color interior, called "bark" or "orange peel."

A Radford Pottery vase of gray with white raised decorations. It is 7 inches high. Lincoln's profile appears on one side, an eagle on the other. The vase is unmarked except for the number 12 incised on the bottom. (Authors' collection)

Zanesville jasperware was made in royal blue, light blue, olive green, two shades of gray, and sometimes trimmed with pink or light yellow brown. The jasperware was marked with an incised number.

Other wares were made at the Zanesville pottery, possibly as experiments to determine the production for the Clarksburg plant. Listed in the ledgers of 1903 are jasperware, glazed jardinieres, etched vases, blended vases printed in black figures, and pitchers of light green dipped in enamel (*A. Radford Pottery, His Life and Works* by Fred Radford, p. 15).

The Clarksburg factory made several different lines under the direction of Albert Radford. One was Ruko, an art pottery similar to Weller's Louwelsa line. The name Ruko is impressed on the base of most pieces. Another, Radura, was a matte glazed line in green, dark blue, black, light blue, red, pink, yellow, brown, lilac, light lavender, or tan. The glaze was developed by Radford's son, Albert E. Radford. Thera was another of the lines from the Clarksburg plant. It too is a matte glaze, similar to Lonhuda. And Velvety Art Ware was included. It is a colored ware with hand-painted designs. Records show it was made in pink, green, purple, light blue, and yellow green (*A. Radford Pottery, His Life and Works* by Fred Radford, p. 25).

In 1971, Fred Radford, grandson of Albert Radford, started to reproduce the Zanesville jasperware. He used the original molds and original clay formulas and made six different vases. All these pieces are marked as reproductions, dated, and numbered.

Bibliography

Pottery Collectors' Newsletter (April 1972).

————, (September 1972).

Purviance, Evan, "American Art Pottery," *Mid-America Reporter* (November 1972), 7.

Radford, Fred W., *A. Radford Pottery, His Life and Works.* Privately Printed: Fred W. Radford, 1973.

Schneider, Norris F., "Many Small Art Potteries Once Operated in Zanesville," *Zanesville Times Recorder* (February 4, 1962).

Marks:

REDWING STONEWARE

Used between 1878 and 1892.

RED WING

The Red Wing Stoneware Company was started in 1878 in Red Wing, Minnesota. The company went through a

Left to right: Weller pottery Coppertone vase with frog, 9 inches high; Dickensware vase showing Dombey and son, 9 inches; Louwelsa vase, 4½ inches; russet matte vase, 6 inches. (Smithsonian Institution).

Tiles made about 1900 by Moravian Pottery and Tile, Doylestown, Pennsylvania.

(Below left) An incised and carved vase signed Jervis. (Collection of Ann Koepke). (Below center) Pisgah Forest Pottery vase, 14½ inches high. (Smithsonian Institution). (Below right) Rookwood vase showing a full length figure of an Indian. It is called "Pablino Diaz Kiowa." Grace Young decorated the vase in 1901. This same vase was pictured in the book *The Pottery and Porcelain of the United States* by Edwin Barber, page 479, second edition, 1901. (Paul Brunner collection).

Green matte glazed vases, left to right: Teco, 11¼ inches; Fulper, 11¼ inches; Denver, 8½ inches; Grueby, 11½ inches. (Smithsonian Institution).

Brown glazed pieces, left to right: Roseville, signed "RRW," 5¼ inches; Lonhuda, 1893; 5½ inch diameter, Weller, 9 inches; Rookwood, 1901, 5 inches; Owens, signed "JB CH," 5 inches. (Smithsonian Institution).

Left to right: Yellow vase, 3½ inches, Hampshire; dark vase, 7½ inches, Hampshire; fish, 6 inches long, Marblehead; vase, 3¾ inches high, Marblehead; vase drip glaze, 5 inches high, Clifton, 1906. (Smithsonian Institution).

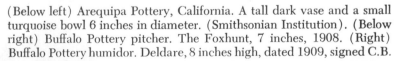

(Below left) Arequipa Pottery, California. A tall dark vase and a small turquoise bowl 6 inches in diameter. (Smithsonian Institution). (Below right) Buffalo Pottery pitcher. The Foxhunt, 7 inches, 1908. (Right) Buffalo Pottery humidor. Deldare, 8 inches high, dated 1909, signed C.B.

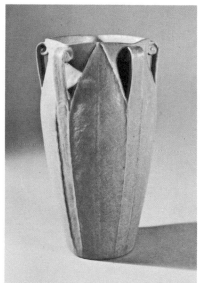

Haviland Art pottery vase. Sang-de-boeuf piece with bronze doré mount, 3½ inches high. Made by Chaplet. (Jean d'Albi, Limoges, France).

(Below left) Buffalo Pottery pitcher. Mason design showing adaptation of Willow pattern. 7 inches. (Below right) Chelsea Keramic Art teapot. 7 inches, olive green, 1880–1888, marked CKAW. (Smithsonian Institution).

(Top) A crystalline glazed Fulper vase, 8½ inches high. (Bottom) Grueby Faience vase, 1897.

(Above left) "Jazz" is a bowl made at the Cowan Pottery by Victor Schreckengost in the 1920s. (Western Reserve Historical Society, Cleveland, Ohio). (Above right) The bowl is 13½ inches by 10 inches wide and 3 inches deep; the cream-colored lady flower holder is 10 inches high. Both are marked Cowan. The rust-colored figure of "Adam" is 13½ inches high. It is signed R. G. Cowan. (Western Reserve Historical Society, Cleveland, Ohio). (Left) "Moses" is the 18½-inch-high brilliant blue figure, designed by Alexander Blazys and made at the Cowan pottery in 1930. The blue Cowan vase made by Edward Winter has an experimental enamel finish. It was unsuccessful because the finish flaked off. It is 5½ inches in diameter and 6¼ inches high. (Western Reserve Historical Society, Cleveland, Ohio).

Middle Lane Pottery (or Brouwer), East Hampton, New York. Pink vase 7½ inches high, center vase 8½ inches high, vase with mouse in cheese, 3½ inches high. (Smithsonian Institution).

Jugtown pottery made in the twentieth century. (North Carolina Museum of Art).

(Above left) Jugtown drip glazed jar, 5⅛ inches high, early twentieth century. (Estate of Miss Esther Bloxton, North Carolina Museum of Art). (Above center) Knowles, Taylor, and Knowles Lotus ware pottery. This vase is called Parmian 500 in the catalogue. (Paul Brunner collection). (Above right) Lotus ware vase, called Syrian 505 in the catalogue. (Paul Brunner collection). (Below left) McCoy jardiniere marked "Loy-Nel-Art," 9 inches high, 11 inches in diameter. (Authors' collection). (Below right) Matt Morgan plaque marked with a paper label. Green iridescent glaze. (Paul Brunner collection).

(Left) Newcomb Pottery. Vase 11¾ inches high signed Mazie T Ryan, about 1897–1910 and vase 8¼ inches high, matte glaze, signed Henrietta Bailey, about 1910. (Smithsonian Institution). (Right) George Ohr puzzle jug in snake decoration, 9¼ inches high. (Authors' collection).

(Left) Pauline pottery unmarked matte glazed plate. (State Historical Society of Wisconsin). (Above) Pauline pottery chocolate pots. (State Historical Society of Wisconsin). (Below left) Pauline pottery pitcher decorated with arabesques and grotesques from William Blake, about 1903. (State Historical Society of Wisconsin). (Below right) Pauline pottery vase of deep blue. Marked with the crown trademark. Made for M. F. & Co., indicating that it was sold by Marshall Field. (State Historical Society of Wisconsin).

(Above left) Mosaic Tile Company tile of Woodrow Wilson. (Mr. and Mrs. Charles Klamkin). (Above center) Matt Morgan bottle. Marked with the incised Matt Morgan mark, a paper label, and the artist's initials DR, 5½ inches high. (Paul Brunner collection). (Right) Owens vase, 13 inches high. (Authors' collection).

(Above left) Roblin redware vase, 2½ inches high. (Smithsonian Institution). (Above right) Roblin vase, 2½ inches high. (Smithsonian Institution). (Left) L. C. Tiffany pottery, New York City, about 1905. (Smithsonian Institution).

(Above) Weller vase, 12¼ inches high. "TA-WITS-NEN-UTE" written in glaze on side. Marked AF Best in the glaze, with "Weller" impressed on the bottom. (Paul Brunner collection). (Right) Weller-Sicard plaque, 13 by 16 inches, iridescent glaze. (Smithsonian Institution). (Below) Weller-Sicard vase, about 1903. It is 26⅝ inches high. (Smithsonian Institution).

Left to right: Weller-Sicard vase, 8½ inches, signed Sicardo on side; Weiller LaSa vase, 8½ inches, paper label; Weller-Sicard vase, 6 inches, signed on side. (Authors' collection).

(Left) Rookwood stein picturing Thomas Jefferson. It is signed "M. A. Daly, 1896." (Collection of Paul Brunner). (Above left) Rookwood mug, 5½ inches high, signed Truesdale, 1892. (Paul Brunner collection). (Above right) Rookwood puzzle mug, 5 inches high, signed "SL" [Sturgis Laurence] after Gritzner," 1899. (Paul Brunner collection).

(Above left) Rookwood vase, "Three Finger Cheyenne," 1899, signed "Hurly, 80 B," 7 inches high. (Paul Brunner collection). (Above right) Rookwood vase, "Eagle Deer Sioux," signed "SL, 1900, 707 AA," 9 inches high. (Paul Brunner collection).

(Right) Rookwood vase, "Rushing Eagle, Sioux," signed "Sturgis Laurence, 1899." (Paul Brunner collection).

(Top left) Rookwood pottery pitcher 9⅝ inches high, 1885; 7⅞-inch plate signed A R Valentien, 1895; vase, 8½ inches high, 1886. (Smithsonian Institution). (Top right) Rookwood vase with braided silver wire trim, 6½ inches. The piece is dated 1894 and signed K C M. (Paul Brunner collection). (Center left) Left to right: Rookwood pottery vases 1894, 1903, 1905, 1907 (5½ inches), 1910. (Smithsonian Institution). (Center right) Rookwood bookend dated 1919. It is 5½ inches high. (Authors' collection). (Left) Rookwood Ewer with daisy decoration. (Smithsonian Institution). (Bottom center) Rookwood vase marked "Conjuring Bear—Sioux." The bottom of the vase is marked ADS 90 2 C with the date 1901. The piece is 9 inches high. (Paul Brunner collection). (Bottom right) Rookwood stein picturing John Calhoun, dated 1896 and signed "M A Daly 820 10F." (Paul Brunner collection).

(Above) Rookwood basket with Tiger Eye glaze. It is dated 1886 and signed A M B 45 D R. (Paul Brunner collection).

(Top left) Rookwood vases 1922, 1923, 1924, 1952, 1953 (5 inches). (Smithsonian Institution). (Center left) Bathroom of Rookwood tiles made ca. 1925. (Mrs. S. A. Horvitz). (Bottom left) Rookwood vase 16½ inches high made in 1907 by the famed Japanese artist Shirayamadani. (Western Reserve Historical Society, Cleveland, Ohio). (Bottom right) Rookwood vase marked with 8 flames and the Japanese signature of Shirayamadani. The vase is 14 inches high and 11 inches in diameter. (Western Reserve Historical Society, Cleveland, Ohio).

(Left top) Rookwood vases: blue 9½ inches high dated 1925; deer decoration 6 inches high dated 1934; and a 6-inch-high piece dated 1915. (Western Reserve Historical Society, Cleveland, Ohio). (Left bottom) Rookwood 16-inch-high vellum vase dated 1915, 7 inches in diameter, and a rook 3 inches high and 4 inches long dated 1913. (Western Reserve Historical Society, Cleveland, Ohio). (Above) This 10-inch vase was signed by Valentien in 1882. It bears the rare "Rookwood Pottery Cin. O." mark. (Western Reserve Historical Society, Ohio).

A Grueby vase of matte green glaze, 8 inches high, and a larger Van Briggle Indian vase. (Western Reserve Historical Society, Cleveland, Ohio).

(Left) Weller wisteria vase, 9 inches high and a smaller Weller vase marked Ferrell. (Authors' collection). (Right) Weller plaque with painted design of an Apache child. The picture was copied from a photograph by Edward S. Curtis in 1903. (Paul Brunner collection).

(Right) Grueby tile, 13 inches square, made in 1906. (Smithsonian Institution). (Far right) Van Briggle vase, Despondency, in a 1969 version. (Authors' collection).

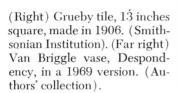

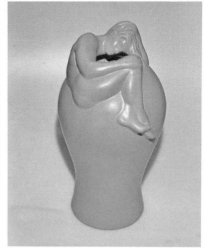

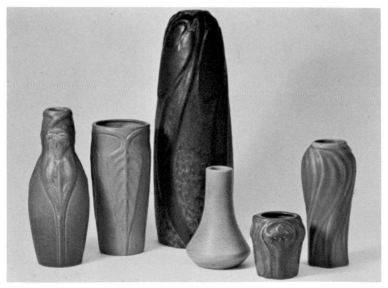

Van Briggle vases: The relief-decorated vase with daffodils is marked 1903. It is 9½ inches high. The all yellow matte glaze vase is dated 1901, and the 15-inch-high green mottled vase is marked 1904. The other three vases are undated. (Smithsonian Institution).

Van Briggle pottery. The candlesticks are almost identical except for the glaze colors. The vase is dated 1912. (Authors' collection).

(Right) Cambridge tiles made in Covington, Kentucky, about 1887–1899. (The Smithsonian Institution).

(Below) An American Encaustic 6-inch-square tile. (Authors' collection).

(Below) Two matching Cambridge tiles, each 6 inches by 9 inches. The wreath was part of a fireplace tile trim. (Authors' collection).

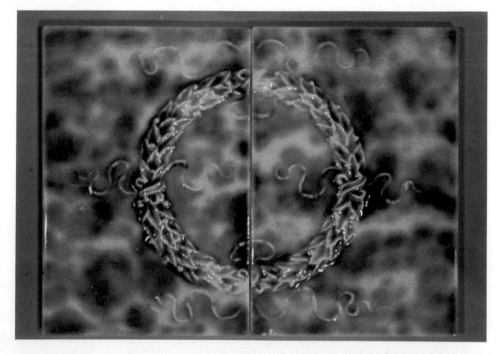

(Right) Tile made by Arthur Osborne for the J. and J. G. Low Art Tile Works. (Robert Koch collection). (Below) Tiles by J. and J. G. Low Art Tile Works, Chelsea, Massachusetts, from 1881–1885. Several are marked on the face with the Arthur Osborne "AO." (Smithsonian Institution). (Below right top) Tile with a 6-inch edge featuring a raised head. It is unmarked but probably made by the J. & J. G. Low Company. (Authors' collection). (Below right bottom) 6-inch tile by the Providential Tile Works, New Jersey.

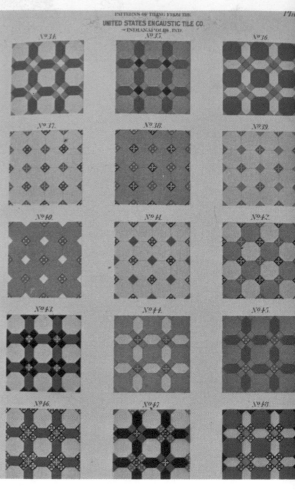

(Above left) Page from the catalogue of the United States Encaustic Tile Co., Indianapolis, Indiana. (Above right) Page from the catalogue of the United States Encaustic Tile Co., Indianapolis, Indiana.

Six-inch tile by the Providential Tile Works, New Jersey.

Stamped in black ink.

RumRill
451

Incised.

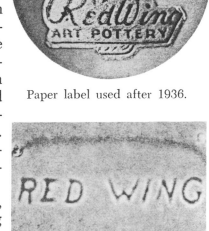

Paper label used after 1936.

period of competition and mergers with other potteries in the area and by the 1920s, the Red Wing Union Stoneware Company began making pottery. At first, they made flowerpots and vases decorated with cattails, leaves, flowers, and cranes. The pieces had a green stain over a tan background. As their sales climbed, the firm expanded their art pottery line and made ashtrays, cookie jars, jardinieres, mugs, candlesticks, trays, bowls, and other items. From about 1930 to 1938 or 1939, Red Wing made pottery for George Rumrill, which he sold as Rum Rill pottery.

The firm began making dinnerware during the 1930s, and in 1936 they changed their name from Red Wing Union Stoneware Company to Red Wing Potteries, Inc.

Their dinnerware was made from imported clays from several other states. The local clays had been suitable for stoneware, but they were too impure for dinnerware.

Red Wing Potteries closed in 1967. One reason was labor trouble, but actually the many imported dinnerwares had taken a great share of their business.

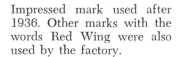

Impressed mark used after 1936. Other marks with the words Red Wing were also used by the factory.

(Below left) An olive green glaze with yellow highlights covers the raised designs of lions and foliage. The 8-inch-high vase bears a stamped mark, "Red Wing, Union So———." (Authors' collection)   (Below right) A medium maroon matte glaze covers the raised, swirled ribbing of this Rum Rill vase. The piece is incised with a handwritten mark, "RumRill 451." (Authors' collection)

(Below) This green crystalline glazed vase decorated by bell-shaped flowers is 8½ inches long by 3½ inches high. It is marked Rum-Rill. (Collection of LeRoy Eslinger)

A 12-inch-high vase with black glossy glaze and an incised circle mark, "Red Wing Art Pottery." (Collection of LeRoy Eslinger)

Bibliography

Dommel, Darlene. "Red Wing and Rum Rill Pottery," *Spinning Wheel* (December, 1972), 22–24.

———, "Red Wing Pottery," *The Antique Trader* (October 23, 1973), 59.

Schneider, Norris F., correspondence with authors.

Letter from A. E. Hull to Norris F. Schneider (August 10, 1960).

PAUL REVERE POTTERY

The Paul Revere Pottery was formed from a group of amateurs working to learn a trade and to keep "occupied" in the manner of the settlement house movement. Their pottery was made in several locations in or near Boston from 1906 to 1942.

Edith Brown and Edith Guerrier, a librarian in Boston, suggested in 1906 that members of The Saturday Evening Girls Club make pottery. The club was located in a settlement house in Boston. The two women had seen pottery made in Switzerland and thought the girls would find the work interesting, cultural, and financially rewarding. The women studied potting and glazing and in about a year bought a kiln and hired a pottery chemist from the Merrimac Pottery.

(Left) A Saturday Evening Girls Club member decorating a piece of Paul Revere pottery.

(Below) A tea set in the Greek key border design made in 1914. (*House Beautiful*, August, 1914)

In 1907, a group of Italian and Jewish immigrant girls were trained in pottery making at the summer camp at Chestnut Hill. It was found impractical and the group moved to the Hill Street Settlement House. The girls were daughters of immigrant families in the Boston area. The hope was that the settlement house could "keep them off the streets." The Library House, a settlement house, had been sponsored by wealthy Bostonians and many activities were available. Lectures, readings, classes in music, dancing, six glee clubs, and other entertainments were pursued. The Glee Club concerts and the reading-class plays were given to the public and the money helped to support the settlement house.

By 1912, the pottery was an important activity at the house. At first, the girls worked in the basement of a home and at the North Bennett Street Industrial School, but Mrs. James J. Storrow, one of the founding backers of the settlement house, financed a brick house at 18 Hull Street. This was in the North End of Boston, near the Old North Church where Paul Revere had seen his signal lanterns.

The pottery made by the teenage members of The Saturday Evening Girls Club was popular and sold well. Over two hundred girls worked on the pottery, although only about ten were active at any one time.

A paper label and pottery mark.

(Below) An oatmeal set in the duck pattern made in 1914. (*House Beautiful*, August, 1914)   (Right) Bread and milk set in rabbit design made by Paul Revere Pottery in 1914. (*House Beautiful*, August, 1914)   (Bottom right) Porridge set and bread and milk bowl made by Paul Revere Pottery.

(Above) The pine tree vase. (*House Beautiful*, 1914)

(Left) The chrysanthemum vase was offered in a catalogue as "VCCd vase, 9 in., blue green and cream $50.00 less 40%." The catalogue also states that "any item displayed may be obtained in any of the colors shown in the center color plate." (The catalogue also shows some pieces that were pictured in an article about the pottery in 1914; the cover picture of the catalogue appears in a 1922 article.) (*House Beautiful*, August, 1914)   (Top right) The Paul Revere Pottery offered this vase about 1910. It is 5^{11}/$_{16}$ inches high. It has incised and painted decorations of yellow daffodils and green leaves on a blue background. The vase is marked with the initials "AM" (Albina Mangini?). (Private collection, picture from The Art Museum, Princeton University, Princeton, New Jersey)   (Above) Incised and painted roosters decorate the outside of this bowl. Note the incised and painted motto on the inside. Yellow, black, and white matte glazes were used. The vase is 5½ inches in diameter. It was made about 1910. On the bottom of the bowl are the marks 1.10, and the artist's initials, CG, in a vertical rectangle, and also part of the original paper label with an SEG within a sketch of a bowl and the price, $2.50. (Newark Museum, Newark, New Jersey)

Working conditions were excellent. The pottery rooms were decorated with flowers and someone read aloud to the girls while they worked. They had an eight-hour day with a half day off on Saturday and two weeks paid vacation. The group worked with a potter, a designer, and a kiln operator. New girls sat next to the more experienced girls so that they could learn the trade quickly. Some of the girls planned to earn a living as potters while others joined the group just to keep occupied during their teenage years.

The popularity of the pottery made expansion necessary, and in 1917 the firm built its own building on Nottingham Hill in the Aberdeen District of Brighton, Massachusetts. There is some confusion in the records, but it seems Mrs. Storrow still supported the group at this time. The new building was an English-style house set on a hill. Edith Brown was the main designer of the pottery and she added the expenses of a clean, attractive factory plus a living wage to the cost of the pottery. She felt many people preferred to buy products made under good working conditions. The pottery remained active and it had many girls working.

Miss Brown died in 1932 and the Paul Revere Pottery continued without her, but it finally closed in 1942. Mrs. Storrow, the financial angel for the firm, died in 1944.

Product

The Paul Revere Pottery made a wide variety of art pottery, but the main lines offered for sale were children's dishes and tiles. Their glazes were matte finished in solid colors. Decorations were outlined in black and filled with color. Yellow, green, blue, tan, and a metallic gunmetal shade were used. Pale cream lined with green or blue, gunmetal lined with red, blue, yellow, maroon, green, or brown were featured in the dishwares. Bread and milk sets consisting of a plate, bowl, and pitcher were made for children. Chickens, rabbits, nursery rhymes, ducks, roosters, boats, flowers, trees, cats, windmills, and even special order pieces with the owner's name and birth date were used as designs. The flower vases were decorated with large flowers, especially chrysanthemums, iris, nasturtium, wild roses and clover. All types of bowls were made, from salad bowls to individual open salt dishes. Also in the line were plates, coffee cups, saucers, cream pitchers, sugar bowls, egg cups, platters, milk or water pitchers, mugs, honey jars, salts and peppers, toilet sets for chil-

(Left) This 9-inch-high vase is glazed in powder blue with a white design. It was made before 1916. (The Smithsonian Institution)
(Right) Artist "EL" initialed this gray blue, black, and white glazed plate. The design shows conventionalized flowers. A white crackle glaze was used. It is marked with the original paper label for the bowl shop and shows the price as $2.50. (Newark Museum, Newark, New Jersey)

dren, flower vases, lamps, desk sets, candlesticks, and paperweights. Full luncheon and dinner sets were sold in stock patterns and to special order. If a piece broke, a replacement could be purchased to match.

Tiles were made in great variety. The most interesting were those that pictured Boston street scenes, Paul Revere's house, the Old South Church, the Schoolmaster's house, the Eliot house and others, made to be used on fireplace mantels. Other tile sets showed the three ships of Columbus and a thirteen-tile set of the ride of Paul Revere. The tiles were four or five inches square with matte surfaces. The designs were drawn on the soft clay, then color was added in natural tones.

The factory made bisque doll heads for a short period during World War I. They were made with socket necks to fit either a bisque doll shoulder or a papier-mâché torso. But even after the heads were fired, the wigs and eyes never arrived from Europe, and no heads were ever completed for sale. Some of these heads were found in the river in 1950.

Bibliography

Binns, Charles F., "Pottery in America," *The American Magazine of Art* (V. 7, No. 4) (February, 1916), 131.

Blasberg, Robert W., "Paul Revere Pottery," *Western Collector* (V. VII, No. 1), (January, 1969), 13–16.

Brown, Edith, "The Story of Paul Revere Pottery," *Craftsman* (V. 25), (November, 1913) 205–207.

Crowley, Lilian H., "It's Now the Potter's Turn," *International Studio* (V. 75), (September, 1922), 539.

Edson, Mira B., "Paul Revere Pottery of Boston Town," *Arts and Decoration* (V. 1), (October, 1911).

Little, Flora Townsend, "A Short Sketch of American Pottery," *Art & Archaeology* (V. 15), (May, 1923), 219.

Northend, Mary Harrod, "Paul Revere Pottery," *House Beautiful* (V. 36), (August, 1914), 82.

Paul Revere advertising brochure (date unknown).

"The Paul Revere Pottery, An American Craft Industry," *House Beautiful* (V. 51), (January, 1922), 50.

Pendleton, Margaret, "Paul Revere Pottery," *House Beautiful* (V. 32), (August, 1912), 74.

Pochmann, Ruth Fouts, "The Paul Revere Pottery, 1912–1942," *Spinning Wheel* (November, 1963), 24.

"The Story of Paul Revere Pottery," pamphlet (date unknown).

Wallach, Mrs. Philip, correspondence to Mr. Jacoby, Director of North Bennett Street Industrial School.

ROBLIN POTTERY

Mrs. Linna Irelan established an art pottery in San Francisco about 1899. While visiting in Cincinnati, she had seen the work of the Cincinnati Pottery Club and thought that it would be a worthwhile project for some women in California. She could not find anyone to join her, but in 1899, Alexander W. Robertson (see Dedham Pottery) joined her and they formed the A. W. Roblin Pottery. The name was from A. W. Robertson and Linna.

One type of Roblin Pottery was a faience with glazes of green, tan, dull blue, or gray. The pieces resembled the works of the Chelsea Keramic Co. of Massachusetts. Another type was made of red clay that was found in Monterey County, California. The pieces were fired once and sometimes decorated with white slip in engobe style. The finish was satin. Decorations were usually animal shapes,

Impressed Roblin marks.

An assortment of Roblin ware as shown in *Keramic Studio*, January, 1902.

such as lizards, frogs, horned toads, and birds, or flowers, mushrooms, and toadstools.

Robertson threw all of the pieces on a wheel. Mrs. Irelan decorated the pieces without the use of molds. She used only wooden tools to do the modeling, relief, and incised work. All the clay and glaze material came from California.

The Roblin Pottery was almost completely destroyed in the San Francisco earthquake of 1906, and went out of business in April of that year.

Pieces of Roblin Pottery were marked with the word Roblin and an impressed figure of a bear. Sometimes, Robertson's name and some numbers were also impressed.

Bibliography

Barber, Edwin, *Marks of American Potters,* Philadelphia: Patterson and White, 1904, p. 166.

Benjamin, Marcus, "American Art Pottery—Part III," *Glass and Pottery World* (April, 1907), 35.

Evans, Paul F., "The Art Pottery Era in the United States 1870 to 1920, Part, Two," *Spinning Wheel* (November, 1970), 52.

Hawes, Lloyd E., M.D., *The Dedham Pottery and the Earlier Robertson's Chelsea Potteries*, Dedham, Massachusetts: Dedham Historical Society, 1968, 27.

Irelan, Mrs. Linna, "Roblin Ware," *Keramic Studio* (V. 3, No. 9), (January, 1902), 190.

ROOKWOOD POTTERY

The Rookwood Pottery was founded in 1880, but to completely understand the history of the pottery, it is necessary to go back a few years to discover some of the influences on Maria Longworth Nichols, the founder.

Maria Longworth was born in 1849 to a wealthy Cincinnati family. She attended a private school and had a usual education for a lady of her day. She married Colonel George Ward Nichols in 1867 and they later had a son and a daughter. It has been said that the marriage was "not a happy one."

Mrs. Nichols first started decorating china in 1873. A neighbor, Karl Langenbeck, had been given a set of china decorating paints. Mr. Langenbeck, Mrs. Nichols, and another neighbor, Mrs. Learner Harrison, started decorating china. When Maria Eggers started a china decorating class in Cincinnati in 1874, Mrs. Nichols and others joined the group. Artistic inspiration came to Mrs. Nichols in the form of some Japanese design books that were given to her by a friend in 1875. It was the first time she had seen this style of design and after viewing the Japanese exhibit at the Philadelphia Centennial Exposition in 1876, she decided to form an American pottery company to make similar wares. The same exhibition also had some fine examples of Haviland art pottery and it was this pottery that inspired the glazing techniques used by Mrs. Nichols.

At first, Mrs. Nichols was going to hire Japanese workmen and set up a pseudo-Japanese pottery, but later dismissed the idea. She and her friends continued to experiment with "underglaze" decoration and they tried to adapt the methods seen on the Haviland works from Auteuil (see Haviland Pottery).

China decorating was becoming an industry and a mania among people of means. M. Louise McLaughlin

Artists and Decorators (* indicates an artist listed in Edwin Barber's *Marks of American Potters*):

*Edward Abel.** About 1890–1892.

*Louise Abel.** (1894–   ). 1920–1928, 1929–1932, 1953–?

*Howard Altman.** 1899–1904.

*Lenore Asbury.** 1894–1931, did occasional work in other years.

𝔍𝒜

*Fanny Auckland.** Daughter of William Auckland, first thrower at Rookwood. About 1881 to about 1884. Did incised decoration.

D. B. 1882. Unknown.

M.B.

M. B. 1884–?

CAB

Constance Amelia Baker.
1892–1904.

C. J. Barnhorn. 1914, name
on garden fountain.

Elizabeth Barrett. 1943–
1948. Married Jens Jensen,
1931.

J.B. *I.B.*

Irene Bishop. (1880–1925).
1900–1907. Married Ed-
ward T. Hurley, 1907.

C.FB

Caroline F. Bonsall. 1902–
1905.

AMB
AB

Anna Marie Bookprinter.
(1862–1947). 1884–1905.
Married Albert R. Valen-
tien, 1887. Signed work
A.M.V. after marriage.

EWB

Elizabeth Weldon Brain.
1898– about 1902.

Alfred Laurens Brennan.
(1853–1921). At Rook-
wood from 1881 to 1883 or
1884. Recorded as designer
of a few early shapes.

WHB

W. H. Breuer. 1881–1884.

C.P.C.

C. P. C. 1882.

Alice E. Caven. 1917–1919.

Arthur P. Conant. 1915–
1920s. Husband of Patti M.
Conant.

Patti M. Conant. 1915–late
1920s. Wife of Arthur P.
Conant.

D·C

Daniel Cook. (1872–
1950s?). 1893–1894. Also
worked at Owens.

Catherine Pissoreff Covalenco.
(1896–1932). About 1925–
1928.

S.E.C.

*Sara Elizabeth (Sallie)
Coyne.* 1880–? 1891; dec-
orator 1892–1931.

Catherine Crabtree. About
1924.

E.B.I.C.

E. Bertha I. Cranch. A rela-
tive of Edward P. Cranch.
1887.

CRANCH

Edward Pope Cranch.
(1809–1892). Part-time
decorator 1880 to 1890.
Used black etched lines on
light clay body.

Cora Crofton. 1886 to about
1892.

A.D.

A. D. Unknown. 1916.

Matthew Andrew Daly.° (1860–1937). 1882–1903. Worked at Matt Morgan Art Pottery.

VBA VBD

Virginia B. Demarest.° 1900–1903.

Mary Grace Denzler. 1913–about 1915.

Charles John Dibowski.° 1892, 1893. Also may have worked at Lonhuda.

E.D. E.D.

Edward George Diers.° (1871–1947). 1896–1931.

Cecil A. Duell. (1889–1946). About 1907 to about 1914. His wife, Cathryn A. Duell, worked at Rookwood but was not a decorator.

J. E. Unknown. 1882.

Lorinda Epply. (1874–1951). 1904–1948.

H. F. Unknown.

M.L.F.

M.L.F. Unknown. 1900.

Henry François Farny, c. 1880.

Rose Fechheimer.° (1874–1961). 1896–1906.

E.R.F.

Edith Regina Felten.° 1896–1904.

K.F.

Kate Field. c. 1880.

E.D.F.

Emma D. Foertmeyer.° 1887–1892.

ITF

Mattie Foglesong. 1897–1902.

Laura A. Fry.° (1857–1943). 1881–1887, part-time; 1892, Lonhuda Pottery.

L F

Lois Furukawa. (1912–   ). 1942–1948.

AG

Arthur Goetting.° (1874–?). Summer of 1896.

K.G

Katherine de Golter. Not an artist at Rookwood, but member of Women's Pottery Club, c. 1880. Decorated Rookwood blanks.

G.H.

Grace M. Hall.° About 1902–1905. About 1910–1912.

LEH

Lena E. Hanscom. About 1902–1907.

JH

Janet Harris. (1907–   ). 1929–1932.

VEH WEH

William E. Hentschel. (1892–1962). 1907–1939. Kenton Hills Pottery in Erlanger, Kentucky.

*Katharine Leslie Hickman.°
1895–1900.*

/ ticks

Orville B. Hicks. Only his name and mark are known.

ȮH   N.J.H.

N. J. Hirschfeld.° About 1882–1883, Matt Morgan Art Pottery.

A. B)H.

Alice Belle Holabird. About 1880. Not an artist at Rookwood, but a member of the Women's Pottery Club. Decorated Rookwood blanks.

L4

Loretta Holtkamp. About 1920 in glaze room. Decorator about 1943 to 1953.

⊦B-

R. Bruce Horsfall.° (?–1948). 1893–1895.

H.H

Hattie Horton.° 1882–1884.

A.H.

Albert Humphreys.° (1864–1926). About 1882–1884.

*Edward Timothy Hurley.°
(1869–1950). 1896–1948.*

Joseph Jefferson. Before 1905; the famous actor who visited frequently and enjoyed decorating plaques.

Jens Jacob Herring Krog Jensen. 1928–1948. Married Elizabeth Barrett 1931.

KJ

Katherine Jones. 1924–1931.

ETK

E. T. K. 1887. Unknown.

F.E.K.

Florence Kebler. About 1880; not an employee.

MᵥᵗKeenan

Mary Virginia Keenan. About 1880; not an employee but a member of the Women's Pottery Club.

Flora R. King. (1918–   ). 1945. Twin sister of Ora King.

Ora King. (1918–   ). Rookwood 1945–1946; 1947–1948. Twin sister of Flora King.

WK.

William Klemm.° About 1900 and 1902.

Charles Klinger. About 1924.

K
F D K

Mrs. F. D. Koehler.° About 1886 and 1890.

SL

*Frederick Sturgis Laurence.°
1895–1904.*

ECL

Eliza C. Lawrence.° (?–1903). 1900–1903.

LEY

Kay Ley. About 1945–1948.

L N.L

Elizabeth Neave Lingenfelter Lincoln. (1880–1957). 1892–1931.

CCL

Clara Christiana Lindeman.° 1898 until after 1907. Sister of Laura E. Lindeman.

L.E.L. *LEL*

Laura E. Lindeman.° 1899 until after 1905. Sister of Clara C. Lindeman.

Elizabeth Neave Lingenfelter.° See Elizabeth Neave Lingenfelter Lincoln.

TOM

Tom Lunt.° 1886–1890.

HM.

Helen M. Lyons. About 1913–after 1915.

AM

A. M. Unknown. 1901.

S. N. M.

S. N. M. Unknown. 1882.

EM

Elizabeth F. McDermott. About 1912–sometime after 1915.

MHM

EHM

Margaret Helen McDonald. (1893–1964). 1913–1948.

W.P.M°D.

WPM°D **WPM°D**

WD

William Purcell McDonald.° (1865–1931). 1882 to 1931.

M

Charles Jasper McLaughlin. (1888–1964). 1913–1920.

S. M.

Sadie Markland.° (?–1899). 1892–1899.

K.C.M.

Kate C. Matchette.° 1892.

ÆM

Ruben Earl Menzel. (1882–   ). In the clay department 1896. Began decorating and signing his work about 1950 to 1959.

Ferdinand Mersman. Did Garfield vase and pitchers.

M

Marianne Mitchell.° 1901–1905.

/M

Herman Milton Moos. 1926.

7M

Albert Cyrus Munson.

C.N

C.CN

Clara Chipman Newton.° (1848–1936). 1881–1884.

N⊔ **hN**

Maria Longworth Nichols. (1849–1932). 1880–1890.

E.N.

Edith Noonan. (1881–?). 1904–1910. Married Stanley Gano Burt 1910.

E. N.

Elizabeth Nourse. Not an employee.

M.M.

Mary Madeline Nourse.° (1870–1959). 1891–1905.

AFP

A. F. P. Unknown. c. 1907.

NP.

MLP. **MP**

Mary Louella Perkins.° About 1886–about 1898.

B

Pauline Peters-Baurer.° About 1893 or 1894.

O. Geneva Reed Pinney.° See Olga Geneva Reed.

Agnes Pitman. About 1880, not an employee.

Albert Pons. About 1904 until about 1911.

John Wesley Pullman. (1886–1931). 1926–1931.

Marie Rauchfuss. ° (1879–?). 1899–1903. Worked at Weller and Owens.

Olga Geneva Reed. ° (1873–?). 1890–1903. Married Mr. Pinney in 1890s. Second marriage to Matt Daly in 1928.

Wilhelmine Rehm. (1899–1967). 1927–1932, 1935, and 1943–1948.

Martin Rettig. ° (1869–1956). 1883.

Frederick Daniel Henry Rothenbusch. ° 1896–1931.

Jane Sacksteder. (1924–?). 1945–1948.

S.S.

Sara Sax. ° 1896–1931.

V. S.

Virginia Scalf. Only her name and mark are known.

Charles (Carl) Schmidt. ° (1875–1959). 1896–1927.

A.D.S.

Adeliza Drake Sehon. (?–1902). 1896–1902.

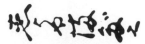

David W. Seyler. Not an employee, but a sculptor who used the pottery after 1937.

Kataro Shirayamadani. ° (1865–1948). 1887–1915, 1925–1948.

M·H·S

Marian Frances Hastings Smalley. ° (1866–1957). 1899–1902. Married Francis William Vreeland 1903.

a₃s

A·B·S

Amelia Browne Sprague. ° 1887–1903; about 1930. Also worked at Lonhuda.

Carolyn Stegner. ° (1923–   ). 1945–1947.

S

C.F.S.

C.S.   C. S.

Caroline Frances Steinle. ° (1871–1944). 1886; decorator 1892–1925. Also worked at Roseville.

M L S

Maria Longworth Nichols Storer. ° See Maria Longworth Nichols.

H·R·S

Harriette Rosemary Strafer. ° (1873–1935). At Rookwood 1890–1899.

H. Pabodie Stuntz. ° About 1892, 1893.

Jeannette Swing.* (1868–?). 1900–1904.

Mary A. Taylor.* (1859–1929). 1883–1885.

V.T.

Vera Tischler. (1900–   ). 1920–1925.

C.S.T.

CSJ

Charles Stewart Todd. (1885–1950). 1911–1920s.

Sara Alice Toohey.* 1887–1931.

A.R.V.

Albert Robert Valentien.* (1862–1925). 1881–1899, 1900–1905.

a.m.V.

Anna Marie Valentien.* See Anna Marie Bookprinter.

AVB A·B· A·V·B

Artus Van Briggle.* (1869–1904). Avon Pottery until 1887. Rookwood 1887–1899. Van Briggle Art Pottery in 1901–1904. Married, 1903.

L·V·B

Leona Van Briggle.* 1899–1904. Younger sister of Artus Van Briggle.

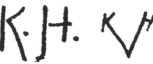

Katherine Van Horne. About 1907–1917.

F.V.

Francis William Vreeland.* (1879–1954). 1900–1902. Married Marian Smalley, 1903.

L. E. W. Unknown. 1882.

M.H.W.

M. H. W. Unknown. 1882.

M.R.W.

M. R. W. Unknown. 1886.

John Hamilton Delaney ("Dee") Wareham.* (1871–1954). 1893–1954.

H.W.

Harriet Wenderoth.* 1881–about 1885.

H.E.W.

Harriet (Hattie) Elizabeth Wilcox.* 1886–1907. ?–1930.

Edith L. Wildman. About 1911–about 1913.

Alice Willitts. About 1906.

Delia Workum. (1904–   ). 1927–1929.

K. Y. Unknown. 1905–1906.

Grace Young.* (1869–1947). 1886–1904. Also worked at Roseville.

C Z

Clotilda Marie Zanetta. (1890–?). About 1943–about 1948. Also worked at Weller, Roseville.

Josephine Ella Zettel.* (1874–1954). From 1892–1904.

Unknown. 1907.

Unknown. 1917.

Unknown. 1889.

Unknown. 1906.

Unknown.

Unknown.

Unknown. 1943.

Marks: There are five distinctive Rookwood marks: the factory mark, the clay or body mark, the size mark, the process mark, and the decorator mark. (The decorator marks have already been provided.)

Factory Marks:

Painted or incised, before 1882.

Painted or incised, before 1882.

Stamped or in relief, before 1883.

Printed in black underglaze, 1880–1882.

Impressed, 1883.

Stamped, c. 1883.

Stamped, c. 1883.

Found on Garfield Memorial Pitcher, 1881–1882.

Incised mark found on an unglazed pitcher.

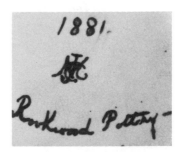

Blue underglazed mark found on stein.

Paper label used at World's Columbian Exposition, 1893.

M L S
1897

Maria Longworth Storer's initials (not really a factory mark).

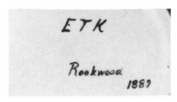

ROOKWOOD 1882

Impressed, name and date, 1882–1886.

Rare mark written in blue underglaze found on blue stein.

Incised by artist Alfred Brennan in 1883.

Impressed monogram, 1886.

Flame added each year to 1900.

Roman numeral given last two digits of year after 1900.

Special pieces fired for 50th, 60th, 70th anniversary. Printed on ware.

75th anniversary. Printed on ware.

ROOKWOOD CINTI, O

After 1942.

ROOKWOOD POTTERY STARKVILLE MISS

Impressed paper label, 1962–1967.

Clay Marks: A letter was impressed on the base of the piece from 1883 to 1900 to tell the color of the clay used.

G Ginger.   **S** Sage green.

O Olive.   **W** White.

R Red.   **Y** Yellow.

Impressed in pieces made after 1914 to indicate "soft porcelain."

Size Marks: Sizes are marked A through F. A new piece was made and given the letter C or D; then larger pieces could be marked A or B, smaller ones, E or F. Not all shapes were made in all sizes. A double letter, such as BB, was used if a size fell between two existing sizes. XX indicated a piece larger than A or smaller than F.

Each pattern had a number and all were recorded in a shape book. The numbers went from 1 through 7199. A few of the later novelties had no number.

Process Marks: Strange marks were put on a very limited number of experimental pieces. The meaning of all is not known. These are the ones listed by Edwin Barber in 1904:

Trial for new glaze.

X15X

Trial for new decorating technique.

Stanley Burt trial mark.

Trial mark by Joseph Banley, Sr.

Other process marks.

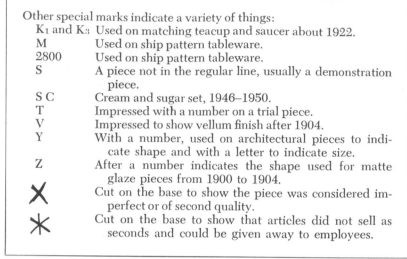

Other special marks indicate a variety of things:

K₁ and K₃	Used on matching teacup and saucer about 1922.
M	Used on ship pattern tableware.
2800	Used on ship pattern tableware.
S	A piece not in the regular line, usually a demonstration piece.
S C	Cream and sugar set, 1946–1950.
T	Impressed with a number on a trial piece.
V	Impressed to show vellum finish after 1904.
Y	With a number, used on architectural pieces to indicate shape and with a letter to indicate size.
Z	After a number indicates the shape used for matte glaze pieces from 1900 to 1904.
X	Cut on the base to show the piece was considered imperfect or of second quality.
✳	Cut on the base to show that articles did not sell as seconds and could be given away to employees.

If a tile was part of a set to make a larger design, the tiles in the set were numbered with the pattern number, the letter Y, and a 1, 2, 3, etc.; one number for each tile in the completed set. A few artists from 1885 to 1900 added extra letters when signing a piece. The meaning of these letters is unclear.

(see Pottery Club of Cincinnati), of Cincinnati, published several books about china painting and working on glazing techniques. Her pieces were probably the first underglaze art pottery wares made in the United States. Miss McLaughlin founded the Women's Pottery Club in 1879 and for some unknown reason, Mrs. Nichols was not a member. Miss McLaughlin had originally worked at the Coultry Pottery, using yellowware, but she soon moved to the Frederick Dallas Pottery.

Using a kiln with a high heat Mrs. Nichols began her own experiments at the Dallas Pottery. Because the Dallas kiln was too hot, Miss McLaughlin had a special one built for her pieces. Mrs. Nichols heard about the new kiln so she too had a special kiln built for her work. Miss McLaughlin sent work to Thomas C. Smith and Sons of Greenpoint, New York, to be fired; Mrs. Nichols sent her pieces to Lycett's in New York City for firing. The working arrangements at the Dallas Pottery seem odd in that Miss McLaughlin and her group worked in one room and Mrs. Nichols and her group in another. The two rooms at the Dallas Pottery were entered through the same yard, but each group remained completely independent.

Mrs. Nichols at first used graniteware that was made at the Dallas Pottery, but it did not take the colors. Later she tried Rockingham clays. She finally was able to make pieces with cobalt blue, black, and then with the help of Joseph Bailey, the superintendent, she developed dark green, claret brown and, at last, light blue and light green. This limited palette was discouraging for the artist, but in 1880, her father suggested if she really wanted to have a pottery, she could use an old schoolhouse that he had purchased at a sheriff's sale.

The schoolhouse pottery was a solution to many of the problems at the Dallas Pottery. Mrs. Nichols could make her own clay mixtures, colors, glazes, and even control the heat of the kiln. She talked to Mr. Bailey of the Dallas Pottery and he helped her to decide what equipment was needed. She tried to hire him, but he would not desert his employer of fifteen years, so she hired his son, Joseph Bailey, Jr.

The schoolhouse was transformed into a working pottery and named "Rookwood" because it reminded Mrs. Nichols of the Wedgwood Pottery of England and her father's country home near a crow- (rook)-filled woods. Henry Farny, a Cincinnati artist, designed the trademark, which was a kiln and a spray of fruit blossoms with two rooks.

Just as the pottery was being completed in October, legal problems with T. J. Wheatley (see Wheatley Pottery) started and the unfinished pottery was threatened with closure.

However, Mrs. Nichols kept on with her project and continued to hire workmen and artists, and in November of 1880 the first pieces were fired. The Rookwood Pottery made several types of wares from the very beginning. Commercial tableware was for household use. It was made of a white granite and had a cream-colored body. Some yellow clay wares were also made. The art pottery made by Mrs. Nichols and some artwork made by outside amateurs were all fired at the Rookwood Pottery. Mrs. Nichols furnished the biscuit pottery to the amateurs for their decoration and she also fired the finished pieces. There was no working space at the factory for the artists, but Mrs. Nichols was happy to help them in other ways.

In 1881 Clara Chipman Newton was hired to handle the office details. Edward Cranch worked part time for the pottery handling the administrative problems. Both worked part time as decorators. Although not officially Rookwood employees, James Broomfield, Henry Farny, and Ferdinand Mersman (see Cambridge Art Tile Works) also worked as artists.

(Top) This plain 3-inch-high gray unglazed pitcher has the rare kiln mark used in 1881 and 1882. (Collection of Paul Brunner)   (Bottom) Stein made in 1882. It has white dogwood on a dark blue glazed body. The piece is marked "ETK Rookwood 1882" (see photo in listing of marks). (Collection of Paul Brunner)

(Top) Painted underglaze decorations of spiders in a web adorn this basket in beige, black, and white. It is 20 inches long, 8¼ inches high. The piece is marked "MLN" for Maria Longworth Nichols. It is also marked with the impressed "Rookwood, 1882." (Cincinnati Art Museum)   (Bottom left) Tan flowers and gray leaves decorate this cream-colored pitcher. It is 8¼ inches high. The piece is marked "Rookwood, 1882" with the artist's initials, "D.B." (Barrett-Durkes)   (Bottom right) This dark aquamarine vase in pilgrim bottle shape is 11 inches high, 9 inches wide. It has pink and white flowers with green leaves. The piece is marked "Rookwood, 1882 A.R.V." and has the anchor mark. (Authors' collection)

(Top left) Clara Chipman Newton decorated this stein with blue decorations on a cream body. It was made in 1881 and is marked with the script words Rookwood Pottery (see photo in listing of marks). (Collection of Paul Brunner)   (Center left) This unglazed pitcher has incised decorations made with tools similar to those used to tool leather. The piece is marked with the very rare and early script mark incised on the bottom: "Rookwood Pottery Cin" (see photo in listing of marks). (Collection of Paul Brunner)   (Bottom left) An early printed decorated Rookwood plate pictured in *Popular Science Monthly*, January, 1892.

By 1881, the Rookwood Pottery was making quantities of dinnerware, often decorated with underglaze blue or brown prints of birds, fish, or other animals. The high-relief decorated vases, such as the Garfield Vase, were made by Ferdinand Mersman at this time, while Mrs. Nichols was making Japanese-inspired artware. Even some "printed ware" was made.

In June of 1881, after the death of Frederick Dallas and the closing of the Dallas Pottery, Joseph Bailey, Sr., became the superintendent of the Rookwood Pottery. He stayed until 1885 when he left for Illinois, and returned in 1886.

In the summer of 1881 the pottery was enlarged and space was provided for the Rookwood School for Pottery Decoration. Mrs. Nichols hoped the school would be financially successful and thought it would furnish more decorators for the pottery.

That same year, a decorating department was formally organized, and Albert R. Valentien, Laura A. Fry, Harriet Wenderoth, W. H. Breuer, Alfred Brennan, and Fanny Auckland (then twelve years old) worked in the department. William P. McDonald and Matthew A. Daly joined the decorators in 1882 and, soon after, Martin Rettig, Albert Humphreys, and N. J. Hirshfeld were hired.

Even though the Rookwood Pottery was expanding and selling as much pottery as it was producing, the firm was not financially successful. Mrs. Nichols's father, who had paid for the original equipment and the building, continued backing the pottery until his death in December of 1883.

In 1883 William Watts Taylor joined the pottery as administrator and partner. He had no previous knowledge of the pottery business and his only concern was that of a businessman. One of his first changes in the Rookwood operation was to close the Rookwood School for Pottery Decoration. The Pottery Club continued to use the space, but because the members bought pieces for decoration and had them fired at the Rookwood Pottery, there is some confusion about the early wares. The biscuit wares were stamped with the name Rookwood plus the date. The staff decorators usually signed the pieces. Therefore, some of the marked Rookwood pieces dating from 1882 to 1885 were decorated by artists who were not part of the pottery staff.

William Taylor analyzed the problems of the firm and changed some of the marketing methods. He started

(Top) This Rookwood vase is signed "ARV 1883 Rookwood." The artist was Albert Robert Valentien.

(Bottom) Birds fly over blowing weeds on this blue and beige vase with gold highlights. It is marked "Rookwood, 1884." Although the piece has no artist's signature, the bird design was used by Albert Valentien on other pieces. (Authors' collection)

keeping records showing the types of Rookwood that sold quickly, and the unpopular numbers were discontinued.

A discovery by Laura Fry in 1883 led to the "Rookwood Standard Glaze." She used an atomizer to apply color to the green clay body. This made a more even glaze and more delicate shading possible.

An accident in the kiln produced another glaze, the gold-flecked "tiger eye" glaze. The glaze had gold streaks beneath the colored glaze. When the result was less dramatic and gold flecks appeared, it was called "Goldstone." The search for the reason why some pieces glazed as Tiger Eye led to the belief that a chemist was needed. Mrs. Nichols's old neighbor, Karl Langenbeck, was hired around January, 1885.

After her husband died in 1885, Mrs. Nichols spent less time at the pottery, and Joseph Bailey, Sr., returned to his job as superintendent in 1886. Mrs. Nichols married Bellamy Storer in March of 1886 and left for a lengthy honeymoon in Europe. The firm continued to produce new types of wares and new styles of design, and a Japanese artist, Kataro Shirayamadani, joined the decorating staff. By the end of 1888, the firm was making enough money to pay back the losses of earlier years.

In 1889, the Rookwood Pottery gained international renown with a Gold Medal at the Exposition Universelle in Paris and the First Prize Gold Medal at the Exhibition of American Art Industry in Philadelphia. Maria Nichols, now Mrs. Storer, retired from the Rookwood Pottery in 1890 and transferred her interests to Taylor. He organized a stock company called the Rookwood Pottery Company. New buildings were constructed and the firm moved to its new location on the summit of Mount Adams overlooking Cincinnati.

Rookwood had several displays in the World's Columbian Exposition held in Chicago in 1893. They won a bronze medal, the only award given. The publicity helped the sales of Rookwood and many European museums bought examples.

New lines were made and in 1894, Sea Green, Aerial Blue, and Iris were put into production. Stanley Burt had been hired by Rookwood in 1892 as a chemist and he was able to take over in 1898 when Joseph Bailey died.

The decorating department began to make portraits in 1897. Dogs and other animals, historical figures, actors, birds, as well as flowers, and Indians appeared in the standard glaze vases.

(Below, top) This pair of pilgrim bottles come in a basket. Each bottle is marked "Cranch, Rookwood, 1884." At the bottom of the front of the bottles it says "Three wise men of Gotham went to sea in a bowl." (Collection of Paul Brunner)   (Below, bottom) The turtle swims on a glossy green blue glaze. The 6½-inch-diameter plate is marked "WMcD" (artist W. P. McDonald) and "RW" and has the incised mark "Rookwood 1885." (The Smithsonian Institution)

(Right) Three green crabs are pictured on an orange and brown ground on this 5¼-inch-high Rookwood vase. It is marked "Rookwood 1885, 142 C" and has the artist's initials, ARV. (The Smithsonian Institution)   (Bottom right) This sage green crackle, glazed vase is decorated with an owl and a pine branch. It is 10½ inches high. The vase is impressed "Rookwood 1885" and has the incised marks "S, ARV" (for Albert Valentien). (The Smithsonian Institution)

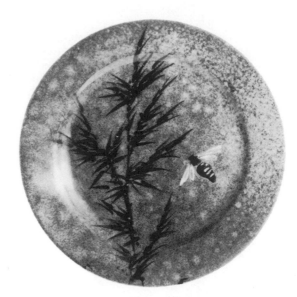

(Top left) Another 6¼-inch-diameter plate by W. P. McDonald has a butterfly design. The orange and yellow butterfly is on a glossy green background with brown grass. It is marked "Rookwood 1885, 202, McD." (The Smithsonian Institution) (Top right) A bumblebee is the decoration on this Rookwood plate. The plate has a speckled brown green glossy glaze and is marked with the impressed "Rookwood 1885 C 3 2" (in triangular formation) and the incised initials "MR" for artist Martin Rettig. (The Smithsonian Institution) (Right) Three early Rookwood pieces. *Left:* 9⅝-inch pitcher with brown and gold flecked glaze dated 1885; *Center:* yellow and beige plate with white and brown branches, 7⅞ inches in diameter, by A. R. Valentien, dated 1895; *Right:* yellow and green 8½-inch vase marked 1886. (The Smithsonian Institution)

The Indian portraits were copied from contemporary photographs of Indians circulating in stores at the time. We have discovered copies of Indians photographed for the book *Indians of Today* by George Bird Frinnell, 1900, and also from *North American Indian* by Edward S. Curtis. Both of these books were also inspirations for pieces decorated at the Weller Pottery.

Portraits did not sell well and by about 1903 were discontinued.

The pottery expanded its building in 1899. Once again, in 1900, an international exhibition helped the sales of Rookwood. The Paris Exposition awarded them several medals including one gold medal. In 1901 the Pan American Exposition in Buffalo, New York, awarded more prizes for the firm.

(Top left) This jardiniere was made from white clay with a bright amber glaze. The oak leaves are green, brown, and yellow. The 11⅝-inch-high piece is marked "Rookwood 1886 130W." (The Smithsonian Institution)   (Top right) The chrysanthemum pitcher is 17 inches high. It is marked "MAD," for artist Matthew Daly, and dated 1887. The white dogwood vase on a turquoise and gold matte glaze is dated 1886. It is marked LAF for artist Laura A. Fry.   (Right) The Rookwood pottery made many special order pieces to commemorate events of importance. This mug dated 1888 was made for the City of Cincinnati. (Collection of Paul Brunner)

Decorative architectural tiles were made for the first time in 1902, and by 1903 architectural tiles had been ordered for use in the New York City subway. Once again, the factory had to expand and a New York office was opened to sell tiles. Garden pottery was added to their lines in 1906.

Mr. Taylor died in November of 1913. His will provided that the Rookwood Pottery stock be given to a board of trustees to hold until it went to the Cincinnati Museum Association twenty-one years later. The trustees were to use all of the profits to improve the company and they could sell stock only to Rookwood employees. Taylor also left some money to be distributed to the employees who had worked there for more than five years.

The Rookwood Pottery Company continued under the direction of the board of trustees and Joseph Henry Gest as president. Since 1902, Gest had worked part time for both Rookwood and the Cincinnati Art Museum, as a director.

The general pottery lines continued, adding new de-

211

This 6-inch-diameter vase has an orange brown glaze that in some spots shows flecks of gold. It was designed by Artus Van Briggle and is dated 1887. The swastika (not visible here) and spider decorations are Indian inspired. The same motif occurs on page 274. (Collection of Mrs. Sam Horvitz)

signs, as well as many new ones for the architectural line. In 1915, "Rookwood Soft Porcelain" was introduced. It had a semitranslucent body that glazed with rich color. Crackle-type glazes could also be used. And "Jewel Porcelain," a series of new glazes, appeared.

In 1920, a special order was filled for a dozen service plates. This order led to the production of Rookwood's blue and white ship dinnerware sets. During that same year, "Tiger Eye" glaze was revived in several new colors, even a yellow green; it was a crystalline glaze and not the same as the original Tiger Eye. It was discontinued about 1950.

The firm also made garden pottery, fountains, tiles, lamp bases, sculpture, and mass-produced pieces.

A decision of the U.S. Board of Tax Appeals in 1928 ruled that the Rookwood Pottery owed $19,873 in back income taxes. This in addition to the Depression left the Rookwood Pottery with little cash reserve. The architectural tile department closed in the 1930s. Art pottery was a luxury that only few could afford so the artist-decorated expensive lines were discontinued in 1937. Some lower-cost pieces were made with flowing glazes.

Henry Gest had resigned as president in 1934 and John D. Wareham succeeded him. Wareham had already worked for the Rookwood Pottery for forty-one years as a decorator and vice president.

The Rookwood Pottery was no longer a leader in design and the financial problems grew until the firm went into receivership in 1941, preceding a series of liquidation sales. The Rookwood Pottery was sold for $60,500 to a group headed by Walter E. Schott, a Cincinnati auto dealer. Wareham continued as director.

Plans were made to reopen the plant. In November, 1941, production resumed. But by the end of 1942, the pottery was turned over to the Institutum Divi Thomae, a nonprofit organization. It sold the operation of the pottery to Sperti, Inc., and in 1943 production resumed on a small scale. Part of the plant was reserved for the manufacture of wooden blocks for water conduits used in army camps. The decorating staff was reassembled and John W. Milet was appointed to manage the pottery for Sperti, Inc. Artist-decorated pottery was made from 1944 to 1949.

When World War II had ended, Rookwood production continued. Some changes had been made in the glazes because many of the chemicals had been unavailable. The quality of the glaze declined and by 1947 the decorated

(Top left) Bats and weeds and clouds on a dark green background are the improbable decoration on this 9-inch-long basket. The edges are touched with overglaze gold. The interior is tan. The piece is incised "Rookwood 1892" and the initials ARV also appear. (Authors' collection)   (Top right) This 6-inch-high vase has underglaze decorations of strawberries and leaves in yellow, brown, orange, and green. The piece is marked with the RP flame mark and 7 flames (1893) and the symbols "304" and "W." The incised letters CS are included for artist Caroline Steinle. The vase also has the original paper label with the picture of the kiln and the crow. The label reads "Rookwood Pottery, Cincinnati U.S.A. World's Columbian Exposition 1893." (The Smithsonian Institution)   (Left) This vase was made of cream-colored clay covered with glaze shading from red brown to green, then black. It is 17¼ inches high. The piece is impressed with the RP flame mark and 9 flames (1895) and the artist's signature, Shirayamadani. (Smithsonian Institution)

(Top) This 6-inch jug with the ear of corn decoration is glazed brown. It is dated 1894 and has the artist's initials, HEW, for Harriet Elizabeth Wilcox.   (Bottom) Birds and rushes decorate this cream to orange 9-inch-high vase. It is signed with the incised initials ARV (Albert R. Valentien) and the incised name Rookwood and date 1885. (Authors' collection)

pieces were of poor quality. The staff of artists was discontinued in 1949. Less and less of the property was used for making pottery and for a time only unglazed bisque pieces were made for amateurs to decorate. These pieces are marked with the Rookwood mark and the date.

James Smith bought the property in 1956 and tried to rebuild the Rookwood reputation. He failed and late in 1959 the pottery was sold to the Herschede Hall clock firm. The pottery moved to Starksville, Mississippi, and about twelve hundred molds dating back to 1882 were shipped to the Starksville plant. The pottery at the new plant did not sell well and it was closed in 1967.

In 1971, Briarwood Lamps, Inc., of Starkville, bought the assets of the Rookwood Pottery Company, including three thousand block molds, five thousand glaze and clay formulas, the trademark, and the medals won by the company.

Modern copies of the Rookwood standard glaze were made during the late 1960s. These pieces are marked with the 1880–1886 dates and impressed. Some have the RP symbol and a year in the 1890s indicated by the flames on the mark. A few 1897 Indian head decorated mugs and some other popular late items were made. Artists' signatures such as Maria Longworth Nichols, MAD, MR, and others have been appearing. The collector should be careful when buying Rookwood or any other art pottery. Forgeries are not too difficult to recognize if you are familiar with the authentic pieces.

Special Items

The Rookwood Pottery made decorative vases, tiles, and plaques through most of its years. In addition, some specialty items were made.

Architectural Faience: Architectural faience was part of the business at the Rookwood Pottery from 1903 to the 1940s. The most important years for production of tiles was from 1907 to 1913. Rookwood tiles included mantels, mantel facings, wall panels, drinking fountains, architectural reliefs for building exteriors, plain and decorated tiles. The tiles were made in sizes from two by three inches to twelve by eighteen inches. During a peak year, thirty colored glazes were made, 145 different decorative tiles, and hundreds of special tiles for borders, and so on. The tiles were made with matte finish.

Lamps: The lamps made at Rookwood were an important

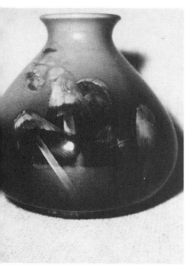

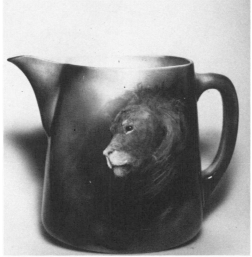

(Top left) Mushrooms are painted on this 7½-inch brown glazed vase. It is marked with the flame mark for 1896 and the numbers "815." The initials of A. R. Valentien are incised on the bottom. (Barrett-Durkes) (Top center) A pensive lion is on the side of this 8½-inch ale pitcher. The piece has the RP flame mark and 9 flames (1895). (Collection of Paul Brunner)   (Top right) This small, 4½-inch-high vase has the standard brown glaze and a yellow leaf decoration. It is marked with the flame mark for 1898. (Authors' collection)   (Bottom left) Incised lines outline stylized flower decorations on this vase by W. P. McDonald. It was made in 1899. (Cincinnati Art Museum)   (Bottom right) This unglazed gray pitcher has a portrait bust of Garfield on one side, an eagle on the other. It is 10 inches high. The piece is marked with the RP flame mark with 9 flames (1895) and the impressed letter S. (Smithsonian Institution)

(Left) Sarah Sax was the artist for this 6¼-inch mug. It is decorated with underglaze gooseberries and leaves of green and orange on a brown background. The mug has the RP flame mark and 13 flames (1899), the symbols "659," "C," and the cipher "SAX." (The Smithsonian Institution)   (Right) *Left:* A 6¼-inch-high vase made by Rose Fechheimer in 1898. *Right:* A 7¼-inch-high ewer made in 1901 by Jeannette Swing. Both pieces have the standard brown glossy glaze and yellow decorations.

part of the early lines, and included kerosene and electric types. The firm made the pottery bases and the metal mounts. They were still making lamps from their vases in the 1920s. The customer could choose a vase, then the pottery would drill and mount it. These lamps were marked Rookwood Pottery on the metal base. Later a paper label was used.

Metal Mounts: During the years 1894 to 1897, the Rookwood Pottery had its own staff to make and attach the metal mounts to lamps and other pieces. Pewter mounts for jug and lamp fittings were made. Silver deposit work was also done. E. H. Asano, a Japanese metalworker, was hired and in 1899 a new metal mounting department was formed to do metal overlays by the electrodeposit method; copper and silver deposits were formed. In 1902, after an absence, Mr. Asano returned to Rookwood to resume his work, but he soon left for Japan. There is no information about him after this time. On some of the silver overlay that was made from 1892 to 1895 the name Gorham Silver is found.

A catalogue dated about 1900 states: "Metals applied appropriately to reliefs modeled by artists in connection with painted decorations characterize another type of Rookwood. This method gives the piece a variety and

This 6-inch-high Rookwood vase has the flame mark for 1900 and the cipher "JEZ" for artist Josephine Ella Zettel.

richness of texture and color, while retaining the unity of design usually lost in metal mounting."

Novelties: Many novelty items were sold by Rookwood in the later years. Bookends first appeared in 1908. A few new designs were added each year until eighty-five bookend designs were made. Other novelties made by the pottery included candlesticks, flower holders, figurines, candy boxes, ashtrays, inkwells, and wall sconces. Design ideas were taken from any source. One early bowl was actually molded from a melon. In the 1940s, a bust of a woman was made by making a mold of an Italian majolica bust.

Wall Plaques: Wall plaques were made as early as 1896.

(Below, top) *Left:* An iris glazed vase decorated with a flock of gray crows. The 8½-inch piece has the flame mark for 1903 and the initials of artist Edward Hurley. *Center:* The 5½-inch-high cachepot is decorated with iris glaze in peach and gray and decorated with blossoms and leaves in pink and green. It has the impressed mark for 1889 and the initials of artist Anna Marie Valentien. *Right:* The 8½-inch-high vase is standard glaze with stylized blossoms and leaves of green and brown. It has the artist's signature for Olga Geneva Reed.   (Below, bottom) *Left:* An iris glazed vase with yellow to green glaze and crocuses and leaves in blue and green. The piece has the impressed factory mark for 1904 and the artist's initials for Rose Fechheimer. *Center:* The basket has tiger eye glaze with sprays of yellow three-leafed clovers. It is dated 1886 and was made by Anna Marie Bookprinter. *Right:* The vase has standard brown glaze with pansies and leaves of yellow, brown, and green. It is signed by the artist Harriet E. Wilcox and has the impressed factory flame mark for 1890.

(Above) This vase with the raised molded design of a woman is glazed with matte white and light blue glazes. It is 5½ inches high. The piece is marked with the impressed flame mark and 14 flames (1900), the symbols "T1228" and the incised cipher of "WMcD" for designer William P. McDonald. (The Art Museum, Princeton University, Princeton, New Jersey)

(Below) This matte glazed ashtray with a molded design of a woman was made in 1901. It has the artist's initials "AMV" for Anna Marie Valentien. (Collection of Paul Brunner)

(Top left) This molded vase with poppy seed pod decoration is in red, green, and purple matte glazes. It is 7½ inches high and has the 1901 flame mark and the signature of John D. Wareham. (Collection of the Museum of Modern Art, New York) (Left) Kataro Shirayamadani, the famous Japanese artist at the Rookwood Pottery, made this modeled and painted vase. Geese in white and tan are seen against a matte green glaze. The 10½-inch-high vase was made in 1901. (The Art Museum, Princeton University, Princeton, New Jersey) (Top right) Daffodils of white and yellow on a matte blue background are seen on this 5⅜-inch-high vase. It was executed in 1901 by Mary Nourse. (Collection, The Museum of Modern Art, New York)

At first, these plaques were part of the experimental work for the Architectural Faience Department. Some of the earliest plaques (c. 1899) were decorated with copies of well-known oil paintings by masters such as Van Dyck, Rembrandt, Hogarth, and Franz Hals. We have seen one decorated with an Indian head. Another, marked Sturgis Lawrence, 1903, had a landscape with a glossy finish.

In 1904, the vellum glaze was perfected and the vellum scenic tiles were an important product of the Rookwood Pottery until almost 1950. Most of the vellum plaques show landscape scenes.

The plaques were almost always sold in oak frames and were expensive to make. The sizes ranged (without frame) from four by eight to fourteen by sixteen inches. Some round and oval plaques were also made.

A word of warning to the collector. Reproductions of these vellum plaques have been produced about 1970. These were made by transferring an etched design in black or blue to a white tile. A little pink color was added and the result appeared to be a winter landscape. The entire plaque was then sprayed with a vellumlike matte overglaze and fired. These can be detected if they are compared with the originals.

Clay, Glaze, Design: The clays used in the early years came from a variety of sources. Local Ohio clays were used. Various colors of clay and even artificially tinted clays were tried. Red clay from Buena Vista, Ohio, chocolate-colored clay from Ripley, Ohio, yellow clay from Hanging Rock, Ohio, and white or cream clay from Chattanooga, Tennessee, were used by 1902. Most of the clays tended to be in the red to yellow color range so the standard glaze of the dark brown shade seems a logical choice.

The sea green glaze was used on a mixture of clay said to be from Chattanooga and Virginia. The mixture was a dull but not dark green. The copper in the clay reacted with the tin in the glaze and made some of the glaze colors turn pink on some pieces as early as 1898. This was one of the "happy accidents" that led to new glaze discoveries.

In 1910, William Watts Taylor, head of the Rookwood Pottery, wrote a description of the process of making some of the artware.

To start with the raw materials: these consist, for the body, of various plastic clays combined with flint and spar. These clays are mainly drawn from mines in the Ohio Valley. Clays even from the same mine vary more or less. This fact and their constantly varying adjustment to the glaze require the continual vigilance of the chemist. When these mixtures are decided, they are weighed with water into a great churn-like mixer, out of which they pass to the sifter of fine silk bolting cloth, and are pumped into vats where they settle to the consistency of very thick cream. This cream is what potters know as "slip" and if vases are to be made from clay in that state, it is done in plaster molds by a process known as "casting." The other process is to form them on the potter's wheel. For this enough water must be taken from the slip to stiffen it to the consistency of dough. This is done in presses worked by a steam pump. The operation of the potter's wheel is what is known as "throwing," and the process was used, essentially as it is today, at least twenty-two hundred years before the Christian Era. It is a simple application of the laws of centrifugal

Tiger Eye is one of the most famous glazes used at the Rookwood Pottery. This vase has the gold crystals showing the glaze clearly near the top left-hand side of the picture. The $8\frac{7}{16}$-inch-high vase is decorated with black and dark brown birds flying over the waves. It is marked with a paper label "Rookwood Pottery Cincinnati U.S.A., exhibited at Pan Am Exp. Buffalo, 1904 Louisiana Purchase Expo St. Louis, SPU Universal Exposition Paris." The label has the printed kiln and letters. (Cooper-Hewitt Museum of Design, Smithsonian Institution, New York)

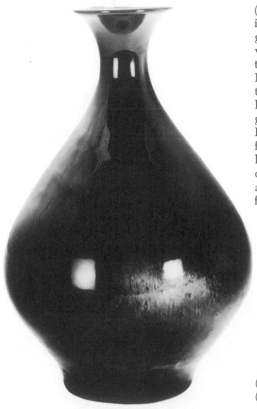

(Top left) In 1904, Charles Schmidt made this dark glazed iris vase. The 10¾-inch-high piece is decorated with underglaze peacock feathers in blue, green, yellow, and black. The vase has the RP mark and 14 flames (1900), "940 C W" and the cipher "CS" in a circle. It has a paper label, "Rookwood Pottery Cincinnati USA, 1904 Louisiana Purchase Exposition." (The Smithsonian Institution)   (Center) Pale violets in lifelike colors are the decoration on this glazed pink to gray iris vase. It is 5½ inches high, marked with the initials LNL for artist Elizabeth N. Lincoln, and the RP flame mark for 1905. (Authors' collection)   (Right) Queen Anne's lace is represented on the glazed iris vase with pink to gray coloring. The 10-inch-high vase has the flame mark for 1906 and the symbols 821 C W. It is marked with the initials L. A. for artist Lenore Asbury. (Authors' collection)

(Left) Another tiger eye glaze vase. It is on a red clay body. (The Art Institute of Chicago)

and centripetal force, which swing the planets in their courses, and I know of no mechanical operation which is so immediately creative, or so full of poetic suggestion. It has the added interest that no other material than clay can be worked in this way. Unfortunately the continuance of so beautiful a craft is threatened by the very quality which recommends it to the artist. So responsive is the clay upon the wheel to the lightest touch of the thrower's hand, that no two pieces can be made precisely alike and this is fatal to that uniformity of shape which seems the sad necessity for commercial work. In the use of this process, and in the treatment afterward of the clay pieces, made either in this way or by casting, Rookwood departs from the methods of commercial production. Here, instead of drying the pieces at once for the kiln, they must be kept moist in what are known as damp rooms until needed for the decorator. We will follow them next to the studios where you will see them placed on whirlers ready for the artist. The palette consists of a glass plate on which the colored slips look much the same as oil colors. The design is first sketched on the piece with India ink, which, being a vegetable color, subsequently fires out and can therefore be freely used and the outlines followed or not as the artist thinks best. He then proceeds with the painting, mixing his slips and laying them on the pieces. They are all, of course, in slight relief, and during the painting or when it is finished, are gone over more or less with modeling tools. Ready at hand is an atomizing cup which must be constantly used to keep the piece itself and the color palette at the right point of moisture. The colors in the clay are very different from what they appear after firing. To allow for this transposition of color, as it were, into another key; to use the slip so that they may not crack or peel off, requires long practice and constant vigilance. The failures are frequent even with the most experienced, and often disheartening. For the raw material, so to speak, of the design, there must be available thousands of drawings and photographs from nature, either made by the artists themselves, or carefully selected from other sources. These are never literally copied, but serve only as authentic records of details and characteristics of the subject, which may be conventionalized wholly, or in part, or rendered much as in nature. After the piece is finished, which may take only a few hours or many days of time, it is slowly dried and is then ready for the firing. The pieces are placed in fire clay boxes called saggers, and these are piled in the kiln one upon the other with lutings of soft clay between to form flame-tight joints. The door of the kiln, when full, is bricked up, and the firing proceeds for from twenty-four to thirty-six hours, after which the kiln is allowed three or four days to

This ad appeared in the *Sketch Book* in the early 1900s. The same vase was offered in a 1904 mail-order catalogue for the Rookwood Pottery. It was described as 8½ inches high and for sale at $40.

Rookwood made outdoor pottery. This garden fountain, 35 inches high, is dated 1914. It is impressed with the factory mark and C. J. Barnhorn. (Taylor & Dull)

cool. The pieces are then taken out and dipped in the various glazes.

When the raw glaze has been thus applied to a piece and you see it slowly drying for the kiln, the color and decoration disappear, except as the latter may be traced through the slight reliefs. They look exactly as though they had received a heavy coat of ordinary whitewash. But what happens when they go back again into the fire is the transmutation of this whitewash into a glass or glaze, through which you can see again all the colors and decorations. This is true of all the varieties of Rookwood except the mat glazes. In these you do not see through the glaze at all, and therefore when they are used, no painting or coloring in clay is done. You will observe how radically this difference in method distinguishes the mat glazes from the others. The decorations, if any, on the clay pieces are entirely plastic, consisting of incised lines or modeled reliefs. Apart from these the artistic interest is now transferred entirely to the glaze itself, and the body, instead of being an integral part of the decorative medium, becomes merely a support for the glaze surface. The painting is done on the biscuit pieces with the various colored mat glazes in their raw state. When fired, these glazes are crystalline in structure, and though not the least transparent, admit of a certain interpenetration of light upon which much of its effect depends. The charm of texture is the highest quality of a fine mat glaze, and through this the colors play delightfully. (*Forensic Quarterly*, Sept., 1910, Vol. 1, no. 4, p. 203–218, University of the South, Sewanee, Tenn.)

The clays used in the 1960s were from Georgia, Tennessee, and Florida. Over forty thousand glaze formulas were listed at the factory and over five hundred glazes were in daily use in the 1936 period. Rookwood pottery changed with the times in clay, glaze, and design.

Lines

The dates given are the earliest known for the line. The quotations are from Rookwood catalogues of 1896, c. 1902, 1904, c. 1915, and from advertisements.

Aerial Blue. "Mono-chromatic ware with a quiet decoration in celestial blue on a cool, grayish white ground," 1896.

Aurora Orange. Textured surface like an orange peel, vellum finish in shades of yellow and orange, c. 1943.

Aventurine. A rich red, 1930.

Bisque. Unglazed finish, mainly found on early pieces.

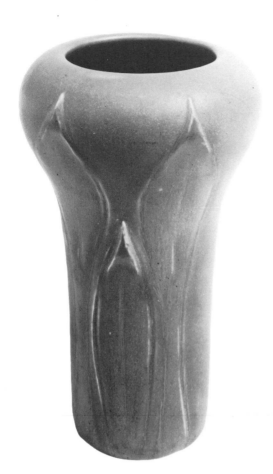

(Top left) The 1907 RP mark is on the bottom of this 7¾-inch-high matte green vase. It is marked with an unknown artist's signature. (The Smithsonian Institution)   (Top right) An example of the silver overlay used on pieces of Rookwood in the early 1900s. This vase is signed by Matthew A. Daly.   (Right center) Part of a 12-plate dinner set. The 3-inch plates are in salmon glaze, the 9-inch, in blue green glaze. Each is decorated with slightly different flowers and leaves.   (Right) Stylized peacock feathers in brown, yellow, green, brown, and orange decorate this 7³⁄₁₆-inch vase. It has the RP mark and 14 flames, the Roman numeral XI (for 1911), 939 D, V and the artist's initials SAX (Sara Sax). A price sticker shows the vase originally cost $15. (Newark Museum, Newark, New Jersey)

(Above) Rookwood potters took inspiration from many sources. *Left:* The bronze-color glazed bust has the 1912 flame mark and the symbols II 2026. The flower-decorated bust, used as a model, was once in the office of the secretary of the Rookwood factory. It is an Italian faience. (Collection of Paul Brunner)   (Below) An owl decorates this pink matte glazed vase. It was made in 1916. (The Brooklyn Museum)

Brilliant. A glaze name referred to in an article by Susan Stuart Frackelton in 1906, *Sketch Book,* Vol. 5, July.

Butterfat. A matte glaze with a greasy look made in shades of yellow, c. 1930.

Cameo. Slip painted decoration under a clear glaze, later called Standard Glaze.

Celadon Glaze. Rich green glaze, c. 1930.

Conventional Mat Glaze. "This type is a mat glaze with flat, conventional decoration in colors. This new type of Rookwood appeals to a taste for simple, flat decorations rather than naturalistic treatment, and reflects an important movement in modern art," 1904.

Coramundel. Glaze to copy Tiger Eye, 1930s.

Crystal Glaze. Transparent glaze over incised designs or colored clay, developed 1943.

Crystalline. A glaze name referred to in an article by Susan Stuart Frackelton in 1906, *Sketch Book,* Vol. 5, July. Also mentioned as a new glaze in a booklet put out by the factory about 1930.

Flambé. Red glaze of Chinese type, c. 1920 [mentioned in Starkville, Miss., leaflet of late 1960s].

Flowing Glaze. "This deep and heavy glaze has a quality resembling in many respects some of the old Chinese. It has a similar luminosity and at the same time a peculiar richness of texture. The decoration is painted upon the piece in slight relief, in forms and colors so simple that the glaze may flow pleasantly over them." c. 1907.

Goldstone. "Resembling the glistening of golden particles in aventurine, but rather more limpid (than Tiger Eye) by reason of the glaze. Both the Tiger Eye and Goldstone are seen on dark grounds." 1896.

Incised Mat Glaze. "Derives its name from the incised decoration. This type is made in reds, blues, yellows, greens, etc. in a multitude of shapes; sometimes in single colors, sometimes in a combination of two or more colors." 1904.

Iris. "Designates a large class of effects with a considerable range of color based upon a warm gray tone. Delicate pinks, soft blues and greens, creamy whites and yellows, play tenderly into the gray scheme. In these lighter wares a more crisp decoration is used." 1904 (first made in 1896).

Jewel Porcelain. A semiporcelain, with incised lines for embossed decorations. Characterized by rich, heavy color glaze. 1920 to 1960s.

Lagoon Green. Blue blended to green, semi gloss glaze, slightly mottled.

Lagoon Green. Yellowish green over brown decorations, 1943.

Limoges Style. Decoration called by this name in the early 1890s. It was the application to wet clay pieces of metallic oxides mixed with clay and water, or "slip."

Lustre. Undecorated or with incised designs glazes with rainbow luster.

Mahogany. Slip painted decoration on dark brown ground later called Standard Glaze. 1884.

Majolica. Dark green, red, yellow, blue, and black heavy gloss glaze. Used primarily on bookends and figurines.

Mat Glazes. "Distinguished by the absence of gloss. Their texture is in itself delightful, a pleasure to the eye and to the touch, whether the surface be decorated or not. The glaze is no longer designed merely to protect the colors beneath, nor to reveal them as though swimming in a lustrous depth, but is now itself the dominating interest.

"Rookwood Mat possesses hitherto unknown range of color in glazes of astonishing variety of texture. Now it seems solid as quartz, and partaking of its crystalline

(Top) A dark olive green mottled glaze was used for this bookend of a girl seated on a bench. The 5½-inch-high piece has the 1919 flame mark. (Authors' collection)   (Bottom) A very dark olive green glaze resembling aged bronze covers this 3½-inch figurine of two geese. It has the 1912 flame mark. The design is by Sarah Toohey. (Collection of LeRoy Eslinger)

This eagle bookend is glazed with a bronzelike olive green color. The artist's mark for William McDonald is incised on the back of the 6-inch piece. On the bottom is the flame mark for 1931 and the number 2623. (Collection of LeRoy Eslinger)

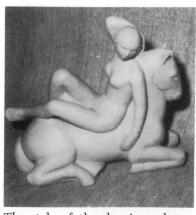

The style of the day in sculpture can be seen in this 1940 Rookwood unglazed figurine. It is 9½ inches long and 9½ inches high. (Barrett-Durkes)

structure; again one sees a more mellow surface suggesting that of firm, ripe fruit, or again it suggests the quality of old ivory, or of stained parchment; but always showing a slight translucency, a sense of depth, and a pleasure in the feel of it which makes it delightful to the touch.

"On many pieces decoration of flowers is applied or other subjects broadly painted or modeled. Others are treated with simple incised designs, yet always emphasizing those qualities of texture and color which give this type of Rookwood its fine distinction." 1904. First made in 1896.

Mat Glaze Painting. "A mat glaze with decorations painted in rich, warm reds, yellows, greens, and blues, a process of the greatest difficulty, suggestive of glowing enamels, but with a mat texture," 1904.

Modeled Mat. Mat glaze with modeled decoration, 1904.

Ombroso. "[This] type of glaze was brought out in 1910. The colors are usually in quiet tones of gray and brown, with occasional accents of other colors (green, blue or yellow), and the decorations, if any, of relief modeling or incised designs." c. 1915. *Arts and Decoration,* Vol. I, Sept., 1911, pg. 449: "Three vases delicately modeled and decorated in a simple and exquisite manner, the result lightly touched with color. In the examples of the true Ombroso ware no color is used, except that in the glaze itself, which is modified by the forms and the chemical changes due to the effect of the fire upon the texture and color, but does away with the necessity of painting, either in mineral colors or with the colored slip." 1904.

Oxblood. A red crystalline glaze with a gold or silver glitter, 1920. A 1930 Oxblood line was made with no glitter.

Porcelain. A semi-porcelain covered with glossy glaze, at first plain or low relief designs. By 1923, painted with slip on biscuit piece. Pieces are marked with the impressed letter P on the base. 1916.

Sea Green. "The name of a variety of Rookwood in which a limpid, opalescent sea-green effect is attained. Beautiful combinations of rich, deep blues, and greens, relieved with glowing touches of golden yellow, red and other warm colors marked this variety." c. 1907. Devel-

(Top left) This tile was molded, then painted with the decoration of a crow on a tree branch and the word Rookwood. It is blue, brown, green, and tan in matte glazes. The tile is 4½ inches high and 8¾ inches wide. It has the original $3.00 price sticker. (Newark Museum, Newark, New Jersey)   (Bottom)   In 1924, this pottery sign was made to be placed in jewelry store windows. It is glazed tan and black. (Top right) This Rookwood tile with raised decoration has a yellow ground with blue and green relief areas. It is 6 inches by 6 inches. (The Smithsonian Institution)

oped in 1894. Often marked with incised or impressed letter G.

Smear Glaze. A reference in a catalogue about 1902 mentions an earlier effort at a dull finish or Smear Glaze. It was a different method than the mat glaze developed by 1900.

Solid Color. "Pieces comprise many of the richest and deepest reds and browns, some so intense that only actual sunshine will reveal the elusive hue. Others are covered with feathery mottlings, one color often playing almost imperceptibly through another with occasionally a pleasant grayness of surface as though catching light. Some are combinations of gray greens and browns. There have also been a few small pieces of brilliant red, some of the 'Sang de Boeuf' quality, others lighter." 1896.

Standard Glaze. "The term given the type which first matured (first produced at the pottery). It is the familiar low-toned ware, usually yellow, red and brown in color, with flower and figure decoration. It is characterized by a luxuriant painting in warm colors under a brilliant

Blue stylized daisies with brown stems are applied underglaze on this cream-colored vase. The entire piece is covered with a clear bubbled glaze. It is 5½ inches high. The 1943 flame mark appears with the symbols 6185 F and an unknown artist's cipher that may be "H A." (Authors' collection)

glaze. From a comparatively light and golden scheme the color arrangement varies to deep, rich red, brown, and green combinations in mellow tones." c. 1907.

Tiger Eye. "Takes its name from a strange luminosity of the glaze in places where one catches glimpses of mysterious striations, which seem to glow with a golden fire, indefinable in words. These happy accidents of the kiln are necessarily very rare," 1896; "the fire always contributing its uncertain element to enhance or disturb the artists' calculations. Tiger Eye was first made at Rookwood in 1884 and is the earliest of the class of crystalline glazes since so extensively made at Sèvres, Copenhagen, and Berlin, though none have attained this particular effect." c. 1907.

Vellum. "This variety of Rookwood Mat Glaze differs from all others, and was first exhibited at the St. Louis Exposition, 1904. It is the fruit of long experiment, and technically considered, is an achievement worthy to be first shown at a World's Exposition, so radical is the departure it makes from any previously known types.

"The name Vellum conveys some idea of its refinement of texture and color. Devoid of lustre, without dryness, it partakes both to the touch and to the eye of the qualities of old parchment. The mat glazes hitherto known have permitted, by reason of their heaviness, of but little decorations other than modeling or very flat and broad painting. The refinements of rendering so generally esteemed in ceramics have been impossible in that medium. The Vellum on the contrary retains for the artist all those qualities possible hitherto under brilliant glaze alone. It is therefore within bounds to say that Rookwood, in developing this new ware, has taken a step forward as remarkable as any in its history." 1904.

Water Color. Writer's name for a design type that resembled a water color painting with an indistinct outline, c. 1924.

Wax Mat. Soft waxy surface, sometimes looks curdled, mat glaze, c. 1930. Developed by Stanley Burt and John Wareham.

Wine Madder. Shades of maroon to blue purple with an orange peel finish, 1943.

Bibliography

Alexander, Mary L., "New Crystal Glaze Described as

Rookwood's Masterpiece," *The Enquirer,* Cincinnati (December 2, 1943).

Antiques, "Nineteenth-century View of Rookwood" (January, 1962), 118.

The Antique Trader, "Rookwood—One of America's Finest Potteries" (August 29, 1972), 2.

Architectural Record, "Rookwood Pottery" (V. 17), (April, 1905).

Arts and Decoration, "Ombroso Pottery, A Recent Rookwood Product" (V. 1), (September, 1911), 449.

Barber, Edwin, *The Pottery and Porcelain of the United States,* New York: G. P. Putnam's Sons, 1909, pp. 276–303, 332, 479–483.

Bopp, H. F., "Art and Science in the Development of Rookwood Pottery," *Bulletin of the American Ceramic Society—Communications* (V. 15), (December, 1936) 443–445.

Bowdoin, W. G., "Some American Pottery Forms," *The Art Interchange* (April, 1903), 87.

Brush and Pencil, "Latter-Day Developments in American Pottery—III" (v. 9), (1902), 353–360.

Cincinnati Enquirer, "Auto Dealer Is New Owner of Pottery, Attorney Reveals" (October 1, 1941).

———, "Rookwood Works Bankrupt, Voluntary Petition States; List of 95 Creditors Filed" (April, 17, 1941).

Cincinnati Times-Star, "Late Master of Rookwood in His Will Provided for the Famous Pottery and also for Relatives and Employees" (November 19, 1913).

———, "Provision for Rookwood" (November 19, 1913).

———, "Rookwood Pottery Soon to Be Reopened" (September 30, 1941).

Clark, Edna Maria, *Ohio Art and Artists,* Richmond, Virginia: Garrett & Massie Publishers, 1932, pp. 158–165.

Clark, Robert Judson, *The Arts and Crafts Movement in America 1876–1916,* Princeton, N.J.: Princeton University Press, 1972, pp. 119, 120, 122–125, 133, 150–154.

This 1946 vase is glazed pale blue to pink with green and pale mauve flowers. It is 9½ inches high. The piece is incised 778, and has the painted marks 400A and the cipher CS for artist Charles Schmidt. (Authors' collection)

Craftsman, "The Potters of America: Examples of the Best Craftsmen's Work for Interior Decorations: Number One" (V. 27), (December, 1914), 295.

Crowley, Lilian H., "It's Now the Potter's Turn," *International Studio* (V. 75), (September, 1922), 539.

Cummins, V. R., "Rookwood Pottery (New Monograms)," *Pottery Collectors' Newsletter* (V. 1, No. 9), (June, 1972), 119.

Davis, Chester, correspondence with authors.

————, "The Later Years of Rookwood Pottery 1920–1967," *Spinning Wheel* (October, 1969), 10–12.

Fawcett, Waldon, "The Production of American Pottery," *Scientific American* (V. 83) (November 10, 1900), 296–297.

Frackelton, Susan Stuart, "Rookwood Pottery," *Sketch Book* (V. 5), (July, 1906), 273–277.

Freeman, Helen, "The Rookwood Pottery in Cincinnati, Ohio," *House Beautiful* (V. 47), (June, 1920), 499–501.

Hall, Foster E. and Gladys C., "The Rookwood Pricing Formula" (leaflet).

House Beautiful, "Rookwood Pottery" (V. 4) (1898), 120–129.

Hungerford, Nicholas, "The Work of American Potters, Article Three—The Story of Rookwood," *Arts & Decoration* (V. 1), (February, 1911), 160–162.

Independent, "Rookwood Pottery, A Woman's Contribution to American Craftsmanship" (No. 77), (March 16, 1914), 377.

Jervis, W. P., "*A Pottery Primer,*" Oyster Bay, New York: O'Gorman Publishing Company, 1911, pp. 175–178.

Keramic Studio, "Louisiana Purchase Exposition Ceramics—Rookwood Pottery" (V. 6), (January, 1905), 193–194.

————, "An Historical Collection of the Rookwood Pottery" (May, 1906–April, 1907), 274.

Kircher, Edwin J., *Rookwood Pottery, An Explanation of Its Marks and Symbols,* 1962, privately printed.

Kircher, Edwin J., and Agranoff, Barbara and Joseph,

Rookwood, Its Golden Era of Art Pottery 1880–1929, privately printed, 1969.

Koch, Robert, "Rookwood Pottery," *Antiques* (March, 1960), 288.

Ladies' Home Journal, "A View of the Rookwood Pottery, October, 1892."

Laing, Trudy, "Rookwood Art Pottery," *The Gallery* (Jan.–Feb., 1972), 11.

_____, "Rookwood Art Pottery Exhibited at Frame House Gallery, Oct. 3–Nov. 7," *Tri-State Trader* (November 20, 1971), 19.

_____, "Rookwood's Japanese Artist." (publication unknown), (April, 1972).

Lansdell, Sarah, "Rookwood Pottery Having a Revival," *Pottery Collectors' Newsletter* (V. 1, No. 2), (November, 1971), 13.

Little, Flora Townsend, "A Short Sketch of American Pottery," *Art & Archaeology* (V. 15), (May, 1923), 219.

Macht, Carol M., "Rookwood Pottery," *Ceramics Monthly* (January, 1966), 29.

Nelson, Marion John, "Indigenous Characteristics in American Art Pottery," *Antiques* (V. LXXXIX, No. 6), (June, 1966), 846.

P-B Enterprises, *Catalog of Rookwood Art Pottery Shapes, Part 1,* privately printed, Kingston, New York, 1971.

_____, *Catalog of Rookwood Art Pottery Shapes, Part 2, 1907–1967, Shapes 1303 to 7301,* privately printed, Kingston, New York, 1973.

Peck, Herbert, *The Book of Rookwood Pottery,* New York: Crown Publishers, Inc., 1968.

_____, "The History and Development of Rookwood Bookends," *The Antique Trader* (February 20, 1973), 48.

_____, "New Evidence Points to Alfred L. Brennan as Creator of Famous Rookwood." *Pottery Collectors' Newsletter* (V. 1, No. 8), (May, 1972), 110.

_____, "Rookwood Pottery and Foreign Museum Collections," *Connoisseur* (September, 1969), 43.

This matte glazed tile with raised pink tulips and green leaves on a cream ground is 6 inches square. It has the impressed marks RP 416 G627X and blurred numerals that appear to be 1847. (Authors' collection)

———, "Rookwood Pottery Paperweights," *Pottery Collectors' Newsletter* (V. 2, No. 2), (November, 1972), 17.

———, "Rookwood Pottery, Plaques and Tiles," *Pottery Collectors' Newsletter* (V. 2, No. 5), (February, 1973), 56.

———, "Some Early Collections of Rookwood Pottery." *Auction* (September, 1969), 20–23.

Peck, Herbert and Margaret, correspondence with authors.

The Popular Science Monthly, "Recent Advances in the Pottery Industry" (January, 1892), (V. 40).

Pottery Collectors' Newsletter, "Rookwood Paperweights" (V. 2, No. 3), (December, 1972).

———, "June Auction Notes" (V. 1, No. 10), (July, 1972), 142.

———, "Pottery Party Line" (V. 1, No. 7), (April, 1972), 100.

Rawson, Jonathan A., Jr., "Recent American Pottery," *House Beautiful* (V. 31), (April, 1912), 148.

Ray, Marcia, "ABC's of Ceramics," *Spinning Wheel* (April, 1968), 21.

Rookwood Factory Catalogues. (assorted, dates unknown).

Ruge, Clara, "Development of American Ceramics," *Pottery & Glass* (V. 1, No. 2), (August, 1908), 3.

———, "American Ceramics—A Brief Review of Progress," *International Studio* (V. 28), (March, 1906), 21–28.

Scribner's Magazine, "The Field of Art—American Pottery, Second Paper" (V. 33–44) (March, 1903), 381.

Sheridan, Millicent M., "Rookwood—A Good Field to Explore," *Hobbies* (V. 57), (July, 1952), 84, 99.

Shull, Thelma, "Rookwood Pottery," *Hobbies* (V. 47), (October, 1942), 66–67.

Sketch Book (advertisement), (V. 5), (1906), xiii.

Spinning Wheel, "Letter to the Editor" (March, 1970), 45.

Stout, Wilber, R. T. Stull, Wm. J. McCaughey, D. J. Demerest, "Art Pottery," *Geological Survey of Ohio,*

Columbus, Ohio: J. A. Bownocker, State Geologist, 4th Series, Bulletin 26, 1923.

Taylor, William Watts, "The Rookwood Pottery," *The Forensic Quarterly,* University of the South, Sewanee, Tennessee (V. 1, No. 4), (September, 1910), 203–218.

Trapp, Kenneth R., "The Bronze Work of Maria Longworth Storer," *Spinning Wheel* (September, 1972), 14–15.

_____, "Japanese Influence in Early Rookwood Pottery," *Antiques* (January, 1973), 193–197.

_____, "Rookwood's Printed-Ware," *Spinning Wheel* (January, February, 1973), 26–28.

Vlissingen, Arthur Van, Jr., "Art Pays a Profit," *Factory and Industrial Management* (V. 79), (February, 1930), 301–303.

Yaeger, Dorothea, "Rookwood, Pioneer American Art Pottery," *American Collector* (July, 1943), 8–9, 19.

ROSEMEADE WAHPETON POTTERY

The Rosemeade Wahpeton Pottery Company was started by Laura (Meade) Taylor and Robert Hughes in Wahpeton, North Dakota, in 1940. Miss Meade had been a student at the University of North Dakota where she studied pottery with several artists; she demonstrated a potter's wheel at the World's Fair in New York in 1939.

The Rosemeade Pottery used North Dakota clay. Many types of birds, vases, salt and pepper shakers, and cream and sugar sets were made. The pieces were brightly colored but had a matte glaze similar to Van Briggle's. Their pieces were marked on the bottom with the name Rosemeade in black or blue lettering or with a paper sticker.

Laura Meade married Robert Hughes in 1943. She died in 1959 but the pottery continued operating until 1961. Rosemeade pieces were sold at their salesroom until 1964.

Bibliography

Weiss, Grace M., "A Native of North Dakota: Rosemeade Pottery." *The Antique Trader* (February 27, 1973), 68.

ROSEVILLE POTTERY

The Roseville Pottery was incorporated in 1892. They began by buying the J. B. Owens factory started in 1885.

Artists, Directors, and other Personnel:

EA

E. A. (Elizabeth Ayers). Also worked at Lonhuda, Weller.

GA

G. A.

V. ADAMS
A

Virginia Adams. About 1911 (Rozane). Also worked at Owens, Weller.

AB   **AB**

A. B.

mB

M. B.

FEST

A. F. Best. Also worked at Owens, Weller.

Jenny Burgoon.

B

John Butterworth. Also worked at Weller (?), Owens (?).

F. S. Clement. President, 1931.

A.P.

Anna Dautherty (?). Also worked at Weller.

When Roseville Pottery incorporated, George F. Young of Lower Salem, Ohio, who tried teaching, selling Singer sewing machines, and held other jobs without success, became the secretary and general manager. C. F. Allison was president, J. F. Weaver, vice president; Thomas Brown, treasurer, and J. L. Pugh became a member of the board of directors.

The firm started manufacturing a line of stoneware jars, flowerpots, and cuspidors. In 1898, they bought a second plant, the Midland Pottery, and more stoneware was made. The Linden Avenue plant, built for Clark Stoneware Company in 1892 in Zanesville, Ohio, was sold to the Roseville Pottery. Painted wares were made at the Linden location until 1900, when the glazed Rozane was developed. There is much confusion among the early reports of the Roseville Pottery plants. The Zanesville Chamber of Commerce Booklet of 1918 says: "The company began operations in Roseville, where they operated two plants. In 1898, they built a pottery in Zanesville, and a little later another one, still continuing the plants at Roseville."

In 1902 the Muskingum Stoneware Plant in Zanesville became part of the Roseville Pottery. By 1910 all of the work in the town of Roseville was terminated and the entire Roseville Pottery operation was located in Zanesville.

At no time did the Roseville Pottery make artware in Roseville. All of their early production was devoted to utilitarian wares such as stoneware and painted flowerpots.

At Zanesville, George Young had decided to make art pottery at the Roseville Pottery and he hired Ross C. Purdy to create a line. Purdy made a ware that was similar to the other underglaze slip-decorated brown-colored wares then popular, and it was named "Rozane" for Roseville and Zanesville; the name Rozane was used as the mark. Later, a light background Rozane was made, and thereafter also other lines with the same mark. Other marks were also used.

John Herold, hired as a designer and art director in 1900, created the Rozane Mongol line and the pottery began making a competing art line for each new product produced by the Weller Pottery Company. A Japanese artist, Gazo Fudji, was hired to help add oriental designs to the ware. Frederick Rhead, who had worked for S. A. Weller, was art director from 1904 to 1908. He developed

Anthony Dunlevy.

E. Dutro.

Charles Duvall.

Katy Duvall.

![HE]

Hattie Eberlein. Also worked at Owens.

![M F]

M. F.

![F]

Bill Farnsworth.

![Ferrell FF]

Frank Ferrell. Hired as art director 1917–1954. Developed Pinecone, Ferrella. Also worked at Weller, Owens, Peters & Reed.

Gazo Fudji. Japanese artist, about 1900. Woodland line, Fujiyama, Rozane, Fudji.

![G]

Gussie Gerwick.

![Goldie]

Goldie.

C. H. On 1906 Rozane ware.

![W. P. Hall]

William Hall. Marked W. H.; also worked at Weller (?).

![J.H. J. H.]

John J. Herold. (1871–1923). Hired 1900, designer, art director. Created Rozane Mongol. He was a chemist who later started the Herold China Company at Golden, Colorado. It later became Coors China Co. Also worked at Owens (?), Weller (?).

![M-H]

Madge Hurst. Also worked at Weller.

Joseph Imlay. (Josephine (?) Imlay)

![J. I.]

Josephine Imlay. Decorated Rozane. Also worked at Weller.

George Krause. About 1915, technical supervisor.

H. L.

Harry Larzelere. Also worked at Owens.

![L L Leffler L. V. & C V]

Claude L. Leffler. Also worked at Weller.

![M]

L. McGrath. Also worked at Weller (?).

![B MALLEN BM]

B. Mallen. Also worked at Owens.

![M]

Mignon Martineau.

Madeline Menet.

Walter Meyers. Worked on 1906 Rozane ware.

![HM]

Hattie Mitchell (?). Also worked at Owens (?), Weller.

L. Mitchell
L M *LM*

Lillie (Lilly) Mitchell. Also worked at Weller.

ℳ

Gorden Mull. Modeler (Married Grace Neff).

Helen Myers.

M·M

M. Myers. Also worked at Weller.

W. MYERS

Walter Myers.

Grace Neff. Artist, decorator, 1911 (Married Gorden Mull)

Christian Nielson. Modeler and designer.

KO

K. O. Unknown.

C. E. Offinger. Technical supervisor 1900 to 1915. Died in 1962.

Pillsbury

H H

Hester Pillsbury. Also worked at Weller.

Ross C. Purdy. (1875–1949). Artist, developed Rozane.

RᴸS *ℬ*

R. Lillian Shoemaker (?). Also worked at Owens.

AS

Allen Simpson.

H

Helen Smith. Also worked at Owens, Weller.

F

Fred Steel(e). Also worked at Weller.

T *F*
TS

Tot Steele. Also worked at Owens, Weller.

CFS. *S*

Caroline Frances Steinle (?). Also worked at Rookwood.

F Rhead

Frederick Hurten Rhead. (1880–1942). Art director 1904–1908. Developed Della Robbia, Aztec, Olympic. Had worked for Weller and Avon Faience, 1902, 1903, American Encaustic Tiling Company, about 1910, University City, Missouri, studio potter in Santa Barbara, California, about 1914.

H Rhead

Harry Rhead. (1881–1950). 1908 art director. Developed Carnelian, Pauleo, Donatello, Mostique; 1908–1920 Roseville, 1922–1923 Mosaic Tile Company, 1923 Standard Tile Company, South Zanesville, Ohio.

Lois Rhead. Also worked at AET Co.

F

C. Minnie Terry. Also worked at Owens (?), Weller.

M. T.

Madeline Thompson (?). Also worked at Weller (?).

Mae Timberlake
M. T. *S*

Mae Timberlake. Also worked at Owens, Weller.

S.T. *S/T*

Sarah Timberlake. Also worked at Owens, Weller.

C U

C. U. Unknown.

Arthur Williams. Also worked at Owens.

Robert O. Windisch. President, 1938–1954.

Mrs. Anna Young. President, 1931.

George F. Young. Treasurer, General manager 1885–(?).

Russell Young. General manager, 1918–(?).

Clotilda Zanetta. Also worked at Rookwood, Weller.

Marks:

ROZANE
RPCo

Impressed mark used before 1905. Also used on other lines without the word "Rozane."

AZUREAN

Impressed mark. Sometimes appears with RPCo mark.

Paper sticker, which was printed in red ink.

Impressed marks first used in 1904.

ROZANE "OLYMPIC" POTTERY

Black ink stamp used after 1905 and before 1939. A description of the scene is printed on the bottom of each piece.

ROSEVILLE POTTERY CO. ZANESVILLE, O.

Red ink stamp mark used after 1905 and before 1939.

Impressed mark or paper sticker in green ink used before 1905 (Rozane I; Della Robbia).

Black ink stamped mark used before 1906.

Ink stamped in black, blue, or green. This mark was used after 1914 until 1930, and may possibly have been used as early as 1910.

Gray on black aluminum foil sticker used from 1914 to 1934. Possibly appeared as early as 1912.

Impressed mark used from the 1930s. The numbers represent the pattern number and the size in inches.

Raised mark used during the 1950s.

Impressed mark used from 1914.

Raised mark used from 1939 to 1953. The numbers represent the pattern number and size in inches.

Raised mark used during the 1950s.

Impressed mark used from 1915.

Raised mark used from 1939 to 1953. Numbers represent pattern number.

ROSEVILLE PASADENA PLANTER U.S.A.

Raised mark used during the 1950s.

Raised mark used after 1935 until 1954.

Gray paper sticker used from 1917. The same sticker in gold was used on the Pinecone line during the 1930s.

Blue ink stamp used from 1939 to 1953.

Raised mark used after 1935 until 1954.

the Della Robbia and Olympic lines. When Rhead left to pursue his career in teaching in St. Louis, Missouri, his brother Harry, from England, replaced him.

In 1917 the Muskingum plant burned and that entire operation was moved to the Linden plant. Frank Ferrell was hired as art director, remaining in that post until 1954. He developed the Pinecone line, which derived from ideas he had suggested at the Weller Plant. It became the most popular line ever made at Roseville. (Later it was redesigned by Ferrell for Peters and Reed and was called Moss Aztec.)

In 1918, the new trademark, "Roseville U.S.A.," was adopted and George Young turned the general manager's job over to his son Russell T. Young. In 1931 Russell's mother, Anna Young, became president. The name of the firm was changed to Roseville Pottery, Inc. In 1938 her son-in-law, F. S. Clement, became president. After his death, Frederick J. Grant succeeded him and then Robert P. Windisch held the job until he left in 1954. That year the Roseville Pottery, Inc., including all designs, the plant, everything, was sold to the New England Ceramics Company, after which it was sold to Franklin Potteries of Franklin, West Virginia. By 1954, all Roseville Pottery production had stopped.

Twenty-two different shapes and sizes in jade green, celestial blue, and temple white were made in this Ming Tree line. This vase is 6½ inches high. It is marked "20, Roseville, U.S.A." (Collection of Donald Alexander)

Product

A contemporary description of the work at the Roseville Pottery appeared in *The Southwestern Book,* December, 1905, Vol. II, No. 12, "A Visit to Some Zanesville Potteries," by Lura Milburn Cobb.

We went first to the Roseville potteries, which occupy a large group of buildings, wherein is manufactured a great variety of ware, including washstand sets, jardinieres, and art ware. Over three hundred persons are employed at this plant, and about five thousand pieces of finished ware are turned out every day.

As our time was limited, and we were both very fond of art pottery, my friend and I visited only the rooms in which the art ware is manufactured.

Our guide led us from room to room, showing and explaining to us the various processes through which the clay passes, until it is ready for the admiring purchaser.

We learned that the Ohio clays naturally run to golden browns and yellows, that can be preserved unaltered through the intense heat of the firing to which the ware is subjected.

(Top left) These seven Apple Blossom vases are decorated with white flowers on pink ground. Each piece is marked with the raised Roseville USA mark. (From the collection of J. Walter Yore Company, Toledo, Ohio)　　(Left) This 7½-inch-high Gardenia vase is decorated with a white flower on green ground. It is 13 inches wide. (Collection of J. Walter Yore Company, Toledo, Ohio)　　(Top right) Five pieces of Snowberry pattern Roseville pottery. The pieces are decorated with white berries on pink to red ground. Each piece bears the raised Roseville USA mark. (Collection of J. Walter Yore Company, Toledo, Ohio)

(Left) Pink flowers on green ground decorate these Clematis pieces. Each has the raised Roseville USA mark. (Collection of J. Walter Yore Company, Toledo, Ohio)　　(Bottom left) *Top; left to right:* An 8-inch-high Bittersweet basket decorated with orange berries on gray ground and marked with raised Roseville USA 809-8. The Bittersweet flower bowl is 7 × 2½ inches. It is decorated with orange berries on gray ground and marked Roseville USA 826-6. *Bottom:* White flowers on a pink ground decorate the 13-inch-wide Iris vase. It is impressed Roseville USA 362-10. The 8-inch-high Iris vase is decorated with white iris on blue ground. Roseville 9-228 is impressed on the bottom. (Collection of J. Walter Yore Company, Toledo, Ohio)　　(Bottom right) A selection of Freesia pattern items. They are variously decorated with pink, yellow, or white flowers on green, orange, purple, brown, or blue background. (Collection of J. Walter Yore Company, Toledo, Ohio)

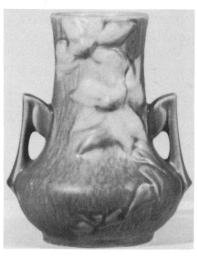

(Top left) These large and small Zephyr Lily vases have white flowers on blue background. The raised Roseville USA mark appears on the bottom. (From the collection of J. Walter Yore Company, Toledo, Ohio)   (Top center) Over 50 shapes were made in the Freesia pattern. This lamp base is 13 inches high. It is marked "20, Roseville, U.S.A." (Collection of Donald Alexander)   (Top right) Wincraft line, made about 1948. This 18½-inch vase features a raised tulip. It is marked "23 Roseville, U.S.A. 279-18." Advertisements for the line show pieces with other flowers or even geometric designs. It came in apricot, chartreuse, and azure blue. (Collection of Donald Alexander)   (Bottom left) This Clematis line vase has a green background. It is 7½ inches high, marked "20, Roseville, U.S.A." (Collection of Donald Alexander)   (Bottom right) Yellow sunflowers and green leaves cover this Sunflower line vase. The unmarked vase is 6¼ inches high. (Collection of Donald Alexander)

241

Spires of the flower decorate this Foxglove line jardiniere and pedestal. The piece is 24 inches high. It is marked "20 Roseville, U.S.A." (Collection of Donald Alexander)

Most of the potteries use clay from the neighboring hills, but to produce certain kinds of ware, and certain color effects, other ingredients are added; sometimes clays from other sources are used entirely or mixed with the native clays.

The abundant supply of natural gas at Zanesville is a potent factor in the manufacturing of all kinds of pottery. By its use degrees of heat are attained that would be impossible by other methods of firing, and the buildings are kept clean and free from dust.

Led by our guide, we viewed with interest the processes through which the clay is taken, from the time it reaches the factory, fresh from the neighboring hill, until it is transformed into a thing of beauty, fit to grace an artistic home.

The clay is pulverized and thoroughly washed, filtered and mixed with water, to a certain consistency. It is then, either by hand or machine, pressed into a mold, made of plaster of paris. This mold absorbs the water, making a body of clay next to the mold. After three or four minutes, the liquid that remains is poured out. The shell thus left is the future vase. It goes to the finisher who sponges and smooths off all defects.

The underglaze artware is sprayed with a clay liquid in mineral colors, and we marveled at the rapidity with which the blending is done by the young girls in charge of this branch of the work. We were allowed to stand and watch the decorators at work, painting from nature or copy, in mineral colors, giving to each article with skillful fingers its own individual crown of beauty.

After being decorated, the piece is taken to the dry room, where it stays until the water has all evaporated, and then is placed in the kiln.

We were surprised to find how large the kilns are, some of them being twenty feet high inside. The men have to climb on ladders to put on the top of the tall columns of saggers, or boxes of clay, which contain the precious ware. At the right time, after the ordeal by fire, each article is dipped in a liquid glass solution called glaze, and after this, fired for the second time, and is then a finished product.

We were told that we had seen the usual process of manufacturing artware, but variations of this and different processes are used, to produce other efects, and that the artist chemists are allowed to experiment, and often achieve wonderful results.

The greatest care in every detail must be exercised in order to secure perfection.

Most of the decorators were women, and I observed women and girls at work in many other rooms. Such employment must be very pleasant, congenial and suitable, bringing them into constant contact with beauty, in form and color, and it demands the care, patience and attention to detail which women are fitted by nature to give to their work.

Other sources say the pieces were made from American clays, mainly Ohio and Tennessee. The earliest pieces were painted clay. The artwares were made with almost every type of decorative detail, slip decoration, decals, freehand decoration, incised or embossed designs. A few lines such as Aztec were decorated by slip; that was squeezed from a bag, just as we today decorate with cake frosting.

(Top left) These Water Lily vases are decorated with yellow or lilac flowers on orange to brown, or pink to green ground. Each piece is marked with the raised Roseville USA mark. (From the collection of J. Walter Yore Company, Toledo, Ohio)   (Bottom left) A selection of Magnolia vases. White flowers appear on pink, blue, green, or orange ground. Roseville USA in raised letters appears on each piece. (From the collection of J. Walter Yore Company, Toledo, Ohio)   (Top right) Orange berries decorate these five Bushberry vases. The background colors are green to either orange or blue. The raised Roseville USA mark is on each piece.

(Left) This 4¼-inch-high vase is from White Rose line. It is green and pink with dull white flowers. (The Smithsonian Institution)   (Below) These Pinecone vases and candlesticks have pinecone decoration on orange to brown ground. The right-hand vase has a high-gloss glaze. The line was marked in many different ways. (From the collection of J. Walter Yore Company, Toledo, Ohio)

(Left top) This Cherry Blossom vase is 5¼ inches high. It is unmarked, made about 1932. (Collection of Donald Alexander)   (Left bottom) Roseville's 7-inch-long pottery sign advertisement.   (Below left) Laurel line was often marked like this 6¼-inch vase, with a silver-colored paper sticker (Collection of Donald Alexander)   (Below center) This 7¼-inch Baneda line vase is unmarked. The vase has a mottled red background with red berries and green leaves. (Collection of Donald Alexander)   (Below right) *Top:* Three vases and a pair of candlesticks in the Moss pattern. The pieces are decorated with moss on pink to green ground and marked with the impressed Roseville mark. *Bottom, Left to Right:* Pink and white flowers decorate the 8-inch-high and 7-inch-wide green Foxglove vase. It carries the raised Roseville USA 373-8 mark. The 3-inch-high Foxglove vase is decorated with pink and white flowers on a blue ground and marked Roseville 659-3. The 6-inch-high shell-shape Foxglove vase is decorated with pink flowers on rose to brown background. Roseville USA in raised letters and 166-6 appears on the bottom. (Collection of J. Walter Yore Company, Toledo, Ohio)

The pottery used more modern methods through the years and by 1920 the handmade art pottery was replaced by commercial pottery produced by machine to be sold in quantity. Embossed designs with little freehand decoration were favored.

Lines (The date represents the catalogue year when line was shown—or, if in parentheses, an approximation from other sources).

Antique Green Matte. Overall design of raised vines, solid green matte glaze. 1916.

Apple Blossom. Colored background of blue, coral, or green; relief apple blossom spray. 1948.

Artcraft. (1930)–1934.

Artwood. 1951.

Autumn. Red, yellow background, green landscape. 1916.

Aztec Art. May have been made about 1904 (1910 catalogue listing); base color beige, cream, or gray, decoration stylized, almost brushstroke patterns resembling leaves, flowers, or geometric patterns.

Azurine (Azurean?). Made in 1904. Blue background decorated with ships, scenes, portraits, or flowers, high-gloss glaze, marked R. P. Co. on some pieces.

Azurine Orchid Turquoise. Solid high-gloss colors of blue, orchid, or turquoise, unmarked. 1952.

Baneda. Incised band with raised leaf decoration on mottled ground. (1933).

Bittersweet. Shaded background, relief bittersweet in natural shades. (1940s), 1951.

Blackberry. Mottled green line with blackberry leaves and berries at top. (1930s), 1932.

Bleeding Heart. Shaded gray background, relief bleeding hearts. 1938, 1940.

Blue Ware. High-gloss glaze, blue background, underglaze decorating. 1910.

Burmese Green. Busts of Burmese man and woman (bookends). 1950.

Bushberry. Dark green rough background; relief bushberry spray in natural colors. 1941.

Cameo Line. Dark green or beige matte finish background with a border of trees and girls holding hands. 1910–1915.

(Top) Earthtones color this Florentine vase with raised panels of fruit. The unmarked piece is 8½ inches high. (Collection of Donald Alexander) (Bottom) This Rozane Ware vase should not be confused with the other patterns named Rozane. It was made about 1917. The flowers are yellow, pink, and lavender, the leaves green. The background is cream-colored. The 8¼-inch vase is marked with a blue ink circular stamped mark, "Roseville Pottery, Rozane Ware." (Collection of Donald Alexander)

The Roseville Pottery made many experimental pieces that were never accepted for commercial production. These three vases, front and back view, are all samples that were rejected in the late 1930s. *Vase #1:* High-bush cranberry in red and yellowish green. *Vase #2:* Hawthorn blossom. *Vase #3:* Arrowhead. (Collection of Mary and Terry Turan, Mostly Pottery, Wilmington, Illinois)

(Bottom left) These four Jonquil vases feature white jonquils on green to orange ground. They are unmarked. (Collection of J. Walter Yore Company, Toledo, Ohio)   (Bottom right) *Top:* These brown to green Sylvan flower bowls have a barklike appearance. They are unmarked. *Bottom:* These Dahlrose vases are decorated with white flowers on brown ground. The Dahlrose pattern was first made in 1924. The pieces are marked with paper stickers. (From the collection of J. Walter Yore Company, Toledo, Ohio)

Carnelian. Developed by Harry Rhead (first line 1910–1915); drip glaze decoration over matte glaze on specially shaped pieces marked with the Rv cipher. Second line 1916, textured glaze, blended color.

Cherry Blossom. Pink, brown, buff, yellow, blue. 1932.

Chinese Red. See Rozane Mongol.

Chloron. Dark green background, matte finish, and embossed decoration on cream ground. The mark Chloron in a semicircle appears on some of pieces. 1907.

Clemana. Yellow beige background, pastel raised floral decoration. 1936.

Clematis. Green, brown, or blue background; relief clematis flowers, 48 items. 1944–45.

Coat-of-Arms. Banner and shield design, black and red on cream (1916).

Columbine. Shaded background in red, blue, or brown; relief columbine spray, 44 items. 1941.

Corinthian. Fluted with a wreath border, developed under George Young. (1916–1930?).

Cornelian or Cornelian Twist. Muddy green glazed ware, gold edges. (1900).

Cosmos. Earthtone background: several ridges as part of design around center of vase; raised cosmos flower decoration. 1939.

Cremo. Three colors blended together, green at base, yellow center, rose top. (1910–1915).

Cremona. Pink and yellow background, small raised flowers and leaves. (1924–1930).

Crystal Green. 1939.

Crystalis. Crystaline glazed undecorated pieces. 1906.

Dahlrose. Daisylike flowers on a mottled beige and cream background (1924–1928).

Dawn. Pale matte glaze with raised floral decoration. 1937.

Della Robbia. Developed by Frederick Rhead, background was cut away and Greek, Persian, or conventional decorations remained. Overglazed. Later Sgraffito decoration was added to some pieces. 1906.

Dogwood I. Developed by Frank Ferrell. Large dogwood flowers on matte ground (1916–1918).

Dogwood II. White dogwood flowers in mottled light blue backgound, high gloss. 1928.

Donatella. Geometric designs of tulips and rectangles; cream background (1914).

(Top) This 3-inch-high bowl is in the Persian pattern, made about 1916. It is marked only with the number 14 in red ink. (Collection of Donald Alexander) (Bottom) The 10-inch-diameter tray, powder dish, hair receiver, and ring tree form a dresser set made about 1916. The pattern is Forget-Me-Not. The pieces are unmarked. (Collection of Donald Alexander)

Tea sets were made in the Landscape pattern about 1915. This teapot, sugar bowl, and creamer (top to bottom) show views of windmills and ships in blue on a cream background. The pieces are unmarked. (Collection of Donald Alexander)

(Left top) A selection of Donatello pieces. The Donatello pattern was introduced in 1915. These unmarked pieces are decorated with orange and green scenes on white ground. (From the collection of J. Walter Yore Company, Toledo, Ohio)   (Left center) More Donatello pieces with orange and green decoration on white ground. (From the collection of J. Walter Yore Company, Toledo, Ohio)   (Left bottom) This 2¼-inch-high Juvenile cup has an orange band on cream ground. The Sunbonnet Baby is dressed in a blue dress and yellow bonnet. The cup is marked RV on the bottom. (Collection of J. Walter Yore Company, Toledo, Ohio)

(Above left) This 10½-inch-high Della Robbia vase is decorated with raised fish. The piece is signed "ED" by the artist and has the Rozane Ware seal. (Collection of Donald Alexander)

(Above right) This 8-inch Mostique vase is unmarked. It is 8 inches high. The Mostique line was made about 1915. (Collection of Donald Alexander)

(Right) The red crackle glazed line called Pauleo was made about 1914. This Pauleo vase, 12 inches high, is impressed "16 Rv." (Collection of Donald Alexander)

(Top left) Mottled pink, green, and cream matte glaze covers this candleholder of the Carnelian line. The piece is 3 inches high and 4½ inches in diameter. It is marked with a blue underglaze "Rv." (Authors' collection)   (Center left) This first Carnelian line ewer is 10 inches high and marked "16, 17" and "Rv." There is also a paper sticker. (Collection of Donald Alexander)   (Bottom left) A Della Robbia vase, pictured in the 1906 catalogue, with incised and painted underglazed decorations of flowers and leaves in blue, green, yellow, and orange. This 11-inch piece has a glossy glaze. It is marked with the Rozane Ware disc in relief and the artist's initials, "W. M." (The Art Museum, Princeton University, Princeton, New Jersey)

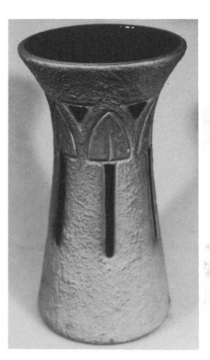

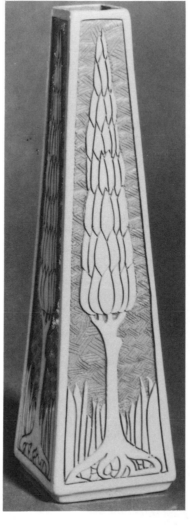

(Above) Yellow, blue, and green glazed geometric designs appear on the unglazed gray background of this Mostique vase. The interior is glazed green. The unmarked piece is 12 inches high. (Authors' collection)   (Left) Frederick H. Rhead designed this vase made by C.H. about 1906–1908. It is decorated with brown and buff cypress trees. The glossy glazed piece is 10½ inches high. (The Art Museum, Princeton University, Princeton, New Jersey)

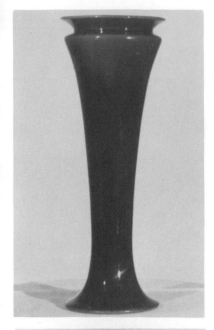

(Top) A dark red glaze is the only decoration on this Rozane Mongol vase. It is 14 inches high. The piece is marked with the Rozane Mongol seal and the number 6. (Collection of Donald Alexander) (Bottom) This 14-inch vase of deep red is undecorated. It is the Rozane Ware Mongol 1 line. (The Smithsonian Institution)·

Donatello. Developed by Harry Rhead in 1915. He copied the decoration from a Czechoslovakian jardiniere. It has a fluted top and bottom, and a molded strip featuring cherubs and trees. Glazed green and brown shades on white background. Early pieces had matte glaze, later pieces had semigloss or glossy glaze.

Dutch. Colored decals of Dutch people; blue edging (1900).

Earlam. Two-toned mottled glaze with slight incised ridge at neck of vase. 1930.

Falline. Beige with peapodlike decorations. 1933.

Ferrella. Introduced about 1930 and named for Frank Ferrell. Shell-like border and a mottled body, green and brown with ivory shells and other colors, openings at the top between shells.

Florane. Plain matte glazed ware. Middle period.

Florentine. Rough mottled panels and perpendicular flower clusters. 1924–1928.

Forest. Earthtone body with raised scenes of forest. Middle period.

Forget-Me-Not. Blue or lavender flowers and green leaves in swag border, gold trim, cream background. (1916).

Foxglove. Solid color background; relief foxglove stalk. 1942.

Freesia. Brown, green, orange, purple, or blue background; relief flowers, yellow, pink or white. 48 shapes. 1945.

Fuchsia. Slightly mottled background, in dark browns, grays, fuchsia leaves and a few drooping blossoms in natural shades. 1938.

Fugi. See Rozane Woodland.

Futura. Modern shapes and designs in blended glaze. 1924–1928.

Gardenia. Shaded pastel background in green, gray, or tan; relief white gardenia flower and green leaves. 1950.

Glossy Pinecone. Probably another name for Pinecone II.

Glossy White Rose. Probably same as White Rose but with glossy finish.

Holland. Dutch boy and girl on light-colored stoneware. 1930.

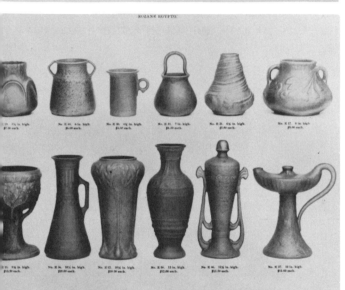

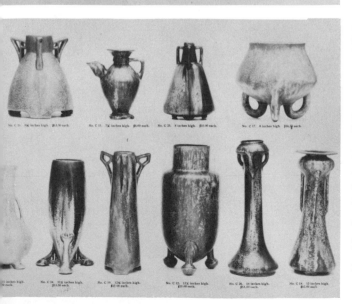

(Top left) A page from the 1906 Roseville catalogue showing the Della Robbia line. Note the original price. (Ohio Historical Society)   (Center left) A page from the 1906 Roseville catalogue showing the Rozane Egypto line. (Ohio Historical Society)   (Left) A page from the 1906 Roseville catalogue showing the Crystalis line. (Ohio Historical Society)

(Above left) A Dutch mother and two children are shown in a decal on this pitcher. The line was introduced about 1900. The figures are multicolored, and a thin blue line appears near the top. The 12-inch-high pitcher is unmarked. (Collection of Donald Alexander)   (Above right) This Rozane Woodland vase is 6½ inches high. It is marked with the Rozane Woodland seal and the artist's initials, M B. The line was made about 1904. (Collection of Donald Alexander)

About 1900 the Cornelian or Cornelian Twist line was introduced. This 6-inch pitcher has no mark. It has a dull green glaze and gold trim. (Collection of Donald Alexander)

Holly. Red to green matte glaze on carved holly leaf decoration. 1915.

Imperial I. Small band of floral or geometric motifs at the neck on a green or blue mottled background. 1916–1919.

Imperial II. Textured matte glaze of red and blue, green and orange, yellow and violet, or white and pink. 1924–1928.

Iris. Earthtone background, raised iris decoration in earthtones. 1939.

Ivory. White glaze. 1916. Another line called ivory was offered in 1940.

Ixia. Beige matte background shaded to darker color at base, floral spray. 1937.

Jonquil. White and yellow jonquils and leaves on mottled light brown body. 1931.

Juvenile. Decal decoration on light ground.

Landscape. 1916 matte glaze; 1915 brown or blue decal landscapes of Holland; 1920 glossy glaze.

La Rose. Creamy matte background, delicate floral drape in pastel colors. 1924–1930.

(Below left) *Left to Right:* A Rozane Royal 8-inch vase of crackled gray and green glaze; a Rozane Ware Egypto vase inscribed "More Light to Goethe," 3¾ inches high; and an orange and brown urn with orange flowers. It is marked R. P. Co. and is in the Rozane Royal line. (The Smithsonian Institution)   (Below right) A page from the 1906 Roseville catalogue showing the Rozane Royal, light glazed pieces. (Ohio Historical Society)

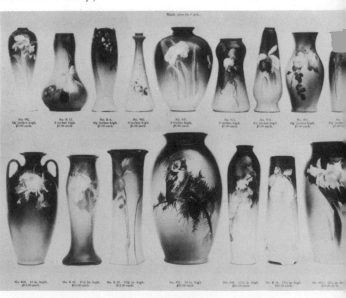

Laurel. Medium brown background, stylized laurel branches in wood tones. Vertical panels of three incised bands. 1934.

Lombardy. Scalloped top, paneled, square feet, various colors. 1924–1928.

Lotus. Petals of lotus surround the opening of the vase like an opening lotus flower. 1951.

Luffa. Solid color glaze. 1934.

Luster. Metallic luster glaze of orange, purple, or yellow. 1921.

Magnolia. Rough background, tan, blue, or green, relief magnolia in shaded white glaze. 65 items. 1943–1944.

Matte Green. See Antique Green Matte.

Mayfair. Solid color glaze. Late period.

Medallion. Oval cameo decal decoration with gold floral swags. 1916.

Ming Tree. Tortured branch shapes in the oriental manner and irregularly shaped pieces; green, blue, or white. 1949.

Mock Orange. Light background, modern shapes, relief mock orange blossoms. (1946?) 1949.

Moderne. Modern shapes, solid color. 1936.

Monticello. Mottled brown, green, band of darker shade, small modern decoration on band, running over edge of band. 1931.

Morning Glory. Pastel shade background, overall design of raised morning glories on vine. 1935.

Moss. Shaded pink to white or green to white background, raised decoration of Spanish moss in natural colors. 1936.

Mostique. Flower or conventional incised designs and a pebbly matte background. Almost art deco in appearance. 1915.

Mowa. Shades of red, glossy glaze. 1917.

Normandy. Grapes and leaves in top band, fluted matte glaze. 1924–1930.

Nursery. Nursery rhyme motifs (1920).

Old Ivory. Ivory color, no design. (1916).

Olympic. Decorated with Greek mythological scenes made by black line transfer and overglazed. Decorations were not handmade. One of the rarest Roseville lines. Marked Rozane Olympic Pottery. A description

A portrait of Maude Adams decorates this Rozane vase with dark glaze. The 13-inch-high piece is marked "Rozane RPCo 812." It is signed with the artist's initials, "AD." (Collection of Donald Alexander)

(Top left) M. Timberlake signed this dark Rozane vase. It is 10 inches high. (Collection of Donald Alexander)   (Bottom left) This 10-inch-wide by 9-inch-high Rozane jardiniere has a brown to green to mahogany glaze with orange and green floral decoration. The artist's cipher, WH(?), appears at the base. The impressed Rozane mark and "40 4 RPCO," and "2" are on the bottom.   (Center) W. Myers signed this dark glazed 16-inch Rozane ewer. It is marked "1 Rozane RP Co 858." A very similar piece appears in the 1906 catalogue as "Rozane Royal, dark." (Collection of Donald Alexander)   (Right) This 18½-inch-high vase is Rozane Royal with a dark glaze. It is marked "Rozane, RP Co. 865." The vase is signed by the artist Myers. (Collection of Donald Alexander)

of the scene is printed in black on the bottom of each piece.

Opac Enamel. Plain green, yellow, or red glaze (1900).

Orian. Plain color, geometric designs, blue, yellow, purple, or brown. 1935.

Panel. Dark green background, panel design with raised colored fruit or nude women pictured in panel. 1920.

Pauleo. Designed by Harry Rhead. 1914. Named for George Young's daughter-in-law Pauline and his daughter Leota. Oriental shape with a red crackled glaze, metallic brown luster overglaze. It was very expensive. A later version of this line had a marbelized finish. It is marked "Rv" (the v is within the loop of the R) or "Pauleo Pottery" within an impressed circular seal.

Peacock. An umbrella stand (?).

Peony. Shaded earthtones of brown, green, or coral, rough background, relief peony in yellow, brown or green ground. 65 shapes. 1942.

Persian. Persian type motif on light color matte background. 1916.

Pinecone I. Developed by Frank Ferrell about (1917)? it was not made until 1935.

Pinecone II. Glossy glaze. (1945)–1953.

Poppy. Pale green, yellow, earthtone background, raised poppy spray in pastel shades. (1930).

Primrose. Pastel background, globular-shaped vases, raised primrose decoration. 1934.

Raymor. Ovenproof tableware. 1952.

Romafin. Restaurant serving dishes, reddish brown outside, white interior. (1918).

Rosecraft. Lusterware developed by Harry Rhead. Plain classic shape, undecorated. 1916–1917.

Rosecraft Hexagon. Dark green, black matte background, hexagonal-shaped body, decoration of bleeding hearts in a lighter color. 1924–1928.

Rosecraft Vintage. Black background with art nouveau curved border of browns and yellows. (1916) 1924–1928.

Rouge Flambé. See Rozane Mongol.

Royal Capri. Metallic luster on modern petal-formed vase.

Rozane Crystalis. Crystalized flowing glaze (1907).

Rozane Egypto. Made by John Herold by 1905. Egyptian-shape vases covered with relief decorations and matte green glaze.

Rozane Fuji. See Rozane Woodland.

Rozane Grecian. Blue background and classical white figures, early line.

Rozane Mara. An iridescent metallic line similar to Weller's Sicardo. Most of it is unsigned. Developed by John Herold about 1904.

Rozane Matte. Matte glaze, slip decorated. 1920s.

Rozane Mongol. Dark red crystalline glaze. A few pieces were made with a solid red glaze or a silvery overlay. Sometimes called Chinese Red or Rouge Flambé. Developed by John Herold. (1900–1904).

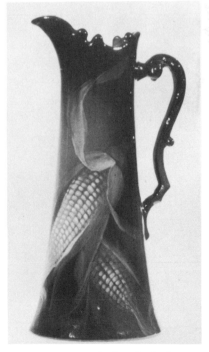

V. Adams signed this dark Rozane Royal 15½-inch tankard. It is marked "5, Rozane Royal" with the usual Rozane emblem. (Collection of Donald Alexander)

Rozane I. First pieces were made with dark backgrounds and underglaze slip painting. Finished piece had a high gloss finish. Pieces decorated with portraits, animals, or flowers. Marked R. P. Co. or Rozane R. P. Co. Later the Rozane line used either a light or dark background and the name was changed to Rozane Royal. The name Rozane Ware written over a rose in a double circle was being used on this ware by 1905.

Rozane Ware. Raised roselike flowers in pastel colors surrounded by green leaves. Stippled cream background. Stamped Roseville Pottery Rozane Ware (1917).

Rozane Woodland. Gazo Fudji created the Rozane Woodland line about 1905 to compete with Dickens Ware by Weller. Sgraffito decorations (incised designs) surrounded the glazed design. Small dots made with a needle as a background, colored flowers. Matte finish. Gray, yellow, or brown shades for the background; decorations are brown or russet. When the dots were omitted the ware was called Fujiyama or Rozane Fudji. These pieces were decorated with geometric designs or insects. "Fujiyama" sometimes appears stamped on the bottom.

Russco. Modern shapes, solid color glaze. 1934.

Savona. Solid-colored shiny glaze with fluting at bottom, grapes at the top. 1924–1930.

Silhouette. Modern-shaped pieces with nude females in panels. (1940).

Snowberry. Shaded background, in blue, green, or rose, relief snowberry branch. 52 pieces. 1947.

Sunflower. Mottled background in earthtones with natural color sunflowers in raised design. (1930).

Sylvan. Owls and leaves on rough background. Developed by Frank Ferrell about 1918 (1930).

Teasel. Plain flowing line shapes with raised teasel spray in shaded monotone glaze. 1938.

Thorn Apple. Pastel glaze, raised thorn apple branch as decoration. 1937.

Topeo. Perpendicular relief, 1934.

Tourist. Decorated with decals of automobiles on a cream background, matte finish. (1906–1916)?

Tourmaline. Shaded blue vase with ridged banding at neck. 1933.

Tree Branch. In relief as decoration or handles. 1940–1945.

Tuscany. Pastel, glossy glaze, embossed grapes and leaves. 1924–1930.

Velmoss I. Red roses on cream matte background. 1916–1919.

Velmoss II. Green leaves, three stripes in center, green, blue, or red background, orange interior matte glaze. 1935.

Victorian. 1924–1930.

Volpato. Fluted like Donatello but the border is a wreath. The pieces are green glazed. (1916 or 1918–1921)?

Water Lily. Shaded rough background in blue, brown, or rose, relief water lilies. Over 50 items. 1943.

White Rose. Solid background in coral, blue, or brown, relief white roses. 50 items. 1940.

Wincraft. Modern shapes, background shades to brown at bottom, relief floral or animal decoration, high gloss glaze apricot, chartreuse, or azure blue. 1948.

Windsor. Blue or brown background, leaves or geometric designs. 1931.

Wisteria. Mottled earthtone body with lavender wisteria on green vine at neck. 1933.

Zephyr Lily. Shaded background of blue, brown, or green, relief zephyr lily. 52 items. 1947.

Bibliography

Alexander, Donald E., *Roseville Pottery for Collectors*, Privately published: Donald E. Alexander, Richmond, Indiana, 1970.

(Left) A page from the Roseville 1906 catalogue showing the Rozane Royal dark glazed pieces. (Ohio Historical Society) (Above) An ear of corn decorates this Rozane Royal mug. It has the dark glaze, and is 6 inches high. The mark is "5 Rozane Royal Scene" and the piece is signed by the artist V. Adams. (Collection of Donald Alexander)

J. Imlay is the artist who signed this Rozane Royal vase with the light glaze. It is 8½ inches high. The mark is "5," plus the Rozane Royal emblem. (Collection of Donald Alexander)

Barber, Edwin, *Marks of American Potters,* Philadelphia: Patterson and White, 1904, p. 139.

Bulletin of the Department of Commerce and Labor, "American Art Pottery," *American Pottery Gazette* (V. V, No. VI), (August 10, 1907).

Clark, Robert Judson, *The Arts and Crafts Movement in America 1876–1916*, Princeton, N.J.: Princeton University Press, 1972.

Clifford, Richard A., *Roseville Art Pottery,* Winfield, Kansas: Andenken Publishing Company, 1968.

Cobb, Lura Milburn, "A Visit to Some Zanesville Potteries," *The Southwestern Book* (V. II, No. 12), (December, 1905).

Henzke, Lucile, "Roseville Pottery, Part One," *Spinning Wheel* (November, 1969), 16–17, 56.

————, "Roseville Pottery, Part Two." *Spinning Wheel* (December, 1969), 22–24.

Jervis, W. P. *A Pottery Primer.* New York: O'Gorman Publishing Co., 1911.

Ohio Historical Society Library Files, "Patterns Manufactured by Roseville Pottery Incorporated."

————, Rozane Ware Catalog.

Pottery Collectors' Newsletter, "Answers" (V. 1, No. 4), (January, 1972), 52.

Purviance, Evan, "American Art Pottery," *Mid-America Reporter* (April, 1972), 17.

————, "American Art Pottery," *Mid-America Reporter* (May, 1972), 15.

————, "American Art Pottery," *Mid-America Reporter* (June, 1972), 14.

————, "American Art Pottery," *Mid-America Reporter* (August, 1972), 28.

————, "American Art Pottery," *Mid-America Reporter* (September, 1972), 4–5.

Purviance, Louise and Evan, and Norris F. Schneider, *Roseville Art Pottery in Color,* Des Moines, Iowa: Wallace-Homestead Book Co., 1970.

The Roseville Pottery Company, *"Rozane Ware Catalog,"* 1906.

Schneider, Norris F. "Roseville Pottery," *Western Collector* (July, 1969), 302–307.

―――, "Veteran Mosaic Tile Employee Compiles Outstanding Display" *Zanesville Times Recorder* (October 30, 1960).

Spinning Wheel, "Roseville Pottery" (April, 1968), 21.

Stout, Wilber, R. T. Stull, Wm. J. McCaughey, D. J. Demerest, "Art Pottery," Geological Survey of Ohio. Columbus, Ohio: J. A. Bownocker, State Geologist, 4th Series, Bulletin 26, 1923.

Turan, Terry and Mary, correspondence with authors.

Zanesville Chamber of Commerce, Booklet, 1918, "The Roseville Pottery Company."

RUM RILL POTTERY. See RED WING, SHAWNEE

SHAWNEE POTTERY

The Shawnee Pottery was not an art pottery, but it was the final chapter in the history of several potteries. Shawnee was organized after the close of the American Encaustic Tiling Company in 1935. Their president Addis E. Hull, was the son of the founder of the Hull Pottery Company. He had held that position for six years, later going to Western Stoneware Co. of Monmouth, Ill. Shawnee was named for a Shawnee arrowhead found at the site of the pottery plant, and their first trademark was an Indian profile on an arrowhead. Shawnee pottery sold well, partly because of the anti-German and Japanese feelings and the "buy American" movement. The factory made pieces for S. S. Kresge, S. H. Kress, F. W. Woolworth, McCrory stores, Sears, and other outlets that sold their low-priced commercial pottery.

At first, the customer had furnished the designs. Then from 1938 to 1942, Rudy Ganz was their designer. Louis Bauer, later with Hull Pottery, also was a designer and Ed Hazel designed from 1942 to 1944.

In 1938 or 1939, George Rumrill of the Rum Rill Pottery Company of Little Rock, Arkansas, stopped buying from the Red Wing Pottery of Minnesota and started to buy from Shawnee. Mr. Rumrill designed the pieces Shawnee made for him.

Shawnee continued to make pottery until early 1961. Most of the pieces were kitchenware and inexpensive dinnerware and premiums. During World War II, from 1942 to 1946, the firm was engaged in special defense work.

Some pieces were marked Shawnee, many were marked with a paper label. Kenwood was a mark used by a division of the Shawnee Pottery.

Bibliography

Collectors' Weekly, "Shawnee Pottery" (December 1, 1970), 11.

Field, Zane, "Shawnee, Last Made in 1961, Is Suggested," *Collectors' Weekly* (December 1, 1970), 1.

Hull, A. E., correspondence to Norris F. Schneider (August 10, 1960).

Ohio Historical Society Files, ads and catalogues (undated).

Schneider, Norris F., "Shawnee Pottery," Zanesville *Times Recorder* (October 16, 1960 and October 23, 1960).

Schweiker, Malcolm A., correspondence to Norris F. Schneider (August 3, 1960 and August 11, 1960).

Weiss, Grace M., "Shawnee Pottery" *The Antique Trader* (June 5, 1973), 55.

SHAWSHEEN POTTERY

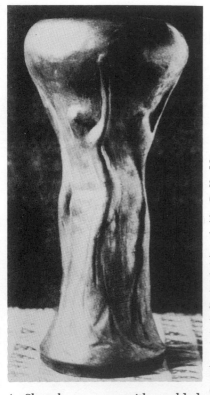

A Shawsheen vase with molded decoration shown in *Keramic Studio,* May, 1911.

Shawsheen pottery was first made in Billerica, Massachusetts, during the spring of 1906. The firm moved to Mason City, Iowa, in 1907. Mr. and Mrs. Edward Dahlquist, who founded the company, had been trained as potters. Edward Dahlquist had studied at the Minneapolis School of Art, the Chicago Art Institute, and the Art Students League in New York. His pastels had been displayed in a Boston gallery. Mrs. Dahlquist also studied at the Minneapolis School of Art and the Chicago Art Institute. She took special instruction from Lucy Perkins, a potter, in New York City.

The early pottery done at Shawsheen was hand coiled, but after moving to Iowa, the potters made many pieces on a wheel. They did all the designing, throwing, decorating, glazing, and firing. The firm went out of business in 1911.

Bibliography

Keramic Studio, "Shawsheen Ware" (V. 13), (May, 1911–April, 1912), 104–105.

STOCKTON TERRA COTTA

REKSTON

Impressed Stockton mark.

The Stockton Terra Cotta Company was established in Stockton, California, in 1891. It was founded by a group of Stockton businessmen who were convinced by Charles Bailey that a California pottery could be a successful business. Bailey had worked as the manager of the majolica department of the Excelsior Pottery Works in Trenton, New Jersey, and in Ohio. He represented various potteries in the East, and while traveling in California, he felt that it was a logical place for an art pottery factory because of the nearby clay beds and cheap transportation.

The firm started making drain and sewer pipe and other terra-cotta ware from clays that were found in Calaveras County, California.

The company began to make art pottery in 1897. The ware was called Rekston. The name is supposed to have come from the letters in Stockton Terra-Cotta.

Rekston ware was made with heavy colored glazes in mottled and blended colors. They made vases, pitchers, jardinieres, flowerpots, pedestals, umbrella stands, bowls, and tea sets. Dark green, brown, pale pink, rose, spattered gold, and yellow were some of the colors used. Some of the decorations were raised. Pieces were marked with the round symbol of the firm and the name Rekston.

The company had a fire on November 17, 1902, and the pottery was never rebuilt.

(Right) A Stockton dark brown pitcher.   (Below) Stockton sugar bowl, creamer, and teapot with raised ivy leaf pattern around the sides. (Thelma Shull, *Victorian Antiques*)

Bibliography

Barber, Edwin, *Marks of American Potters*, Philadelphia: Patterson and White, 1904, pp. 164–165.

Evans, Paul F., "The Art Pottery Era in the United States, 1870 to 1920, Part One," *Spinning Wheel* (October, 1970), 52.

Shull, Thelma, "The Stockton Art Pottery," *Hobbies* (V. 54), (August, 1949), 94–95.

——, *Victorian Antiques*. Rutland, Vermont: Charles E. Tuttle Company, 1963.

TECO GATES

Teco marks, stamped on the bottom. The name "Teco" was found in advertising brochures as late as 1958 but the product is of different quality from the original Teco art pottery.

William D. Gates was born in Ashland, Ohio, in 1852. In 1853 his family moved to Illinois where he was educated in the Illinois public schools. He received his degree from Wheaton College, Illinois, in 1875. Gates moved to Chicago to study law, but before he finished, his father died and he returned home to spend two years settling the estate. In 1878, he returned to Chicago and in 1879, he was admitted to the bar. He practiced law for several years, but when an opportunity arose to make more money, he began a tile business with a plant in Terra Cotta (Crystal Lake), Illinois, and an office in Chicago.

In 1881 Mr. Gates founded the Terra Cotta Tile Works in Terra Cotta, Illinois, where he obtained a grist mill. With good clay deposits on the property and the grist mill wheels to grind the clay, Gates went into the manufacture of architectural terra-cotta bricks, drain tile, and pottery; terra-cotta architectural pieces were in great demand by builders. The pottery built a chemical laboratory and kilns and Gates continued experimenting with art pottery. In 1902, the Teco line was introduced. The name Teco came from "te" in terra and "co" in cotta. The pottery, known as the American Terra Cotta and Ceramic Company, had money, space, equipment, and many talented artists so that none of the art pottery was produced until their experiments assured them of a superior product. Elmer Gorton, a graduate of the Department of Ceramics at Ohio State University, and Paul and Ellis Gates, sons of William Gates, also graduates of the Department of Ceramics at Ohio State, worked at the pottery. Many artists and architects were employed as designers, including T. Albert, Fritz Albert, J. K. Cady, N. L. Clark, W. J. (I. ?) Dodd, A. L. Dort, architect Max Dunning, W. K. Fellows,

(Top left) The A.T.C. and C. Company plant in Terra Cotta, Illinois. (Bottom left) Two Teco matte green pottery vases meant for the garden, as pictured in *Keramic Studio*, February, 1905.   (Top right) Three Teco porcelain vases with crystalline glazes shown in *Keramic Studio*, February, 1905.   (Bottom right) A tile decoration by Hardesty Gillmore Maratta for Teco Gates Pottery as shown in *Sketch Book*, October, 1905.

N. Forester, Mrs. F. R. Fuller, architect Hugh M. G. Gardner, Ellis D. Gates, H. H. Gates, William D. Gates, O. Giannini, Mr. Hals, J. L. Hamilton, R. A. Hirschfeld, architect W. L. B. Jenney, architect W. K. Fellows, architect W. B. Mundie, Hardesty Gillmore Maratta, architect George C. Nimmons, Blanche Ostertag, Christian Schneider, Howard V. Shaw, Holmes Smith, and M. P. White. Schneider, who was also a modeler for the company, was loaned to Louis Sullivan, the famous architect, to help with his modeling of architectural details. The architects may have been working on specific buildings and were at Teco only to design special items for their own projects.

The experiments with the art pottery frequently had to wait for available time as the work with the architectural terra-cotta was of prime importance. Marbled or mottled surfaces were tested. The art pottery tried a similar glaze. Their green matte was popular, but red, buff, and brown finishes were also made. A metallic luster was discovered in 1898 by chance, and experiments were repeated until the glaze was finally perfected. Another accident caused a piece of pottery to be covered with a glaze having

A selection of Teco ware pictured in *Pottery and Glass*, December, 1908.

NEW DESIGNS IN TECO POTTERY FOR WEDDINGS, BIRTHDAY GIFTS, CARD FAVORS AND AS A HOME DECORATION.

Why not handle an advertised Pottery of merit, where each design is prized as an object of art? TECO POTTERY with its soft mossy green color and originality of design cannot be duplicated or successfully imitated.

We sell to only one and the best dealer in art goods in each town. Write for catalog and particulars regarding Teco agency for your city.

THE GATES POTTERIES
602 Chamber of Commerce Building
Potteries, Terra Cotta, Ill.   CHICAGO, ILL.

An advertisement from *Pottery and Glass*, November, 1909.

minute crystals. Once again, more experiments were needed to improve the quality and standardize the finish. Gates even invented a machine to throw three streams of different colors of glaze to produce a mottled effect, as well as developing a more efficient pressing machine and a turned kiln.

Teco pottery was offered for sale in ads reading *"The Gates Pottery, Chicago, Illinois"* rather than the firm name. Ads and articles about Teco and its production have been found dating up to 1923. No one seems to be sure of the date production was stopped.

The pottery buildings were purchased in 1929 by George A. Berry, Jr. He renamed the company the American Terra Cotta Corporation and made architectural terra-cotta, ceramic wares, and some ornamental pottery. The company diversified and started The American Steel Treating Company, which is still operating.

Product

The first experimental Teco pottery was in subdued tones of red, then in buffs, and then in browns. After this, the pottery made some pieces with a marbelized finish similar to those they were using on architectural pieces.

An experimental metallic luster glaze was made in 1898 and later a crystalline glaze appeared after an accident in an experiment. These glazes were perfected and also used

on a porcelainlike body. The green matte glaze of other
art potteries such as Grueby was popular with customers,
so Teco developed a green glaze that was "strongly suggestive of Grueby pottery in tone and finish, but again this
was a matter of accident and not of deliberate imitation"
(*Brush and Pencil,* Vol. 9, 1902). This was a soft moss
green crystalline color on a stonewarelike body. At the St.
Louis exposition in 1904, some of the Teco pottery with
the green crystalline glaze was on display. The famous
vases in the Pompeian room of the Auditorium Annex
were made with this peculiar metallic green glaze. The
vases were designed and made by William Gates and
were seven feet in height. It was because they had kilns
large enough to fire architectural pieces that large-sized
Teco pieces were possible.

An interesting type of clay picture that was occasionally
used in a fireplace mantel was made at Teco from about
1905. The pictures were painted with colored slip of
differently colored liquid clay. The surface was unglazed
when it was fired. One of these pictures was made of tiles
three feet wide and eighteen inches high. Each finished
view was composed of a group of these with sometimes as
many as seven or eight tiles being used. Hardesty Gillmore Maratta was the artist who did most of the tile
"painting."

The Teco pottery line included over five hundred designs by 1911. New colors were added including platinum
gray, blue, red, purple, yellow, and several peculiar
shades of green and four shades of brown. A few "freaks
of the kiln" were sold with metallic blue and purple or
starred crystallization patterns.

At first, Teco was influenced by the natural woodland
and lake setting of the pottery building. Designs suggesting aquatic plants such as lilies, lotuses, flower petals,
leaves, branches, stalks, and buds were made. One popular vase resembled an ear of corn.

Almost all of the early pieces of Teco art pottery were
flower vases. There were also garden ornaments in the
line and they were usually of classical design. Soft stone
gray pieces for the yard were made in 1911. Garden fountains were made using several types of glaze. A fountain
might be of buff-colored clay with a wreath glazed in red,
green, or orange.

Tile was also produced at this time. Mantels were made
of many colored tiles in green, brown, orange, blue, and
gray tones. Landscape decorations were often part of the

A Teco green matte glazed vase,
10¾ inches high by 3¼ inches in
diameter. The vertical Teco mark
is on the bottom. (The Smithsonian
Institution)

design. Some of the tiles were in low relief. The famous Teco green glaze was used for many tiles.

The firm also made tableware and full tea sets in gray and light pinkish beige.

Teco pottery vases were made with molding and by throwing on the wheel. The clays used were of many colors including red, yellow, buff, and blue, and these were carefully mixed with other minerals for the desired effect. Almost all the clay came from near or in Brazil, Indiana. (A very complete description of the making of a vase in 1905 can be found in "Sketch Book," Sept., 1905, Vol. 5, *Our American Potteries, Teco Ware,* by Susan Stuart Frackelton, pp. 13–19.)

Bibliography

Arts and Decoration (Vol. 1), (March, 1911), 229.

Barber, Edwin, *Marks of American Potters,* Philadelphia: Patterson and White, 1904.

Bulletin of the Department of Commerce and Labor, *American Pottery Gazette* (Vol. V, No. VI), (August 10, 1907).

Chicago Historical Society, various clippings from their files.

Clark, Robert Judson, *The Arts and Crafts Movement in America 1876–1916,* Princeton, N.J.: Princeton University Press, 1972.

Craftsman, ad. (Vol. 7.), (1905).

Crosby, Charles, "The Work of American Potters, Article Four—How Teco Came to Be," *Arts and Decoration* (V. 1), (March, 1911), 214–215.

Crowley, Lilian H., "It's Now the Potter's Turn," *International Studio* (V. 75), (September, 1922), 539.

Edgar, William Harold, "Another American Pottery Where Artists Are in Close Communion with Nature and Mechanical Facilities Are Extraordinary," *Pottery and Glass* (V. I, No. 6), (December, 1908), 14–16.

———, "The Teco Pottery," *International Studio* (V. 36) (January, 1909, Supplement), xxvii–xxix.

Frackelton, Susan Stuart, "Our American Potteries, Teco Ware" *Sketch Book* (V. 5), (September, 1905), 13–19.

———, "Our American Potteries, Maratta's and Albert's

(Above) Black highlights are on this 13¼-inch-high green glazed vase. It was made about 1910 and has the stamped vertical Teco mark. (Collection of Mr. and Mrs. John Keefe)   (Below) Slight ribbing decorates this light green matte glazed vase marked "Teco 363." It is 4¾ inches high by 4¼ inches wide. (Authors' collection)

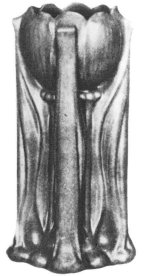

A selection of Teco Ware pictured in *Arts and Decoration*, March, 1911.

Work at the Gates Potteries," *Sketch Book* (V. 5), (October, 1905), 73–80.

Gray, Walter Ellsworth, "Latter-Day Developments in American Pottery—II," *Brush and Pencil* (V. 9), (1902), 289–296.

Industrial Chicago (V. 1), (1891), 789.

Jervis, W. P., *A Pottery Primer,* New York: O'Gorman Publishing Co., 1911.

Keramic Studio, "Teco Ware" (V. 6), (February, 1905), 219.

Little, Flora Townsend, "A Short Sketch of American Pottery," *Art & Archaeology* (V. 15), (May, 1923), 219.

Pottery and Glass (V. III, No. 5), (November, 1909) 103.

———, (November, 1911), 36.

Pottery Collectors' Newsletter, "Teco Potteries, Terra Cotta, Illinois" (V. 1, No. 3), (December, 1971), 31–32.

———, "Teco Potteries, Terra Cotta, Illinois: More on Teco Pottery by a Teco Collector" (V. 1, No. 11), (August, 1972), 151–152.

Rawson, Jonathan A., "Teco and Robineau Pottery," *House Beautiful* (V. 33), (April, 1913), 151.

Ruge, Clara, "American Ceramics—A Brief Review of Progress," *International Studio* (V. 28), (March, 1906), 21–28.

This blue green matte glazed vase has the Teco impressed mark. It is 3¾ inches high by 5½ inches wide. (Authors' collection)

_____, "Development of American Ceramics," *Pottery & Glass* (V. 1, No. 2), (August, 1908), 3.

Sketch Book (V. 5), (1906), ad., xi.

Stuart, Evelyn Marie, "About Teco Art Pottery" *Fine Arts Journal* (V. 20), (June, 1909), 341–345.

_____, "Teco Pottery and Faience Tile," *Fine Arts Journal* (V. 25), (August, 1911), 99–111.

Williams, Margaret Gates, correspondence to Mr. Jedlic.

The incised Tiffany mark.

TIFFANY POTTERY

The varied works of Louis Comfort Tiffany are well known to most collectors. He was one of the greatest of the American artists making glass, pottery, jewelry, enamel on copper, tombstones, paintings, and other salable works of art. However, it is his pottery that is of interest here.

The Tiffany metal furnaces of Corona, New York, were started in 1898 and experiments in making pottery began the same year. It was not until the St. Louis Exposition in 1904 that Tiffany pottery was put on display. The three pieces used at the exhibit were ivory-glazed white semiporcelain clay from Ohio and Massachusetts. In 1905, his firm began to make its own lamp bases for the Favrile glass shades. The bases were deep ivory-shaded brown. Later bases were green, and a few white or coated with bronze. Many had matte glazes. All were marked "LCT" on the bottom. The pottery bases were only a limited success, and most of the lamp bases made by Tiffany were of enameled metal rather than pottery.

Limited quantities of art pottery were made and sold by

(Below) A selection of Tiffany pottery pictured in *Pottery and Glass*, August, 1908.   (Left) This vase with molded decoration of tulips is glazed in mottled green semigloss glaze. It is 11 inches high. The piece is marked with the incised LCT cipher and the etched mark "P1341 L.C. Tiffany Favrile Pottery." (The Art Museum, Princeton University, Princeton, New Jersey)

Left: A covered jar glazed green-buff with a pattern of hibiscus blossoms and leaves. It is 9 inches high. The Tiffany monogram mark appears on the bottom. *Center:* Lions, hearts, and lozenges decorate this ocher glazed 6½-inch vase. It has an impressed Tiffany monogram. *Right:* Fern fronds are the molded design on this buff glazed 10-inch vase marked with the impressed Tiffany monogram. (Taylor and Dull)

An artichoke blossom was the inspiration for the molded design on this semigloss mottled green vase. It is 11 inches high. The bottom is marked "P 952 L.C. Tiffany, Favrile Pottery." (Philadelphia Museum of Art Collection)

Tiffany & Co. and the Tiffany Studios. Some were thrown on the wheel, most cast in molds. "The main body of the pieces are in porcelain (really a semiporcelain), but for the plastic decorations, other clays were also used. Slender forms, which often approach those of the Favrile glassware were most often chosen. The glass shows only the plant motifs [not true; other motifs were used for glass] in the forms of the objects themselves, but in the ceramics the motifs of plants are also used for the decorations. Water plants, the lotus, the poppy, and many kinds of creepers including the Fuchsia, are employed with good taste." (*Pottery and Glass,* Aug. 1908, Vol. 1, No. 2, p. 5)

The pottery was also decorated with a variety of grains, jack-in-the-pulpits, ferns, natural shapes such as the mushroom, Queen Anne's lace, or tree branches or leaves, birds, and insects. Near Eastern motifs were used. A few pieces also had abstract designs. The early wares were colored a deep ivory and shaded to brown. Later, green shades in varicolored glaze were used on the outside of pieces, which were glazed inside with green, brown, or blue. Some pieces have code numbers or letters incised. A few pieces are marked with variations of an inscription written into the glaze, such as "L. C. Tiffany Favrile Pottery" or "P." Matte crystalline and iridescent glazes were used. Blue, red, and dull bronze were tried. Bronze pottery was perfected about 1910. One type was made with

(Top left) Seed pods are the molded decorations on this green semigloss and orange matte glazed vase. It is 5⅛ inches high. The bottom is marked with the incised cipher LCT. (The Art Museum, Princeton University, Princeton, New Jersey)   (Top center) Purple and russet green glazes decorate this 4¾-inch vase by the Tiffany Studios. (Collection, The Museum of Modern Art, New York)   (Top right) This 4⅝-inch vase is Tiffany Favrile pottery. It is 4⅝ inches high. (Metropolitan Museum of Art, Gift of the Louis Comfort Tiffany Foundation)

Left: This buff ewer with molded cattails is 12¼ inches high. It has the impressed Tiffany cipher; *Center:* Molded stalks are on this ocher vase, 10½ inches high, marked "Tiffany Favrile P 276"; *Right:* Molded pussywillows decorate this 9½-inch buff vase. It is impressed with the Tiffany monogram. (Taylor and Dull)

a metal sleeve that was shrunk onto the clay while another was electroplated.

Only glazed pottery was sold at Tiffany and Company. The unglazed pottery was at the Tiffany Studios and it could be ordered in a special color or bisque ware. The pottery production stopped by 1920.

As with the bases, the pieces are marked with the letters "LCT" scratched into the bottom clay.

Bibliography

Clark, Robert Judson, *The Arts and Crafts Movement in America 1876–1916*, Princeton, N.J.: Princeton University Press, 1972, pp. 164, 166–167, 168.

Eidelberg, Martin P., "Tiffany Favrile Pottery, A New Study of a Few Known Facts," *The Connoisseur* (September, 1968), 57–61.

Koch, Robert, *Rebel in Glass*, Crown Publishers, 1967.

———, *Louis C. Tiffany's Glass • Bronzes • Lamps*, Crown Publishers, 1971.

Ruge, Clara, "American Ceramics—A Brief Review of Progress," *International Studio* (V. 28), (March, 1906), 21–28.

———, "Development of American Ceramics," *Pottery & Glass* (V. 1, No. 2), (August, 1908), 3.

VAN BRIGGLE POTTERY

Artus Van Briggle was born in Felicity, Ohio, on March 21, 1869. His parents, Eugene and Martha Bryan Van Briggle, came from Holland. They claimed the two Pieters and Jan Breughel, the famed Flemish painters, as ancestors.

The date was changed each year. From 1900 to 1920, incised.

Even as a child, Artus was a talented artist. He worked in Cincinnati and studied there at the Academy of Art. About 1886, he worked with Carl Langenbeck of the Avon Pottery, and by 1887 joined Mrs. Storer of the Rookwood Pottery. In 1893, he studied in Paris at the Julian Art Academy under Jean-Paul Laurens and Benjamin Constant. During that period he went to the Beaux Arts to study clay modeling and in the summer of 1894 was in Italy studying painting. Back in Paris in 1895, he became engaged to a talented artist, Anne Louise Gregory.

Two other Van Briggle incised marks.

The time that he spent in France influenced Van Briggle in many ways. He became familiar with the Art Nouveau styles, which he later adapted. He saw Chinese pottery of the Ming dynasty and determined to reproduce the matte or dead glaze of that earlier period. And he became familiar with the works of the Berlin and Sèvres porcelain factories, and was greatly influenced by their designs.

Artus returned to Cincinnati in 1896. He worked at the Rookwood factory as a painter and decorator and also at his own studio.

Used after 1920, incised "U.S.A." was added to the mark from 1922–29.

Because of tuberculosis he had contracted as a boy, in 1899 he decided to move to Colorado Springs, Colorado, for his health. He worked at Colorado College and at a home studio experimenting with the local clay and glazes. In August, 1901, the first pieces were fired at the Van Briggle Pottery located at 615 North Nevada Avenue, Colorado Springs. By Christmas of that year, he was selling his pottery. It was during that same year that he exhibited in Paris and his vase "Despondency" was later purchased for the Louvre for $3,000.

His wife, Anne Gregory Van Briggle, was born in Plattsburgh, New York, July 11, 1868. As a young girl, she lived with an aunt and studied painting in New York City from 1889 to 1893. In 1894, Anne and her aunt went to Paris where Anne had her own studio. She did a portrait of Artus in Paris, and the two became engaged in 1895. But Anne did not move with him to Colorado Springs until 1900 when she obtained a job as art supervisor in the high school.

It was not until 1902 that they married. She worked with him at the pottery until Artus died on July 4, 1904. At the time, they employed fourteen workmen.

Anne continued the pottery after the death of her husband, and a memorial building, the Van Briggle Art Pottery, was begun in 1907 and completed in 1908. It stood at 300 West Uintah Street, Colorado Springs. Young artists were trained at a school of design at the pottery to continue the work of Artus Van Briggle. In 1908 Anne Van Briggle married Etienne A. Ritter of Denver, Colorado. She died November 15, 1929.

The pottery went into bankruptcy and in 1913 was taken over by Ede F. Curtis. C. B. Lansing took it over from 1915 to 1919 when he sold it to I. F. Lewis of Springfield, Missouri. A fire destroyed part of the plant in June, 1919, but it was rebuilt.

The Van Briggle Pottery continued making their typical matte glazed wares. When the factory became too small, in 1955, a building of native stone was built at 600 South 21st Street in Colorado Springs. Pottery is still being made and sold from this address.

The Van Briggle Pottery Company won many awards, including gold, silver, and bronze medals at the Paris Salon in 1903 and 1904; other medals at the Saint Louis

(Top) Anne Gregory at the studio about 1900.   (Bottom) Artus Van Briggle's portrait by Anne Gregory in 1894.

(Top) Artus Van Briggle working on his famous Toast Cup in 1900 in Colorado. The boy is William C. Holmes.   (Center) Workmen in the first Van Briggle studio, 500 Block North Nevada Ave., Colorado Springs, 1901.   (Bottom) In the 1900s, Artus Van Briggle *(left)*, Harry Bangs (in bowler hat), and an errand boy. Among the vases are the Toast Cup and the Lady of the Lily.

This 15-inch vase is decorated with conventionalized leaves. The glaze is light and dark mottled matte glaze. The vase is incised "AA Van Briggle 1904 106." It also has a paper label, "5915, $50 p 106 $20." Notice that the same vase appears in front of the kiln door in the preceding picture. (Smithsonian Institution)

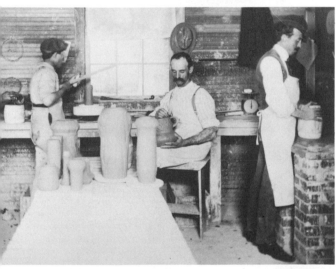

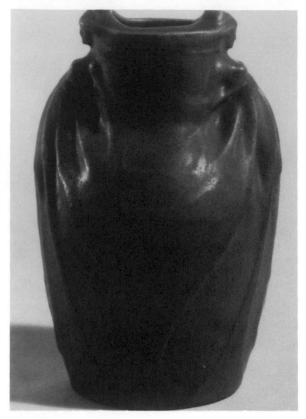

(Top left) A Van Briggle stoppered jug with green matte glaze and raised designs. Around the neck it says "Fire Water." The piece is incised "1902 AA." (See photograph of Van Briggle decorated vase of spiders shown in the Rookwood entry.) (Smithsonian Institution) (Top right) Two women form the handles of this green matte glazed vase. It is 7¾ inches high, marked "AA" in a rectangle, "Van Briggle, Colorado Springs, 1906." (The Art Museum, Princeton University, Princeton, New Jersey)   (Left) This dark green glazed vase is unmarked but the design and technique identify it as Van Briggle pottery made about 1902. It is 5 inches high. The spiderlike decoration is on one side, the Indian symbol on the other. The clay used for this vase is very yellow. (Authors' collection)   (Below) This pottery plate with molded designs of poppies is glazed light green. The 8⅝-inch plate is marked "AA" in a rectangle, "1902, III 20." (The Art Museum, Princeton University, Princeton, New Jersey)

Exposition, 1904, and at the American Pacific Exposition, 1905; and an award at the Arts and Crafts Exhibition, Boston, 1906.

Product

The clay used at the Colorado Springs pottery came from a nearby deposit located within five miles of the plant. The deposits of clay ranged from dark red to cream buff. Clay from Georgia and England were also used. And

(Left) This grass green matte glazed vase has a glossy glazed interior. It is 10½ inches high. The vase is incised "1902 A III." (Smithsonian Institution)   (Center) Yellow daffodils, aqua, and magenta matte glaze decorate this 9½-inch vase. It is marked "AA Van Briggle 1903 III 161" and has a paper label, "No 5308, $12, $8, p. 161."   (Right) A Van Briggle vase with molded design of flowers and leaves. The matte glaze is green and red. The 11⁵⁄₁₆-inch vase is marked with the incised AA in a rectangle and "Van Briggle, 1903, III, 233." (Newark Museum, Newark, New Jersey)

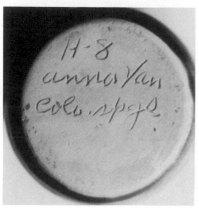

This pitcher is marked "Anna Van H-8." The 6¼-inch-high piece has a green crystalline glaze, of the type used since 1955. (Collection of LeRoy Eslinger)

for all of the needed clay preparation, the plant had electrical power and machinery.

A great variety of pieces were made at the pottery including all types of glazed terra-cotta for mantels, chimney tops, roof tiles, tile for interior decoration, building exterior, dry press tile for fireplace hearths, wall fountains, garden decoration, and even flowerpots.

The glazes varied, the most famous the turquoise Ming (a blue matte glaze still in use) and Persian Rose (a two-tone rose to maroon shade). Van Briggle also used green, brown, purple, pink, red, blue, lavender, plum, cardinal red, brown, yellow, mustard, black, gray, green, and other colors. A few pieces were done with two colors. An early article (*Keramic Studio,* May, 1905) mentions a "quaint all over pattern like figures from a cashmere shawl." All other reports are of pieces decorated with a single color. Van Briggle "adorned his creations with the precious and semiprecious stones of Colorado" (*Pottery and Glass,* August, 1908, p. 7). In 1912, it was noted: "within the last three years it [Van Briggle Pottery] has been making an iridescent glaze which takes a third firing. The color is put on by hand, making the design more pronounced yet in complete harmony with the colors of the vase" (*House Beautiful,* April, 1912, "Recent American Pottery" by Jonathan A. Rawson Jr.). The glaze was not applied by dipping, but was sprayed on with an atomizer. (A more complete description of the technical aspects of making the pottery is in *Transactions of the America Ceramic Society,* Vol. X, 1908, pp. 65–75.)

Mountain Craig Brown, the brown and green glaze favored at Van Briggle Pottery after 1922, was discontinued in 1935. A flood destroyed much of the pottery and some of the glaze formulas were lost. The brown glaze and the molds for a piece known as "Old Man of the Sea" were the two most important losses to the flood. A white glaze called "moonglow" was in use about 1946. Persian Rose glaze was used until 1969 when it was discontinued.

Lamp bases were produced by 1919. Lampshades using grasses and butterflies and local flowers were designed to blend with the bases.

We have seen a piece of bronze-plated Van Briggle pottery marked "Van Briggle, 702 S.W." (The firm did some silver plating and made "solar apparatus" used in the treatment of T.B. c. 1915–1919—from letter to author from Mr. C. B. Lansing by Alice Lansing, Aug. 13, 1973.)

Several prominent designs made by the Van Briggle

(Left) An unusual Van Briggle pottery vase with aqua matte glaze and bronze mountings. The bronze resembles mistletoe with seed pearl berries. The 8½-inch vase is marked "AA" in a rectangle, "Van Briggle, 1904, V 275." (The Art Museum, Princeton University, Princeton, New Jersey) (Right) A greenish yellow semimatte glaze was used on a brown clay body for this 7½-inch vase. It is marked "AA" in a rectangle, "Van Briggle 1905 V 95." (The Art Museum, Princeton University, Princeton, New Jersey)

A photograph of some Van Briggle pieces that appeared in a German publication about 1901. Notice, *from right to left*, Lorelei, the Toast Cup, and Lady of the Lily. The later version of the Lady of the Lily did not include the flowers on the base.

(Left) Lady of the Lily has been made at the Van Briggle Pottery since 1901. This is a vase with turquoise matte glaze made in 1970. An example in mountain craig brown appeared on a color postcard about 1935, priced at $42.00. (Authors' collection) (Right) The Lorelei vase has been made since 1901. This turquoise example was made in 1970. It is 10½ inches high, marked "Van Briggle Colo. Spgs." (Authors' collection)

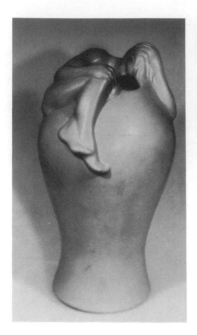

(Left) Despondency, the vase with a man curled around the top, has been made since 1903. This turquoise matte glazed vase is 16 inches high. (Authors' collection)   (Above) The Siren of the Sea has been made since 1904. The frog flower holder in the center of the vase is a separate piece. A 1935 postcard lists the vase at $42.50. (Authors' collection)

(Left) Anna Van vase with turquoise matte glaze. This vase is 16½ inches high. It has been made since about 1925 and is still available at the factory. (Authors' collection)   (Center) Raised stems and flowers decorate this dark maroon vase. It is marked "Van Briggle 1916." It is 7¼ inches high. (Authors' collection) (Right) An unusual light pink matte glaze is on this 8-inch-high vase. It is marked in the Van Briggle square symbol "Van Briggle, Col. Spgs. 666 16." (Authors' collection)

Pottery Company through the years should be mentioned. All have been made continually since they originated. "Lorelei" was first exhibited in 1903 at the Paris Art Salon. The original is now in the South Kensington Museum in London. The vase shows a figure of a woman draped around it and incorporated into the design. A picture of the vase appeared in *Brush and Pencil,* Oct. 1901. In the "Lady of the Lily" vase, which dates from 1901, the lady is leaning against it.

The "Siren of the Sea" was an award winner at the St. Louis Exposition in 1904. It is a shell-shaped vase topped by a reclining mermaid.

"Despondency" won first prize at the Paris Salon in 1903. It is now in the Louvre Museum in Paris.

The "Toast Cup" is a large cup with pinecone decorations and a woman on one side. It was made in 1900. This cup has not been copied in later years. "Anna Van," a vase held by a standing lady was made later on. It was sculptured by Artus Van Briggle and found in his attic workroom after he died. It does not seem to have been in production until 1925.

Many hundreds of other designs for vases, lamps, bookends, ashtrays, cups, and other items have been made through the years. Almost all of them were of a single color matte glaze with a raised decoration and of art nouveau inspiration.

Marks

The famous "AA" mark was used by Artus and Anne Van Briggle on the very first pieces made in Colorado. It was incised in the clay with the date and the words "Van Briggle." The mark appears with some variations because it was always incised by hand.

The "AA" is sometimes in a rectangle, sometimes a trapezoid, sometimes alone.

Many of the pieces were dated from about 1900 to 1920. Stock numbers were put on the bottom with a stamp from 1910 to 1920. The letters "U.S.A." followed the mark from 1922 to 1929. After 1920, the words "Colorado Springs, Colorado" were added to the mark. This was sometimes done in an abbreviated form.

The girls who worked in the pottery sometimes listed other things on the bottom of a piece. The words "Colo Sprgs" were written in script or print, depending on the girl; "Original" means the piece was turned on a wheel and not made in a mold; "Hand carved" means that the

(Top) Green and dark brick red matte glaze covers this 11½-inch-high vase. (Authors' collection) (Bottom) Another vase with raised swirl decoration and the dark red and green matte glaze made by the Van Briggle Pottery. (Authors' collection)

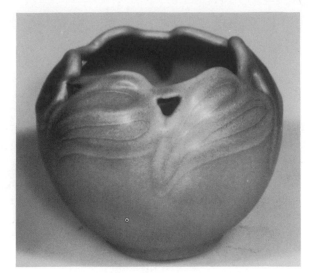

(Left) The characteristic maroon and dark blue matte glaze covers this 4½-inch vase. It has raised leaf decorations and buds. It is marked "Van Briggle, Colo. Spgs." (Authors' collection)   (Above) A vase of the 1950s, "Design 847." The catalogue called it "An example of eyelet embroidery in clay. Height 4 inches Width 5 inches $3.85." This piece is turquoise, but the catalogue mentions that it was also available in "Persian Rose" or "Moonglow." (Authors' collection)

(Below) This quarter-moon vase was a popular design by Van Briggle Pottery in the 1940s. It appeared in a sales brochure as "A Crescent for Medium Stems, No. 324, Height 8 inches $5.75." It is glazed with the maroon matte glaze called "Persian Rose." (Authors' collection)

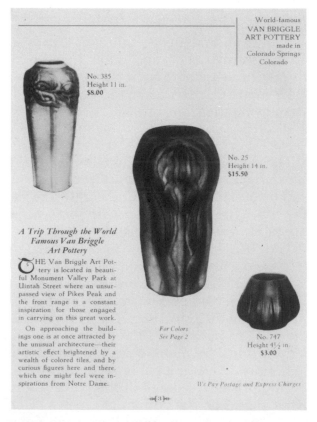

Page from a Van Briggle catalogue dated 1925.

World-famous
N BRIGGLE
T POTTERY
e in
orado Springs
Colorado

No. 833
Height 5½ in.
$1.50

No. 858
Height 3 in.
$3.50

Ship Book Ends
Height 3 in.
$3.75 Pair

No.808
Height 7 in.
$8.00

No. 684
ight 3½ in.
$1.50

Pay Postage and Express Charges

Upon entering the reception room, the visitor is assigned to a party which is in charge of a competent guide and the trip through the plant, from that moment is a very interesting experience.

The first process is preparing the clay. This particular clay is found in one place only, in Black Canyon, just west of the famous Garden of the Gods. This body of clay was discovered by Artus Van Briggle in 1897. After dissolving and filtering this clay is then ready for use in the throwing and casting rooms.

In the throwing room one

World-famous
VAN BRIGGLE
ART POTTERY
made in
Colorado Springs
Colorado

No. 15
Height 13 in.
$10.00

No. 792
Height 7 in.
$2.50

No. 733
Height 3½ in.
$2.75

For Colors
See Page 2

No. 860
Height 8½ in.
$6.00

No. 589
Height 3 in.
$3.50
Flower
Holder Included

may see the oldest art in history, which is "throwing on the potter's wheel". This is a very interesting phase of art pottery making, and it is indeed interesting to see an art potter deftly shaping the crude clay into beautiful and graceful forms.

A corps of highly trained artists are continuously engaged in their work of finishing the pieces. The pieces are carefully redesigned by these artists, after which they are placed in the drying room and thoroughly dried, preparatory to the first firing. The pieces are then placed in the mammoth kiln where the ware is

rld-famous
N BRIGGLE
T POTTERY
e in
orado Springs
Colorado

Dog
Book Ends
Height 5 in.
Pair $5.00

No. 139
Height 14 in.
$10.00

No. 520
Height 6½ in.
$12.00

No. 645
Height 4½ in.
$1.00

169
ight
3 in.
2.00

No. 661
Height 7 in.
$3.75

For Colors
See Page 2

fired the first time. This kiln has a capacity of 4,000 pieces. It is a muffled type kiln. The fire is confined between two walls and does not come in contact with the ware, itself. This kiln is fired to 1,400°, an operation which requires thirty hours. After the ware is unloaded from this kiln it is then ready for the glaze and color laboratories.

The famous Van Briggle glazes and colors are produced by a secret method and are the only glazes and colors of their kind being produced in the world, today. These glazes and col-

World-famous
VAN BRIGGLE
ART POTTERY
made in
Colorado Springs
Colorado

No. 695
Height 4 in.
$2.50

No. 822
Height 7 in.
$2.75

No. 18
Height 3 in.
$3.00—
Flower Holder
Included

For Colors
See Page 2

No. 754
Height 9 in.
$12.50

No. 863
Height
7½ in.
$3.00

No. 510
Height 4½ in.
$6.00

We Pay
the Postage
Charges

ors are a reproduction of an old 14th century Chinese process which was a lost art until rediscovered by Artus Van Briggle. The coloring process requires artists of unusual ability, as the coloring is by thought and not by sight. The colors do not appear until the ware is again fired, which is the next operation.

The kiln used for the last firing is another mammoth kiln, even larger than the first. This kiln is of the same type, being muffled, so that the fire does not come in contact with the ware, being the same principle

Pages from a Van Briggle catalogue dated 1925.

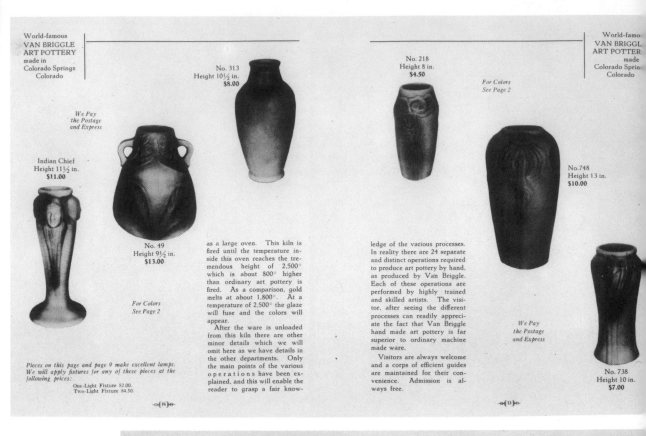

World-famous
VAN BRIGGLE
ART POTTERY
made in
Colorado Springs
Colorado

World-famous
VAN BRIGGLE
ART POTTERY
made
Colorado Springs
Colorado

No. 313
Height 10½ in.
$8.00

No. 218
Height 8 in.
$4.50

*For Colors
See Page 2*

*We Pay
the Postage
and Express*

Indian Chief
Height 11½ in.
$11.00

No. 49
Height 9½ in.
$13.00

*For Colors
See Page 2*

No. 748
Height 13 in.
$10.00

*We Pay
the Postage
and Express*

No. 738
Height 10 in.
$7.00

as a large oven. This kiln is fired until the temperature inside this oven reaches the tremendous height of 2,500° which is about 800° higher than ordinary art pottery is fired. As a comparison, gold melts at about 1,800°. At a temperature of 2,500° the glaze will fuse and the colors will appear.

After the ware is unloaded from this kiln there are other minor details which we will omit here as we have details in the other departments. Only the main points of the various operations have been explained, and this will enable the reader to grasp a fair knowledge of the various processes. In reality there are 24 separate and distinct operations required to produce art pottery by hand, as produced by Van Briggle. Each of these operations are performed by highly trained and skilled artists. The visitor, after seeing the different processes can readily appreciate the fact that Van Briggle hand made art pottery is far superior to ordinary machine made ware.

Visitors are always welcome and a corps of efficient guides are maintained for their convenience. Admission is always free.

Pieces on this page and page 9 make excellent lamps. We will apply fixtures for any of these pieces at the following prices:
One-Light Fixture $2.00.
Two-Light Fixture $4.50.

·◦{ 8 }◦·

·◦{ 9 }◦·

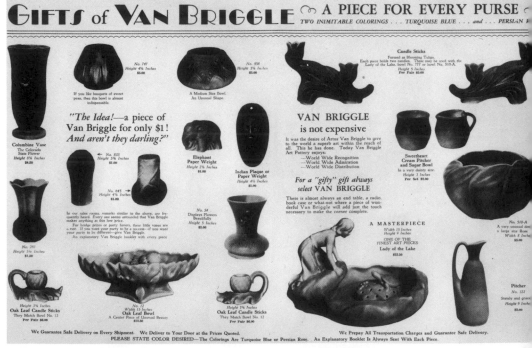

GIFTS of VAN BRIGGLE A PIECE FOR EVERY PURSE
TWO INIMITABLE COLORINGS . . . TURQUOISE BLUE . . . . and . . . PERSIAN R

*"The Idea!—a piece of
Van Briggle for only $1!
And aren't they darling?"*

VAN BRIGGLE
is not expensive

It was the desire of Artus Van Briggle to give to the world a superb art within the reach of all. This he has done. Today Van Briggle Art Pottery enjoys:
—World Wide Recognition
—World Wide Admiration
—World Wide Distribution

*For a "gifty" gift always
select VAN BRIGGLE*

There is almost always an end table, a radio, book case or what-not where a piece of wonderful Van Briggle will add just the touch necessary to make the corner complete.

A MASTERPIECE
ONE OF THE
FINEST ART PIECES
Lady of the Lake

Columbine Vase
The Colorado
State Flower

Candle Sticks

Sweetheart
Cream Pitcher
and Sugar Bowl

Oak Leaf Candle Sticks

Oak Leaf Bowl
A Center Piece of Unusual Beauty

Oak Leaf Candle Sticks

Pitcher
No. 322

We Guarantee Safe Delivery on Every Shipment.   We Deliver to Your Door at the Prices Quoted.
We Prepay All Transportation Charges and Guarantee Safe Delivery.
PLEASE STATE COLOR DESIRED—The Colorings Are Turquoise Blue or Persian Rose.   An Explanatory Booklet Is Always Sent With Each Piece.

Pages from a Van Briggle catalogue dated 1930.

(Facing page) Pages from a Van Briggle catalogue, date unknown, probably about 1940.

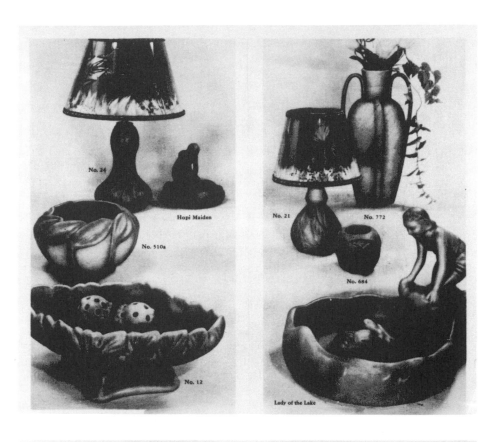

No. 24

Hopi Maiden

No. 510a

No. 12

No. 21　No. 772

No. 684

Lady of the Lake

No. 747

Damsel of Damascus

No. 54

No. 797

No. 847

No. 505

No. 44

No. 777

No. 281

No. 645

No. 754a

WE PAY THE TRANSPORTATION

No. 647
Height 4" $1.90

FOR SHORT STEMS

No. 734
Width 6" $3.40

PANSY BOWL
No. 19
Height 3" $2.15

FOR YOUR ROSES

No. 822
Height 7" $4.05

These popular pieces have been chosen to appear in this pamphlet because they are useful, beautiful and ornamental. A history booklet will be sent with each piece. This booklet enhances the value of the gift you may send. We always remove all price tags and never include any bills or price sheets.

FOR VERY SHORT STEMS
No. 775
Width 5" $2.15

OAK LEAF PATTERN

No. 778
Width 8" $7.70

Any of the pieces shown may be had in the Turquoise, the Persian Rose or the Moon-Glow colorings. Please state your choices.

PLEASE STATE YOUR CHOICE OF COLORING — THE PRICES SHOWN ARE PREPAID PRICES.

GRACEFUL BUD VASE
No. 468
Height 7" $3.65

A CRESCENT FOR MEDIUM STEMS
No. 124
Height 8" $5.75

No. 150
Height 5" $6.75

A Useful Sweet Pea Bowl
No. 858
Width 6" $4.55

The Very Useful Pattern
No. 54
Height 5" $3.15

A LOVELY FLOWER BOWL

Useful as Well as Ornamental
No. 885
Height 5" $3.80

A Masterpiece . . .
LADY OF THE LAKE
Width 15" $16.50

World Famous *Van Briggle* Art Pottery

At the foot of the rockies
COLORADO SPRINGS, COLORADO

ART POTTERY BY VAN BRIGGLE

is a gift supreme for all occasions. Christmas, the sweet girl graduate, the lovely spring bride. Birthday gifts, showers, party favors and bridge prizes are always on the list. Van Briggle is exclusive, you won't find it in stores, send your order direct. We prepay the transportation on all orders and guarantee safe delivery and complete satisfaction. World famous Van Briggle is enduring, artistic, practical and exquisitely beautiful.

GIFT SHIPPING SERVICE

Gifts of Van Briggle will be beautifully wrapped to suit any occasion and shipped prepaid to the recipient. You may send your card to be enclosed with your gift or we will include an appropriate card with your message as you may direct. You will find our gift shipping service most convenient and completely satisfactory. Just write your directions and our gift shopper will personally handle your order.

COLORINGS

The three imitable colorings of Van Briggle are: the EVER POPULAR TURQUOISE which is like a sky on a perfect day, the RICH PERSIAN ROSE which has the warmth and depth of a beautiful sunset and the MOON-GLOW WHITE which is comparable to the silvery white in a harvest moon. All the pieces and lamps shown in this pamphlet are available in any of the three colorings you may choose.

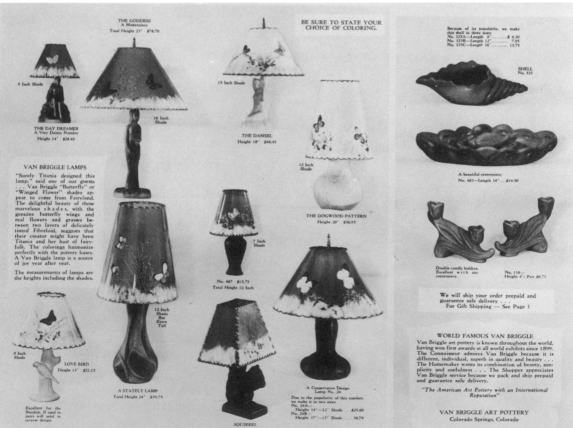

THE GODDESS
A Masterpiece
Total Height 23" $78.70

BE SURE TO STATE YOUR CHOICE OF COLORING.

9 Inch Shade

THE DAY DREAMER
A Very Dainty Number
Height 14" $28.40

18 Inch Shade

15 Inch Shade

THE DAMSEL
Height 18" $48.45

12 Inch Shade

THE DOGWOOD PATTERN
Height 20" $56.95

Because of its popularity, we make this shell in three sizes:
No. 525A—Length 8" $4.30
No. 525B—Length 12" 7.95
No. 525C—Length 16" 13.75

SHELL
No. 525

A beautiful centerpiece.
No. 483—Length 14" $14.50

VAN BRIGGLE LAMPS

"Surely Titania designed this lamp," said one of our guests . . . Van Briggle "Butterfly" or "Winged Flower" shades appear to come from Fairyland. The delightful beauty of these marvelous shades, with the genuine butterfly wings and real flowers and grasses between two layers of delicately tinted Fibreloid, suggests that their creator might have been Titania and her host of fairyfolk. The colorings harmonize perfectly with the pottery bases. A Van Briggle lamp is a source of joy year after year.

The measurements of lamps are the heights including the shades.

7 Inch Shade

No. 467 $15.75
Total Height 12 Inch

12 Inch Shade But Extra Tall

9 Inch Shade

LOVE BIRD
Height 13" $21.15

Excellent for the Boudoir. If used in pairs will send in reverse design.

A STATELY LAMP
Total Height 24" $39.75

SQUIRREL
Height 13" $28.45

A Conservative Design
Lamp No. 24
Due to the popularity of this number, we make it in two sizes.
No. 24A—
Height 14"—12" Shade ... $25.80
No. 24B—
Height 17"—15" Shade ... 36.70

Double candle holders. Excellent with any centerpiece.
No. 116—
Height 4", Pair $6.75

We will ship your order prepaid and guarantee safe delivery . . .
For Gift Shipping — See Page 1

WORLD FAMOUS VAN BRIGGLE

Van Briggle art pottery is known throughout the world, having won first awards at all world exhibits since 1899. The Connoisseur admires Van Briggle because it is different, individual, superb in quality and beauty . . . The Homemaker wants its combination of beauty, simplicity and usefulness . . . The Shopper appreciates Van Briggle service because we pack and ship prepaid and guarantee safe delivery.

"The American Art Pottery with an International Reputation"

VAN BRIGGLE ART POTTERY
Colorado Springs, Colorado

design was carved into the piece; "Hand decorated" means there was slip decoration.

Code numbers have appeared on some early pieces before 1904. The most reliable information suggests that "III" was the code for Artus Van Briggle, while "II" was for the work of Harry Bands; a "I" was for the pieces turned out by Anne Van Briggle. The name of an artist appears on a very few pieces. One piece we have seen is marked F.L.

(Top) This 9½-inch vase is one of a pair. Both are glazed in dark maroon matte glaze. Raised flowers and stems are the decoration. One is marked "Van Briggle, Colo. Spgs.," the other "Van Briggle U.S.A." (Authors' collection)

(Bottom) Conventionalized flowers decorate this 2½-inch dark maroon matte glazed vase. (Authors' collection)

Bibliography

American Pottery Gazette, The, "Van Briggle Pottery" (V. 4, No. 3), (November 10, 1907), 42.

Barber, Edwin, *Marks of American Potters,* Philadelphia: Patterson and White, 1904, pp. 166–167.

———, *The Pottery and Porcelain of the United States,* New York: G. P. Putnam's Sons, 1909, pp. 299, 480, 566–567.

Bayer, Ralph E., "Van Briggle Pottery," *The Western Collector* (March, 1969), 110–115.

Bogue, Dorothy McGraw, *The Van Briggle Story,* privately printed by author, 1968.

Bowdoin, W. G., "Some American Pottery Forms," *The Art Interchange* (April, 1903), 87.

Clark, Robert Judson, *The Arts and Crafts Movement in America 1876–1916,* Princeton, N.J.: Princeton University Press, 1972, pp. 158–163.

Crowley, Lilian H., "It's Now the Potter's Turn." *International Studio* (V. 75), (September, 1922), 539.

Galloway, George D., "The Van Briggle Pottery," *Brush and Pencil* (V. IX, No. 1), (October, 1901), 1–8.

Keramic Studio, "Pottery at the Arts and Crafts Exhibit, Craftsman Building, Syracuse" (May, 1903–April, 1904), 36.

Kistler, Ralph H., correspondence with authors.

Koch, Robert, "The Pottery of Artus Van Briggle," *Art in America* (V. 52, No. 3), (June, 1964), 120–121.

Laing, Trudy, "Young Van Briggle, Artist Probed Glaze Secrets," *Collectors' Weekly* (June 13, 1972), 1–3.

(Facing page) Pages from a Van Briggle catalogue dated 1945.

Lansing, Mrs. Charles B., correspondence with authors.

Rawson, Jonathan A., Jr., "Recent American Pottery," *House Beautiful* (V. 31), (April, 1912), 148.

Riddle, Frank H., "The New Pottery and Art Terra Cotta Plant of the Van Briggle Pottery Company at Colorado Springs, Colo." *Transactions of the American Ceramic Society* (V. X), (1908), 65–75.

Ruge, Clara, "American Ceramics—A Brief Review of Progress," *International Studio* (V. 28), (March, 1906), 21–28.

———, "Development of American Ceramics," *Pottery & Glass* (V. 1, No. 2), (August, 1908), 3.

Russack, Fran, correspondence with authors.

Scribner's Magazine, "The Field of Art—American Pottery" (November, 1902), 637.

Van Briggle Art Pottery, misc. leaflets, booklets, etc.

VOLKMAR POTTERY

Charles Volkmar was born in Baltimore, Maryland. His grandfather was an engraver and his father a portrait painter so it was natural that he be trained as an artist. Charles went to Paris to study under Antoine-Louis Barye, the bronze sculptor, and Henri Harpignies, the landscape painter. He returned to the United States after fifteen years "partly for the purpose of voting for the second term of Lincoln, getting married, and other commendable enterprises" (*International Studio*, Jan., 1909, Vol. XXXVI, No. 143, pp. 75–80). He later returned to Paris where he became interested in pottery and underglaze painting. By 1875, he was exhibiting his oil paintings and pieces of pottery. Many other artists also were painting designs for French potters at this time.

Volkmar returned to the United States in 1879 and set up a kiln in Greenpoint, New York. He made vases and tiles with underglaze decorations, and then moved to Tremont, where he continued to make the same type of underglaze decorated pieces, working with limited colors. In 1883 he made a series of "barbotine" vases, a slipware-decorated faience.

In 1888 he started to make tile at the Menlo Park Ceramic Works in Menlo Park, New Jersey, with J. T. Smith. They made enameled terra-cotta tiles for the Rockefeller mansion at Tarrytown, New York, tiles that matched the

Marks:

Incised monogram used between 1879 and 1888.

Raised letters used in 1895.

VOLKMAR & CORY

Raised mark used in 1895.

Volkmar & Cory, 1896.

marble and onyx used on other walls in the building. Their tiles were installed in a number of buildings, including the Boston Public Library and the National Bank Building in New York City.

In 1895, Volkmar organized the Volkmar Keramic Company and Smith continued at the Menlo Park Ceramic Works.

Volkmar started his new company in Brooklyn, New York, and continued to make tiles. He made a series of plaques with underglazed blue designs, usually of historic buildings or persons. The company also made loving cups, beer mugs, and plates, all of them in the same type of blue decoration.

Mr. Volkmar joined Kate Cory in 1896 and, under the name Volkmar and Cory in Corona, New York, worked together for a few months making plaques.

Alone again, Volkmar made plain pieces with colored glazes. The ware was thin and light. A few examples from this period had painted decorations, usually landscapes. He also made an underglazed ware called "Crown Point."

In 1903, Volkmar moved his pottery to Metuchen, New Jersey, where the company was known as Charles Volkmar and Son. (Volkmar's son, Leon, became a teacher of pottery at the Industrial School of the Pennsylvania Mu-

I V

Incised or relief mark used between 1896 and 1903.

Incised or relief mark used from 1896 until after 1903.

(Left) Although blue and white plates were made at the Volkmar Ceramic Company in Brooklyn about 1895, this 11½-inch-diameter plate was made at Corona, New York, by Volkmar and Cory about 1896, probably a continuation of the series. (The Smithsonian Institution)   (Right) Another type of blue and white plate by Volkmar is this 8½-inch one. (The Smithsonian Institution)

(Left) Volkmar made this matte green glazed vase at Metuchen, New Jersey, about 1910. It is 6 inches high and marked with an incised V. (Newark Museum, Newark, New Jersey)   (Right) Hand-painted birch trees in brown, green, and blue semimatte glaze decorate this 7¾-inch-square tile. It is marked "Volkmar Kilns, Metuchen, N.J." on the back. A V in the lower right-hand corner is painted on the face of the tile. (Newark Museum, Newark, New Jersey)

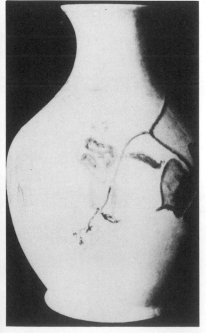

A vase by Charles Volkmar pictured in *The International Studio,* January, 1909.

seum by 1905.) Art pottery was made and it included vases and bowls with a matte finish in dark gray, green, blue, dark red brown, and pink. Some pieces had linings of a brighter color such as orange. He also made decorative underglaze paintings of ducks, foliage, or other natural subjects. Several underglaze decorations were made with a firing between each painting. One of his pupils, Jan Hoagland, did some of the designing.

The last known working date of the pottery is 1911, though it is unknown when it actually closed.

Bibliography

Barber, Edwin, *The Pottery and Porcelain of the United States,* New York: G. P. Putnam's Sons, 1909, p. 377.

———, *Marks of American Potters,* Philadelphia: Patterson and White, 1904, pp. 82–83.

Clark, Robert Judson, *The Arts and Crafts Movement in America 1876–1916,* Princeton, N.J.: Princeton University Press, 1972, pp. 128, 180–181.

International Studio, "Notes on the Crafts and Industrial Arts" (V. 25), (March, 1905), 9–11.

Jervis, W. P., *A Pottery Primer*, New York: O'Gorman Publishing Co., 1911, p. 181.

Keramic Studio, "Louisiana Purchase Exposition Ceramics—Charles Volkmar" (V. 6), (March, 1905), 251.

Ruge, Clara, "Development of American Ceramics," *Pottery & Glass* (V. 1, No. 2), (August, 1908), 3.

————, "American Ceramics—A Brief Review of Progress," *International Studio* (V. 28), (March, 1906), 21–28.

Scribner's Magazine, "The Field of Art—American Pottery, Second Paper" (V. 33–44), (March, 1903), 381.

Walton, William, "Charles Volkmar, Potter," *The International Studio* (V. 36, No. 143), (January, 1909), 75–80.

WELLER

About 1873 Samuel A. Weller opened a small factory at Fultonham (Muskingum County), Ohio, where he started to make plain unpainted flowerpots and other wares. He soon began decorating the pots with house paint and sold them door to door in nearby Zanesville. He also made stoneware on a kick wheel. By 1882, the pottery was so successful that Weller moved into a frame building on Pierce Street on the river. In 1888 he leased an extra warehouse on South Second Street and by 1890 he had built a new pottery at Pierce Street and Cemetery Drive. In 1891, he purchased the plant that had been used by the American Encaustic Tiling Company located on Sharon Avenue. During these years he made painted flowerpots, jardinieres, hanging baskets, umbrella stands, and other pottery pieces.

In 1893 an addition was built on the old plant and the first artwares were made. Samuel Weller had seen the Lonhuda ware at the Chicago World's Fair and he was so impressed that he hired William Long of the Lonhuda Pottery in Steubenville, Ohio. Within the year, Lonhuda was being produced. Although Long left the pottery in 1895, Weller continued to make a very similar artware that he named "Louwelsa." Louwelsa glaze is characterized by its slight brittleness. It has been known to "explode" if the piece is subjected to too high or too low temperature.

Just after Long left, Charles Babcock Upjohn was hired as art director and designer. He introduced the Dickensware in 1900, but left the firm in 1904. In 1902, Weller

Decorators and Artists (* from Edwin Barber's *Marks of American Potters*):

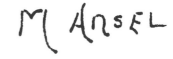

Abel. May have been Edward Abel, Louise Abel, or unknown.

*Virginia Adams.** Also worked at Owens, Roseville.

W. Allsop.

M. Ansel.

ЕА

*Elizabeth Ayers.** Also worked at Lonhuda, Roseville.

A

Ruth Azline. Also worked at Mosaic Tile.

J. B. About 1902 (Dickens).

M. B. Signed on Rozane.

O.B

O. B. Unknown.

A3

A. F. Best (?) Also worked at Owens, Roseville (?).

E·B

L. B.

*Lizabeth Blake.** May also be Elizabeth Blake.

Florence Bowers (?).

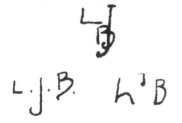

*Levi J. Burgess.** 1905–1907. (Louwelsa & Dresden). Burgess was the son of Samuel Weller's sister. He lived in Zanesville and worked at the studio as an artist from 1905 to 1907. He traveled, opened an art emporium in 1909, a decorating business in 1912, and a tearoom a few years later. He moved to Cincinnati where he was a commercial illustrator. He died in 1943. Burgess decorated many of the vases with Indian head decoration.

hired Jacques Sicard and his assistant, Henri Gellie, from France. They made the Sicard line, a pottery with a metallic luster, but they left Weller in 1907 and took the secrets of the glaze with them.

During all those years, the Weller Pottery continued making a variety of other art potteries. The Aurelian, Auroral, Turado, and Eocean lines were introduced. Etna, Floretta, Jap-Birdimal, Dresden, Etched Matt, Hunter, and L'Art Nouveau were made before 1906.

In 1915 the Weller pottery was considered by some the largest art pottery in the world. Weller had over forty salesmen and hundreds of workmen.

However, the prestige lines of pottery were discontinued at the end of World War I and a more commercial line was substituted. Weller started making wares that would compete with each of the new Roseville Pottery items, with at least one new line appearing each year.

Weller bought the Zanesville Art Pottery on Ceramic Avenue in 1920 and enlarged it in 1924. During the 1920s John Lessell (Lassell) designed and made the LaSa line which had a metallic overglaze decoration of trees and landscape. He also designed the Chengtu and Lamar lines.

In 1925 the pottery was changed from a sole proprietorship to a company, becoming the S. A. Weller Company. Samuel Weller died October 4, 1925, and his nephew, Harry Weller, became the president of the firm. A fire destroyed one of the three Weller plants in 1927 but it was rebuilt by 1931. Harry Weller died in an automobile accident on September 25, 1932, and the firm was headed by two of Samuel Weller's sons-in-law, Frederick Grant and Irvin Smith.

The pottery lines became less elaborate during the depression years and the demands were small. Two plants were closed in 1936 and all the pottery was made at the one remaining plant on Ceramic Avenue. Business improved during World War II, but after the war, foreign competition took over the American pottery market. By 1945, some of the space in the pottery was leased to the Essex Wire Company, and in 1948 the Weller Pottery ceased manufacturing.

The following article, "Our American Potteries—Weller Ware," by May Elizabeth Cook, appeared in *Sketch Book,* Vol. 5, May, 1906.

Seven miles from Zanesville, in a log cabin, twenty-one feet square, was the first fire kindled in 1872, in one small kiln. Motive power for crushing clays, hauling the finished products to nearest market was supplied by an old white horse. Common red ware alone was made, viz., crocks, tile, etc,. from clay found around Zanesville.

Mr. Weller's pottery is now known as one of the large potteries of the world, having floor space of three hundred thousand feet. Twenty-five kilns with natural gas for fuel (which is, by the way, the ideal fuel for firing kilns, as the temperature is the most even to be obtained) are glowing night and day. Hundreds of skilled workmen are employed. The great room in the first story where the clays are first made ready for the artist modeler is of surpassing interest.

The clay body used in the manufacture of the Weller pottery is a combination of several clays, both native and foreign. These have been most carefully tested by chemical analysis and fire tests, until a satisfactory body has been found for the decoration and glaze desired. First there must be found a perfect harmony in body and glaze; and where such a variety of ware in under glaze decoration, matt and luster is made, a great number of tests, in fact hundreds for body, glaze and color must be made. The clay for art pottery, into the composition of which, pipe clay, koalin, quartz and feldspar enter, is prepared with especial care. These ingredients are thoroughly mixed in a blunger, a machine not unlike a great churn with paddles to cut and blend the clays. Water is added, and as the blunger turns, the clay and water [are] thoroughly mixed into a "slip" and . . . carried from the blunger to a cylindrical sieve, of one hundred meshes to the inch.

The liquid clay or "slip," as it is technically known, is then pumped by hydraulic pressure into presses where the superfluous moisture is pressed out, and we then have great cakes of fine plastic body, blue-gray in color.

From the presses the clay is carried to great pits to be "aged"; it then is ready for the hand of the modeler. Mr. Weller is utilizing every appliance that modern mechanics can supply to facilitate the work of his artist ceramists. The modeling and moulding rooms are on the second floor and are quite picturesque with the many workers in their white blouses and caps. Some are busy at the wheels, while others bearing long boards filled with moulds gracefully balanced on their heads, walk rapidly to the drying rooms where the moulds are placed on shelves to dry.

There is quite a fascination in watching the expert moulder at his wheel, known as a "jigger." The moulds, made of plaster of Paris three inches thick, are in two parts, tightly bound together by a strap, and placed on the rapidly revolving wheel. From a great box of very soft clay, placed at his right, the moulder throws into the mould with his hand the needed amount of clay, then quickly inserts a shaped paddle suspended above the

John Butterworth (?). Also worked at Roseville, Owens (?).

C. Unknown.

M. C. Unknown.

Sam Celli.

Charles Chilcote. 1904. He was an apprentice to Mr. Upjohn and also worked at Owens (?) and Zane.

Laura Cline.

K. Coyleone.

Anna Dautherty.° (Dickens, Louwelsa). Also worked at Roseville (?).

Frank Dedonatis (Donatis ?).

Anthony Dunlavy.° 1901 (Dickens).

Tony Dunlavy. 1923 (Lamar).

C. A. Dusenbery.

W. E. Unknown.

Dorothy England. See Dorothy England Laughead.

I. F. c. 1909 (Dickens 2nd).

Frank Ferrell.* (Louwelsa). Worked at the time of Sicard. Also at Roseville, Owens, Peters & Reed.

Charles Fouts (?). Also worked at Owens.

Henry Fuchs. Head of the decorating studio, 1925.

G. (Louwelsa).

C. G. (Dickens).

Henri Gellie. 1901–1907. Gellie came to the Weller pottery as an assistant to Jacques Sicard. He returned to France in 1907, was wounded in World War I at the Battle of Verdun, and died of pneumonia at the end of the war.

Mary Gillie.* (Jap Birdimal, Aurelian).

Charles Gray (?). Also worked at Owens.

J. H. Unknown.

K. V. H. Unknown.

V. M. H. Unknown.

William F. Hall (?). Also worked at Roseville.

Delores Harvey. (Aurelian). Also worked at Owens.

Albert Haubrich.* (1897–1903). (1901, Louwelsa and Eocean). Haubrich was born in Biersdorf, Germany, on July 8, 1875. His family moved to Steubenville, Ohio, and in 1897 he started working for the Weller Pottery Company as a decorator. He also worked for Owens. Later he went to work for Albert Radford as manager of the decorating department of his newly opened pottery in Clarksburg, West Virginia. Radford died and the firm closed. Haubrich's activities from 1904 to 1920 are unknown. Records show that he moved to Columbus, Ohio, in 1920 where he operated his own business as an interior designer. He died in 1931.

John Herold (?). Also worked at Owens (?) and Roseville.

Hugo Herb. Also worked at Owens.

Hood (Hudson).

Roy Hook (?). Also worked at Owens.

Madge Hurst.* (Aurelian). Also worked at Roseville.

W. I. (Aurelian).

Josephine Imlay.* Also worked at Roseville.

E. J. (?). Unknown.

Anna Jewett.

Karl Kappes.* (Louwelsa). Artist.

L. Knaus. 1902. Applied glaze.

Joe Knott (?).

E. L. Unknown.

J. B. L. (Dresden).

S. L.

S. L. (Louwelsa).

W. L. (Louwelsa).

X L

X. L. Unknown.

**LaSa
Lessell
JL**

John Lassell (also spelled Lessell). Born in Mettlach, Germany, 1871; died, 1926. Worked for Weller from the early 1920s to 1925. He had worked in Bohemia and moved to the United States to take a job in the J. B. Owens Pottery of Zanesville, Ohio. He was made head of the Weller decorating department during the early 1920s. Mr. Lassell created several lines including LaSa, Marengo, Chengtu, and Lamar. He left Weller and started a pottery in Newark, Ohio, in 1925, the year before his death.

D

Dorothy England Laughead (also Dorothy England). She worked as a decorator, modeler, etc., in 1925. In 1938, she married Laughead and used both her maiden and married names in her signature.

**C L Leffler
C. L.**

Claude Leffler. (Hudson). Also worked at Roseville.

AV

A. V. Lewis (?). Also worked at Owens.

William A. Long. Worked 1893–1894 (*See* Lonhuda Pottery). Long worked for Samuel Weller for one year making Lonhuda Pottery, then he left to make the same type of pottery at the J. B. Owens Company and then to the Denver China and Pottery Company. From 1905–1908, he was at the Clifton Art Pottery Company of Newark, New Jersey. He returned to the Weller factory from 1909 to 1915.

Rudolph Lorber. 1905 to after 1919. He was born in Vienna, Austria, educated in Bohemia, worked in England, and moved to Zanesville in 1905. Lorber was in charge of modeling the new lines.

C B M

C. B. M. Unknown.

Margret McGinnis.

L. McGrath (?). Also worked at Roseville.

L McLain

L. McLain.

**McLaughlin
SL**

Sarah Reid McLaughlin. Worked at Lonhuda and made Louwelsa.

Lelia Meloy.

Hattie Mitchell. (Dickens, Aurelian). Also worked at Roseville.

**L Mitchell
L M**

Lillie Mitchell. Also worked at Roseville.

**M Mitchel
M**

Minnie Mitchell.

Morris

Morris.

M

Gordon Mull. Designer, 1902. Also worked at Mosaic Tile Co.

M-M

M. Myers. Also worked at Roseville.

hP.

Lizzie Perone.

E.L.P. ELP

Edwin L. Pickens. (Dickens, Dickens 2nd line). Plant supervisor.

MP PP

Mary Pierce. (Louwelsa). Also worked at Owens.

HP JP

Hester W. Pillsbury. (Hudson). Also worked at Roseville.

C. a. R

C. A. R. Unknown.

Albert Radford. (*See* Radford Pottery.) Radford had worked at the Wedgwood Pottery in England, then in Trenton, New Jersey, and Broadway, West Virginia. He worked in Tiffin, Ohio, and made Radford Pottery, then joined the Weller Pottery as a modeler. For a short time, he was superintendent of the J. B. Owens Pottery of Zanesville, Ohio. In 1903, he was making his own pottery in Zanesville and in 1904 moved to Clarksburg, West Virginia.

Marie Rauchfuss. Before 1899 (?). Worked at Rookwood 1899–1903. Also worked at Owens.

F Rhead

Frederick Hürten Rhead. (Jap Birdimal). Born 1880, died 1942. (His brother, Harry Rhead, was the art director of the Roseville Pottery from 1908 to 1920). Frederick Rhead came from Staffordshire, England, in 1902. He created the Jap Birdimal line in 1904 for Weller. In later years, he worked as art director at the Roseville Pottery (1904–1908). When he left, his brother took over this position. He also worked at Peoples University of St. Louis, Missouri from 1908 to 1911, the Arequipa Pottery in San Francisco, California (1911–1914); Rhead Pottery, Santa Barbara, California; American Encaustic Tiling Company of Zanesville, Ohio (1920–1927), and the Homer Laughlin China Company of East Liverpool, Ohio thereafter.

Eugene Roberts.[*] (Hudson). Also worked at A.E.T. Co.

Harry Robinson (?).

Hattie M. Ross. Also worked at Owens.

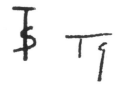

D. S. Unknown.

LRS. (Jap Birdimal).

Aloysius J. Schwerber. 1901. He became a potter and plant foreman.

Norman Scotthorn (?).

SICARD

Jacques Sicard. 1901–1907. Sicard worked at the Clement Massier Pottery in Golfe Juan, France. He developed the metallic luster used on the famous Sicardo or Weller Sicard line. Sicard had heard about William Long being dismissed after Samuel Weller learned Long's secrets of glazing Lonhuda ware. It was at this point that Sicard was determined to keep his own secrets and supposedly worked in a secret room; each morning he would plug up the holes that Weller had drilled the night before. Sicard returned to France in 1907 and operated a pottery in Golfe Juan, until he died in 1923.

Helen Smith. 1897 (Utopian). Also worked at Owens, Roseville.

Irvin Smith.

Amelia B. Sprague.

Fred Steel. Also worked at Roseville.

Ida Steele. 1899. (Utopian).

Tot Steele.[*] Also worked at Owens, Roseville.

William H. Stemm. (Eocean). Also worked at Owens.

E. Sulcer. (Louwelsa).

C. T. (Louwelsa).

L. B. T. Unknown.

wheel, pressing it against the sides of the revolving mould until an even thickness of clay adheres to the sides. Then the superfluous clay in the bottom is lifted out, inside of the base smoothed, and before one can draw a long breath a workman is carrying away the mould to the drying room and another form almost finished is whirling around on the jigger.

The absorption of the moisture by the plaster mould, soon gives the clay sufficient consistency to take the necessary shape. Subsequent shrinkage allows its removal from the mould. After a partial drying, the vase or jardiniere is dressed or smoothed and has its decorations applied and the ware then goes again to the drying room. If it is to be decorated in relief, or with handles or feet, they are applied at that stage. If to receive the underglaze decoration, it is taken when bone dry to the studios where the backgrounds are applied. These are sprayed on through an atomizer by compressed air, the vase standing upon a wheel that turns slowly. From this studio it goes to another where the design suited to its form is painted on with liquid clays, in which the colors have been thoroughly blended with the "slip." This process is called by the French "pâte-sur-pâte," and is seen in its greatest beauty in the exquisite work of Solon, the noted artist of the Sèvres and Minton Potteries.

After the decoration is applied, the vase is ready for glazing, which in this case will be a bright, clear glaze. This ware with the underglaze decoration is the first art pottery made by Mr. Weller. Its pretty name, Louwelsa, is a combination of the name of his little daughter, Louise, who was born at the time these first experiments were perfected, the first syllable of Mr. Weller's name, and his initials. The usual backgrounds on this ware are orange, shading into the browns with decorations in lighter tones of the same colors and green. The Aurelian, which was the second ware produced, is similar to the Louwelsa in effect, both background and decoration being painted on in rich mahogany tones.

These first experiments were quickly followed by others known as the Jap-Birdimal, Golbrogreen, Eocean, Sicardo, Oriental, Monochrome, Hunter, Floretta, L'Art Nouveau, Dickens and Perfecto, and were the results of many experiments made by artists of various nationalities employed by Mr. Weller. French, Japanese, Austrian, German and American craftsmen work side by side in the studios, though in reality each is in a little world of his own, working out his dreams in form and color, entirely oblivious of all around him. The Eocean ware mentioned has an underglaze decoration on white clay body. The backgrounds are beautifully blended from pinkish fawn color at the

C. Minnie Terry. ° Also worked at Roseville, Owens.

M. T.

Madeline Thompson (?). Also worked at Roseville (?).

Mae Timberlake

Mae Timberlake. (Pictorial, Hudson, and Louwelsa). Also worked at Roseville, Owens.

Sarah Timberlake. Also worked at Owens, Roseville.

H + U

H. U. Unknown.

Charles Babcock Upjohn. (Dickens). Born 1866, died 1953. Worked at Weller from 1895 to 1905. Upjohn had gone to the Peekskill Military Academy and later worked in the architecture firm of his father. In 1890, he went to Liberia to build missions, but he became ill with malaria. He studied art in England, France, and Italy, where he spent much time recovering from his illness. Upjohn apprenticed to the sculptor Karl Bitter. Although he was red-green color-blind, he was employed by Samuel Weller as art director and designer in 1895. It is believed that in 1904, he left Weller and opened his own pottery in Zanesville, Ohio. In 1905 he worked as a designer for the Trent Tile Company of Trenton, New Jersey. After ten years with the firm, he joined the faculty of Columbia University as an art and ceramics professor.

K. W.

K. W. Unknown.

KAW

K. A. W. Unknown.

L W

L. W. Unknown.

Art Wagner. 1920 (?)–1948. Decorator. Later worked for Mosaic Tile Company.

Naomi Walch (Truitt). 1927–1936.

Carl Weigelt.

Henry Weigelt. 1920s. Worked on Lamar line.

Carrie Wilbur.

Edna Wilbur.

A Wilson

Albert Wilson.

H.W.

Helen B. Windle.

C.Z.   CZ

Clotilda Marie Zanetta. Also worked at Rookwood, Roseville.

base into soft blue grays. The decorations are in harmonious tones of pinks, grays, and browns. The designs used are flowers, birds, animals, and one special decoration is known as the Dickens ware, having figures in low relief from Cruikshank's illustrations of Dickens's stories. The floral decorations on this delicate background are particularly good. The Sicardo ware is of special note. It is the crowning product of the metallic luster studio, under the directorship of Monsieur J. Sicard, formerly an associate of Clement Massier, a famous ceramist of Golfe-Juan, France.

M. Sicard, after coming to the Weller Pottery, experimented in the metallic lusters for two years, aided in every way by Mr. Weller, until he achieved the beautiful luster known as Sicardo. The forms which he uses are those thrown on the potter's wheel, and this method, or modeling by hand, gives a character and purity of line to a vase thus made, which can never be obtained by the commercial method of moulding.

The metallic lusters require, not only the fine color sense of the artist, but the skill and knowledge of the chemist; these gifts M. Sicard happily possesses. Accustomed to the use of peat or dead brushwood to fire the kilns in France, M. Sicard could with difficulty be persuaded to use the natural gas in the kilns in which the luster ware was to be fired. In his first experiments, he insisted on firing the kilns with the wild growths found along the roadsides around Zanesville. Was it not a pretty thought that the wild blossoms, having caught all the glow and richness of the summer, in rainbow tints, should through sacrificial fires transfer their glory to the moulded clay? The large show-room devoted to the Sicardo ware would indicate most satisfactory results from the complicated experiments requiring such care in decoration and firing. Beautiful forms with exquisite tones of flame, rose, blue, green, bronze, purple and crimson, melting into one another like colors in an opal, or in the great arch of the rainbow, are most harmonious and restful. To obtain this beautiful luster, the vases are first treated all over with a metallic preparation, and then decorated in conventional designs, in long flowing lines and curves, with chemically prepared pigments. This glaze is fired at a very high temperature, resulting in a texture and lustrous, changing color much like the Tiffany glass.

Mr. Weller is to be congratulated upon his past successes and the promise of greater ones in the future. At the Weller Pottery both thought and money are being expended most liberally for experiments. A great future and a great opportunity lie before these practical ceramists of our day.

Marks:

Impressed mark used on Lon-
huda pottery made at the
Weller factory by William
Long.

Incised mark recorded in Barber. However, a 1905 Wel-
ler catalogue advertised the
line as Eocean.

Aurelian
WELLER
Incised early mark.

Incised.

SICARDO-WELLER

AURELIAN

LOUWELSA

**SICARDO
WELLER.**

LOUWELSA
WELLER

DICKENS WARE
WELLER

TURADA
WELLER

LOUWELSA
WELLER

FLORETTA
WELLER

WELLER

Eleven impressed Weller
marks.

Two marks rubber-stamped in
dark ink.

Two marks in relief.

Weller Pottery
Since 1872

Weller
Pottery

Two incised marks.

(Left) Impressed.   (Center) Rubber stamped in dark ink.   (Right)
Written under glaze.

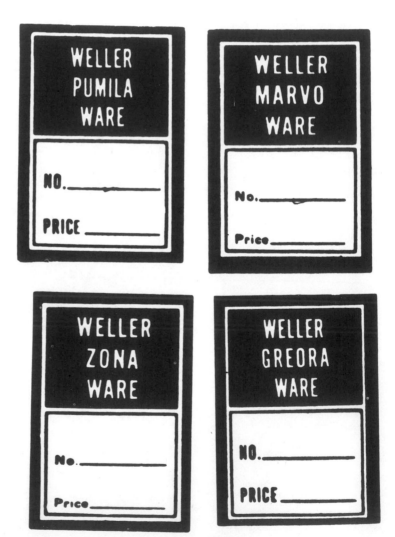

Various labels used on different Weller lines.

Lines

There have been so many lines offered by the Weller Company during its years of operation that a complete list is probably impossible. The following is a compilation of the lines offered, approximate date, where possible (early period: pre-World War I; middle period: 1920–1930; late period: 1930–1948), artists and modelers who worked on the line, where known, and a description of the line.

Alvin. Matte glaze, molded raised decoration with fruit, branches, or vines, c. 1928.

Anco. Ivory-colored, traditional designs.

Ansonia. Matte glaze in blue or gray. Made to appear hand turned with small ridges in the design (called Fleron if colored green), middle period.

Arcadia. Matte or glossy glaze, molded leaves, flowers, form irregular edges, late period.

Arcola. Matte glaze, light or dark colors, realistic grapes on vines or roses in relief, middle period.

Ardsley. Raised cattails and leaves, water lilies, form body of vase, matte glaze, 1928.

Art Nouveau. Matte or high gloss glaze, light color molded decoration, typical art nouveau decorations featuring women with flowing hair, tendrils, etc., 1910. Usually marked.

Atlantic. Matte glaze, tinted and molded fruit, flowers, leaves, middle period.

Samuel A. Weller, the founder of the Weller pottery.

(Right) Frederick Rhead was the designer of this Weller pottery plaque. It has painted underglaze decoration of poppy flowers and seeds in shades of brown, green, white, and blue. The 10½-inch plaque is incised "Weller Faience" on the back. The name "Rhead" appears in sgraffito on the front. (The Art Museum, Princeton University, Princeton, New Jersey) (Below) A selection of vases with raised figure decoration as pictured in *Pottery and Glass*, August, 1908.

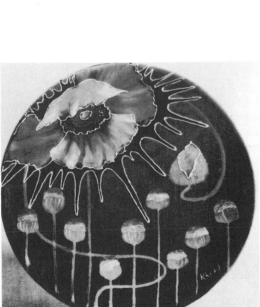

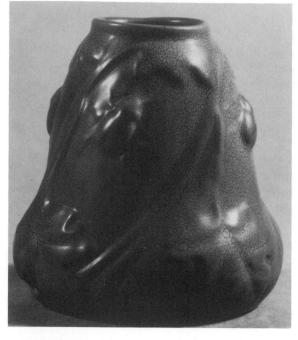

(Top left) A molded design of leaves and beetles is glazed blue gray and brown on this matte finished vase. It is 5 inches high. The vase is impressed "Weller." (The Art Museum, Princeton University, Princeton, New Jersey)   (Top right) Three-dimensional frogs climb this Weller vase made about 1905. The 7¾-inch vase has a matte green glaze. It is marked with the impressed name "Weller." (The Smithsonian Institution)   (Center left) A Weller matte green vase and candlestick as pictured in *Pottery and Glass*, March 9, 1909.   (Center right) Matte green finished pottery shown in an advertisement for Weller pottery, *American Pottery Gazette*, August, 1905. (Reproduction from the collection of the Library of Congress)   (Left) This chocolate brown glazed vase has plant figures in low relief. Made about 1905, it is 6 inches high, marked with the impressed name "Weller." (The Smithsonian Institution)

(Top left) This vase was made in the form of a bivalve mollusk shell resting on a low pedestal base. It is 6¾ inches high, has a matte glaze, and was made about 1900. The piece is impressed "Weller." (The Smithsonian Institution)   (Top center) An early unsigned Weller vase. It is blue with yellow and green glaze on the raised flowers. It is 4½ inches high. (Authors' collection)   (Top right) This matte glazed vase was modeled in the form of a plant about 1900. It is 7½ inches high. (The Smithsonian Institution) (Far left) Raised lavender and tan flowers decorate this Weller vase made about 1896–1905. It is 10 inches high. (The Smithsonian Institution)   (Left) This Weller Sicardo vase is of copper red iridescent glaze. It is signed on the side "Sicard, Weller" (see lower left of picture). The interior is glazed blue. The vase is 7 inches high. (Authors' collection)

(Top) This 7-inch-high Turada piece was originally a lamp base. (Bottom) This Weller Louwelsa clock is 6 inches high. It has the artist's signature, LJB (or LBJ), on the side.

Atlas. Star-shaped top, semigloss, angular sides, many colors, late period.

Aurelian. Brushed background, high-gloss brown glaze background similar to Louwelsa, brighter colors, red, yellow, brown, 1898–1910, sometimes marked "Aurelian" in script.

Auroro. (variants called Auroral, Aurora, Auroso). Mottled pastel background, gray, pink, overall crazing, fish, flower decorations, slip decorations, high gloss, 1904.

Baldin. Matte or glossy glaze, apples on branch, sometimes shaded blue background, other colors, middle period.

Barcelona. Matte glaze, pink to yellow, pink at base, flower decorations, ridges to imitate hand-thrown pottery, matte glaze, middle period.

Bedford. Glossy glaze, molded flowers on stems, dark colors, middle period.

Bedford Green Matte. Green matte glaze, molded flowers on stems, middle period.

Besline. Luster glaze, monochrome, overglaze woodbine decoration.

Blo'red. Blue glaze with red, high-gloss glaze, middle period.

Blossom. Pink flowers, green leaves, blue or green matte glaze, late period.

Blue and Decorated. Matte cream or blue background glaze, slip decoration, flowers or parrots, in shaded blue, cream pink, middle period.

Blue and Ivory. Tinted apple or pinecone decoration, blue background, middle period.

Blue Drapery. Dark blue matte glaze, red roses, pastel flower, draped vertical folds, c. 1920.

Blue Ware. Dark blue matte glaze, embossed medieval figures with plants in light colors, middle period.

Bo-Marblo. Luster glaze, tree design, middle period.

Bonito. Matte cream glaze, flowers, middle period.

Bouquet. Molded dogwood blossoms, a lily of the valley, matte glaze, late period.

Bradley. Fluted garden pots, middle period.

Breton. Matte glaze, band of stylized flowers and leaves in center, middle period.

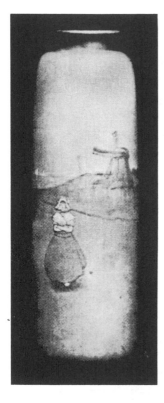

(Top left and center) Dresden line vases from an article in *Pottery and Glass*, November, 1909. (Reproduction from the collection of the Library of Congress) (Top right) A Weller LaSa vase, 7 inches high. The words "Weller LaSa" are printed on the lower part of the vase, below the tree decoration. (Bottom left) Weller plaque modeled by Jacques Sicard in 1907. It is 13 by 19 inches. The plaque has the typical Weller Sicard iridescent glaze. (The Smithsonian Institution) (Bottom right) This Weller vase by Jacques Sicard was made about 1901–1907. It features a design of honeysuckle blossoms in iridescent glaze. The piece is 5½ inches high. It is marked with the impressed name "Weller" and an incised "53." (The Art Museum, Princeton University, Princeton, New Jersey)

(Top left) This Weller Louwelsa vase pictures a Newfoundland dog. It is 15 inches high. (Top center) Impressed on the bottom of this jug type vase are the symbols "Louwelsa Weller 614 10." The 6½-inch piece is glazed brown to green with orange and green flowers. It is also marked with the cipher for C. Minnie Terry. (Collection of LeRoy Eslinger) (Top right) A Weller Louwelsa vase, 3½ inches high, decorated with pansies. (Center left) Yellow orange flower on brown to green ground decorate this Louwelsa 13-inch-wide, 10-inch-high vase. It is marked with the impressed block letters "Louwelsa Weller" and signed by the artist, M. Mitchell. (Collection of J. Walter Yore Company) (Center right) Orange flowers on a brown ground decorate this Louwelsa 14-inch-wide vase. It is marked with the impressed block letters "Louwelsa Weller." (Collection of J. Walter Yore Company) (Left) Yellow flowers on dark green ground decorate this Dickens ware 12-inch-wide, 12-inch-high vase. It is marked in block letters Dickens ware Weller 350 8. (Collection of J. Walter Yore Company)

Brighton. Figurines, natural colors, birds, glossy glaze, middle period.

Bronze Ware. Metallic-looking mottled glaze, middle period.

Burnt Wood. Realistic-looking tan and brown ware with the appearance of burnt wood. Lighter color designs carved out of clay, 1909, middle period.

Cameo Jewel (Cameo). White "jewels" in relief, pastel green, blue, coral used for background, semimatte, late period.

Chase. Relief white dogs and hunter on horseback, dark blue matte background (similar to Wedgwood jasper in appearance), late period.

Chelsea. Band of flowers near top, dark color to accent fluted sides, matte glaze, middle period.

Chengtu. Matte glaze, orange red, 1920–1925, developed by John Lessell.

Chinese Red. Red glaze developed by Lessell, c. 1920 (perhaps Chengtu).

Clarmont. Dark background, raised flowers, vines, grapes on band, raised small "beads" near the top, bottom.

Classic. Evenly placed relief vines forming arches at the top of the piece with cutout areas beneath the vine, plain light colors, c. 1920, middle period.

Claywood. Similar to Burnt Wood, middle period.

Clinton Ivory. Raised, molded trees, plants, other decorations, matte glaze, ivory with brown overtones, middle period.

Comet. Matte glaze, stars scattered on surface, pastel or white glaze, late period.

Coppertone. Blotchy semigloss green over brown glaze, yellow shading, figures of frogs, etc., and vases decorated with lifelike frogs, fish, animals, plants, middle period.

Cornish. Relief decoration of leaves and berries, largest leaves near the top, mottled background, middle period.

Cretone. Human features on vases, late period.

Crystalline. Columns of overlapped leaves, matte glaze, late period.

Darsie (Dorsey ?). Looped cords with tassels, matte glaze, solid color, late period.

Brown cherries and green leaves decorate this brown Louwelsa vase. It is 11 inches high and is incised "Weller Louwelsa" in a circle, "4, 431." (Collection of LeRoy Eslinger)

A Weller Louwelsa vase with clover decorations.

(Left top) Orange flower on dark blue green ground decorates this Dickens ware 11-inch-wide, 7-inch-high vase. It is marked with the impressed block letters Dickens ware Weller (Collection of J. Walter Yore Company) (Left center) *Left:* Weller matte glazed Dickens ware vase 8¾ inches high. *Right:* Dick Swiveller is pictured on this glossy glaze Dickens ware vase. It is 10½ inches high and was made about 1906. (The Smithsonian Institution) (Left bottom) Pink and white flowers on green to gray ground decorate this 9-inch-wide, 7½-inch-high Eocean vase. It has no marks. (Collection of J. Walter Yore Company) (Right top) Flying ducks are incised on this blue to mustard Dickens ware mug. (The Smithsonian Institution) (Right bottom) Eocean ware from an advertisement in *American Pottery Gazette,* August, 1906. (Reproduction from the collection of the Library of Congress)

(Above) Two undated catalogue pages circa 1920 showing Weller
Lamar ware. (Ohio Historical Society Library)   (Top right) This
Marengo lamp base is decorated with bright red and white trees and
landscape on a pink background. The 7-inch piece is signed Lessell
at the base but with no mark on the bottom. (Collection of LeRoy
Eslinger)   (Bottom right) Applied dark and pastel glazes form the
raised flowers on the Rochelle line vase. It is 10 inches high and has
no mark. (Collection of LeRoy Eslinger)

Some of the new superbly decorated Eocean ware which ranks high among the very finest art ware made in America. From S. A. WELLER, Zanesville, O., and seen in the showroom of CHARLES H. TAYLOR 57 Park Place, New York.

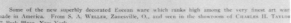

(Above left) Undated catalogue page circa 1920 showing jardinieres and pedestals in several patterns. (Ohio Historical Society Library) (Above right) Undated catalogue page, circa 1920, showing Eocean wares. (Ohio Historical Society Library)

(Left) Eocean ware *(top)* and Dickens ware *(bottom)* from an advertisement for Weller pottery, *American Pottery Gazette*, August, 1905. (Reproduction from the collection of the Library of Congress) (Below) Weller Muskota vase with squirrel, 8 inches in diameter.

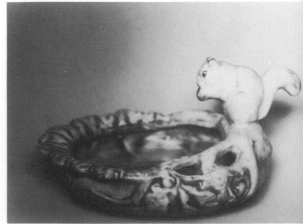

Delsa. Relief flowers and leaves, matte glaze, leaf handles, late period.

Delta. Blue slip decorations on blue background, matte glaze, middle period.

Dickens Tobacco Jars. Admiral, Turk, Chinaman, Irishman.

Dickens Ware. First line: solid dark brown, green, or blue background resembling Louwelsa, occasionally a shaded background, slip decorations, flowers, 1897–1898, marked "Dickens Ware," developed by Mr. Upjohn. *Second line:* shaded background matte or high gloss glaze; graffito decoration of scenes from Dickens, also Indians, monks, fish, birds, golfers, drinking scenes, historical scenes; colors used were dark red brown, green, gray, turquoise, and pink. Marked "Dickens Ware," sometimes has artist's name, 1897–c. 1905, developed by Mr. Upjohn. *Third line:* dark background shaded to light, similar to *Eocean* line, high gloss, relief figures. On one side are figures from Dickens's stories. Reverse side has a raised black disc with the name of the scene, sometimes a raised white disc with the profile of Dickens. Marked "Weller," created by Frederick Hürten Rhead, 1910.

Dorland. Scalloped top, ribs, matte glaze, late period.

Drapery. See *Blue Drapery.*

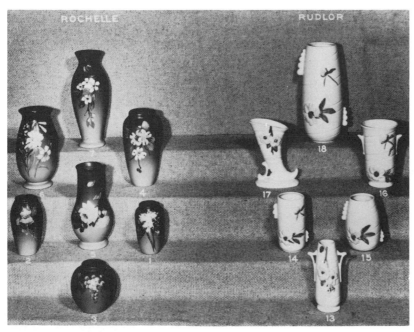

Undated catalogue page circa 1920 showing Rochelle and Rudlor lines. (Ohio Historical Society Library)

This 16½-inch-high vase is glazed from dark gray to light gray to pink. It has dogwood flower decorations in natural shades. The vase is signed Leffler at the base. The bottom is incised "Eocean Weller" in script. (Collection of LeRoy Eslinger)

Dresden Ware (also called Holland). Dutch scenes, slip painted, blue, blue figures, matte glaze, 1907–1909.

Dugan. Relief flowers on low bowls, middle period.

Dupont Ware. Relief roses, colored background, middle period.

Eclair. High relief roses, white or dark glossy background, middle period.

Elberta. Buff-colored bands on green matte background.

Eldora. Ribbing at bottom, flowers in band at top, matte glaze, colored background, middle period.

Eocean (Eosian). Underglaze slip decoration, birds, animals, fish, flowers, character study, light eggshell shaded to blue gray or brown background, high gloss, 1898–1915, marked "Eocean Weller."

Eocean Rose. Same as Eocean except shaded from gray to pink, usually marked "Eocean Rose Weller."

Etched Matte. Incised decoration, matte gray glaze, similar to second line Dickens, early period.

Ethel. Cream-colored background, matte glaze, oval medallion with profile of woman's head (said to be Ethel Weller), roses on stems, bands on cross-hatching top and bottom, c. 1915.

Etna. Light blue to gray shaded to dark at the top, high gloss, flowers or grapes molded, colored, 1906, mark "ETNA" scratched into base.

Euclid. Matte glaze, no decoration, middle period.

Evergreen. Green blue matte finish, ribbed, late period.

Fairfield. Similar to Donatello pattern by the Roseville factory, band of cherubs at top, fluted base, matte finish, middle period.

Flemish Ware. Matte glaze, embossed decorations of parrots, cows, grapes, roses, apples, birds, or nymphs, c. 1920 (?)–1928 (name seems to have been used for other wares too).

Fleron. Green glaze, made to look hand turned (called Ansonia if blue or gray) middle period.

Floral. Ribbed background, blue, green, or white background pastel colors, floral decoration, semigloss, late period 1931–1948.

Florala. Cream background, raised molded flowers, pastel tints in rectangular panels, matte glaze, middle period.

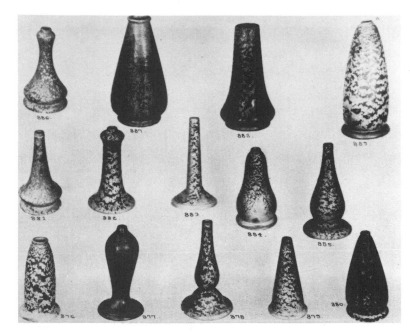

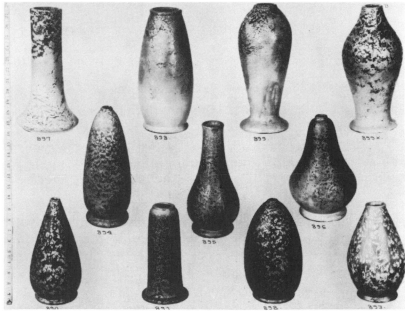

(Left) Two undated catalogue pages showing frosted matte ware. (Ohio Historical Society Library) (Below) A 12½-inch-high vase in the Etched Matte line. It has an orange matte glaze and incised decorations. The vase is impressed "Weller." (Collection of LeRoy Eslinger)

Florenzo. Pastel flowers on a ribbed background of cream edged with green, matte glaze, middle period, 1928.

Floretta. Brown or pastel background, underglaze flowers or fruit in low relief, or incised like second line Dickens, high gloss glaze or matte finish, marked "Floretta Weller" in a circle, impressed, 1904.

Forest. Polychrome, tinted color, matte or shiny glaze, hand-decorated forest scenes, c. 1920.

Forest View. Forest scenes, leaf and berry decoration.

Frosted Matte. Mottled, almost metallic-looking in many colors, green, yellow, purple, blue, pink, middle period.

Fruitone. Upright streaks of color, shaded like a piece of fruit, late period.

(Right) Undated catalogue pages circa 1920 showing the Hudson line. (Ohio Historical Society Library) (Above) This Weller Etna line vase with thistle decoration is 8½ inches high. It has the word Weller incised on the side of the vase (at lower right corner of picture).

Fudzi. Listed in 1906 catalogue, description unknown.

Geode. Cream glaze, fluting, scalloped top, 1936.

Glazed Hudson. See Hudson.

Glendale Ware. Scenes of birds with nests, branches, plants, Indians, slightly raised on sky-blue background, matte glaze, 1928.

Gloria. Matte glaze, beige, black berries in relief.

Golbrogreen (Gold-Green?). Gold shaded to green, matte glaze, early 1907 period.

Golden Glow. Mottled background, leaves, applied handles.

Graystone. Outdoor pottery line resembling granite.

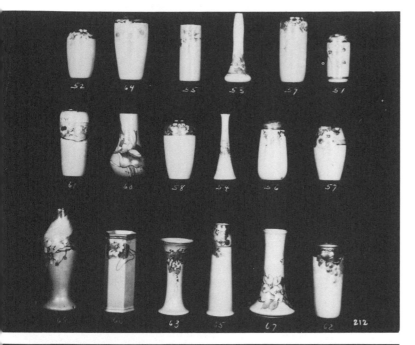

Greenaways. Gray to pink, landscapes, windmills, sea scenes, similar to Dresden ware, 1909.

Greenbriar. Pink over green glaze, glossy, made to resemble hand turning, middle period.

Greora. Orange brown mottled with shades of green semigloss, middle period.

Hobart. Vellum finish, monochrome green, white, human and animal figures, flower holders, 1928 (if shaded glaze, called Lavonia).

Holland. See Dresden Ware.

Hudson. Matte glaze, underglaze slip-painted decorations, realistic flowers, birds, etc., early and middle peri-

(Left top) Undated catalogue page circa 1920 showing the glazed Hudson line. (Ohio Historical Society Library)   (Left bottom) Undated catalogue page circa 1920 showing the Marvo line. (Ohio Historical Society Library)   (Right top) This vase is impressed with the name "Weller." It has a raised iris decoration in pale pink shades on a gray background. It is 8 inches high. (Authors' collection) (Right bottom) This unmarked vase is Burntwood Line with a fish decoration. It is 2 inches high. (Authors' collection)

(Above and on facing page) Three undated catalogue pages circa 1920 showing the Weller Knifewood line. (Ohio Historical Society Library) (Right) Undated catalogue page circa 1920 showing Muskota ware. (Ohio Historical Society Library)

ods (Glazed Hudson is the same with a glossy finish).

Hunter. Brown background, slip decorations of outdoor subjects, birds, butterflies, etc., glossy glaze, early 1907 period, signed "Hunter."

Ivoris. Ivory background color, relief flowers, semigloss, late period.

Ivory. Cream color tinged with brown, relief decorations, cupids, swags, etc. matte glaze, 1928.

Jap Birdimal. Brown, blue, gray, terra-cotta, greenish yellow background, decorations of birds, trees, animals,

314

Japanese women. Designs were incised then inlaid with slip, covered with high gloss glaze. 1904, created by Frederick Rhead, sometimes marked Weller, Rhead.

Jet Black. Matte black, late period.

Jewel. See *Cameo Jewel.*

Juneau. White matte glaze, late period.

Kenova. Relief decorations of flowers, woman's head, birds, middle period.

Kitchen Gem. Utility line.

Klyro Ware. Seven-inch bud vases, two flowers and perpendicular green lines, middle period.

Knifewood. Looks like carved wood, colored decorations, dogs, swans, other animals, matte glaze, middle period.

Lamar. Deep red background with black scenery, trees, middle period, designed by John Lessell.

L'Art Nouveau. See *Art Nouveau.*

Lasa. Metallic glaze in gold, reddish gold, silver background, landscape decorations, marked on side near base, 1900–1925, created by Art Wagner.

Lavonia. Matte or glossy glaze, pink shaded to blue, fluted pieces (see *Hobart*), middle period.

Lessell (Lassell). Hand-decorated metallic luster, trees on rose gold, silver background, 1920. (Marbelized).

Lido. Pastel, relief leaf decoration or just draped, middle period.

Lonhuda. Brown glazed line, 1894, impressed mark.

Lorbeek. Cream color, modernistic, middle period.

This 11-inch-high Burntwood vase is decorated with birds and flowers. It is marked Weller on the bottom. (Collection of LeRoy Eslinger)

(Top) This claywood dish is 4½ inches in diameter. It is unsigned. (Authors' collection) (Center) A 7-inch-high Pinecone line Weller vase. (Bottom) This unmarked vase has an almost black matte glaze around the spider web. It may be Weller claywood design or it may be a copy by another factory. (Authors' collection)

Loru. Raised leaf design near base, matte finish, late period.

Louella. Same as Blue Drapery except in pink, gray, or brown, middle period.

Louwelsa. Shaded fall-colored background of brown, yellow, green, slip decorated with flowers, fruit, Indians, dogs, very similar to Lonhuda, high gloss glaze, 1895–1918, sometimes marked Louwelsa.

Louwelsa Matte. Slip decorated, pastel matte finish.

Lustre. Plain luster glaze, no decoration, middle period.

Luxor Line. Imitation bark with relief flowers, middle period.

Malta Ware. Flower holder shaped like birds or figures, pastel, 1928.

Malvern. High relief realistic leaves and flowers on rough background, matte finish, middle period.

Manhattan. Different color background, traditional stylized flowers and leaves, matte or glossy glaze, middle period, c. 1920.

Marbelized (Lessell Ware). Luster background decorated with trees, mountains, pink, orange, blue, lavender, gray, or purple luster, middle period, sometimes marked Lessell on side.

Marne. Outdoor pottery sundials and birdbaths, etc., middle period.

Marvo. Raised ferns and leaves, light green, tan, matte glaze, 1928.

Matte Floretta. See *Floretta.*

Matte (Mat) Green. Slightly shaded dark green, matte glaze, raised designs of leaves, natural forms, 1905.

Melrose. Pastel-colored realistic cherries, grapes, or roses in relief, cream background, tinged with color, irregular shape to vase, middle period.

Mi-Flo. Flowers, leaves, or diagonal panels in relief, matte glaze, late period.

Mirror Black. Black glaze, plain, middle period.

Monochrome. Matte glaze, solid color, early period (1907).

Morocco. Tree, fruit in carved relief on black or red background, middle period.

Muskota. Flower holders in bird, animal, human shapes, bowls, jars, light or dark colors, glossy glaze, 1928.

Neiska. Mottled finish, matte glaze, found on Ivoris, Velva shapes, late period.

Nile. Matte glaze, drip decoration, middle period.

Norona (Narona). Ivory-colored background, classic figures, fruit, or flowers in relief, decorations accented with rubbed brown color, wax, 1909.

Norwood. Art Nouveau patterns in relief, stippled background, dark, matte background, 1909.

Noval. Brown background or white with black edging, applied roses, fruit, middle period.

Oak Leaf. Matte glaze, raised oak leaves and acorns, late period.

Ollas Water Bottle. Water bottle of gourd shape with stem top, plate painted yellow, green, etc., late period, designed by Mrs. Dorothy England Laughead.

Oriental. Variation of Jap Birdimal, early period.

Orris. Relief flowers and leaves, basket weave background on some pieces, middle period.

Panella. Nasturtiums or pansies in relief, matte finish, late period.

Paragon. Stylized impressed flowers and leaves, matte glaze, late period, c. 1920.

Parian. Hanging wall baskets, ivory, impressed leaves, geometric designs, matte glaze, late period.

Pastel. Modern shapes, pastel colors, matte glaze, late period.

Patra. Scalloped top, mottled, design at bottom, round texture, matte finish, middle period.

Patricia. Swan handles, leaves, glossy pale cream glaze, sometimes tinted, late period.

Pearl. Matte glaze, cream color, decorated with loops of pastel colored beads, relief decoration, middle period, c. 1920.

Perfecto. Unglazed, painted decoration, early (1907) period.

Pictorial. Underglaze slip decoration, landscapes, usually pastel, middle period.

Pierre. Basketweave decoration, dinner sets, late period.

Pinecone. Pinecone decoration in panel, light color, matte glaze, middle period.

Pumila. Matte glaze, relief leaves or blossoms, form irregular edge at top, late period, 1928.

(Top) This Weller coppertone vase is 6½ inches high. (Bottom) This Weller vase with a mottled green glaze is from the Coppertone line. It is 6 inches high, signed "Weller Handmade." (Authors' collection)

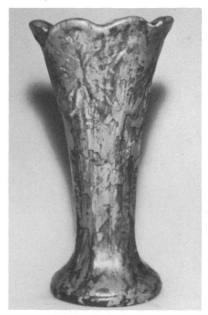

(Top) Stylized decorations in gold, blue, and maize on a crackled cream matte glaze decorate this Weller vase. The artist's name, Ferrell, is in color on the side of the vase. (Authors' collection) (Bottom) A vase from the "Blue and Decorated" line. The body is cream-colored crackle glazed, and the trailing blossom decorations are pink and gray. The 10-inch-high vase is marked Weller. (Authors' collection)

Racene. Modern-style deer and leaves, late period.

Ragenda. Draped folds over piece to make design, dark matte glaze, middle period.

Raydence. Solid color glaze, flowers at bottom, fluted top, middle period.

Reno. Plain dark bands decorate middle of light piece, middle period.

Roba. Raised flowers and leaves, realistic coloring, looped on crinkled background, matte glaze, late period.

Rochelle. Slip designs, low relief, high gloss glaze, similar to Eocean, middle period.

Roma. Garlands of flowers or other motif on plain background, cream, brown, black, or green, matte glaze, middle period, c. 1919. May be several types—another had raised naturalistic flowers and stems tied with bow on matte vase, some had cattails, kingfishers.

Roma Cameo. See *Cameo Jewel.*

Rosella. Mugs, pitchers, fluted near base, narrow flower bands, middle period.

Rosemont. Low relief decoration, flowers, birds on dark high-gloss glaze or rose petals on light background, middle period.

Rudlor. Relief flowers on horizontal spiral, ribbed piece, matte glaze, late period.

Sabrinian. Seashell-like piece, sea horse handle, matte glaze, pastel shades, middle period.

Scenic. Matte glaze, blue or green, scenes of nature, late period.

Selma. High-gloss glaze on the Knifewood line, middle period.

Seneca. Pastel or dark colors, glossy glaze, no decoration, middle period.

Sicardo. Iridescent glaze of metallic shadings in greens, blues, crimson, purple, coppertones, with vines, flowers, stars, free-form geometric lines, 1902–1907, created by Jacques Sicard and Henri Gellie, usually signed on surface of piece "Weller-Sicard" or "Sicardo."

Silvertone. Matte glaze, pink, blue, green, lavender, realistic cast flowers, fruits, or butterflies, middle period.

Softone. Drapery design with folds, semimatte glaze, pastel, late period.

Souevo. Indian tupe decoration, incised, matte glaze, 1909.

Stellar Black. Black with white stars and comet or white with blue stars and comet, matte glaze, middle period.

Sydonia (Sudonia ?). Shell-like shape, leaves at base, middle period.

Teakwood. Dark background woodlike surface, flowers, fruits, birds, women's heads, "carved" on surface, matte glaze, middle period.

Terose (Tearose). Kitchen wares, white matte glaze, plain or ribbed, middle period.

Terra-Cotta. Outdoor birdhouses, baskets, gray, rough surface, middle period.

Ting. White or ivory vase, Chinese shape on black pottery base, like teakwood, late period.

Tivoli. Glossy cream-colored piece with black edging on some, borders of flowers, middle period.

Tupelo. Perpendicular bands of flowers, grapes, pastel colors, ribbed, middle period.

Turada. Background brown, black, dark blue, lacy decoration of white, pale orange, light blue, incised then inlaid with slip, high gloss glaze, 1897–1898, usually marked "Turada."

Turkis. Unknown.

Tutone. Flowers and leaves in relief, matte glaze, assorted colors, middle period.

Underglaze Blue Ware. Mottled dark blue glaze, similar to Coppertone, middle period.

Velva. Stylized relief flowers and leaves in panels, brown or beige background, late period.

Velvetone. Blended colors of green, pink, yellow, brown, green, matte glaze, 1928.

Voile. Matte green-gray background, low relief, fruit trees in tinted colors, 1928.

Warwick. Matte, fruit trees modeled, middle period.

Wayne Ware. Ivory with green interior, matte glaze, jardinieres and pedestals, 1928.

Weller Etched Matte. See *Etched Matte.*

Weller Matte Green. See *Matte Green.*

Wild Rose. Light pink shaded, matte background, roses applied or later cast, middle period.

Woodcraft. Natural-looking tree stumps, logs, wooden surface with realistic animal decorations, polychrome colors, matte glaze, 1928.

This 15½-inch-high vase has a matte blue background with lifelike colored irises. It is signed Pillsbury on the side, near the base. (Authors' collection)

The name "Timberlake" is signed on the side of this 7-inch vase. It has an aqua to pink crackled matte glaze with pink and white dogwood blossoms. (Authors' collection)

Wood Rose. Roses for decoration, middle period, oaken bucket background.

Zona. Red apples, green leaves, stems (same design, made by Gladding, McBean & Co. of California as "Franciscan ware"), designed by Rudolph Lorber, 1920.

Zona (later). Jars, baskets, pitchers, decorated with kingfisher, cattails, in panels, low relief designs.

Zona Baby Line. Baby dishes.

Bibliography

American Pottery Gazette (August 5, 1905), p. 41.

————, (August 10, 1906), p. 29.

————, (March, 1909), p. 29.

Antique Trader, The, "Weller Pottery" (May 16, 1972), p. 53.

Barber, Edwin, *Marks of American Potters,* Philadelphia: Patterson and White, 1904. p. 131.

————, *The Pottery and Porcelain of the United States,* New York: G. P. Putnam's Sons, 1909, pp. 509, 563.

Clark, Edna Mavia, *Ohio Art and Artists,* Richmond, Virginia: Garrett & Massie Pub., 1932.

Clark, Robert Judson, *The Arts and Crafts Movement in America 1876–1916,* Princeton, N.J.: Princeton University Press, 1972.

Cobb, Lura Milburn, "A Visit to Some Zanesville Potteries," *The Southwestern Book* (V. II, No. 12), (December, 1905).

Cook, May Elizabeth, "Our American Potteries—Weller Ware," *Sketch Book* (V. 5), (May, 1906), 340–347.

Fruge, Eliose, "Third Line Weller Is Rarest," *Collectors' News,* date and page unknown.

Garrett, Brice, "Weller Ware," *Spinning Wheel* (May, 1965), 8–10.

Hall, Foster and Gladys, "The Weller Pricing Formula," date unknown.

————, Correspondence to "Pottery Party Line," *Pottery Collectors' Newsletter* (V. 2, No. 2), (November, 1972), 24.

Henzke, Lucile, "Weller's Dickens Ware," *Spinning Wheel* (October, 1968), 16–18.

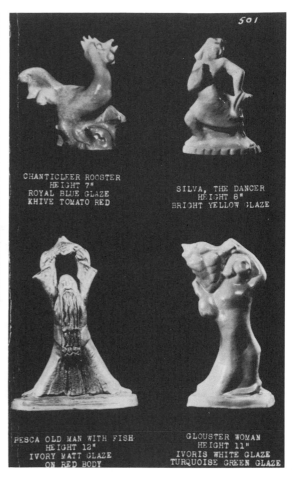

CHANTICLEER ROOSTER
HEIGHT 7"
ROYAL BLUE GLAZE
KHIVE TOMATO RED

SILVA, THE DANCER
HEIGHT 8"
BRIGHT YELLOW GLAZE

PESCA OLD MAN WITH FISH
HEIGHT 12"
IVORY MATT GLAZE
ON RED BODY

GLOUSTER WOMAN
HEIGHT 11"
IVORIS WHITE GLAZE
TURQUOISE GREEN GLAZE

_____, "Weller's Sicardo," *Spinning Wheel* (September, 1969), 26–28, 67.

Markham, Kenneth H., "Weller Sicardo Art Pottery," *The Antiques Journal* (September, 1964), 18.

Pottery and Glass, "New Jardinieres, Flower Pots, Etc." (V. III, No. 2), (August, 1909), 65.

_____, (V. III, No. 5) (November, 1909), 232–234.

Purviance, Evan, "American Art Pottery," *Mid-America Reporter* (December, 1971), 8.

_____, "American Art Pottery," *Mid-America Reporter* (January, 1972), 30.

_____, "American Art Pottery," *Mid-America Reporter* (February, 1972), 13.

_____, "American Art Pottery," *Mid-America Reporter* (March, 1972), 10.

Purviance, Louise, "American Art Pottery," *The Antique Reporter* (April, 1973), 4.

(Top left) Floral line examples in red and green decoration with white ground. The pieces on the bottom row are marked with the impressed word "Weller." The pieces on the top row are unmarked. (Collection of J. Walter Yore Company) (Bottom left) These two animals are Weller Coppertone pieces. The frog is 4 inches high, incised "Weller Pottery" in script. The 4-inch-long, 2-inch-high turtle is stamped "Weller Pottery" in black ink. Both pieces have the typical green mottled glaze. (Collection of Les Senders, Senders Antiques) (Right) Page from an undated catalogue showing four figures made by the Weller Potteries. (Ohio Historical Society Library)

(Left) This advertisement from *Tile and Tile Work*, April, 1930 shows "Venetian Canal Scene," a special installation of tile made for The Carmichael Tile Company of Birmingham, Alabama, at the Weller Potteries. (Ohio Historical Society Library)   (Right) This advertisement for Weller tiles appeared in *Tiles and Tile Work*, June, 1930. It emphasizes that each installation is one of a kind and will not be duplicated.

Purviance, Louise and Evan and Norris F. Schneider, *Zanesville Art Pottery in Color.* Leon, Iowa: Mid-America Book Company, 1968.

———, *Weller Art Pottery in Color,* Leon, Iowa: Mid-America Book Company, 1971.

Ray, Marcia, "ABC's of Ceramics, Part Thirteen," *Spinning Wheel* (July–August, 1968), 32.

———, "ABC's of Ceramics, Conclusion," *Spinning Wheel* (September, 1968), 38.

Ruge, Clara, "American Ceramics—A Brief Review of Progress," *International Studio* (V. 28), (March, 1906), 21–28.

———, "New Features in Domestic Potteries," *Pottery and Glass* (V. II, No. 3), (March, 1909), 129–130.

Schneider, Norris F., "Albert Haubrich, Weller Pottery Decorator," *Pottery Collectors' Newsletter* (V. 1, No. 8), (May, 1972), 107–108.

————, "Plant Ceased Work in 1948," *Zanesville Times-Signal* (April 13, 1958).

————, "Weller Pottery," *Zanesville Times-Signal* (March 16, 1958 and April 6, 1958).

————, "Sicardo Ware, Potter Guards Secret Process," *Zanesville Times-Signal* (March 30, 1958).

Stout, Wilber, R. T. Stull, Wm. J. McCaughey, D. J. Demerest, "Art Pottery" *Geological Survey of Ohio*, Columbus, Ohio: J. A. Bownocker, State Geologist, 4th Series, Bulletin 26, 1923.

Zanesville Chamber of Commerce Booklet, "S. A. Weller Potteries," 1918.

WHEATLEY POTTERY

Thomas J. Wheatley was one of many people influenced by the work of the Pottery Club of Cincinnati (see) and M. Louise McLaughlin (see Rookwood). He also experimented at the pottery of P. L. Coultry about 1879, forming a brief partnership with Mr. Coultry. In 1880, Wheatley established his own firm, T. J. Wheatley & Co., in Cincinnati. He built a kiln on Hunt Street, where he did his own preparation of clay, and his own molding, glazing, and firing. It is interesting that contemporary sources comment that he "has been unselfish in regard to his discoveries of modes and processes, freely communicating them to any who wish to learn and who are welcomed to work at his establishment" (*Harper's New Monthly Magazine*, May, 1881, p. 840). Nevertheless, he once threatened to file suit to keep other potters from using his patent on glazing. His improvement in underglaze decoration was patented on September 28, 1880,* and he made some of the largest pieces ever produced in his time. His wares were varied—some covered with a mottled green matte glaze, others with a shiny glaze and floral decorations. The pieces were marked with a paper label or with an incised signature T.J.W.C. Although Wheatley had his own company, he also worked for the Cincinnati Art Pottery Company (see) from 1880 to 1882. And some-

*Miss McLaughlin claimed to have developed the method first, but she had never filed for a patent.

(Top left) John Rettig signed this 13⅛-inch-high vase made by T. J. Wheatley. It has wild roses painted underglaze on a blue background. The bottom of the vase has the incised mark "T. J. Wheatley, 1879." (Cincinnati Art Museum, Cincinnati, Ohio) (Bottom left) A Wheatley Pottery dark and light green vase. It is 12 inches high, marked only with a paper sticker. (The Smithsonian Institution) (Above) A green matte glaze covers this 14-inch-high vase made by the Wheatley Pottery Company about 1905. (The Smithsonian Institution) (Below) A Wheatley label featuring the mark.

WHEATLEY.
No 237943
Price
CINCINNATI, O.

time between 1893 and 1905 his own company must have suspended business because in Barber's 1905 edition, it is mentioned that Mr. Wheatley "has recently resumed the making of art pottery." It is recorded that the Cambridge Tile Manufacturing Company bought the Wheatley Pottery in 1927.

Bibliography

Antiques, "Wheatley Pottery Co." (June, 1966), 850.

Barber, Edwin, *The Pottery and Porcelain of the United States,* New York: G. P. Putnam's Sons, 1909.

ZANE POTTERY (1920–1941)

Zane Pottery was officially founded in January, 1921. The owners, Adam Reed and Harry McClelland had purchased the Peters and Reed Company and changed the name. McClelland had begun working for Peters and Reed in 1903 and by 1909 was the company secretary. He became the president of Zane Pottery in 1920. After Reed died, McClelland bought all of the outstanding stock and he became the sole owner. He enlarged the plant and added art pottery while continuing to make flowerpots.

The Zane Pottery made a full line of garden flowerpots, decorative garden pieces, jars, vases, birdbaths, and art pottery. They used a handpress method. The firm had a line called Greystone, but the Weller Pottery had copyrighted that name so Zane changed the name of its line to Stonetex.

There are no known catalogs of Zane art pottery. Some of the lines they have been known to make are Crystaline, a semimatte orange and green glazed ware; Drip, a line covered with one color glaze and a dripped glaze of a second color at the top; Powder blue, a blue matte finish; and Sheen, a four-color line with a semimatte glaze.

McClelland died in 1931 and his wife became president. In 1941, the family sold the plant to Lawton Gonder and he changed the name to the Gonder Pottery. See Gonder Pottery and Peters and Reed.

ZANESVILLE ART POTTERY (1900–1920)

The Zanesville Art Pottery was founded in 1900 by David Schmidt in Zanesville, Ohio. He had moved from Germany to Pittsburgh, had been a roofer, then imported and sold slate for roofs. In 1900, he changed the Zanesville Roofing Tile Company to the Zanesville Art Pottery Company. The firm made faience, umbrella stands, jar-

This 7-inch-high La Moro vase has a green to brown to orange glaze with yellow violet decoration. The artist's cipher "L.F." appears on the rim of the base. The bottom is marked with an impressed "LA MORO 885." (Authors' collection)

This green to orange glazed La Moro vase is decorated with a yellow Black-eyed Susan. The 10-inch piece is impressed LA MORO on the bottom with the numbers "8 11 5", and the artist's initials "C.S." is on the bowl part of the vase. (Authors' collection)

dinieres, and pedestals. The art pottery was dark brown with Indian heads, flowers, and other underglaze decorations. Its famous art line was called La Moro. Two known artist's marks used in La Moro are CS and LE. The artists' names are unknown.

The firm was destroyed in a fire in 1901, but rebuilt. In 1910, another fire and another rebuilding took place. In 1920, the plant was sold to S. A. Weller and it became the Weller Plant No. 3.

Albert Radford, of England, worked at the Zanesville Art Pottery as general manager in 1901. He started his own firm in 1903 (see A. Radford Pottery). Otto and Paul Herold, nephews of David Schmidt, worked at the pottery for about six years. Otto worked at the Roseville Pottery from 1914–1918, moved to the American Encaustic Tile Company, then to the Zane pottery. Paul moved to Chicago and became an artist. In 1936, the two Herold brothers founded their own firm, LePere Pottery. It worked until 1962.

Bibliography

Barber, Edwin, *The Pottery and Porcelain of the United States,* New York: G. P. Putnam's Sons, 1909.

Purviance, Evan and Louise, *Zanesville Art Tile in Color,* Des Moines, Iowa: Wallace-Homestead Book Co., 1973.

Purviance, Louise and Evan and Norris F. Schneider, *Zanesville Art Pottery in Color,* Leon, Iowa: Mid-America Book Company, 1968.

Schneider, Norris F., "Many Small Art Potteries Once Operated in Zanesville," *Zanesville Times Recorder* (February 4, 1962).

"Zanesville Art Pottery," *Zanesville Times-Signal* (November 11, 1956).

Zanesville Chamber of Commerce Booklet, "The Zanesville Art Pottery Company" (1918).

POTTERY TILES

ALHAMBRA TILE COMPANY
Newport, Kentucky

Established 1892.

AMERICAN ENCAUSTIC TILING COMPANY

English-made tiles for flooring and walls were selling so well in the United States that in 1874 a group of Zanesville, Ohio, men decided to try making tiles locally. F. H. Hall began experimenting with the tiles. He had the financial backing of Benedict Fischer and G. R. Lansing of New York City, both eventually becoming officers in American Encaustic. Mr. Hall was evidently successful in making tiles from Ohio clay. In 1875 the *Zanesville Courier* mentioned that Mr. Hall had patented his system of tile manufacturing. No more is known of Hall and he is not listed in the city directories.

The American Encaustic Tiling Company was founded in 1875, and in 1876 Gilbert Elliott came from England to supervise their tile production. In 1877 he planned and directed the manufacture of their first commercial installation of tile, which was for the floor of the Muskinghum County Courthouse in Zanesville. The firm must have been producing tile in quantity because in 1877 they bought land for more kilns. The building, with six kilns, was finished in 1879. During the same year the American Encaustic Tiling Company Ltd. was incorporated, with Benedict Fischer president, George R. Lansing treasurer, and William G. Flammer secretary.

George A. Stanberry probably joined the company in 1876. He was a mechanical engineer, born in Zanesville, but he evidently had worked in Europe. He developed the machinery that made it possible for the firm to produce floor tiles in quantity. By 1879 he was general superintendent of the plant.

The problem facing the company was to convince American architects that the locally made tiles were of the same quality as those from Europe. To prove themselves, the company not only made the tile. They laid it and guaranteed it. It was not too long before their tile was accepted, and by 1880 the floor of the New York State Capitol Building in Albany, New York, consisted of American Encaustic Tiling Company tiles.

The first glazed tile was made at the plant in 1880, and

American Encaustic marks. (Smithsonian Institution)

Mark on jasper ware tiles.

Mark on pieces modeled by Herman C. Mueller before 1893.

Paper label.

by 1881 embossed tiles were being made. The firm continued to grow and by 1889 the owners decided to move the plant to New Jersey. But the citizens of Zanesville raised forty thousand dollars to keep the plant in Zanesville where a new factory site was purchased in 1890. The citizens gave the company the land for the site, developed the gas, and furnished free water and adequate railroad lines. The new plant, the largest tile works in the world, was opened in 1892. At the dedication, fifteen thousand souvenir tiles were distributed.

The factory made tiles of all types. In 1893, Edwin Barber wrote in his book, *The Pottery and Porcelain of the United States:*

Encaustic or inlaid floor tiles are made by both the plastic and the damp-dust processes, and the geometrical designs for these are prepared by competent designers who are employed by the company for this purpose. Relief tiles are also made here to a large extent, designed by Mr. Herman Mueller. . . . Special designs have been produced in single panels, twelve by 18 inches in dimensions, of which we have seen some female water carriers of Grecian type. Plastic sketches of large size have also been executed for special orders. Among other styles produced at this factory are imitation mosaic tiles, damask, and embossed damask-finished tiles. By a peculiar treatment, pictures and portraits are also reproduced on a plain surface. . . . Some of the most artistic productions of this factory are the eight, ten and fifteen tile facings, with raised designs of classic female and child figures. . . . This company has recently produced a new style of unglazed floor tiling, in elegant designs and attractive coloring which is designated by the name and trademark of "Alhambra." . . . The tinted arabesque designs are inlaid to the depth of about one eighth inch, simulating mosaic work.

The firm was making 6 by 6 inch tiles in 1906, but a while later, changed to 4¼ by 4¼. In 1909, George Stanberry died and Harry D. Lillibridge became plant superintendent. In 1919 American Encaustic had a shop in New York City where workmen cut tiles for mosaic work. That year they also purchased a plant in California. The firm continued to prosper. Half the tiles used in the Holland tunnel in New York City were made by the American Encaustic Tiling Company.

The firm started to make faience tiles by the 1920s. Frederick Rhead headed the research for bathroom fixtures and soda fountain tiles from 1920 to 1927.

In 1932, the firm began having financial problems and

the California branch of the company was sold. The Zanesville plant was closed in 1935, reopening in 1937 as the Shawnee Pottery (see).

Special Souvenir Tiles

A. E. Tiling Co., Ltd. Paperweight tile; 1896 calendar on back.

Admiral George Dewey. Six-inch plaque in color.

American Encaustic Tile Company. Dedication tile, April 19, 1892; blue glaze 4 by 4 inches.

Association of Interstate Mantel and Tile Dealers. New York, February, 1911, white tile, hand-colored flowers, gold border, 5 by 7 inches.

William Jennings Bryan. Democratic presidential candidate, 1896, 3-inch square, blue glazed, biography pasted on back.

D. W. Caldwell. Portrait, president of Nickel Plate Rail Road, 6-inch square, biography on reverse.

The Courier Company. Zanesville, Ohio, paperweight, 1896 calendar on back.

Walter Crane Tiles. Walter Crane was an English illustrator of books. About 1891, tiles were made from the original plates used to illustrate *The Baby's Opera* and *The Baby's Own Aesop*. At least eleven designs are known. Each tile is marked with the Crane monogram and the letters AETCO on the back. A crane standing on a W inside a C is pictured on the front. Similar tiles were made by the Mosaic Tile Company, but the Crane monogram was omitted.

Cyrene Commandery. November 10, 1902, meeting, Louisville, Kentucky, 2½-inch circle.

Eastern Ohio Teachers Association. Zanesville, November 10–11, 1916, worn on ribbon.

Benedict Fischer. Portrait, founder of A.E.T.C., tile 7 by 9 inches, brown glaze.

The Foraker Club. Zanesville, Ohio. He was governor of Ohio from 1886, aspired to the presidential candidacy

This large tile, 9½ inches by 14 inches, is marked on the back with the AETCo. symbol in a circle in an incised pattern and the painted symbols 8165 Dec. 82. It is a red clay tile with carved decorations. The finished tile is blue, gold, brown, and black. (Authors' collection)

The boy pulling the ram is part of an unglazed terra-cotta tile made by the American Encaustic Tiling Co. It is 6 inches wide by 16 inches long. (The Smithsonian Institution)

(Left top) A fireplace top tile with a peacock and a lounging lady. It is light olive green and measures 6 by 18 inches. (Authors' collection)   (Left middle) Tiles were often made to surround a fireplace opening. This tile was used at the top of the fireplace. It is 6 inches by 18 inches, glazed an olive green. (Authors' collection)   (Left bottom) Campaign tiles and other special tiles were often made by the factory. William McKinley *(left)* and Garrett A. Hobart *(right)* are pictured on these blue glazed intaglio tiles from the election of 1896. The biography of the candidate was pasted on the back of his 3-inch-square tile. (Collection of Charles Klamkin)   (Top right) A white and yellow border edges this polychrome tile marked AET Faience. It is 4 inches square. (Smithsonian Institution)   (Right) William Jennings Bryan was pictured on this intaglio blue glazed tile for the election of 1896. The tile is 3 inches square. (Collection of Charles Klamkin)

in 1903. Date of tile unknown. Circular 3-inch tile set in a badge.

Garret A. Hobart. Republican vice-presidential candidate in 1896 (Vice President 1897 until his death in 1899). 3-inch square, blue glazed.

William McKinley. Republican candidate for president in 1896. 3-inch square, blue glazed.

William McKinley. In color on a blue background.

Republican State Convention. 1896, Zanesville, blue glazed tile 1½ by 3 inches given to delegates.

Arthur Sewall. Democratic vice-presidential candidate in 1896, 3-inch square, blue glaze, biography pasted on back.

Weller's Outing. Buckeye Lake, August 6, 1904, 2-inch circular tile.

Artists, Designers, Supervisors

330

Felix Alcan. Supervised the artists in New York City who cut the mosaics about 1919.

Karl Virgil Bergman. From Brussels, Belgium, 1889–1955. Worked for the Mosaic Tile Company. Worked for American Encaustic Tiling Company until 1919. Left to work in Flint, Michigan, for five years, then founded his own company, Continental Faience and Tile, in Milwaukee, Wisconsin.

Ira Chandler. Designer.

Lillian Cross. Employee whose name was found scratched on the back of tile c. 1903.

Alma Hale.

Ernest R. Hartshorne. From England. Worked about 1910 as head of the design department. Also worked at Mosaic Tile Co.

Von Housenett. An Austrian designer.

Karl Langenbeck. (1861–1938). Born in Cincinnati, Ohio. He was graduated from the College of Pharmacy in Cincinnati, the Polytechnic School of Zurich, Switzerland, and the Technische Hochschule of Berlin. He was the chemist and superintendent of the Rookwood Pottery from 1885–1886. He also founded the Avon Pottery in Cincinnati in 1886. The pottery closed in either 1887 or 1888. From 1890 to 1893, he was the chemist for American Encaustic. In 1894, he helped found the Mosaic Tile Company of Zanesville.

Harry D. Lillibridge. Superintendent in 1909.

Herman C. Mueller. (1854–1941). Some records say 1858, but his obituary says he died in 1941 at 87. Had studied in Nuremberg and Munich. Modeled for the company after 1887, left in 1894 to found Mosaic Tile Company, left Zanesville in 1903 to work at the Robertson Tile Company, Morrisville, Pennsylvania. In 1909, he went to Trenton, New Jersey, to found the Mueller Mosaic Co.

Alfred Nicklin. Nephew of Richard Nicklin, headed the design department after him.

Richard Nicklin. Headed design department.

Christian Nielson. Modeler and designer from 1894 to 1902. He became superintendent of the Roseville Pottery.

Harry M. Northrup. Worked at the Zanesville Art Pottery and then the Mosaic Tile Company until 1917. He went into the service and after the war, returned to the American Encaustic Tiling Company as head of glazing, casting, and decorating. He left to work for the

These two facing tiles were probably made for the sides of a fireplace. The top tiles are 18 inches by 6 inches, the lower decorated pedestal tiles are 12 inches by 6 inches. All of the tiles are glazed a pink brown shade and are marked with one of the American Encaustic Tiling Co. marks. (Authors' collection)

This blue tile 2 inches by 4 inches is unmarked on the back but has the company name and a masonic emblem as part of the design. (Authors' collection)

A sample rack of trim for tiles, probably dating from before 1920. The tile strips can be removed. (Authors' collection)

Roseville Pottery Company in 1935 and then worked for the U.S. Air Force.

Peter Patterson. Designer.

Frank Philo. A ceramicist who later worked in mining and tile manufacturing in California.

Frederick Hürten Rhead. (1880–1942). Came from Staffordshire, England, in 1902. Head of the research department for American Encaustic Tiling Company from 1920 to 1927. He worked for Weller (1902–1904); Roseville Pottery (1904–1908); Peoples University, St. Louis, Missouri (1908–1911); Arequipa Pottery, San Francisco, California (1911–1914); Rhead Pottery, Santa Barbara, California; Homer Laughlin China Company, East Liverpool, Ohio (1927–?).

Lois Rhead. Worked at Roseville and American Encaustic.

Eugene Roberts. Decorator, worked with Frederick Rhead and Harry Northrup. Also worked at Weller.

Mayme Rock. Employee whose name was found scratched on a tile.

George Ruston. English designer.

Henry Scharstine.

Nannie Shunk. Employee whose name was found scratched on the back of a tile, c. 1903.

Leon V. Solon. (1873–1957). Son of Louis Marc Solon. Worked as a designer for American Encaustic Tiling Company in New York City from 1912 to 1925.

Paul Solon. Son of Marc Louis Solon. Worked as designer about the same time as his brother Leon V. Solon (above).

George A. Stanberry (Stanbery). Employee superintendent from about 1876 to 1909.

Walter P. Suter. Designer.

J. Hope Sutor. Artist.

Gertrude Trettipo.

Boris Trifonoff. A Russian designer.

Arthur Wagner. Artist who also worked with Frank Lessell.

Bibliography

Barber, Edwin A., *Marks of American Potters,* Philadelphia: Patterson and White, 1904.

_____, *The Pottery and Porcelain of the United States,* New York: G. P. Putnam's Sons, 1893 (3d and rev. ed. 1909).

Bernard, Julian, *Victorian Ceramic Tiles,* Greenwich, Conn.: New York Graphic Society Ltd.

Davis, Chester, "The AETCO Tiles of Walter Crane," *Spinning Wheel* (June 1973), 18–20.

Evans, Paul F., "Victorian Art Tiles," *Western Collector* (V. No. 11), (November 1967).

McClinton, K. M., *Collecting American Victorian Antiques,* New York: Charles Scribner's Sons, 1966.

Newark Museum Association, *New Jersey Clay Products,* date unknown.

Purviance, Louise and Evan, *Zanesville Art Tile in Color,* Des Moines: Wallace-Homestead Co., 1972.

_____, "American Art Pottery," *The Antique Reporter* (June, 1973).

_____, "American Art Pottery," *Mid-America Reporter* (Dec.–Jan., 1972–73).

Purviance, Louise; Purviance, Evan; and Schneider, Norris, *Zanesville Art Pottery in Color,* Des Moines: Wallace-Homestead Co., 1968.

Schneider, Norris F., "A. E. Tile Company," *Zanesville Times Recorder* May 21, 1961; May 28, 1961; June 4, 1961; October 27, 1963.

_____, "Souvenir Tile," *Zanesville Times Recorder* (October 30, 1966).

Zanesville Chamber of Commerce. "American Encaustic Tiling Company, Ltd.," Booklet, 1918.

ARCHITECTURAL TILE COMPANY
Keyport, New Jersey

Became the Atlantic Tile & Faience Company in 1909 and moved to Mauer, New Jersey, in 1910.

ATLANTIC TILE AND FAIENCE COMPANY
Mauer, New Jersey

See Architectural Tile Company.

This tile is marked "Batchelder, Los Angeles." It is 4 inches square with a Viking ship design in brown with blue. (The Smithsonian Institution)

Beaver Falls marks (the line cut is a raised one).

This stove tile is 2 inches in diameter. It has a dark brown glaze. The back is marked "Beaver Falls" in a semicircle (Authors' collection)

BATCHELDER TILE COMPANY
California

Later became Batchelder Wilson, Los Angeles, California.

BEAVER FALLS ART TILE COMPANY

Francis W. Walker organized the Beaver Falls Art Tile Company Limited in Beaver Falls, Pennsylvania, in 1886. Plain tiles were made at first, but after a few months, embossed intaglio tiles and stove decorations became the company's most important products. Mr. Walker was a chemist and he developed a soft colored glaze that was free from crazing. This made the tiles especially desirable for stove decorations. The glazes were made in pale blue, green, purple, or other pastel shades.

Professor Isaac Broome joined the factory in 1890. He was one of the most famous of the artists who worked at several pottery and tile factories in the United States. Broome was born in Valcartier, Quebec, in 1835. He moved to Philadelphia when he was fifteen and studied art with Hugh Cannon, private tutors, and at the Pennsylvania Academy of Fine Arts. He also studied in Europe for a year and when he returned he tried twice, unsuccessfully, to make terra-cotta vases and architectural pieces. During the same period, Broome did portrait painting and sculpturing and became better established as an artist. In 1875, he went to work for Ott and Brewer of Trenton, New Jersey. He developed an improved kiln and designed many of the best-sculptored pieces made by the firm for the 1876 Centennial. Broome also experimented with ceramics and porcelain. The pieces he designed for the Centennial were so popular that he was sent to the French Exposition of 1878 as "Special Commissioner on Ceramics for the United States Government and the State of New Jersey." The job lasted two years.

In 1883, he joined the Harris Manufacturing Company which soon became the Trent Tile Company of Trenton, New Jersey. (See Trent Tile). He made designs for tiles, marking some with the letter B on the face of the tile. Broome left Trent Tile in 1885 and founded the Providential Tile Works in Trenton, before finally joining the Beaver Falls Art Tile Company.

In 1927, the Beaver Falls Art Tile Company was absorbed by the Robert Rossman Corporation. It went bankrupt in 1930.

Several types of tiles were made by the Beaver Falls Art Tile Company. Many of them had raised designs of heads

(Top left) George Washington and stars decorate this large Beaver Falls tile. Each edge is 12 inches long.   (Top right) Beaver Falls tiles: *Top:* 3⅛-inch-diameter aquamarine tile. There is a B, under the glaze, on the left. The back is marked P53, B.F.A.T. Co.; *bottom left:* 3⅛-inch-diameter aquamarine tile. It is marked B under the glaze at the back of the neck of the figure. The back is marked B.F.A.T. Co.; *bottom right:* 3⅛-inch-diameter aquamarine tile. It is marked B under the glaze on the right near the hatband. The back is marked B.F.A.T. Co. (Barbara White Morse, *Spinning Wheel Magazine*)   (Bottom left) This pair of Beaver Falls tiles are glazed aquamarine. Each is a 5⅞-inch square. There is a B under glaze in the left lower corner indicating the work of Isaac Broome. The tile picturing the woman is marked on the back "A74 B.F.A.T. Co." The other is marked "A75, B.F.A.T." (Barbara White Morse collection) (Bottom right) A lady in a feathered hat decorates this 3-inch-diameter stove tile. It has a green glaze. The tile is marked "Beaver Falls Pa 23 P." (Authors' collection)

or full figures. Large panels representing the Muses were made. They were approximately six inches high and eighteen inches in length, while tiles just showing heads were twelve inches square. The star-studded tile with George Washington is one of the most famous.

Bibliography

Barber, Edwin A., *The Pottery and Porcelain of the United States,* New York: G. P. Putnam's Sons, 1893 (3d and rev. ed. 1909).

Bernard, Julian, *Victorian Ceramic Tiles,* Greenwich, Conn.: New York Graphic Society Ltd., 1972.

Evans, Paul F., "Victorian Art Tiles," *Western Collector,* V, No. 11 (November 1967).

This pair of light blue tiles were designed so that a continuous pattern could be formed when more tiles were added. The 6-inch-square tiles are marked "Beaver Falls Art Tile Co. Ltd. A 156." (Authors' collection)

'Sappho" is the name of this Beaver Falls Art Tile modeled by Isaac Broome. (*Popular Science Monthly*, page 312, January, 1892)

A warrior's head modeled on a 6-inch-square green glazed Cambridge tile. (Smithsonian Institution)

Cambridge label and mark.

McClinton, K. M., *Collecting American Victorian Antiques*, New York: Charles Scribner's Sons, 1966.

Morse, Barbara White, "Tiles Made by Isaac Broome, Sculptor and Genius," *Spinning Wheel* XXIX (January, February 1973), 18–22.

"Recent Advances in the Pottery Industry," *The Popular Science Monthly*, XV (January 1892).

BROOKLYN VITRIFIED TILE WORKS

Established 1898, burned 1906, and reorganized and worked until the end of World War I. See International Tile and Trim Company.

CAMBRIDGE ART TILE WORKS

The Cambridge Art Tile Works started in Covington, Kentucky, in March 1887. Three Cincinnati men, A. W. Koch, F. W. Braunstein, and Heinrich Binz, started the tile works. They planned to make enameled and embossed tiles. Heinrich Binz was a German tilemaker who had been making glazed bricks in Covington with two brothers by the name of Busse.

In 1889, the Cambridge Art Tile Works merged with the Mount Casino Tile Works and formed the Cambridge Tile Manufacturing Company. They used clay from Kentucky and South Carolina. Several talented designers were hired, including Ferdinard Mersman who had worked at the Rookwood Pottery. Mr. Mersman became the principal designer, with Clem Barnhorn as a modeler.

In 1927, the Cambridge Tile Manufacturing Company bought the Wheatley Pottery of Cincinnati, Ohio, moving from Covington to Cincinnati in 1929. At this time, they discontinued the manufacture of art tiles.

Bibliography

Barber, Edwin A., *The Pottery and Porcelain of the United States*, New York: G. P. Putnam's Sons, 1893 (3d and rev. ed. 1909).

Bernard, Julian, *Victorian Ceramic Tiles*, Greenwich, Conn.: New York Graphic Society Ltd., 1972.

Evans, Paul F., "Victorian Art Tiles," *Western Collector*, V. No. 11 (November 1967).

McClinton, L. M., *Collecting American Victorian Antiques*, New York: Charles Scribner's Sons, 1966.

(Top) "Poetry" is a modeled Cambridge tile 6 by 18 inches with a green glaze. (Smithsonian Institution) (Bottom) An assortment of Cambridge Art Tile Works tiles. (Smithsonian Institution). (Right) "Night" and "Morning" are a pair of decorative Cambridge Art Tiles. Each is 6 by 18 inches, glazed light brown. The tiles were modeled by Ferdinand Mersman. (Smithsonian Institution)

"Recent Advances in the Pottery Industry," *The Popular Science Monthly,* XV (January 1892).

CAMBRIDGE TILE MANUFACTURING COMPANY

See Cambridge Art Tile Works.

CANTON ROOFING TILE COMPANY
East Sparta, Ohio

Established before 1913; merged into the United States Roofing Tile Company.

CERAMIC TILE WORKS
Toledo, Ohio

A short-lived company that failed in 1892.

Enfield mark.

The Enfield Pottery and Tile Works made this 4-inch-square, dark brown and green tile about 1907. (The Smithsonian Institution)

CHELSEA

See Dedham Pottery in art pottery section.

COLUMBIA ENCAUSTIC TILE COMPANY
Anderson, Indiana

Established 1889 by B. O. Haugh and George Lilly. They made unglazed floor tiles, enameled tiles, and opaque embossed enamel tiles. The plant burned in 1892 and was rebuilt. In 1897 it became the National Tile Company.

EMPIRE FLOOR AND WALL TILE COMPANY
Zanesville, Ohio

Worked from 1907 to 1928.

ENFIELD POTTERY AND TILE WORKS
Enfield, Pennsylvania

Established 1906.

FAIENCE MANUFACTURING COMPANY
Greenpoint, New York

Worked from 1880 to 1892.

GENERAL TILE
Zanesville, Ohio

No information.

GRUEBY FAIENCE COMPANY

See under art pottery section.

HAMILTON TILE WORKS
Hamilton, Ohio

Several firms were set up and failed a few years later. Hamilton was established 1883 by A. Metzner who made enameled tiles in relief. The company failed in 1896 and reorganized in 1897 as the Hamilton Tile and Pottery Company. In 1901 it became the Ohio Tile Company.

(Left) The Enfield Pottery and Tile Works also made pottery. This cup is 10 inches high. It shows a bicycle rider in a raised design. The glaze is blue green over red clay. The interior is glazed white. The piece is a puzzle jug and water could pour out the holes in the sides or the handle. (The Smithsonian Institution)

HARTFORD FAIENCE COMPANY

Established by W. H. Grueby in 1909.

HYZER AND LEWELLEN
Philadelphia, Pennsylvania

In production before 1870.

INTERNATIONAL TILE AND TRIM COMPANY
Brooklyn, New York

Established 1882. Financed from England. Workers were probably brought from Maw's of Jackfield in Shropshire. In 1888 the company was taken over by the New York Vitrified Tile Works. International Tile and Trim was organized by John Ivory and his father and in 1898 it became the Brooklyn Tile Works.

KIRKHAM ART TILES
Barberton, Ohio

Operated for a few years and closed in 1895. Kirkham was instrumental in the start of the Providential Tile Company.

KIRKHAM TILE AND POTTERY COMPANY
Tropico, California

Established 1898.

LOW

See Low Art Tile under art pottery section.

LYCETT

See under art pottery section.

MATAWAN TILE COMPANY
Matawan, New Jersey

Made tiles on a small scale in 1898 and closed in 1902. After several name changes the firm was reestablished under the same name.

MATAWAN TILE COMPANY
Matawan, New Jersey

Founded in 1902 and closed around the time of World War II. Made white vitreous and encaustic floor and ceramic tiles.

An Enfield Pottery tile fireplace shown in *The American Magazine*, February, 1916.

(Top) Faience Manufacturing Company mark. (Bottom) Printed beneath the glaze. Used for a very short time and on very few pieces.

Faience used this mark between 1886 and 1892. It was penciled above the glaze in various colors.

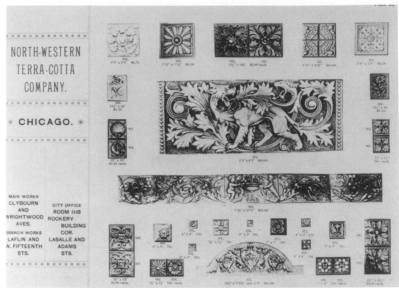

(Right)A page from an undated catalogue of the North-Western Terra-Cotta Company, Chicago, Illinois. (Chicago Historical Society)

MAYWOOD ART TILE COMPANY
Maywood, New Jersey

Originally used as a foundry and machine shop for making iron stoves. In 1891 the company reorganized for tile production and closed in 1905.

McKEESPORT TILE COMPANY
Pennsylvania

Failed in 1895.

MENLO PARK CERAMIC COMPANY
Menlo Park, New Jersey

Established 1888. Charles Volkmar was a partner.

MORAVIAN POTTERY AND TILE WORKS

See under art pottery section.

MOSAIC TILE COMPANY

See under art pottery section.

MUELLER MOSAIC COMPANY

See under art pottery section.

NATIONAL TILE COMPANY
Anderson, Indiana

Established 1897. Still listed as a company in 1914. Used to be the Columbia Encaustic Tile Company.

NEW JERSEY MOSAIC TILE COMPANY
Matawan, New Jersey

Could be either the New Jersey Tile Company of Matawan (1920) or of Trenton.

NEW YORK VITRIFIED TILE WORKS
Brooklyn, New York

Established 1888.

NORTH-WESTERN TERRA-COTTA COMPANY
Clybourn and Wrightwood avenues, Chicago, Illinois

Circa 1930.

OHIO TILE COMPANY

See Hamilton Tile Works under art pottery section.

OLD BRIDGE ENAMELED BRICK AND TILE COMPANY
Old Bridge, New Jersey

Established 1893 by W. E. Rivers.

OWENS TILE COMPANY
Tarrytown, New York

No information.

OWENS TILE COMPANY

See under Owens Pottery in art pottery section.

C. PARDEE WORKS

See under art pottery section.

PARK PORCELAIN WORKS
West Philadelphia, Pennsylvania

Established 1884.

PENNSYLVANIA TILE WORKS COMPANY
Aspers, Adams County, Pennsylvania

Established 1894 for manufacture of encaustic floor tiles.

PERTH AMBOY TILE WORKS
Perth Amboy, New Jersey

Established 1908.

PITTSBURGH ENCAUSTIC TILE COMPANY

Founded 1876. Managed by Samuel Keys in 1876. Became Star Encaustic Tiling in 1882.

C. PARDEE WORKS

See entry in pottery section.

PROVIDENTIAL TILE WORKS

The Providential Tile Works of Trenton, New Jersey, was started in 1885, but their first product was not sold until 1886. Isaac Broome, of the Trent Tile Company, was the first designer and modeler (see Beaver Falls and Trent Tile). Scott Callowhill was another designer and modeler. Mr. Callowhill came from the Royal Worcester Works in England in 1885. He had also worked at Doulton in Lambeth, England, and at the Phoenixville (Pennsylvania) Pottery. Several tiles designed by Mr. Callowhill were listed in Edwin Barber's *The Pottery and Porcelain of the United States.* These included a 6 by 12 inch tile, "Mignon," after Jules Lefebvre and a 6 by 18 inch tile after Benjamin W. Leader's picture "February Fill-Dyke."

Fred Wilde (the Maywood Tile Company in New Jersey and the Robertson Art Tile Company of Morrisville, Pennsylvania) worked for the Providential Tile Works. So did Joseph Kirkham (Kirkham Tile Co., Barberton, Ohio, c. 1895, and Kirkham Tile and Pottery Company, Tropico, California, 1898). Providential made glazed tiles that were either plain or in relief. They experimented with colored glazes on the same piece with the raised portion a different color from the base. Underglaze decoration, gilded, and cloisonné-like decorated tiles were made from about 1890 to 1910. The firm closed in 1913.

Providential marks.

This stove tile was held in place by a screw through the center hole. The 3-inch-diameter tile is glazed pale gray green. It is marked P.T.W. T. N. J. (Authors' collection)

Bibliography

Barber, Edwin, *Marks of American Potters,* Philadelphia: Patterson and White, 1904.

———, *The Pottery and Porcelain of the United States,* New York: G. P. Putnam's Sons, 1909.

Bernard, Julian, *Victorian Ceramic Tiles,* Greenwich, Conn.: New York Graphic Society Ltd., 1972.

McClinton, K. M., *Collecting American Victorian Antiques,* New York: Charles Scribner's Sons, 1966.

Newark Museum Association, "New Jersey Clay Porducts," date unknown.

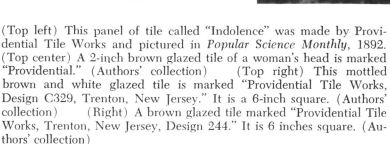

(Top left) This panel of tile called "Indolence" was made by Providential Tile Works and pictured in *Popular Science Monthly*, 1892. (Top center) A 2-inch brown glazed tile of a woman's head is marked "Providential." (Authors' collection) (Top right) This mottled brown and white glazed tile is marked "Providential Tile Works, Design C329, Trenton, New Jersey." It is a 6-inch square. (Authors' collection) (Right) A brown glazed tile marked "Providential Tile Works, Trenton, New Jersey, Design 244." It is 6 inches square. (Authors' collection)

Popular Science Monthly, The, "Recent Advances in the Pottery Industry," (V. 40) (January, 1892), 314.

ROBERTSON ART TILE COMPANY

The Robertson Art Tile Company of Morrisville, Pennsylvania, was started in 1890. In was originally called the Chelsea Keramic Art Tile Works. During the period 1878–1890, George W. Robertson worked with his father and brothers at the Chelsea Keramic Art Works in Chelsea, Massachusetts, and at the Low Art Tile Works in the same town.

About 1893, he started to make etched and relief art tiles; some of the tiles were modeled by Hugh C. Robertson of the Chelsea Keramic Art Works (see). Arthur D. Frost became manager of the tile works after George Robertson left for California in 1895.

Herman Mueller of the American Encaustic Tile Company and the Mosaic Tile Company worked at the Robertson Art Tile Company from 1903 to 1909, when he left to form the Mueller Mosaic Company of Trenton, New Jersey.

The Robertson Art Tile Company is still in existence today, although it is known as the Robertson Manufacturing Company.

There was a Robertson Pottery, founded by Fred Robinson, a brother, in California in 1934.

Robertson Art Tile mark.

Bibliography

Barber, Edwin, *The Pottery and Porcelain of the United States,* New York: G. P. Putnam's Sons, 1909.

Bernard, Julian, *Victorian Ceramic Tiles,* Greenwich, Conn.: New York Graphic Society Ltd., 1972.

343

ROOKWOOD POTTERY

See under art pottery section.

SOUTH AMBOY TILE COMPANY
SOUTH AMBOY, NEW JERSEY

Failed by 1900.

SPARTA CERAMIC COMPANY
EAST SPARTA, OHIO

Founded 1919.

STANDARD TILE COMPANY
SOUTH ZANESVILLE, OHIO

Founded 1923.

STAR ENCAUSTIC TILE COMPANY

**S.E.T.
CO.**

Impressed Star Encaustic mark.

The Star Encaustic Tile Company of Pittsburgh, Pennsylvania, began operating in 1882. The firm was a continuation of the Pittsburgh Encaustic Tile Company Limited. They made unglazed encaustic tile. Some advertisements for the firm appeared in the Pittsburgh city directories of 1884, 1896, and even as late as 1914. There were no ads in the 1926 directory so presumably the firm had closed by that date. Their tiles are sometimes marked S.E.T. CO.

Samuel Keys, an Englishman, was the manager of the firm. He may have been the first man to make tiles successfully in the United States. He started experimenting in 1867, and by 1871 had made satisfactory encaustic tiles. In 1876 he was superintendent of the Pittsburgh Encaustic Tile Company.

Bibliography

Barber, Edwin, *Marks of American Potters,* Philadelphia: Patterson and White, 1904, p. 34.

_____, *The Pottery and Porcelain of the United States,* New York: G. P. Putnam's Sons, 1909, p. 359.

Bernard, Julian, *Victorian Ceramic Tiles,* Greenwich, Conn.: New York Graphic Society Ltd., 1972.

Pittsburgh Directory, 1884, 1896.

Salisbury, Ruth K., correspondence with authors.

TARRYTOWN TILE COMPANY
New York

Failed by 1900.

TRENT TILE COMPANY

The Harris Manufacturing Company of Trenton, New Jersey, was organized in 1882, and soon changed its name to the Trent Tile Company. Isaac Broome was the designer and modeler from 1883 to 1886, when he was replaced by William Wood Gallimore. Gallimore stayed for about seven years. He came from Great Britain where he had experience as a potter and designer at the Belleek Pottery of Ireland and the Goss Pottery of Stoke-on-Trent, England. He also worked at the Ceramic Art Company of Trenton, New Jersey, and others. Edwin Barber, in his *Pottery and Porcelain of the United States,* says: "For six years, he [Mr. Gallimore] was at the Belleek Potteries in Ireland, where he lost his right arm by the bursting of a gun. Since the loss of his arm, Mr. Gallimore has done his modeling with his left hand, and he has accomplished better work with one arm than he did when in possession of both." The Gallimore designs often portrayed boys and cupids.

The firm made dull lustered tiles in a patented form called "alto-relievo" (high relief). They also made glazed and enameled tiles in all sizes plus 6 by 18 inch mantel facings.

The Trent Tile Company went into receivership in 1938. The firm was purchased by the Wenczel Tile Company and is still in business.

Trent Tile marks.

This 6-inch-square Trent tile is made with mottled green and brown glaze. (Authors' collection)

Bibliography

Bernard, Julian, *Victorian Ceramic Tiles,* Greenwich, Conn.: New York Graphic Society Ltd., 1972.

Evans, Paul F., "Victorian Art Tiles," *Western Collector* (V. V, No. 11), (November, 1967).

Hastedt, Karl G., "Wenczel Tile Co," *Trenton* (July, 1957), 6–8, 26–29.

McClinton, K. M., *Collecting American Victorian Antiques,* New York: Charles Scribner's Sons, 1966.

Mitchell, James R., correspondence with authors.

Popular Science Monthly, The, "The Rise of the Pottery Industry" (V. 40), (January, 1892).

Shull, Thelma, "Glass and China Decorative Tiles," *Hobbies* (V. 49), (July, 1944), 64.

Trenton, "An Ancient Art Applied to Modern Sanitation, Trent Tile Company's Products Help Keep Nation Clean" (February, 1928), 4, 21, 24.

(Left) Two tiles listed as "dull finish tiles, Trent Tile Company." (*Popular Science Monthly,* January, 1892)   (Above) This pastoral scene was modeled by William W. Gallimore from a sketch by an artist named Cooper. (*Popular Science Monthly,* January, 1892)

(Left) Golden amber tile, 4¼ inches in diameter, marked "4R20 Trent." It is attributed to the artist Isaac Broome. (Barbara White Morse and *Spinning Wheel Magazine*)   (Above left) A profile of General Grant made by the Trent Tile Company about 1885. (Courtesy of The Brooklyn Museum, Brooklyn, New York)   (Above right) Amber-colored Trent tile 6 inches square. (The Smithsonian Institution)

Stove tile used by the Murdock Company of Boston. It says "May Gode Betide Our Ain Fireside, Murdock Parlor Crate Co.—Boston." The Trent green tile is 4¼ inches wide by 3 inches high. (Authors' collection)

UNITED STATES CERAMIC TILE COMPANY
1375 Raff Rd. SW, Canton, Ohio

Worked 1954 to present. Originally the United States Quarry Tile and the United States Roofing Tile Company (1903– Parkersburg, W. Va., 1909–1926).

UNITED STATES ENCAUSTIC TILE COMPANY

The United States Encaustic Tile Company of Indianapolis, Indiana, started working in 1877. The building was destroyed by fire, but by 1879 a new and larger building was completed. Robert Minton Taylor of England worked at the tile works from 1881 to 1883. In 1886, the ownership changed and the firm was renamed The United States Encaustic Tile Works. The firm name was last listed in the 1934 directory, but a United States Tile Corporation is listed at its address from 1934 to 1937.

The company made floor, wall, and fireplace tile. In 1893, they developed a matte finished glazed tile that was not sold until thirteen years later. The firm made relief tiles in three- and six-section panels. Many of them were made for use on mantels. Ruth M. Winterbotham modeled some of them.

Tile was made for the St. Louis Post Office and the Iowa State House at Des Moines, Iowa. A special tile floor was made for a saloon during the 1890s. It was made to be set with ten- and twenty-dollar gold pieces. According to the story, the floor was popular with customers who liked to walk on money. It was a great idea until the day some workmen stole the floor.

U — S — E — T — W

INDIANAPOLIS.

IND.

United States Encaustic Tile marks.

Bibliography

Bernard, Julian, *Victorian Ceramic Tiles*, Greenwich, Conn.: New York Graphic Society Ltd., 1972.

Landers, Fisk, correspondence with authors.

Popular Science Monthly, "Recent Advances in the Pottery Industry" (V. 40), (January, 1892).

Hamlet and Ophelia are a pair of 6-inch-square brown glazed tiles. The backs of the tiles are marked "U-S-E-T-W Indianapolis Ind." (Authors' collection)

"Twilight" is the name of this mantel tile made by the United States Encaustic Tile Works and designed by Miss Winterbotham. It was part of a series called "Dawn," "Midday," and "Twilight." (*Popular Science Monthly,* January 1892)

A page from the catalogue of the United States Encaustic Tile Co. showing floor tile patterns in 1879. Scale: ¾ inch to a foot. (Photo from the William Henry Smith Memorial Library, Indianapolis, Indiana)

Shull, Thelma, "Glass and China Decorative Tiles," *Hobbies* (V. 49), (July, 1944), 64.

Sulgrove, B. R., *History of Indianapolis and Marion County, Indiana* (1884).

United States Encaustic Tile Works, "Fiftieth Anniversary of the United States Encaustic Tile Works, Indianapolis, Indiana; in Continuous Operation for Fifty Years on the Present Site, 1877–1927," *Fifty Years Ago on Tinker Street in Indianapolis.*

Wright, Martha E., correspondence with authors.

UNITED STATES POTTERY
Bennington, Vermont

No information.

UNITED STATES QUARRY TILE COMPANY
Canton, Ohio

See United States Ceramic Tile Company.

UNITED STATES ROOFING TILE COMPANY

See United States Ceramic Tile Company.

VOLKMAR CERAMIC COMPANY

See under art pottery section.

WELLER POTTERY

See under art pottery section.

WENCZEL TILE COMPANY
Trenton, New Jersey

Established 1915.

WESTERN ART TILE COMPANY

Established 1903 in California by Fred Wilee. See Maywood Art Tile, Providential Tile, Robertson Art Tile.

WHEATLEY POTTERY COMPANY

See under art pottery section.

WHEELING TILE COMPANY
Wheeling, West Virginia

Established 1913.

ZANESVILLE MAJOLICA COMPANY
Zanesville, Ohio

No information.

A stylized flower is centered on this green brown glossy glazed 4-inch-square tile. It is marked "United States Encaustic Tile Co. Indianapolis, Ind." (Authors' collection)

ARCHITECTURAL TERRA-COTTA FACTORIES

BOSTON TERRA-COTTA COMPANY
Boston, Massachusetts

Fiske, Coleman & Co. were the managers and were also associated with the Boston Fire Brick Works, Atwood, and Grueby.

CHICAGO TERRA-COTTA COMPANY

Hired James Taylor, a superintendent of a well-known English works in 1870. Their English methods vastly improved American products.

INDIANAPOLIS TERRA-COTTA COMPANY
Brightwood, Indiana

Established 1886.

LONG ISLAND CITY WORKS

No information.

NEW YORK ARCHITECTURAL TERRA-COTTA COMPANY

Organized 1885.

NORTH-WESTERN TERRA-COTTA COMPANY
Clybourn and Wrightwood Avenues, Chicago, Illinois.

See North-Western Terra-Cotta Company on page 341

PERTH AMBOY TERRA-COTTA COMPANY
Perth Amboy, New Jersey

Incorporated 1879. Produced red, buff, and white terra-cotta. The president of the company was E. J. Hall; vice president, W. C. Hall.

JAMES RENWICK
New York

Architect who experimented with terra-cotta in 1853.

SOUTHERN TERRA-COTTA WORKS
Atlanta, Georgia

Established in 1871 by Mr. P. Pellegrini and Mr. Z. Castleberry.

STEPHENS & LEACH
Girard Avenue and 46th Street, West
Philadelphia, Pennsylvania

Organized in 1886. Changed name to Stephens, Leach & Conkling; then to Stephens, Armstrong & Conkling.

WINKLE TERRA-COTTA COMPANY
Cheltenham, St. Louis, Missouri

Established 1883.

Further Tile Bibliography

Barber, Edwin, *The Pottery and Porcelain of the United States*, New York: G. P. Putnam's Sons, 1909, p. 343.

Bernard, Julian, *Victorian Ceramic Tiles*, Greenwich, Conn.: New York Graphic Society Ltd., 1972.

Binns, Charles F., "Pottery in America," *The American Magazine of Art*, (February, 1916), 131.

Clark, Robert Judson, *The Arts and Crafts Movement in America 1876–1916*, Princeton, N.J.: Princeton University Press, 1972.

Evans, Paul F., "Victorian Art Tiles," *Western Collector* (V. V) (No. 11), (November, 1967).

Federal Writers Project, The, *Matawan 1686–1936*, Matawan, New Jersey: *The Matawan Journal*, 1936.

Forkner, John L., *History of Madison County, Indiana*, 1914, pp. 450, 524.

Forkner, John L. and Byron Dyson, *History of Madison County*, 1897, p. 147.

Kurzon, Mrs. George M., Jr., correspondence with authors.

McClinton, K. M., *Collecting American Victorian Antiques*, New York: Charles Scribner's Sons, 1966.

Newark Museum, The, Mrs. Frank A. Diagaetano, Jr., correspondence with authors.

Newark Museum Association, "New Jersey Clay Products," date unknown.

New York State Historical Association, Peter C. Welsh, Director, correspondence with authors.

North-Western Terra-Cotta Company, supplement to catalogue, date unknown.

Popular Science Monthly, "Recent Advances in the Pottery Industry" (V. 40), (January, 1892).

Public Library of Newark, New Jersey, Charles F. Cummings, correspondence with authors.

Schneider, Norris F., "Souvenir Tile," *Zanesville Times Recorder* (October 23, 1966).

Shull, Thelma, "Glass and China Decorative Tiles," *Hobbies* (V. 49), (July, 1944), 64.

Stark County Historical Society, Gervis Brady, correspondence with authors.

Wires, E. Stanley, correspondence with authors.

MISCELLANEOUS FACTORIES

There is still much to be learned about the American art pottery movement. Tantalizing comments, pictures, lists of names, and other clues appear in old magazines and other sources. Marked pieces of pottery with factory and even city and state information appear, and yet our research has disclosed nothing. These bits and pieces wait for the work of a future enthusiast. Rather than ignore them, we have listed the fragments and the sources in the hopes that someone will learn about the pottery. Some are fairly recent firms, some may not even be makers of art pottery, but we have included any information that seemed promising. Any other information would be welcomed by the authors.

ABINGDON, ILLINOIS

A pottery was working here from about 1930 to about 1950. Some art pottery was made. Pieces are marked Abingdon U.S.A. The company is now called Buggs Manufacturing Company.

AKRON STONEWARE COMPANY
Akron, Ohio

A picture of an artware vase similar to Rookwood Standard glaze, c. 1900, appears on their letterhead. (Blair, C. Dean, *The Potters and Potteries of Summit County 1828–1915* Akron, Ohio: The Summit County Historical Society, 1965.)

ALFRED SCHOOL OF CLAY WORKING
Alfred, New York (1900–c. 1932)

School run by Professor Charles F. Binns until 1932, the first ceramic school in the United States. The College of Ceramics at Alfred still exists and there are many references to it in the literature. The work is not listed in the art pottery section because of its experimental nature.

"I must correct the idea that the New York School of Clay Working was in any sense a factory. Any pottery made by the students was purely experimental in intention. Students have gone out from the school to make names for themselves in teaching and the fine production of pottery." (From a letter by Elsie Binns, daughter of Dr. Charles F. Binns, to the authors dated February 1, 1972.)

A commercial pottery made this iridescent green glazed vase. It is 7½ inches high. A stamped mark on the bottom says "American Art Clay Co. AMACO 15." (Authors' collection)

AMERICAN ART CLAY COMPANY
Indianapolis, Indiana

The American Art Clay Co., Inc., or Amaco, is still in business in Indianapolis. Kenneth E. Smith, the manager, wrote that he has worked for the company for over thirty years and that during that time no commercial wares have been made. The firm makes pottery and metal enameling supplies and equipment. (See American Art Clay Works in entry for Pauline Pottery.)

BENHAM WARE

Benham Ware: impressed mark.

Mr. Charles C. Benham of New York City was probably the first in this country to take up seriously the work of carving ornamental designs on ordinary salt-glazed stoneware. His experiments were commenced previous to the Centennial Exposition in 1876, and were continued until a recent period. Often he has combined the three methods of carving, incising, and painting on the same piece, and he has also made some attempts at actual portraiture, with gratifying success. Mr. Benham was most fortunate in enlisting the sympathy and securing the valuable assistance of Mr. Charles Graham, the well known chemical stoneware manufacturer of Brooklyn, who fitted up a place for his work in his pottery. (Barber, Edwin, *The Pottery and Porcelain of the United States*, New York: G. P. Putnam's Sons, 1909, p. 509.)

(Left) A piece of Bennett Faience pictured in the book *The Pottery and Porcelain of the United States* by Edwin Barber.　　(Right) A group of carved stoneware vases made by Mr. C. C. Benham as pictured in the 1909 edition of *The Pottery and Porcelain of the United States* by Edwin Barber.

The article also describes the graystoneware with blue decorations and several tiles. The same firm is listed with many art potteries in an article from Bowdoin, W. G., "Some American Pottery Forms," *The Art Interchange,* April, 1903, 87.

JOHN BENNETT
New York, New York

Mr. John Bennett, formerly director of the practical work in the faience department of the Lambeth Pottery of Messrs. Doulton & Co. of London, England, came to the United States in the Centennial year and settled for a time in New York City, where he introduced his method of decorating faience under the glaze. He built his first kiln in Lexington Avenue, and afterwards credited others in East Twenty-Fourth Street near the East River. At first he imported English biscuit, but after a time, he employed potters to make the common cream-colored body, as the tint imparted a warmth to his colors. He also used, to some extent, a white body, made in Trenton, N.J. His work was soon in great demand and brought high prices. The shapes were simple and generally devoid of handles or moulded ornaments. The decorations consisted chiefly of flowers and foliage, drawn from nature in a vigorous and ornate style, and painted with very few touches. A background was worked in after the painting, in loose touches and delicate tints, and finally the whole design was boldly outlined in black or very dark color. The glaze was brilliant, even, and firm, and the coloring exceeding rich, the mustard yellows, deep blues, and browns tinged with red giving the ware a bright and attractive appearance. He also produced some pieces in the style of the so-called Limoges faience, by applying colored slips to the unfired clay. About 1882, Mr. Bennett sought retirement on his farm in the Orange Mountains of New Jersey, and although he built a kiln there, he has since done but little in the way of faience decoration. The mark used on the earlier pieces was "J. Bennett, N.Y." and later, "West Orange N.J." (Barber, Edwin, *The Pottery and Porcelain of the United States,* New York: G. P. Putnam's Sons, 1909, pp. 305–308.)

BILOXI ART POTTERY
Biloxi, Mississippi

BRIGHTON POTTERY
Zanesville, Ohio 1905–1906

BRUSH GUILD
Bridgeport, Connecticut or New York, New York

A ware that particularly appeals to the collector is the Brush Guild Pottery, which is made in New York City by Miss Perkins, a pupil of George De Forest Brush, and her mother. Mr. Brush acts as their art counselor and advisor. The pieces made are all after prehistoric patterns, and in a black color which is amply justified from the fact that nearly all the primitive potters used a black coloration in the decoration of their pottery when they produced any. (Bowdoin, W. G., "Some American Pottery Forms," *The Art Interchange,* April, 1903, 89.)

The Brush Guild (Mrs. and Miss Perkins) produces in Bridgeport, Connecticut, brown ware of metallic lustre. (Ruge, Clara, "Development of American Ceramics," *Pottery & Glass,* V. I, N. 2, August, 1908, 6.)

Beautiful brown ware is produced by the Brush Guild. (Ruge, Clara, "American Ceramics—A Brief Review of Progress," *International Studio,* V. 28, p. 27, March, 1906.)

BYRDCLIFFE

"Wares such as Frackleton, Grueby and Byrdcliffe." (Crowley, Lilian H., "It's Now the Potter's Turn," *International Studio* 75, September, 1922, 546.) We have been told it was a communal pottery in Woodstock, New York, in the early 1900s.

PAUL E. COX POTTERY
New Orleans, Louisiana

This was probably a studio pottery. We have seen a marked piece of black glazed ware with a paper label, "The Paul E. Cox Pottery, New Orleans, Louisiana, 3 (7) 8 Pine Street, telephone 6401-W." Mr. Cox had worked at the Newcomb Pottery until 1918. The phone number indicates a date about 1930.

CROWLEY'S RIDGE POTTERY
Bloomfield, Missouri

This pottery made utilitarian and decorative wares from local clays of natural colors. In the 1920s, the pottery was making hand-thrown pieces of marbelized clay. Part of the family moved to the Desert Sands Pottery of Barstow, California, and continued making marbelized wares. (Davidson, Clair., "The Ridge Pottery of Evans Crowley," *Antiques Journal,* August, 1972, 17–18.)

DESERT SANDS POTTERY
Barstow, California

Ferrel and Dorothea Evans made Desert Sands Pottery in Boulder City, Nevada, before 1962. In that year they moved to Barstow and continued to make pottery called Desert Sands. They are from the Evans family connected with the Crowley Ridge Pottery, Bloomfield, Missouri. (Hamm, Jo, "Desert Sands Pottery," *Antiques Journal,* February, 1971, 24–25.)

DESERT SANDS POTTERY
Boulder City, Nevada

This pottery made marbelized wares with glazed interiors, which were marked "Desert Sands Pottery, Hand Made, Boulder City, Nev."

FAIENCE POTTERY COMPANY
Zanesville, Ohio

This company worked from 1902 to 1905.

FAIRHOPE, ALABAMA

This pottery was marked "Pinewood," circa 1918.

THE FLORENTINE POTTERY COMPANY
Chillicothe, Ohio

The Florentine Pottery Company at Chillicothe was formed in 1900 for the purpose of making faience ware. The first manager was George Bradshaw, an English potter, who for some years previously had been managing potteries in Wheeling, Zanesville, and elsewhere in this country. At his death, F. J. A. Arbenz, his assistant, took charge and after much study, he produced a bronze glaze which only an expert could distinguish from the metal. A number of vases and other pieces were sold under the name of "Effeco" ware. As the market for faience ware was limited and as the venture was not financially satisfactory, the company discontinued that line of product in 1905 and began the manufacture of sanitary ware. In 1919, the factory moved to Cambridge, (Ohio). (Geological Survey of Ohio, Bulletin 26, Columbus, Ohio, 1923.)

The Florentine Pottery Co. makes a specialty of faience and art ware, such as vases, pedestals, jardinieres and umbrella stands. The mark is a flowerpot surrounded by the

Desert Sands mark.

"Desert Sands Pottery, Handmade, Boulder City, Nev." is printed in a circle on this marbelized blue, gray, cream, and terra-cotta vase. It has a glazed interior of shiny brown. It is 3 inches in diameter, 2½ inches high. (Authors' collection)

Florentine Pottery mark.

names of pottery and the town. (Barber, Edwin, *Marks of American Potters*, Philadelphia: Patterson and White, 1904, p. 138.)

Fort Hays mark.

FORT HAYS, KANSAS STATE COLLEGE

A marked piece is in the author's collection. "To my knowledge there has never been a commercial pottery at the college but there is a pottery for instructing students in pottery techniques." (Letter of March 28, 1972, to authors from John Carmichael, Kansas State Historical Society, Topeka, Kansas.)

GEIJSBEEK POTTERY
Golden, Colorado

This company began operations in 1899. The products of this company are made from Colorado clays. (Barber, Edwin, *The Pottery and Porcelain of the United States*, New York: G. P. Putnam's Sons, 1909, p. 165.)

Barber also listed the marks used by the company, a gearlike shape with the name Geijsbeek Bros., Denver. The firm made whitewares that were much like modern Delft without a blue decoration and other pieces. Art pottery may have been made for a short time.

GRAND FEU POTTERY
Los Angeles, Calif.

GROTELL

This dark blue glazed vase with all-over decoration of raised leaves is 5 inches high. It is marked with the incised words "Fort Hays, Kansas State College." The mark is not handwritten. (Authors' collection)

Major Grotell was the head of ceramics at Cranbrook Academy in the 1930s and 1940s.

HARTFORD FAIENCE COMPANY
Connecticut

Founded by William H. Graves about 1913.

W. HELD
Pasadena, California

This was probably a studio pottery, c. 1932.

HEROLD CHINA COMPANY
Golden, Colorado

John J. Herold of Zanesville, Ohio, founded the Herold China Company in 1908. Adolph Coors, of beer fame,

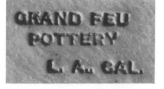

Grand Feu mark (see illustration on page 360).

owned a pottery at this time, and this may be the original name of the Coors Porcelain Works. Art pottery probably was not at the China Company, but Mr. Herold was familiar with the art pottery tradition from Ohio. (Ray, Marcia, "ABCs of Ceramics," *Spinning Wheel*, September, 1968, 37.)

JALAN POTTERY
San Francisco, California

Manuel E. Jalanivich and Ingvardt Olsen joined to make pottery in San Francisco about 1920. Jalanivich had worked under George Ohr and Leon Volkmar. Olsen had worked in Denmark. They used native California clays decorated with Egyptian, Chinese, and Persian inspired designs. The firm moved to Belmont, California, in the early 1940s. Pieces are marked Jalan in incised letters. This was probably a studio potter. (Evans, Paul, "Jalan; Transitional Pottery of San Francisco," *Spinning Wheel*, April, 1973, 24.)

KIRKHAM ART TILE AND POTTERY COMPANY
Barberton, Ohio

The letterhead shows the company as manufacturers of all styles of ceramics, including "limoges" and O. C. Barber, president; George W. Crouse as vice president; Joseph Kirkham, superintendent and ceramist; Joseph B. Evans, art director, and Charles Baird, secretary-treasurer.

LAGUNA POTTERY
California

This company worked about 1915.

Geijsbeek Pottery: Three marks (two printed in black, one in green)

(Left) A pale green, buff, and green vase made by the Grand Feu Pottery. It is called "Sun Ray." It is 2⅛ inches in diameter by 4⅜ inches high. The squat, round vase is also "Sun Ray." It is brown, buff and green, 7½ inches in diameter by 4⅛ inches high. Both vases were acquired by the museum in 1913. (The Smithsonian Institution) (Below) A facsimile of the letterhead of Kirkham, showing tiles and pottery.

This Grand Feu Pottery vase is mottle green brown and violet. It is called "Moss Agate." The vase is 4 inches in diameter by 11¾ inches high. (The Smithsonian Institution)

MARION, INDIANA

There is a green vase with incised decoration in the authors' collection marked Marion, Indiana.

MARKHAM POTTERY

The Markham Pottery was founded by Herman C. Markham of Ann Arbor, Michigan. His son Kenneth worked with him.

Herman Markham was a wood engraver and water colorist. He worked in the Department of Archaeology of the University of Michigan.

The pottery was made of local clay. He tried to develop flower vases that would keep water cool. The original model was thrown on a wheel, then copied in a mold. The pieces were then treated to create unique surface decorations, one called "reseau" the other "arabesque."

There are two general styles of surface, reseau and arabesque. On both the mat glaze is used. In the reseau the texture is fine, the traceries more delicate and slightly raised so that they seem nut-brown and russet; while the traceries, wandering at will and yet with a seeming purpose, are of ochre. Here and there is an elusive tone of green, mysteriously appearing and disappearing.

"Wind-swept-by-the-Sea," we say, as we look at the largest vase in this illustration [not included here]. It is as if the wind, catching up a swirl of green sea water had cast it down upon this stately piece, over mottlings of vari-colored sands and seaweeds.

The arabesque pattern is seen to good advantage in Plates Two and Three [not included]. The vase shown in Plate Two has a background of rough, unfinished texture, while the surface of the relief is smooth. The original color of the vase appears to have been yellow-brown with tones of wine, but back of the raised pattern is an under surface of rich green. It is as if the vase were formed of strata of different colors, and the eating away of the upper surface had revealed the green beneath. The central vase in Plate Three has a background of metallic black, the pattern being in tones of deep orange, red and brown. The first vase on the left is in green and neutral brown, while that

(Left) The treelike design on the vase is incised into the clay. The rather thick walls of the vase and the slightly irregular shape suggest this was a product of a single artist, not a large pottery. On the bottom in handwritten incised letters is "F. N. Marion, Indiana." The 7-inch-high vase has a green matte glaze. (Authors' collection)

on the extreme right, in one color, resembles nothing so much as deeply marked tree bark. (Jarvie, Lillian Gray, "Our American Potteries: The Markham Pottery," *Sketch Book*, V. 5, October, 1905, 123–129.)

Specimens from the Markham kilns at Ann Arbor, Michigan, were of bowls and vases covered with curious forest and autumn leaf effects. The colours were soft, yet brilliant, and artistically mingled. There were copper bronzes, greens, browns and olive greens, combined with reds, yellows and oranges. The suggestions of patterns through the colour are most tantalizing, and one might trace the veins of leaves and forest vistas. (Lovett, Eva, "Fifteenth Annual Exhibition of the New York Society of Keramic Arts," *International Studio*, V. 31, June, 1907, 143.)

I have one piece of Markham that I have seen listed or mentioned only once in a color picture in a 1908 Art magazine. The vases pictured with it are Van Briggle, Teco, Grueby, Newcomb and Rookwood. The vase is in autumnal colors with matt finish. (Letter from Ruth Murphy to *Pottery Collectors' Newsletter*, V. 1, No. 5, February, 1972.)

MIAMI POTTERY
Dayton, Ohio

The Miami Pottery is the product of the Dayton, Ohio Society of Arts and Crafts. It is made from an ordinary yellow clay, found in the valley of the Miami River, and fashioned by hand into simple shapes, and sometimes decorated with modeling in low relief. The chief interest, however, lies in the character of the glaze, which in the most successful pieces, is of a rich dark bronze color, full of life, having a soft luminous quality in its matte surface which is distinctive of the work.

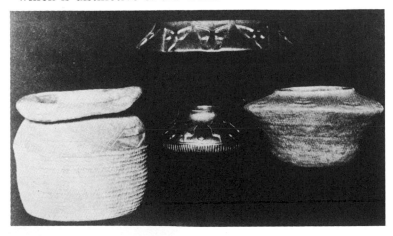

Miami Pottery by Mrs. J. B. Thresher from a photograph that appeared in *Keramic Studio*, May 1903.

Miami Pottery is not the product of experienced crafts-men or accomplished artists. It represents, for the most part, the efforts of young students in the handicraft classes of The Dayton Society, which is under the direction of Forrest Emerson Mann.

As can be seen from the cuts, the designs are unique and artistic, and the work is altogether unusual from amateurs. ("Pottery at the Arts and Crafts Exhibit, Craftsman Build-ing, Syracuse," *Keramic Studio,* May, 1903–April, 1904, 36.

MINERAL AND SANDS (POTTERY) PINTO
(Location and dates unknown)

MOUNTAINSIDE ART POTTERY

Mountainside Art Pottery mark.

Mountainside Art Pottery Studio, Mountain Avenue, Mountainside, New Jersey, Plant at Mountainside, one pe-riodic kiln. Art pottery, vases and statuaries. Owner and Manager, John Kovacs. (*Ceramic Trade Directory, 5th Edi-tion,* 1938, p. 42.)

Seven pieces of Mountainside Pottery are in the collec-tion of the State Museum of New Jersey.

On an impulse I called them [Mountainside Pottery] and discovered that they were still in business making hobby molds. The present owner stated that his father made art pottery from the teens until an indeterminate time after 1938. (From a letter dated November 1, 1972, to the authors from James R. Mitchell, Curator of Decora-tive Arts, State of New Jersey, Department of Education, New Jersey State Museum, Trenton, New Jersey.)

NASH

Mark found on pottery.

NASHVILLE ART POTTERY
Nashville, Tennessee

The Nashville Art Pottery was making in 1886 a fine red ware with good brown glaze, in artistic shapes. Examples may be seen in the Trumbull-Prime collection, now on exhibition at Princeton College. (Barber, Edwin, *The Pot-tery and Porcelain of the United States,* New York: G. P. Putnam's Sons, 1909, p. 334.)

Elizabeth J. Scoville was the founder of the Nashville Art Pottery which was the outcome of an art studio which she had opened for drawing and painting. Her work was

Black and gold leaves decorate this brown glazed redware vase attrib-uted to the Nashville Art Pottery. (The Art Museum, Princeton Uni-versity, Princeton, New Jersey)

gradually extended to modeling and finally a pottery was established, and artistic decorations on pottery were commenced. She hired a potter and fireman to do the heavy work and made her own molds and modelled the forms. This special work extended over about four years from 1885 to 1889. In the year 1888, the "Goldstone" and "Pomegranate" wares were discovered. The former was so called on account of the sparkling golden effect of the rich, dark brown glaze. The clay used was of the common red variety, which, when exposed to a moderate heat, presented no unusual peculiarities, but when a certain glaze was subjected to a high temperature, a remarkably brilliant effect was obtained. The "Pomegranate" ware, so called from its beautiful red color, was the result of an accident. All of the ware in an overfired kiln had been destroyed, with the exception of a single piece in the bottom, which resembled the interior of a ripe pomegranate. The clay was fine and white, and under a special glaze of a solid color, which was fired at a powerful heat, a beautiful red-veined effect was produced, on a mottled pink and blue-gray ground. Experiments were carried on with the native clays of Tennessee, which produced gratifying results, but in the year last named, the pottery was permanently closed as the founder felt herself called to other fields. (Barber, Edwin, *The Pottery and Porcelain of the United States*, New York: G. P. Putnam's Sons, 1909, p. 470.)

Green leaves edged in gold and curved gold lines decorate the surface of this repainted vase by Nashville Art Pottery. It has a yellow glazed interior. (The Art Museum, Princeton University, Princeton, New Jersey)

NATZLER

Otto and Gertrud Natzler are famous studio potters who worked in Vienna in the 1930s, then in America after 1939.

NEILSON POTTERY COMPANY
Zanesville, Ohio

This company worked from 1905–1906.

NORTH CAROLINA STATE COLLEGE

This mark was found on a piece of pottery.

NORWETA

This mark was found on a piece of pottery with crystalline glaze.

ODELL & BOOTH BROTHERS
Tarrytown, New York

At Tarrytown, N.Y. a pottery was started about 1878, under the style of Odell & Booth Brothers. They made majolica and faience, decorated under the glaze. A few

The Nashville Art Pottery made this brown glazed redware pitcher. (The Art Museum, Princeton University, Princeton, New Jersey)

years ago they closed the works, which, after remaining idle some time, were opened and operated by the Owen Tile Co., manufacturers of decorative tiles. (Barber, Edwin, *The Pottery and Porcelain of the United States*, New York: G. P. Putnam's Sons, 1909, p. 308.)

OUACHITA
Hot Springs, Arkansas

The authors own a covered sugar bowl, mottled, green, handled, marked "Ouachita, Hot Springs, Arkansas."

Ouachita mark.

At the Antique show this past summer in Hyannis, I saw a vase (green matt finish with an impressed design) on a Rookwood piece with the regular flame mark. I own a mug in the same green with the exact design but on the bottom, impressed is Ouachita, Hot Springs, Ark. This is puzzling, perhaps an artist left Rookwood and went to Hot Springs. (*Pottery Collectors' Newsletter*, V. 1, No. 5, February, 1972, 67.)

This green matte glazed covered sugar bowl has an incised design of geometric shapes. It is 3¾ inches high by 7 inches wide. The piece is marked on the bottom in impressed letters, "Ouachita, Hot Springs, Ark." (Authors' collection)

The mug is 4 ½ in. tall, 4 ½ in. at base, made in one piece, handle not applied, grayish white clay. (Letter to authors from owner Ellen Donahue, Provincetown, Mass., October 12, 1972.)

PENNSYLVANIA MUSEUM AND SCHOOL OF INDUSTRIAL ART, SCHOOL OF POTTERY
Philadelphia, Penn.

A School of Pottery was added to the course of the Pennsylvania Museum and School of Industrial Art in the autumn of 1903, for the purpose of furnishing instruction in ceramic designing, modelling, decorating, and the manufacture of art pottery. A suitable plant has been constructed, with an up-to-date kiln and the necessary appliances for practical work in pottery making, through all the stages, from the preparation of the clay to the final baking of the ware. The decorations are modelled and carved in relief, and some of them show a marked ability and originality in this style of work. The prevailing color of the glazes is green but there are some beautiful shades of yellow and a variety of blues. The greater portion of the ware possesses a mat surface, but some of the pieces are covered with a brilliant glaze. (Barber, Edwin, *The Pottery and Porcelain of the United States*, New York: G. P. Putnam's Sons, 1909, pp. 569, 570.)

Pennsylvania Museum and School mark.

Similar paragraph and copy of the mark. (Barber, Edwin, *Marks of American Potters*, Philadelphia: Patterson and White, 1904, pp. 36–38.

THE POXON CHINA COMPANY
Los Angeles, California

The Poxon China Co., Vernon, near Los Angeles, Calif., has been organized with a capital of $150,000, to manufacture and deal in general ware. The company is reported to be planning the early operation of a local pottery. It is headed by George J. Poxon, Vernon, and W. J. Charters, Los Angeles. Frank P. Jenal, 621 South Hope Street, Los Angeles, is representative (*Ceramic Age*, July, 1927, 25.)

RAFCO

This mark was found on a piece of pottery.

REDWOOD

"Redwood" is a name that appears on pottery pieces of many types. We have seen examples that are incised like second line Dickensware and other pieces that resemble Louwelsa ware. All sorts of theories exist about the origin of the pottery, much of which is appearing in California.

FREDERICK HÜRTEN RHEAD
Santa Barbara, California

Frederick Hürten Rhead worked as a potter in England, then in the United States at Avon Faience, Weller, and Roseville potteries. He taught at University City Pottery, then in 1911 moved to California. He worked at Arequipa, then incorporated the Rhead Pottery in Santa Barbara.

SHEARWATER POTTERY
Ocean Springs, Mississippi

This family pottery was working in 1935. It was run by Mrs. Anderson, who was trained at Newcomb College, G. W. Anderson, Sr., and their three sons, Peter, who studied at Wayne, Pennsylvania, and at Alfred University, Walter, who studied at the Penn Academy of Fine Arts, and James. The wares were made of local clays, including some clay from the north. The designs are interesting and one of a kind. (*Ceramic Age*, V. 25, No. 4, 1935.)

Unusual shapes are designed by Peter Anderson and covered with his own glazes. Walter I. Anderson carves decorative designs and uses slip to give a soft color and texture. Underglazed figures are created by Walter I. Anderson and James McConnell Anderson. Their pottery is really of the studio type and they have very few stock designs. Many times the designs used have been inspired by the locality and the life of the locality in which the

This terra-cotta vase decorated with a green lamppost is marked "Poxon, Los Angeles." It is 10½ inches high. (The Smithsonian Institution)

Silver Springs, Florida, mark.

(Top) Green, terra-cotta, and cream clays are marbelized on this 4-inch-diameter ashtray. It is marked "Silver Springs, Fla." (Authors' collection) (Bottom) "Silver Springs, Fla." is impressed on the bottom of this marbelized vase of green, terra-cotta, and cream clay. It is 2¾ inches high, 3 inches in diameter. The interior is glazed. (Authors' collection)

Both pottery and porcelain were made at University City Pottery. This pottery bowl with incised and painted decorations is glazed light blue, cream, and pink. It is 4¼ inches in diameter and was made about 1910–1914. It is marked with the cipher UC and 5105. (The Art Museum, Princeton University, Princeton, New Jersey)

pottery is situated. We find the interesting pelican modeled as bookends or just as an ornamental figure. The fish of the sea and the movement of ocean waters are frequently painted or carved on vases and ornaments. Amusing little figures of negroes are created with a real understanding of the negro people.

The Anderson brothers are all artists and their combined efforts result in many beautiful objects. They call their pottery Shearwater and it is on sale in Boston, Philadelphia, and New York as well as in the showrooms at Ocean Springs, Mississippi. (Stiles, Helen E., *Pottery in the United States*, New York: E. P. Dutton & Co., Inc., 1941, p. 190.)

SILVER SPRINGS, FLORIDA

Silver Springs, Florida, was the location of a pottery working in 1938. The company made marbelized wares, often sold as souvenirs.

STEVICK

This mark was found on a piece similar to Cowan Pottery.

SUMMIT CHINA COMPANY
Akron, Ohio

It was listed and a piece pictured in "The Potters and Potteries of Summit County 1828–1915," by C. Dean Blair, Summit County Historical Society, Akron, Ohio, 1965. The firm worked from 1901 to 1915 and used a mark incised "S.C.C. Akron, O."

UNIVERSITY CITY
University City, Missouri

Edward Lewis, who started the American Woman's League in 1907 to educate women, was interested in a book by Taxile Doat, *Grand Feu Ceramics*. Classes were started and Mr. Doat came to University City in 1909. In 1910 Mrs. Adelaide Robineau moved there to teach and work. Frederick Hürten Rhead (who also worked for the Roseville Pottery, the American Encaustic Tiling Company, the Weller Company, and at his own studio in Santa Barbara, California) was another instructor. Overglaze painting on china was the largest part of the work. Some pottery was made and pieces were marked with the cipher UC. The experiment ended in 1914. (See *The Arts and Crafts Movement in America 1876–1916*, edited by Robert Judson Clark, Princeton University Press, 1972, for more information about the porcelain made at University City.)

C. B. UPJOHN POTTERY
Zanesville, Ohio

This company worked from 1904 to 1905.

W. J. WALLEY
West Sterling, Massachusetts

The name of W. J. Walley has been mentioned briefly in connection with West Sterling. He bought the old Wachuset Pottery there before 1890 and continued to operate it alone until his death in 1917. Born in England, August 3, 1852, Walley had come to Canada, working for a time in a glasshouse and then going to Ohio. During the seventies he was employed at the Norton Pottery in Worcester. At West Sterling he continued the flowerpot business in a small way, and also made "art" ware with fancy glazes. Many of his pieces were finished in the green mat glaze so much favored forty years ago. Others were of various shades of blue or of an unglazed terra cotta.... Walley was accustomed to incise his ware with his initials, thus making identification simple. (Watkins, Lura Woodside, "*Early New England Potters and Their Wares,*" Cambridge: Harvard University Press, 1950, pp. 231, 232.)

It is a relief from the general monotony of dull greens, blues, etc. when we encounter Mr. W. J. Walley's rich reds, browns, and purplish browns. (*International Studio,* V. 36, February, 1909, 82.)

WALRATH POTTERY
Rochester, New York

Frederick Walrath was a studio potter who was trained at Alfred University with Charles F. Binns. Walrath taught at the Mechanics Institute in Rochester, New York, and at Columbia University and was a ceramist at Newcomb Pottery. His works were displayed and sold from 1904 until he died in 1920.

Mr. F. E. Walrath exhibits an unusual collection of forms decorated by means of crystallization, also some good work in dull-glazed green ware. (*International Studios,* V. 36, February, 1909, 82.)

WALRICH POTTERY
Berkeley, California

We have seen a piece marked Walrich. Walrich was "owned by J. A. and Gertrude R. Wall. It was first listed

Frederick E. Walrath made this vase at the Walrath Pottery about 1910. It has a painted iris design. The decorations are in brown, purple, yellow green, and green matte glazes. The vase is 9 inches high. It is marked with the incised "Walrath Pottery" and an emblem of four arrows. The original price sticker, "18/6.00," is attached. (Newark Museum, Newark, New Jersey)

in the Berkeley City Directory in 1922 and last appears in 1930." (*Pottery Collectors Newsletter,* V. II, No. 5, February, 1973, 62.)

WANNOPEE POTTERY
New Milford, Connecticut

During this period [1904] "Duchess" ware, characterized by mottled glazes, and porcelain were produced. (Watkins, Lura Woodside. *Early New England Potters and Their Wares.* Cambridge: Harvard University Press, 1950, p. 233.)

The pottery was originally the New Milford Pottery Company. The other wares it made were whiteware and semiopaque china. Duchess ware may not have been an art pottery.

WORCESTER STATE HOSPITAL
Worcester, Massachusetts

Piece listed in exhibit at the Applied Arts Exhibition, Art Institute of Chicago, 1917.

MISCELLANEOUS STUDIO POTTERS

Studio potters' names from lists of exhibits from 1904–1915. Little is known about these artists: Oscar L. Bachelder, Carder, North Carolina (matte glaze, mottled); M. Etta Beede, Minneapolis, Minnesota; Bessie Burdick; Harriet F. Clarke; Russell G. Crook; Marshal Fry, New York; Greenwich House; Handicraft Guild of Minneapolis; Miss Elizabeth Hardenberg; M. M. Heinke; Mrs. I. M. Hibler; Jane Hoagland; Henrietta Ord Jones, St. Louis, Missouri; Christian William Leimbach, Chicago, Illinois; Anna B. Leonard, New York; E. C. Lyon; Miss F. MacDaniel, Garden City, New York; Maud M. Mason, New York; Minneapolis Guild; Emily Peacock; Edith Penman; Lucy Fairfield Perkins, New York; Helga M. Peterson, Chicago (overglaze decorator); Sabella Randolph; Mrs. Sara Wood Safford; Catherine Sinclair.

INDEX

All factory lines such as apple, cherry blossom, etc., are followed by the name of the factory that made the line.
CI refers to Color Illustrations.
Page numbers in bold face refer to illustrations.